T0226226

Communications
in Computer and Information Science 864

Commenced Publication in 2007
Founding and Former Series Editors:
Phoebe Chen, Alfredo Cuzzocrea, Xiaoyong Du, Orhun Kara, Ting Liu,
Dominik Ślęzak, and Xiaokang Yang

Editorial Board

More information about this series at http://www.springer.com/series/7899

Donald Ferguson · Víctor Méndez Muñoz
Jorge Cardoso · Markus Helfert
Claus Pahl (Eds.)

Cloud Computing
and Service Science

7th International Conference, CLOSER 2017
Porto, Portugal, April 24–26, 2017
Revised Selected Papers

 Springer

Editors
Donald Ferguson
Columbia University
New York, NY
USA

Víctor Méndez Muñoz
Escola d'Enginyeria
Barcelona
Spain

Jorge Cardoso
Departamento de Engenharia Informatica
Universidade da Coimbra
Coimbra
Portugal

and

Huawei European Research Center
Munich
Germany

Markus Helfert
Dublin City University
Dublin 9
Ireland

Claus Pahl
Free University of Bozen-Bolzano
Bolzano, BZ
Italy

ISSN 1865-0929   ISSN 1865-0937   (electronic)
Communications in Computer and Information Science
ISBN 978-3-319-94958-1   ISBN 978-3-319-94959-8   (eBook)
https://doi.org/10.1007/978-3-319-94959-8

Library of Congress Control Number: 2018947458

This Springer imprint is published by the registered company Springer Nature Switzerland AG
The registered company address is: Gewerbestrasse 11, 6330 Cham, Switzerland

Preface

The present book includes extended and revised versions of a set of selected papers from the 7th International Conference on Cloud Computing and Services Science (CLOSER 2017), held in Porto, Portugal, during April 24–26, 2017.

CLOSER 2017 received 102 paper submissions from 33 countries of which 28% are included in this book. The papers were selected by the event chairs and their selection is based on a number of criteria that include the classifications and comments provided by the Program Committee members, the session chairs' assessment, and also the program chairs' global view of all papers included in the technical program. The authors of selected papers were then invited to submit a revised and extended version of their papers having at least 30% innovative material.

The 7th International Conference on Cloud Computing and Services Science, CLOSER 2017, focused on the emerging area of cloud computing inspired by some of the latest advances that concern the infrastructure, operations, and available services through the global network. Furthermore, the conference considers as essential the link to services science, acknowledging the service orientation in most current IT-driven collaborations. The conference is nevertheless not about the union of these two (already broad) fields, but about cloud computing where we are also interested in how services science can provide theory, methods and techniques to design, analyze, manage, market, and study various aspects of cloud computing.

The papers selected to be included in this book contribute to the understanding of relevant trends of current research ranging from cloud infrastructure-level virtualization to service science in various application domains. Directions that emerge as being of particular importance are resource elasticity, performance, and energy, and how they are monitored and optimized. Furthermore, how to migrate and architect for the cloud is an ongoing challenge. The effective orchestration and provisioning of cloud services is another specific focus of current research. Recent technology advancements like containers have also being investigated in terms of their benefits as an application deployment framework.

We would like to thank all the authors for their contributions and also the reviewers who helped ensure the quality of this publication.

April 2017

Donald Ferguson
Víctor Méndez Muñoz
Jorge Cardoso
Markus Helfert
Claus Pahl

Organization

Conference Co-chairs

Markus Helfert   Dublin City University, Ireland
Claus Pahl   Free University of Bozen-Bolzano, Italy

Program Co-chairs

Donald Ferguson   Columbia University, USA
Víctor Méndez Muñoz   Mind the Byte and Universitat Autònoma de Barcelona, UAB, Spain
Jorge Cardoso   University of Coimbra, Portugal and Huawei German Research Center, Munich, Germany

Program Committee

Jörn Altmann   Seoul National University, South Korea
Vasilios Andrikopoulos   University of Groningen, The Netherlands
Claudio Ardagna   Universitá degli Studi di Milano, Italy
Danilo Ardagna   Politecnico di Milano, Italy
Amelia Badica   University of Craiova, Romania
Marcos Barreto   Federal University of Bahia (UFBA), Brazil
Simona Bernardi   Centro Universitario de la Defensa, Academia General Militar, Spain
Nik Bessis   Edge Hill University, UK
Luiz F. Bittencourt   IC/UNICAMP, Brazil
Ivona Brandić   Vienna UT, Austria
Anna Brunstrom   Karlstad University, Sweden
Rebecca Bulander   Pforzheim University of Applied Science, Germany
Tomas Bures   Charles University in Prague, Czech Republic
Massimo Cafaro   University of Salento, Italy
Manuel Isidoro Capel-Tuñón   University of Granada, Spain
Miriam Capretz   University of Western Ontario, Canada
Jorge Cardoso   University of Coimbra, Portugal and Huawei German Research Center, Munich, Germany
Eddy Caron   École Normale Supérieure de Lyon, France
John Cartlidge   University of Bristol, UK
Valentina Casola   University of Naples Federico II, Italy
Augusto Ciuffoletti   Università di Pisa, Italy
Daniela Barreiro Claro   Universidade Federal da Bahia (UFBA), Brazil
Thierry Coupaye   Orange, France

António Miguel Rosado da Cruz	Instituto Politécnico de Viana do Castelo, Portugal
Eduardo Huedo Cuesta	Universidad Complutense de Madrid, Spain
Eliezer Dekel	IBM Research Haifa, Israel
Yuri Demchenko	University of Amsterdam, The Netherlands
Robert van Engelen	Florida State University, USA
Ruksar Fatima	KBN College of Engineering, India
Donald Ferguson	Columbia University, USA
Mike Fisher	BT, UK
Chirine Ghedira	IAE, University Jean Moulin Lyon 3, France
Lee Gillam	University of Surrey, UK
Katja Gilly	Miguel Hernandez University, Spain
Dirk Habich	Technische Universität Dresden, Germany
Carmem Satie Hara	Universidade Federal do Paraná, Brazil
Souleiman Hasan	National University of Ireland, Ireland
Benjamin Heckmann	University of Applied Sciences Darmstadt, Germany
Markus Helfert	Dublin City University, Ireland
Mohamed Hussien	Suez Canal University, Egypt
Ilian Ilkov	IBM Nederland B.V., The Netherlands
Anca Daniela Ionita	University Politehnica of Bucharest, Romania
Fuyuki Ishikawa	National Institute of Informatics, Japan
Hiroshi Ishikawa	Tokyo Metropolitan University, Japan
Martin Gilje Jaatun	University of Stavanger, Norway
Keith Jeffery	Independent Consultant (previously Science and Technology Facilities Council), UK
Meiko Jensen	Kiel University of Applied Sciences, Germany
Yiming Ji	University of South Carolina Beaufort, USA
Ming Jiang	University of Sunderland, UK
Péter Kacsuk	MTA SZTAKI, Hungary
Yücel Karabulut	Oracle, USA
M-tahar Kechadi	University College Dublin, Ireland
Gabor Kecskemeti	Liverpool John Moores University, UK
Attila Kertesz	University of Szeged, Hungary
Oleksiy Khriyenko	University of Jyväskylä, Finland
Carsten Kleiner	University of Applied Sciences and Arts Hannover, Germany
George Kousiouris	National Technical University of Athens, Greece
Nane Kratzke	Lübeck University of Applied Sciences, Germany
Miguel Leitão	ISEP, Portugal
Fei Li	Siemens AG, Austria, Austria
Donghui Lin	Kyoto University, Japan
Shijun Liu	School of Computer Science and Technology, Shandong University, China
Yanchen Liu	WalmartLabs, USA
Francesco Longo	Università degli Studi di Messina, Italy
Antonio García Loureiro	University of Santiago de Compostela, Spain

Additional Reviewers

Ankita Atrey	Ghent University, Belgium
Leo Iaquinta	University of Milano-Bicocca, Italy
Neel Mani	Dublin City University, Iceland
Alfonso Panarello	Università degli Studi di Messina, Italy
Plamen Petkov	Dublin City University, Iceland
Eduardo Roloff	UFRGS, Brazil
Giuseppe Tricomi	Università degli studi di Messina, Italy

Invited Speakers

Stefan Tai	TU Berlin, Germany
Francisco Herrera	University of Granada, Spain
Hamido Fujita	Iwate Prefectural University, Japan
Roy Cecil	IBM Portugal, Portugal

Contents

Performance Principles for Trusted Computing with Intel SGX

Anders T. Gjerdrum$^{(\boxtimes)}$, Robert Pettersen, Håvard D. Johansen,
and Dag Johansen

Department of Computer Science, UIT The Arctic University of Norway,
Tromsø, Norway
anders.t.gjerdrum@uit.no

Abstract. Cloud providers offering Software-as-a-Service (SaaS) are
increasingly being trusted by customers to store sensitive data. Companies often monetize such personal data through curation and analysis, providing customers with personalized application experiences and
targeted advertisements. Personal data is often accompanied by strict
privacy and security policies, requiring data processing to be governed
by non-trivial enforcement mechanisms. Moreover, to offset the cost of
hosting the potentially large amounts of data privately, SaaS companies even employ Infrastructure-as-a-Service (IaaS) cloud providers not
under the direct supervision of the administrative entity responsible for
the data. Intel Software Guard Extensions (SGX) is a recent trusted
computing technology that can mitigate some of these privacy and security concerns through the remote attestation of computations, establishing trust on hardware residing outside the administrative domain. This
paper investigates and demonstrates the added cost of using SGX, and
further argues that great care must be taken when designing system
software in order to avoid the performance penalty incurred by trusted
computing. We describe these costs and present eight specific principles
that application authors should follow to increase the performance of
their trusted computing systems.

Keywords: Privacy · Security · Cloud computing
Trusted computing · Performance

1 Introduction

Pervasive computing and the ongoing Internet of Things (IoT) revolution have
led to many new mobile recording and sensory devices that record ever more
facets of our daily lives. Captured data is often analyzed and stored by complex
ecosystems of cloud hosted services. Storing and analyzing large amounts of data
are non-trivial problems. Handling personal data such as smart home monitoring
systems and health tracking, only adds the to this complexity as data processing
might be governed by strict privacy requirements [1].

© Springer International Publishing AG, part of Springer Nature 2018
D. Ferguson et al. (Eds.): CLOSER 2017, CCIS 864, pp. 1–18, 2018.
https://doi.org/10.1007/978-3-319-94959-8_1

The curation and analysis of privacy sensitive personal data on third-party cloud providers necessitate the design of a new Software-as-a-Service (SaaS) architecture that is able to enforce rigid privacy and security policies [2] throughout the entire software stack, including the underlying cloud provided Infrastructure-as-a-Service (IaaS). Commodity hardware components for trusted computing have been available for some time [3,4], but the functionality of existing solutions has been limited to establishing trust and guarantees on the integrity of running software, and rudimentary support for secure code execution (e.g., Intel Trusted Execution Technology).

In 2015, Intel introduced the Software Guard Extensions [5] as part of their sixth generation Intel Core processor micro architecture (codenamed Skylake). Together with complementary efforts by ARM and AMD, SGX is making general trusted computing a commodity, providing confidentiality, integrity and attestation of code and data running on untrusted third-party platforms. SGX is able to deter multiple different software and physical attacks by establishing secure execution environments, or enclaves, of trusted code and data segments inside individual CPUs. While SGX is an iterative technology building upon previous efforts, it is more general in functionality allowing code execution inside enclaves at native processor speeds, a significant performance improvement over previous efforts. SGX is designed with backwards compatibility in mind, allowing developers to port sensitive logic from existing legacy applications into secure enclaves. These properties make SGX a compelling technology for cloud based SaaS hosting privacy sensitive data on untrusted third-party cloud providers. SGX is a proprietary technology and prior knowledge of its characteristics is mostly based on limited documentation by Intel. In particular, little is known about the performance of the computing primitives comprising SGX and how developers should best utilize these to maximize application performance.

This paper provide an in-depth investigation into key performance traits of the Intel SGX platform. We provide a performance analysis of its low-level mechanisms and primitives, and describe several non-obvious idiosyncrasies related to threading, context switching, and memory footprint. From our observations, we derive 1 principles for developing more efficient software on this platform.

The remainder of this paper is structured as follows: Sect. 2 outlines the relevant parts of the SGX micro architecture while Sect. 3 outlines the details of our micro benchmarks. Section 4 provides an informed discussion of our findings and a set of derived principles intended for developers of trusted computing systems. Section 5 details relevant work before concluding remarks.

2   Intel Software Guard Extensions (SGX)

Intel's new general trusted computing platform enables the execution of code on untrusted third-parties at native processor speed. Moreover, the platform preserves the confidentiality and integrity of code and data segments running inside what is referred to as *enclaves*. This section details the core mechanisms comprising SGX, building a foundation for the performance analysis detailed in Sect. 3.

2.1 Enclave Creation

Enclave code and data are distributed to runtime systems in form of a shared library which is bundled together with what the developer reference refers to as the SIGSTRUCT data structure. During the compilation of an enclave, a hash, or measurement, of each code and data segment executable within the shared library is computed and stored together with a signature generated by the developers private key. This bundle is then distributed to the target third-party platform together with the corresponding public key. During initialization, the signature is verified against the public key and the measurement is recalculated and compared with the corresponding value inside the SIGSTRUCT. If the signature matches that of the public key and the integrity of the code and data segments are preserved, the enclave is allowed to execute. This establishes a guarantee that only the expected enclave code and data from the expected enclave author are successfully able to run on the third-party.

2.2 Entry and Exit

Regular application threads are able to enter secure enclaves by invoking the EENTER instruction on a particular logical core. The thread then performs a controlled jump into the enclave code, similar in operation to a call-gate. Threads can only enter enclaves from privilege level 3 (user level).

Software interrupts are prohibited when running in *encalve mode*. As a consequence, no system calls are allowed within enclaves. Applications requesting access to common Operating System (OS) resources such as IO, must therefore explicitly exit the enclave prior to invocation. The application developer explicitly defines these transitions and, in the presence of a potentially malicious OS, all such transitions, parameters to these and responses must be carefully validated.

Although threads cannot be instantiated in enclave mode, SGX allows multiple threads to enter the same enclave and execute concurrently. For each logical core executing inside a particular enclave, a Thread Control Structure (TCS) is required to keep track of thread specific context. Before instantiation, these data structures must be provisioned and stored in the Enclave Page Cache (EPC), comprising pages explicitly set aside for enclaves. The TCS contains an OENTRY field specifying the entry point for the thread, loaded into the instruction pointer upon entry. Stack regions are not explicitly handled by the SGX microcode, however, as Costan and Devadas [6] state, the stack pointer is expected to be set to a region of memory fully contained within the enclave during entry transition. Parameters input to the developer-specified entry points are marshaled and, once the transition is done, copied into enclave memory from untrusted memory. Although not handled by SGX directly, parameter marshaling and stack pointer manipulation are managed under the hood by the SDK implementation which most application authors will use for enclave development.

Threads may transition out of enclaves by means of two different mechanisms, either synchronously trough the explicit EEXIT instruction, or asynchronously by service of a hardware interrupt. Synchronous exists will cause the thread to leave enclave mode, restoring the execution context to its content prior to enclave entry. Asynchronous Enclave Exit (AEX) is caused by a hardware interrupt such as a page fault event. In this case all threads executing on the logical core affected by the interrupt must exit the enclave and trap down to the kernel in order to service the fault. Before exit, the execution context for all logical cores executing within the enclave is saved and subsequently cleared to avoid leaking information to the untrusted OS. When the page fault has been serviced, the ERESUME instruction restores the context and the enclave resumes execution.

2.3 Enclave Memory

During boot-up of the CPU, a contiguous region of memory called Processor Reserved Memory (PRM) is set aside from regular DRAM. Divided into 4 kB pages, only accessible inside the enclave or directly by the SGX instructions, this region of memory is collectively referred to as the EPC. Any attempts to either read or write EPC memory from both privileged level system software or regular user level applications are ignored. Moreover, any Direct Memory Access (DMA) request to this region is explicitly prohibited, deterring physical attacks on the system bus by potentially malicious peripheral devices. Confidentiality is achieved through Intels Memory Encryption Engine (MEE), further preventing physical memory inspection attacks as enclave data is encrypted at the CPU package boundary on the system bus right after the L3 cache.

Much the same as regular virtual memory, EPC pages are also managed by the OS. However, these are handled indirectly through SGX instructions as EPC memory is not directly accessible. The OS is responsible for assigning pages to enclaves and evict unused pages to regular DRAM. Through memory management, the physical limit of 128 MB is evaded by swapping EPC pages and as such there is no practical limit to the size of enclaves. The integrity and liveness of pages being evicted are guarded by an axillary data structure also contained within the PRM, called the Enclave Page Cache Map (EPCM). The EPCM maintains the mappings between virtual and physical addresses of PRM memory. Moreover, it maintains for each page an integrity check and a liveness challenge vector. These precautions guard against a malicious OS trying to subvert an enclave by either manipulating the address translation, explicitly manipulating pages, or serving old pages back to the enclave (replay attacks). In this memory model, only one enclave can claim ownership of a particular page at one given moment, and as a consequence shared memory between enclaves is prohibited. Enclaves are however allowed to read and write directly to untrusted DRAM inside the host process' address space, and therefore two enclaves residing within the same host process are able to share untrusted memory.

Because stale address translations may be exploited to subvert enclave integrity, the processor performs a coarse-grained Translation Lookaside Buffer (TLB) shootdown for each page subject to eviction. Given a page fault event on a particular thread executing inside an enclave, all threads executing on that same logical core must perform an AEX, as described in Sect. 2.2. In order to avoid information leakage stemming from memory access patterns inside enclaves, the lowermost 12 bits of the faulting address, stored in the CR2 registry are cleared. SGX instructions explicitly support batching up to 16 page evictions together at a time, thus curtailing the cost of AEX for each page fault inside an enclave.

2.4   Enclave Initialization

SGX allows the creation of multiple, mutually distrusting enclaves, on the same hardware instance. These can reside in either a single process' address space or multiple. To instantiate enclave system software the OS, on behalf of the application, invokes the ECREATE instruction. This causes the underlying microcode implementation to allocate a new EPC page for the SGX Enclave Control Structure (SECS), identifying each enclave and storing per-enclave operational metadata. Moreover, physical pages are mapped to enclave SECS through the EPCM structure. Before initialization is complete, each separate code and data segment must be added to enclave memory explicitly through the EADD instructions. Similarly, each TCS is added for each logical core expected to execute within the enclave. Once this process is complete the OS issues the EINIT instruction which finalizes initialization and compares the enclave measurement observed to the contents of the SIGSTRUCT. Upon completion, a launch token is generated by a special pre-provisioned enclave trusted by Intel, at which point the enclave is considered fully initialized. Once this process is completed, no further memory page allocations may happen. Intels revised specifications for SGX version 2 includes the possibility for dynamic paging support by means of the EEXTEND command. However, we refrain from further comment, as hardware supporting these features have not yet been released at the time of writing.

Inversely, during teardown of an enclave, the opposite operation is performed. The OS tags each page as invalid, by issuing the EREMOVE instruction. Prior to this, SGX verifies for each page that no threads attributed to that page are executing inside the enclave. Lastly, the SECS is destroyed once all pages referring to it through the EPCM are themselves deallocated.

2.5   Enclave Attestation

In order for applications to securely host privacy-sensitive software components on platforms outside of their administrative domain, we need to establish trust. This can be achieved through remote attestation, a process in which the remote party proves its correctness to the initiator. Assuming an enclave has been created and initialized as outlined above on an untrusted platform, the entity wishing to establish trust with this enclave issues a request for proof. The code inside this enclave then requests a *Quote* from the hardware, which consists of the enclave measurement, in addition to a signature from the hardware platform key. This quote is then sent to the requesting party which can themselves validate the measurement compared to the expected provisioned enclave. Lastly, the quote is sent to Intel for verification through their *Intel Attestation Service*, which validates the signature against their own private key. These two in combination prove to the requesting party that the expected code and data segments are running on a valid SGX-enabled platform.

3   Experiments

The next generation of SaaS systems should be designed from the ground up to utilize trusted computing features in a performance optimal way. Therefore, we conduct a series of micro benchmark experiments on a SGX-enabled CPU to fully understand the micro architectural cost of trusted computing on commodity hardware. Our experimental setup consists of a Dell Optiplex workstation with an Intel Core i5-6500 CPU @ 3.20 GHz with four logical cores and 2×8 GB of DDR3 DIMM DRAM. Dynamic frequency scaling, Intel Speedstep and CStates are disabled throughout our experiments to avoid inaccuracies. We set the PRM size to its maximum allowed 128 MB to measure the peak theoretical performance of the platform. Our experiments ran on Ubuntu 14.04 using the open source kernel module by Intel implementing OS support for SGX[1]. Furthermore, this module has been modified with instrumentation in order to also capture the operational cost from the system perspective. Based on our knowledge regarding SGX, we have derived a set of benchmarks conjectured to capture core aspects of the trusted computing platform. It is worth noting that for all our experiments, more iterations did not yield a lower deviation. We attribute this to noise generated by the rest of the system that while subtle, becomes significant at fine-grained time intervals.

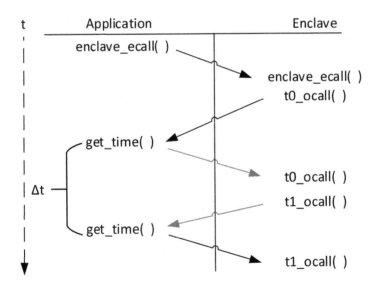

Fig. 1. Sequence of events involved in measuring time spent inside enclaves [7].

---

[1] https://github.com/01org/linux-sgx-driver.

The current generation of SGX does not support the use of the RDTSC instruction or any other native timing facilities inside enclaves. Intel has later released a microcode update to counter this problem, allowing for the RTDSC instruction to execute inside enclaves. We are however unsuccessful, at the time of writing, in obtaining a firmware update specific to our SKU through the correct OEM. Measurements performed throughout the experiments must therefore exit the enclave for each point in time. Consequently, all measurements therefore include the time taken to enter and exit the enclave, described as the sequence of events detailed in Fig. 1.

3.1   Entry and Exit Costs

With SGX, SaaS applications are able to influence the size of their Trusted Computing Base (TCB) by partitioning application logic between trusted and untrusted execution domains. In order to quantify any potential performance trade-off, we examine the associated cost of enclave transitions. An optimal application arrangement should conciser the following trade-off depending on the transition cost: A high cost of transition would necessitate a reduction in the overall amount of transitions and mediating this cost will increase the amount of logic residing within the enclave, thus expanding the TCB. A prominent example at one end of the spectrum is Heaven [8], in which an entire library OS is placed within a secure enclave. Furthermore, details in the Intel Software Developer Manual[2] suggest that the cost of entering an enclave should also factor in the cost of argument data copied as part of the transition into the enclave. Therefore, if the cost of data input to an enclave is high, only data requiring explicit confidentiality and trust should be placed within the enclave.

Figure 2 depicts the measured cost in millisecond latency, as a function of increasing buffer sizes. The cost of entering an enclave is observed to increase linearly with the size of the buffer input as the argument. It is worth mentioning that only buffer input to the enclave is considered. The experiment does not include output buffers or return values from enclaves.

Hosting a buffer inside enclave memory requires that the enclave heap is sufficiently large. Since enclave sizes are final after initialization, we set the heap size to be equally large for all iterations of the experiment. From the graph, we observe that the baseline cost of entering an enclave quickly becomes insignificant as the buffer size increases. This behavior is not surprising, as the overall cost includes the cost of copying memory into the enclaves which invokes the MEE for each page written to the enclave. A curious observation, however, is the fact that the baseline cost only increases linearly for buffers larger than 64 kB. This could be explained by enclaves less than 64 kB being fully provisioned into EPC memory at startup. Whereas for large buffers the cost may be attributed to lazily loaded enclave memory, triggering page faults during the buffer copy operation. This aspect is explored in detail in the following experiment.

---

[2] https://software.intel.com/en-us/articles/intel-sdm.

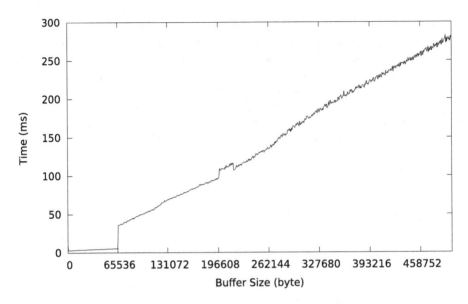

Fig. 2. Enclave transition cost as a function of buffer size [7].

3.2 Paging

Another aspect to consider in the application trade off between TCB and enclave transition cost, is the fact that an increase in TCB would cause an increase in PRM consumption. Moreover, as stated in Sect. 2.3, PRM is a fairly limited resource compared to regular memory and the depletion of this resource will cause system software to evict EPC pages more aggressively. As such, any application utilizing SGX should consider carefully the cost of enclave memory management, more specifically the cost of page swapping between EPC and regular DRAM. Figure 3 illustrates this overhead as observed by both the OS kernel and inside the enclave.

The y-axis is the discrete cost in nano seconds, while the x-axis is time elapsed into the experiment. The SGX kernel module has been instrumented to measure the latency of page eviction denoted by the red dots, and the total time spent in the page fault handler, represented by the black solid line.

From the enclave perspective, the green line denotes the user level instrumentation and represents time spent writing to a particular address in enclave memory. As mentioned in the experimental introduction, measurement primitives are unavailable inside enclaves, and all user level measurements therefore include the cost of entry and exit, including a 4 byte word as parameter input each way.

To induce page faults, the experimental enclave heap size is set to 256 MB, double that of the of the physical PRM size made available by hardware. Moreover, we invoke write operations on addresses located within each 4 kB page sequentially along the allocated memory address space inside the enclave.

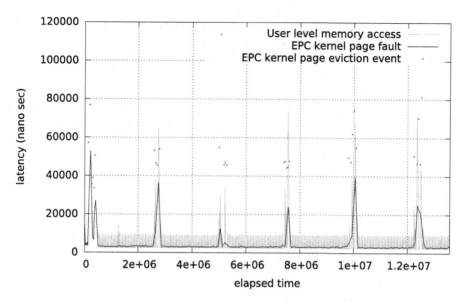

Fig. 3. Paging overhead in nano seconds as a function of time elapsed while writing sequentially to enclave memory [7]. (Color figure online)

Recall from Sect. 2 that all memory for a particular enclave must be allocated prior to initialization. We observe from Fig. 3 that prior to enclave startup, a cluster of page fault events occur at the beginning of the experiment, corresponding with our prior observations. The system is attempting to allocate memory for an enclave of 256 MB while only being physically backed by 128 MB of EPC memory.

The events occurring at user level can easily be correlated with the observations made in the page fault handler. For each increase in latency observed from inside the enclave, a corresponding cluster of evictions occur in the page fault handler. Moreover, the total time spent in the page fault handler coincides with the write overhead observed at user level. Parts of the overhead can be attributed to the fact that page faults cause AEX events to occur for each logical core executing within the enclave, as detailed in Sect. 2.

Moreover, we observe that the SGX kernel module is behaving conservatively in terms of page evictions, and is not exhausting EPC memory resources. As detailed in Sect. 2, the 12 lower bits of the virtual page fault address are cleared by SGX before exiting the enclave and trapping down to the page fault handler. Hence, system software is not able to make any algorithmic assumptions about memory access patterns to optimize page assignment. Furthermore, liveness challenge vector data might also be evicted out of EPC memory, causing a cascade of page loads to occur from DRAM. As a side note, this experiment only uses a single thread, and all page evictions only interrupt this single thread.

In light of the prior discovery, high performance applications should consider tuning the SGX page fault handler to their particular use case, given that the application is able to predict a specific access pattern. Moreover, regardless of access pattern the SGX page fault handler should be optimized to allow exhaustive use of EPC, such that applications running inside enclaves may be less affected by page faults in high memory footprint scenarios.

The initial setup of enclaves will retain large amounts of the pages in EPC memory, alleviating the overhead of paging in certain situations. Moreover, this reduces the execution overhead caused by threads performing AEX. Given that the cost of enclave setup is still a large factor, by the prior statements, it might be advantageous for application developers to pre-provision enclaves.

3.3   Enclave Provisioning

Modular programming and componentized system organization are paradigms commonly used in modern distributed systems. Applications consisting of possibly multiple trust domains and third-party open source components should separate the unit of failure and trust to reduce the overall system impact.

By enabling the creation of mutually distrusting enclaves, SGX is able to support a modular application architecture. Section 2 explains how enclaves might communicate with the untrusted application through well defined interfaces, lending itself to compartmentalization of software into separate enclaves. To capture the cost of using SGX through the scope of a modular software architecture, Fig. 4 illustrates the cost in terms of provisioning latency as a function of enclaves created simultaneously for differently sized enclaves. We observe that the added cost of enclave creation increases linearly for all sized enclaves,

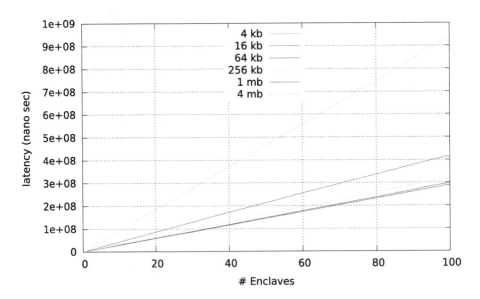

Fig. 4. Latency as a function of number of enclaves created simultaneously, for differing sizes of enclaves [7].

becoming significant for enclaves larger than 256 kB. As detailed in Sect. 2, enclaves are created by allocating each page of code and data to the enclave prior to initialization. During this experiment we observed a significant amount of page faults further attributing to the creation cost. This is expected as the size of enclaves combined with number of instances increases above that of the physically available PRM. Our observations about buffers less than 64 kB from Sect. 3.1 still stands, as we observe that the provisioning cost for enclaves less than 64 kB is nearly identical.

To offset the latency of creation for enclave instances, real-time applications should consider pre-provisioning them. However, as prior experiments show co-locating multiple enclaves in EPC memory might result in additional cost if the memory footprint is large enough.

3.4 Multithreading

The curation and analysis of large amounts of data use concurrency as a measure to speed up processing of data elements. This is especially true for *embarrassingly parallel* computations. One example is the *distinct count* aggregate operation, where a large corpus of data is sectioned into buckets and where each can be counted in parallel. Such computations require parallelism built into the run-time. Fortunately, SGX provides the ability to run multithreaded operations inside the same enclave. However, implementation details reveal that applications with high memory footprint might suffer from extensive page faults, which can act as a barrier and in the worst cases degrade performance significantly. Furthermore, as we argued earlier, applications with multiple tenants might want to isolate analytics execution into separate enclaves, and it is therefore important to consider how threads are delegated inside of enclaves.

To induce a high memory footprint we use the same technique as in Sect. 3.2, where we create an enclave which exceeds in size the amount of available physical PRM. We expect some performance degradation for multiple threads running on the same logical core executing within the enclave. When a page fault occurs, all threads running on the particular core must exit the enclave and block until the page fault is serviced. Our experiment therefore consists of two modes, one where we pin all threads to separate logical cores, and one where we pin all threads to a single core. Both experiments dedicate a single thread to interrogating every 4 kB page of the heap memory causing regular page faults to occur. Our test bench has 4 logical cores so our experiment runs a total of 4 threads simultaneously for both experiments. The remaining threads are just busy-waiting in a loop, measuring the time taken in each iteration. Figure 5 illustrates 4 threads pinned to 4 different cores where core 0 is interrogating memory and causing page faults to occur as illustrated in the green spikes. We observe that there is no co-dependency between threads, and the 3 remaining threads are not impacted by interrupts occurring on the former (Fig. 6).

Our second experiment demonstrates the opposite. We force all 4 threads to be pinned to a single logical core, and as a consequence we observe that thread

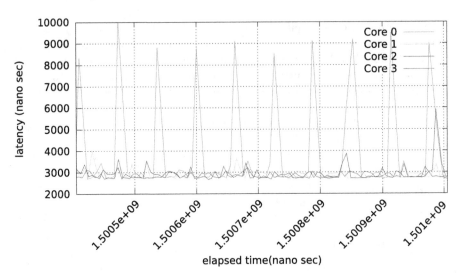

Fig. 5. Execution overhead for multiple threads running on separate logical cores, with page fault events occurring. (Color figure online)

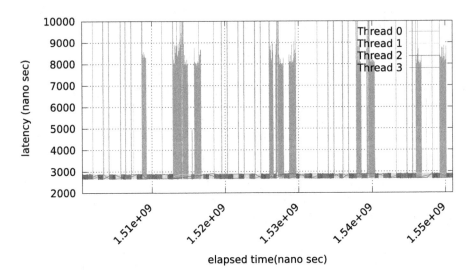

Fig. 6. Execution overhead for multiple threads pinned to a single core, with page fault events occurring.

0, who is causing interrupts to occur, is blocking all other threads from executing while servicing the costly page faults. It is worth noting that this is how threads behave in regular process address space when faced with a hardware interrupt. However, page faults are more costly to perform in enclave memory and more frequent as previous experiments show due to memory footprint constraints. Secondly, we observe that thread scheduling behaves differently as well.

Context switches between threads executing on the same logical core happens multiple magnitudes more infrequently than regular threads executing outside of enclaves. We theorize that this is a design choice when implementing enclave support, because interrupts in enclaves are especially costly. Any context switch would have to be induced by the timer hardware interrupt triggering the thread to exit the enclave, and so it makes sense increasing the scheduler time slices to amortize this cost.

4   Discussion

From the micro benchmarks detailed in Sect. 3, we pinpoint several performance traits of SGX that should be taken into consideration when designing trusted computing-enabled cloud services. We classify these individually as the cost of entering and exiting enclaves, the cost of data copying, the cost of provisioning new enclaves, the cost of memory usage and the cost of multithreaded execution.

Section 2 explained that the transitioning cost is uniform in terms of cost with respect to direction. Moreover, the most significant cost is attributed to the buffer size input as argument to the transition. More specifically, from Fig. 2 we observe a sharp rise in cost when buffer sizes are larger than 64 kB. We conjecture that this is an architectural boundary, where encalves are pre-provisioned, by default, with a given number of pages. Future iterations of SGX may alter this behavior, opting for an increase in pre-provisioned pages. Our principles therefore state:

The Size Principle. *The size of an enclave should not exceed the architecturally determined pre-provisioned memory resources.*

The Cohesion Principle. *Applications should partition its functional components to minimize data copied across enclave boundaries.*

Following the latter principle, a possible component architecture would be to co-locate all application logic into a single, self-sufficient enclave. Haven [8], is a prominent example of this approach. By means of a library OS, a large part of the system software stack is placed within a single enclave, reducing the interface between trusted and untrusted code. However, this approach directly contradicts the observation made in Sect. 3.2 regarding the cost of having a large memory footprint. Since the EPC is a limited resource, the SGX page fault handler promptly pages out enclave memory not being used. However, the paging experiment demonstrates that the available pool of EPC memory is not exhausted, even in the presence of high memory contention. As detailed in Sect. 3.2, the faulting address is not provided as part of the page fault event and the page fault handler is therefore not able to make any assumptions about the memory access patterns. We therefore state that:

The Access Pattern Principle. *Prior knowledge about application's memory consumption and access pattern should be used to modify the SGX kernel module in order to reduce memory page eviction.*

Our experiments have demonstrated that enclave creation is costly in terms of provisioning latency. By pre-provisioning enclaves whenever usage patterns can be predicted, the application is able to hide some of this cost. However, once used, an enclave might be tainted with secret data. Recycling used enclaves to a common pool can therefore potentially leek secrets from one domain to the next; invalidating the isolation guarantees. We therefore state that:

The Pre-provisioning Principle. *Application authors that can accurately predict before-the-fact usage of enclaves should pre-provision enclaves in a disposable pool of resources that guarantees no reuse between isolation domains.*

The cost of enclave creation must also factor in the added baseline cost of storing metadata structures associated with each enclave in memory. Provisioning enclaves must at least account for its SECS, one TCS structure for each logical core executed inside an enclave, and one SSA for storing secure execution context for each thread. [6] details that to simplify implementation, most of these structures are allocated at the beginning of an EPC page wholly dedicated to that instance. Therefore, enclaves executing on 4 logical cores may have 9 pages (34 kB) in total allocated to it, excluding code and data segments. Applications should consider the added memory cost of separate enclaves in conjunction with the relative amount of available EPC. Furthermore, to offset the cost of having multiple enclaves, application authors should consider security separation at a continuous scale. Some security models might be content with role based isolation, rather than call for an explicit isolation of all users individually. We therefore state that:

The Isolation Principle. *Application authors should carefully consider the granularity of isolation required for their intended use, as a finer granularity includes the added cost of enclave creation.*

Executing multiple threads from the same core inside a single enclave degrades the concurrent performance by blocking execution when servicing a page fault. Although regular non-enclave execution behaves similarly, the overhead associated with enclave page faults becomes significant when memory footprint increases. Moreover, latency critical applications will suffer because of the increased time slices of thread interrupts initially thought to amortize the cost of exiting enclaves when switching contexts. From this we deduce that the number of threads executing inside enclaves should never exceed the logical core count for a given system. We therefore establish the following principle:

The Affinity Principle. *Applications should not affinitize multiple threads to the same core.*

Section 3.1 demonstrates the cost of transitioning into and out of an enclave, and it becomes evident that to reduce the transitioning overhead threads should be pinned inside enclaves. Enclave threads should rather transport data out of the enclave through writing to regular DRAM and similarly poll for incoming data. We therefore state:

The Pinning Principle. *Application authors should pin threads to enclaves to avoid costly transitions.*

The prior statements lead us to the following principle:

The Asynchrony Principle. *All execution inside enclaves should be asynchronous.*

Threads should be pinned inside enclaves to amortize transition cost and total thread count should not exceed logical core count. Application authors must therefore be diligent in terms of assigning threads to enclaves. Applications might further isolate contexts based on either user or tenant in different mutually distrusting enclaves, each of which requires a dedicated thread. Core logic executing inside enclaves should remain responsive at all time, servicing both incoming requests and processing data. We therefore state that rather than allocating multiple threads to the same enclave, all execution should be fully asynchronous. This furthermore has the added benefit of high resource utilization improving overall application performance.

At the time of writing, the only available hardware supporting SGX are the Skylake generation Core chips with SGX version 1. Our experiments demonstrate that paging has a profound impact on performance and a natural follow-up would be to measure the performance characteristics of dynamic paging support proposed in the SGX version 2 specifications.

SGX supports attestation of software running on top of an untrusted platform, by using signed hardware measurements to establish trust between parties. For future efforts it would be interesting, in light of the large cost of enclave transition demonstrated above, to examine the performance characteristics of a secure channel for communication between enclaves.

5   Related Work

Several previous works quantify various aspects of the overhead associated with composite architectures based on SGX. Haven [8] implements shielded execution of unmodified legacy applications by inserting a library OS entirely inside of SGX enclaves. This effort resulted in architectural changes to the SGX specification to include, among other things, support for dynamic paging. The proof-of-concept implementation of Haven is only evaluated in terms of legacy applications running on top of the system. Furthermore, Haven was built on a pre-release emulated version of SGX, and the performance evaluation is not directly comparable to real world applications. Overshadow [9] provides similar capabilities as Haven, but does not rely on dedicated hardware support.

SCONE [10] implements support for secure containers inside of SGX enclaves. The design of SCONE is driven by experiments on container designs pertaining to the TCB size inside enclaves, in which, at the most extreme an entire library OS is included and at the minimum a stub interface to application libraries. The evaluation of SCONE is much like the evaluation of Haven, based on running legacy applications inside SCONE containers. While Arnautov et al. [10] make the same conclusions with regards to TCB size versus memory usage and enclave transition cost as Baumann et al. [8], the paper does not quantify this cost. Despite this, SCONE supplies a solution to the entry-exit problem we outline in Sect. 3, where threads are pinned inside the enclave, and do not transition to the outside. Rather, communication happens by means of the enclave threads writing to a dedicated queue residing in regular DRAM memory. This approach is still, however, vulnerable to threads being evicted from enclaves by AEX caused by an Inter Processor Interrupt (IPI) as part of a page fault.

Costan and Devadas [6] describe the architecture of SGX based on prior art, released developer manuals, and patents. Furthermore, they conduct a comprehensive security analysis of SGX, falsifying some of its guarantees by explaining in detail exploitable vulnerabilities within the architecture. This work is mostly orthogonal to our efforts, yet we base most of our knowledge of SGX from this treatment on the topic. These prior efforts lead Costan et al. [11] to implement Sanctum, an alternative hardware architectural extension providing many of the same properties as SGX, but targeted towards the Rocket RISC-V chip architecture. This paper evaluates its prototype by simulated hardware, against an insecure baseline without the proposed security properties. McKeen et al. [12] introduce dynamic paging support to the SGX specifications. This prototype hardware was not available to us.

Ryoan [13] attempts to solve the same problems outlined in the introduction, by implementing a distributed sandbox facilitating untrusted computing on secret data residing on third-party cloud services. Ryoan proposes a new request oriented data-model where processing modules are activated once without persisting data input to them. Furthermore, by remote attestation, Ryoan is able to verify the integrity of sandbox instances and protect execution. By combining sandboxing techniques with SGX, Ryoan is able to create a shielding construct supporting mutually distrust between the application and the infrastructure. Again, Ryoan is benchmarked against real world applications, and just like other prior work, does not correctly quantify the exact overhead attributed to SGX primitives. Furthermore, large parts of its evaluation is conducted in an SGX emulator based on QEMU, which has been retrofitted with delays and TLB flushes based upon real hardware measurements to better mirror real SGX performance. These hardware measurements are present for EENTRY and EEXIT instructions, but do not attribute the cost of moving argument data into and out of enclave memory. Moreover, Ryoan speculates on the cost of SGX V2 paging support, although strictly based on emulated measurements and assumptions about physical cost.

ARM TrustZone is a hardware security architecture that can be incorporated into ARMv7-A, ARMv8-A and ARMv8-M on-chip systems [14,15]. Although the underlying hardware design, features, and interfaces differ substantially to SGX, both essentially provide the same key concepts of hardware isolated execution domains and the ability to bootstrap attested software stacks into those enclaves [16]. However, the TrustZone hardware can only distinguish between two execution domains, and relies on having a software based trusted execution environment for any further refinements.

6   Conclusion

SaaS providers are increasingly storing personal privacy-sensitive data about customers on third-party cloud providers. Moreover, companies monetize this data by providing personalized experiences for customers requiring curation and analysis. This dilution of responsibility and trust is concerning for data owners as cloud providers cannot be trusted to enforce the, often government mandated, restrictive usage policies which accompany privacy-sensitive data.

Intel SGX is part of a new wave of trusted computing targeting commodity hardware and allowing for the execution of code and data in trusted segments of memory at close to native processor speed. These extensions to the x86 ISA guarantee confidentiality, integrity and correctness of code and data residing on untrusted third-party platforms.

Prior work demonstrates the applicability of SGX for complete systems capable of hosting large legacy applications. These systems, however, do not quantify the exact micro architectural cost of achieving confidentiality, integrity and attestation for applications through the use of trusted computing. This paper has evaluated the cost of provisioning, data copying, context transitioning, memory footprint and multi-threaded execution of enclaves. From these results we have distilled a set of principles which developers of trusted analytics systems should use to maximize the performance of their application while securing privacy-sensitive data on third-party cloud platforms.

Acknowledgments. This work was supported in part by the Norwegian Research Council project numbers 263248/O70 and 250138. We would like to thank Robbert van Renesse for his insights and discussions, and anonymous reviewers for their useful insights and comments.

References

1. Gjerdrum, A.T., Johansen, H.D., Johansen, D.: Implementing informed consent as information-flow policies for secure analytics on eHealth data: principles and practices. In: IEEE Conference on Connected Health: Applications, Systems and Engineering Technologies: The 1st International Workshop on Security, Privacy, and Trustworthiness in Medical Cyber-Physical System, CHASE 2016. IEEE (2016)
2. Johansen, H.D., Birrell, E., Van Renesse, R., Schneider, F.B., Stenhaug, M., Johansen, D.: Enforcing privacy policies with meta-code. In: 6th Asia-Pacific Workshop on Systems, p. 16. ACM (2015)

3. Osborn, J.D., Challener, D.C.: Trusted platform module evolution. Johns Hopkins APL Tech. Digest **32**, 536–543 (2013)
4. TCG Published: TPM main part 1 design principles. Specification Version 1.2 Revision 116, Trusted Computing Group (2011)
5. Anati, I., Gueron, S., Johnson, S., Scarlata, V.: Innovative technology for CPU based attestation and sealing. In: 2nd International Workshop on Hardware and Architectural Support for Security and Privacy, vol. 13 (2013)
6. Costan, V., Devadas, S.: Intel SGX explained. In: Cryptology ePrint Archive (2016)
7. Gjerdrum, A.T., Pettersen, R., Johansen, H.D., Johansen, D.: Performance of trusted computing in cloud infrastructures with Intel SGX. In: 7th International Conference on Cloud Computing and Services Science, CLOSER 2017. SCITEPRESS (2017)
8. Baumann, A., Peinado, M., Hunt, G.: Shielding applications from an untrusted cloud with Haven. In: 11th USENIX Symposium on Operating Systems Design and Implementation (OSDI 2014). USENIX Advanced Computing Systems Association (2014)
9. Chen, X., Garfinkel, T., Lewis, E.C., Subrahmanyam, P., Waldspurger, C.A., Boneh, D., Dwoskin, J., Ports, D.R.: Overshadow: a virtualization-based approach to retrofitting protection in commodity operating systems. In: 13th International Conference on Architectural Support for Programming Languages and Operating Systems, ASPLOS XIII, pp. 2–13. ACM, New York (2008)
10. Arnautov, S., Trach, B., Gregor, F., Knauth, T., Martin, A., Priebe, C., Lind, J., Muthukumaran, D., O'Keeffe, D., Stillwell, M.L., Goltzsche, D., Eyers, D., Kapitza, R., Pietzuch, P., Fetzer, C.: Scone: secure Linux containers with Intel SGX. In: 12th USENIX Symposium on Operating Systems Design and Implementation (OSDI 2016), GA, pp. 689–703. USENIX Association (2016)
11. Costan, V., Lebedev, I., Devadas, S.: Sanctum: minimal hardware extensions for strong software isolation. In: USENIX Security, vol. 16, pp. 857–874 (2016)
12. McKeen, F., Alexandrovich, I., Anati, I., Caspi, D., Johnson, S., Leslie-Hurd, R., Rozas, C.: Intel® software guard extensions (Intel® SGX) support for dynamic memory management inside an enclave. In: Hardware and Architectural Support for Security and Privacy 2016, p. 10. ACM (2016)
13. Hunt, T., Zhu, Z., Xu, Y., Peter, S., Witchel, E.: Ryoan: a distributed sandbox for untrusted computation on secret data. In: 12th USENIX Conference on Operating Systems Design and Implementation, OSDI 2016, pp. 533–549. USENIX Association, Berkeley (2016)
14. Ngabonziza, B., Martin, D., Bailey, A., Cho, H., Martin, S.: Trustzone explained: architectural features and use cases. In: 2016 IEEE 2nd International Conference on Collaboration and Internet Computing (CIC), pp. 445–451. IEEE (2016)
15. Shuja, J., Gani, A., Bilal, K., Khan, A.U.R., Madani, S.A., Khan, S.U., Zomaya, A.Y.: A survey of mobile device virtualization: taxonomy and state of the art. ACM Comput. Surv. (CSUR) **49**, 1 (2016)
16. Pettersen, R., Johansen, H.D., Johansen, D.: Trusted execution on ARM Trust-Zone. In: 7th International Conference on Cloud Computing and Services Science (CLOSER 2017) (2017)

About the Complexity to Transfer Cloud Applications at Runtime and How Container Platforms Can Contribute?

Nane Kratzke[✉]

Center for Communication, Systems and Applications (CoSA),
Lübeck University of Applied Sciences, Lübeck, Germany
`nane.kratzke@fh-luebeck.de`

Abstract. Cloud-native applications are often designed for only one specific cloud infrastructure or platform. The effort to port such kind of applications into a different cloud is usually a laborious one time exercise. Modern Cloud-native application architecture approaches make use of popular elastic container platforms (Apache Mesos, Kubernetes, Docker Swarm). These kind of platforms contribute to a lot of existing cloud engineering requirements. This given, it astonishes that these kind of platforms (already existing and open source available) are not considered more consequently for multi-cloud solutions. These platforms provide inherent multi-cloud support but this is often overlooked. This paper presents a software prototype and shows how Kubernetes and Docker Swarm clusters could be successfully transfered at runtime across public cloud infrastructures of Google (Google Compute Engine), Microsoft (Azure) and Amazon (EC2) and further cloud infrastructures like OpenStack. Additionally, software engineering lessons learned are derived and some astonishing performance data of the mentioned cloud infrastructures is presented that could be used for further optimizations of IaaS transfers of Cloud-native applications.

Keywords: Cloud-native application · Multi-cloud · Elastic platform
Container · Portability · Transferability · MAPE · AWS · GCE
Azure · OpenStack · Kubernetes · Docker · Swarm

1 Introduction

This Chapter extends the ideas formulated in [1] and focuses on the complexity to transfer Cloud-native Applications (CNA) at runtime which seems – even after 10 years of cloud computing – to be an astonishingly complex problem [2,3]. It can be hard to operate a CNA across different public or private infrastructures. Very often, because standardization in cloud computing is not very established or in very early stages. A very good case study is Instagram. Instagram had to analyze their existing services for almost one year to derive a viable migration plan how to transfer their services from *Amazon Web Services* *(AWS)*

© Springer International Publishing AG, part of Springer Nature 2018
D. Ferguson et al. (Eds.): CLOSER 2017, CCIS 864, pp. 19–45, 2018.
https://doi.org/10.1007/978-3-319-94959-8_2

to Facebook datacenters[1]. This migration was accompanied by some observable outages for service customers. This phenomenon is called a vendor lock-in and CNAs seem to be extremely vulnerable for it [4]. Therefore, the author proposes to think about the way how to deploy CNAs in order to get migration capabilities across different cloud infrastructures by design. The central idea is to split the migration problem into two independent engineering problems which are too often solved together.

Table 1. Some popular open source elastic platforms. *These kind of platforms can used as a kind of cloud infrastructure unifying middleware.*

Platform	Contributors	URL
Kubernetes	Cloud Native Comput. Found	http://kubernetes.io (initiated by Google)
Swarm	Docker	https://docker.io
Mesos	Apache	http://mesos.apache.org/
Nomad	Hashicorp	https://nomadproject.io/

1. The **infrastructure aware** deployment and operation of elastic container platforms (like the platforms listed in Table 1). However, these platforms can be deployed and operated in a way that they can be transferred across IaaS infrastructures of different private and public cloud service providers at runtime as this contribution will show.
2. The **infrastructure agnostic** deployment of applications on top of these kind of migrateable container platforms. These elastic container platforms can be seen as a kind of cloud infrastructure unifying middleware.

The main point of this contribution is to make use of elastic container platforms that can be used to abstract and encapsulate IaaS infrastructure specifics. That makes it possible to define CNAs that must not be aware about specifics of underlying cloud infrastructures. CNAs are operated on a logical platform and this logical platform is transferable across different public or private IaaS infrastructures. Although this is possible technologically as this contribution will show, almost no recent multi-cloud survey study (see Sect. 6) considered elastic container platforms (see Table 1) as a viable and pragmatic option to support this style of multi-cloud handling. It is very astonishing that this kind of already existing and open source available technology is not considered more consequently (see Sect. 6). That might have to do with the fact, that *"the emergence of containers, especially container supported microservices and service pods, has raised a new revolution in [...] resource management."* [5]. However, container technologies and elastic container platforms gained substantial momentum in recent years and resulted in a lot of technological progress driven by companies

---

[1] To the best of the author's knowledge there are no research papers analyzing this interesting case study. So, the reader is referred to an Wired magazine article: https://www.wired.com/2014/06/facebook-instagram/.

like *Docker, Netflix, Google, Facebook, Twitter*. A lot of these companies released their solutions as Open Source software. Having this progress in mind, we have to state that existing multi-cloud approaches are often dated before container technologies have been widespread and seem very complex – much too complex for a lot of use cases of cloud-native applications. This Chapter considers this progress and presents a software prototype that provides the following:

- Section 4.2 presents a control loop that is able to scale elastic container platforms in multi-cloud scenarios. But the control loop make use of the same features providing scalability to support federation and transferability across multiple IaaS cloud infrastructures as a side-effect.
- The intention of this control loop is to be used in the execution phase of higher-level auto-scaling MAPE loops (monitoring, analysis, planning, execution) [5,6] and to make the necessity for complex and IaaS infrastructure-specific multi-cloud workflows redundant (to some degree).

Section 2 will investigate how CNAs are being build and how to use these insights to avoid vendor lock-in in a pragmatic and often overlooked way. Section 3 will focus requirements which should be fulfilled by multi-cloud capable CNAs and how existing open source elastic container platforms contribute pragmatically to fulfill these requirements in a resilient and elastic way. Section 4 presents a multi-cloud aware proof-of-concept. Several lessons learned from the evaluation, performance analysis and software prototyping are presented in Sect. 5. The presented approach is related to other work in Sect. 6.

Table 2. Cloud Application Maturity Model, adapted from *OPEN DATA CENTER ALLIANCE Best Practices (Architecting Cloud-Aware Applications)* [9].

Level	Maturity	Criteria
3	Cloud native	- A CNA can migrate across infrastructure providers at runtime and without interruption of service **(focus of this Chapter)**
		- A CNA can automatically scale out/in based on stimuli
2	Cloud resilient	- The application state is isolated in a minimum of services
		- The application is unaffected by dependent service failures
		- The application is infrastructure agnostic
1	Cloud friendly	- The application is composed of loosely coupled services
		- Application services are discoverable by name (not by IP)
		- Application components are designed using cloud patterns
		- Application compute and storage are separated
0	Cloud ready	- The application runs on virtualized infrastructure
		- The application can be instantiated from an image or script

2   Commonalities of Cloud-Native Applications

There exist noteworthy similarities of various view points with regard to the vague term CNA [2]. A common approach is to define maturity levels in order to categorize different kind of cloud applications. Table 2 shows a maturity model proposed by the *Open Data Center Alliance*. Common motivations for CNA architectures are software development **speed** (time to market), fault isolation, fault tolerance, and automatic recovery to improve **safety**, and to enable horizontal (instead of vertical) application **scalability** [7]. Fehling et al. [8] proposed the IDEAL model for CNAs. A CNA should strive for an i̲solated state, is d̲istributed, provides e̲lasticity in a horizontal scaling way, and should be operated on an a̲utomated deployment machinery. Finally, its components should be l̲oosely coupled.

Balalaie et al. [10] stress that these properties are addressed by cloud-specific architecture and infrastructure approaches like **Microservices** [11,12], **API-based collaboration**, adaption of **cloud-focused patterns** [8], and **self-service elastic platforms** that are used to deploy and operate these microservices via self-contained deployment units (containers). These platforms provide additional operational capabilities on top of IaaS infrastructures like automated and on-demand scaling of application instances, application health management, dynamic routing and load balancing as well as aggregation of logs and metrics [2]. Some open source examples of such kind of elastic platforms are listed in Table 1.

If the reader understands the commonality that CNAs are operated (more and more often) on elastic – often container-based – platforms, it is an obvious idea to delegate the multi-cloud handling down to these platforms. The question is how to do this? Therefore, the multi-cloud aware handling of these elastic platforms is focused throughout this Chapter.

3   Multi-cloud Specifics

A lot of requirements regarding transferability, awareness and security come along with multi-cloud approaches [13–16]. These requirements will be addressed in this Section. Furthermore it is investigated how already existing elastic container platforms contribute to fulfill these requirements [4]. Impatient readers may jump directly to Table 3 at the end of this Section which summarizes the main points.

3.1   Transferability Requirements

Cloud computing can be understood as a computing model making use of ubiquitous network access to a shared and virtualized pool of resources. Sadly, this conceptual model is quite vague and has been implemented by a large number of service providers in different and not necessarily standardized or compatible ways. So, **portability or transferability** has to be requested for multi-cloud capable CNAs due to several reasons like costs, optimal resource utilization, technology changes, or legal issues [14].

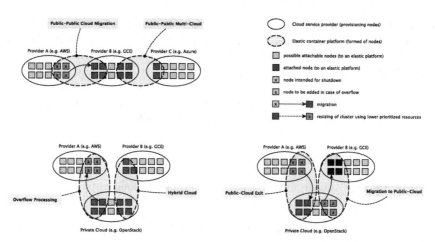

Fig. 1. Deployment options and transferability opportunities: *taken from* [1].

Elastic container platforms (see Table 1) compose container hosts (nodes) into a higher level logical concept – a cluster. Such clusters provide **self-service elastic platforms** for cloud-native applications [7] in an often overlooked way. Some of these platforms are really "bulletproofed". *Apache Mesos* [17] has been successfully operated for years by companies like Twitter or Netflix to consolidate hundreds of thousands of compute nodes. Peinl and Holzschuher [18] provide an excellent overview for interested readers. From the author's point of view, there are the following benefits using these elastic container platforms.

1. The **integration of single nodes (container hosts) into one logical cluster** is mainly done to **manage complexity**. However, it is possible to deploy such clusters across public and private cloud infrastructures.
2. If elastic container platforms are deployed across different cloud service providers they can be still accessed as one logical cluster. And cross-provider deployed elastic container platforms are obviously **vendor lock-in avoiding**.
3. Furthermore, elastic container platforms are **designed for failure** and provide self-healing capabilities via auto-placement, auto-restart, auto-replication and auto-scaling features. They will identify lost containers (due to whatever reasons, e.g. process failure or node unavailability) and will restart containers and place them on remaining nodes. These features are absolutely necessary to operate large-scale distributed systems in a resilient way. However, exactly the same features can be used intentionally to **realize transferability requirements**.

A cluster can be resized simply by adding or removing nodes to the cluster. Affected containers will be rescheduled to other available nodes. In a first step, we simply attach additional nodes provisioned by *GCE* to the cluster. In a second step, we shut down all nodes provided by *AWS*. The cluster will observe node failures and trigger its self-healing features to reschedule lost containers accordingly. From an inner point of view of the platform, rescheduling operations are tasked due to node failures. From an outside point of view it looks like (and in fact **is**) a migration from one provider to another provider at run-time. At this point this should make the general idea clear. All the details will be explained in more details in Sect. 4 and further multi-cloud options like public cloud exits, cloud migrations, public multi-clouds, hybrid clouds, overflow processing and further can be handled using the same approach (see Fig. 1).

3.2 Awareness Requirements

Beside portability/transferability requirements, multi-cloud applications need to have several additional **awarenesses** [16]:

1. **Data Location Awareness.** The persistent data and the processing units of an application should be in the same data center (even on the same rack).
2. **Geo-location Awareness.** To achieve better performance requests should be scheduled near the geographical location of their origin.
3. **Pricing Awareness.** Fiscally efficient provisioning needs information about providers' prices for scheduling operations.
4. **Legislation/Policy Awareness.** For some use cases legislative and political considerations upon provisioning and scheduling must be taken into account. For example, some services could be required to avoid placing data outside a given country.
5. **Local Resources Awareness:** Very often in-house resources should have higher priority than external ones (overflow processing into a public cloud).

Platforms like *Kubernetes*, *Mesos*, *Docker Swarm* are able to tag nodes of their clusters with arbitrary key/value pairs. These tags can be used to encode geo-locations, prices, policies and preferred local resources (and further aspects). So, the above mentioned awareness requirements can be mapped to scheduling constraints for container schedulers of elastic platforms.

For instance, *Docker Swarm* uses constraint filters[2] for that kind of purpose. Arbitrary tags like a location tag "Germany" can be assigned to a node. This tagging can be defined in a cluster definition file and will be assigned to a node in the *install node* step shown in Fig. 4. *Docker Swarm* would schedule a *CouchDB* database container only on nodes which are tagged as "location=Germany" if a constraint filter is applied like shown.

```
docker run -e constraint:location==Germany couchdb
```

---

[2] See https://docs.docker.com/v1.11/swarm/scheduler/filter/ (last access 15th Feb. 2017).

Table 3. Common multi-cloud requirements and contributing elastic platform concepts.

Requirements	Contributing platform concepts
Transferability	- Integration of nodes into one logical elastic platform
	- Elastic platforms are designed for failure
	- Cross-provider deployable (as shown by Sect. 4)
Data location	- Pod Concept (Kubernetes)
	- Volume Orchestrators (e.g. Flocker for Docker)
Awarenesses - Pricing - Legislation/policy - Local resources	- Tagging of nodes with geolocation, pricing, policy or on-premise informations - Platform schedulers have selectors (Swarm), affinities (Kubernetes), constraints (Mesos/Marathon) to consider these taggings for scheduling
Security	- Default encrypted data/control plane (e.g. Swarm)
	- Pluggable and encryptable overlay networks (e.g. Weave for Kubernetes)

Kubernetes provides similar tag-based concepts called *node selectors* and even more expressive *(anti-)affinities* which are considered by the *Kubernetes* scheduler[3]. The *Marathon* framework for *Mesos* uses *constraints*[4]. All of these concepts rely on the same idea and can be used to handle mentioned awareness requirements.

3.3 Security Requirements

If such kind of elastic platforms are deployed across different providers it is likely that data has to be submitted via the "open and unprotected" internet. Therefore elastic container platforms provide encryptable overlay networks which can be used for such kind of scenarios. For instance, *Docker's Swarm Mode* (since version 1.12) provides an encrypted data and control plane and *Kubernetes* can be configured to use encryptable overlay network plugins like *Weave*. The often feared network performance impacts can be contained [19,20].

4 Proof of Concept

This Section presents a software prototype that is implemented in Ruby and provides a command line tool as core component. The tool can be triggered in

---

[3] See https://kubernetes.io/docs/user-guide/node-selection/ (last access 15th Feb. 2017).

[4] See https://mesosphere.github.io/marathon/docs/constraints.html (last access 15th Feb. 2017).

the execution phase of a MAPE auto-scaling loop [5] and scales elastic container platforms according to an execution pipeline (see Fig. 4). The control process interprets cluster description format (the *intended state* of the container cluster, see Appendix 7) and the *current state* of the cluster (attached nodes, existing security groups, see Appendix 7). If the intended state differs from the current state necessary adaption actions are deduced (attach/detachment of nodes, creation and termination of security groups). The execution pipeline assures that

- security groups are established in participating cloud service infrastructures to enable network access control before a node joins the elastic container platform,
- that all nodes are reachable by all other nodes of the cluster adjusting all security groups if a node enters or leaves the cluster,
- that nodes are provided with all necessary software and configuration installed to join the elastic container platform successfully,
- that the elastic container platform is operated in a way that it is providing encrypted overlay networks for containers,
- that removed nodes are drained (graceful node shutdown) in order to initiate rescheduling of workloads to remaining nodes of the cluster,
- that leaving nodes and "empty" security groups are terminated to free resources of IaaS infrastructures.

4.1   Description of Elastic Platforms

The conceptual model shown in Fig. 3 is used to describe the deployment of elastic platforms in multi-cloud scenarios and considers arbitrary IaaS cloud service providers [4]. Public cloud service providers organize their IaaS services using mainly two approaches: project- and region-based service delivery. *GCE* and *OpenStack* infrastructures are examples of project-based approaches. To request IaaS resources like virtual machines one has to create a project first. The project has access to resources of all provider regions. *AWS* is an example for such kind of region-based service delivery. Both approaches have their advantages and disadvantages as the reader will see. However, the approaches are given and multi-cloud solutions must prepared that both approaches occur in parallel. The conceptual model integrates both approaches introducing a concept called District (see Fig. 3).

A District can be understood as a user defined "datacenter" which is provided by a specific cloud service provider (following the project- or region-based approach). So, provider regions or projects can be mapped to one or more Districts and vice versa. This additional layer provides maximum flexibility in defining multi-cloud deployments of elastic container platforms. A multi-cloud deployed elastic container platform can be defined using two definition formats (cluster.json and districts.json). The definition formats are explained in the Appendices in more details.

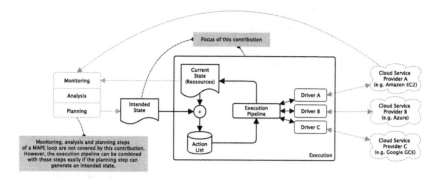

The control theory inspired execution control loop compares the intended state of an elastic container platform with the current state and derives necessary actions. These actions are processed by the execution pipeline explained in Figure 4. The elastic container platform is operated in a set of synchronized security groups across different IaaS infrastructures.

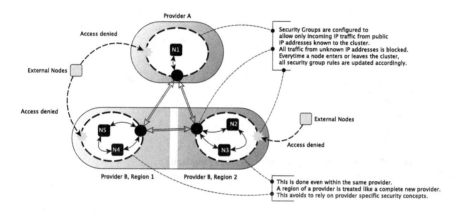

An elastic container platform composed of several nodes is deployed to multiple providers and secured by synchronized security groups (IP incoming access rules) allowing platform internal traffic only. To allow external traffic this must be configured explicitly by the operator and is not done by the execution pipeline or covered by this contribution.

Fig. 2. The execution loop and synchronized security group concept.

An (elastic platform) is defined as a list of `Deployments` in a cluster definition file (see Appendix 7). A `Deployment` is defined per `District` and defines how many nodes of a specific `Flavor` should perform a specific cluster role. A lot of elastic container platforms have two main roles of nodes in a cluster. A "master" role to perform scheduling, control and management tasks and a "worker" (or slave) role to execute containers. The proposed prototype can work with arbitrary roles and rolenames. Role-specifics can be considered by `Platform` drivers (see Fig. 3) in their `install`, `join` and `leave` cluster hooks (see Fig. 4). A typical `Deployment` can be expressed using this JSON snippet.

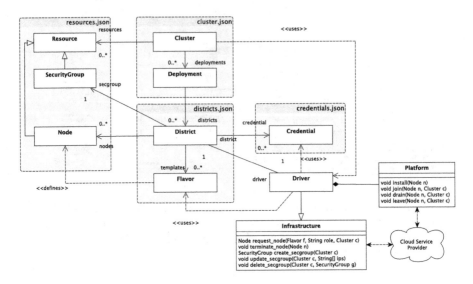

Fig. 3. The conceptual data model: *The relation to descriptive cluster definition formats is shown as well (please compare with Appendices 7, 7, 7, 7).*

```
{ "district": "gce-europe",
  "flavor": "small",
  "role": "master",
  "quantity": 3
  "tags": {
    "location": "Europe", "policy": "Safe-Harbour",
    "scheduling-priority": "low", "further": "arbitrary tags"
  }
}
```

A complete elastic container platform will be composed by a list of such `Deployments`. Machine `Flavors` (e.g. small, medium and large machines) and `Districts` are user defined and have to be mapped to concrete cloud service provider specifics. This is done using the `districts.json` definition file (see Appendix 7). Each `District` object executes deployments by adding or removing machines to the cluster as well as tagging them to handle the awareness requirements mentioned in Sect. 3. The infrastructure-specific execution is delegated by a `District` object to a `Driver` object. A `Driver` encapsules and processes all necessary cloud service provider and elastic container platform specific requests. The driver uses access `Credentials` for authentication (see Appendix 7) and generates `Resource` objects (`Nodes` and `SecurityGroups`) representing resources (current state of the cluster, encoded in a `resources.json` file, see Appendix 7) provided by the cloud service provider (`District`). `SecurityGroups` are used to allow internal platform communication across IaaS infrastructures. These basic security means are provided by all IaaS infrastructures under different names (firewalls, security groups, access rules, network rules, ...). This resources list is used by the control process to build the delta between the intended state (encoded in `cluster.json`) and the current state (encoded in `resources.json`).

4.2 The Control Loop

The control loop shown in Fig. 2 is responsible to reach the intended state (encoded in `cluster.json`, Appendix 7) and can handle common multi-cloud workflows:

- A *deployment* of a cluster can be understood as running the execution pipeline on an initially empty resources list.
- A *shutdown* can be expressed by setting all deployment quantities to 0.
- A *migration* from one `District` A to another `District` B can be expressed by setting all `Deployment` quantities of A to 0 and adding the former quantities of A to the quantities of B.
- and more.

The execution pipeline of the control loop derives a prioritized *action plan* to reach the intended state (see Fig. 4). The reader should be aware that the pipeline must keep the affected cluster in a valid and operational state at all times. The currently implemented strategy considers practitioner experience to reduce "stress" for the affected elastic container platform but other pipeline strategies might work as well and are subject to further research.

Whenever a new node attachment is triggered by the control loop, the corresponding `Driver` is called to launch a new `Node` request. The `Node` is added to the list of requested resources (and extends therefore the current state of the cluster). Then all existing `SecurityGroups` are updated to allow incoming network traffic from the new `Node`. These steps are handled by an IaaS `Infrastructure` driver. Next, the control is handed over to a `Platform` driver performing necessary software install steps via SSH-based scripting. Finally, the node is joined to the cluster using platform (and maybe role-)specific joining calls provided by the `Platform` driver. If *install* or *join* operations were not successful, the machine is terminated and removed from the resources list by the `Infrastructure` driver. In these cases the current state could not be extended and a next round of the control loop would do a retry. Due to its "cybernetic" design philosophy, the control-loop can handle failures simply by repeating failed actions in a next loop.

4.3 IaaS Infrastructures and Platforms

The handling of infrastructure and platform specifics is done using an extendable driver concept (see Fig. 3). The classes `Platform` and `Infrastructure` form two extension points to provide support for **IaaS infrastructures** like *AWS, GCE, Azure, DigitalOcean, RackSpace, ...*, and for **elastic container platforms** like *Docker Swarm, Kubernetes, Mesos/Marathon, Nomad*, and so on. Infrastructures and platforms can be integrated by extending the `Infrastructure` class

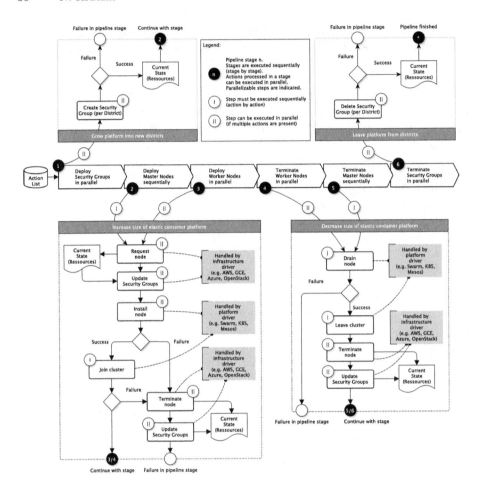

Fig. 4. Execution pipeline.

(for IaaS infrastructures) or `Platform` class (for additional elastic container platforms). The current state of implementation provides **platform drivers** for the elastic container platforms *Kubernetes* and *Docker's SwarmMode* and **infrastructure drivers** for the public IaaS infrastructures *AWS*, *GCE*, *Azure* and the IaaS infrastructure *OpenStack*. Due to the mentioned extension points further container `Platform`s and IaaS `Infrastructure`s are easily extendable.

Table 4 shows how this has been applied for different IaaS drivers. Although only common and very basic IaaS concepts (virtual machine, security groups and IP based access rules) have been used, we can observe a substantial variation in infrastructure specific detail concepts. Even the drivers for *OpenStack* and *Azure* rely on different detail concepts. This is astonishing because both drivers have been implemented using the same cloud library (fog.io). That is why CNAs are prone for vendor lock-in. They bind to these detail infrastructure specifics.

The proposed concept encapsulates all those details in low level infrastructure drivers to make them completely transparent for the platform driver and CNAs being operated on elastic container platforms.

Table 4. IaaS drivers: *The following APIs were used to interact with different cloud infrastructures. In case of GCE the terminal based CLI* gcloud *program is used to demonstrate that the presented approach would even work for infrastructures where no Ruby API is available. Drivers are responsible to launch and terminate nodes (Ubuntu 16.04 LTS) and to synchronize security groups (see Fig. 2).*

Driver	Provider API	Used detail provider concepts
AWS	AWS Ruby SDK	- Keyfile (SSH public/private key)
		- Virtual network + subnet (AWS VPC)
		- Internet gateway + route tables
		- Security group
		- IP based ingress permissions
		- Virtual machines (AWS instances)
OpenStack	fog.io library	- Keyfile (SSH public/private key)
	fog-openstack	- Security group
		- Security group rules
		- External network
		- Floating IPs
		- Fog server concept (virtual machine)
GCE	gcloud CLI	- Keyfile (SSH public/private key)
	(fog.io would work as well)	- Virtual network + subnet (GCE VPC)
		- GCE instance concept (virtual machine)
Azure	fog.io library *with Azure plugin*	- Keyfile (SSH public/private key)
		- Virtual network + subnet (Azure)
	(fog-azure-rm)	- Network interface (Azure)
		- Public IPs (Azure)
		- Storage account (Azure)
		- Security group + rules (Azure)
		- Resource group (Azure)
		- Fog server concept (virtual machine)

See the following urls:
https://github.com/aws/aws-sdk-ruby, https://github.com/fog/fog-openstack, https://github.com/fog/fog-azure-rm, https://cloud.google.com/sdk/gcloud/.

5   Evaluation

The prototype was evaluated operating and transferring two elastic platforms (*Swarm Mode of Docker 17.06* and *Kubernetes 1.7*) across four public and private cloud infrastructures (see Table 5). The platforms operated a reference "sock-shop" application[5] being one of the most complete reference applications for microservices architecture research [21].

Table 5. Used machine types and regions: *The machine types have been selected according to the proposed method by Kratzke and Quint [22]. The OpenStack m1.large and m1.medium are research institute specific machine types and that have been intentionally defined to show maximum similarities with the other mentioned machine types. The OpenStack platform is operated in the author's research institution datacenter and does not necessarily provide representative data.*

Provider	Region	Master node type	Worker node type
AWS	eu-west-1	m4.xlarge (4 vCPU)	m4.large (2 vCPU)
GCE	europe-west1	n1-standard-4 (4 vCPU)	n1-standard-2 (2 vCPU)
Azure	europewest	Standard_A3 (4 vCPU)	Standard_A2 (2 vCPU)
OpenStack	*own datacenter*	m1.large (4 vCPU)	m1.medium (2 vCPU)

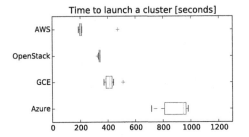 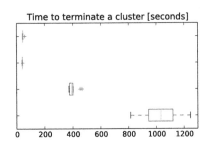

Fig. 5. Launching and terminating times (Kubernetes): *The Kubernetes cluster was composed of one master and five worker nodes. Data of single cloud experiments E1 and E2 (see Table 6) is presented.*

5.1   Experiments

The implementation was tested using a 6 node cluster formed of one master node and 5 worker nodes executing the above mentioned reference application. The experiments shown in Table 6 demonstrate elastic container platform deployments, terminations, and platform transfers across different cloud service infrastructures. Additionally, the experiments were used to measure the runtimes of these kind of infrastructure operations.

---

[5] https://github.com/microservices-demo/microservices-demo (last access 3rd July 2017).

Table 6. Experiments: *Single cloud experiments E1 and E2 were mainly used to measure infrastructure specific timings (see Fig. 5) and have been repeated 10 times.*

Nr.	Experiment	Cloud	Master	Worker	Provider
E1	Cluster launch	single	1	5	AWS, GCE, Azure, OpenStack
E2	Cluster termination	single	1	5	AWS, GCE, Azure, OpenStack

Multi-cloud transfer experiments E3: *Multi-cloud experiments E3 are used to demonstrate the transfer of elastic container platforms at runtime between different cloud service infrastructures and to get a better understanding about runtimes for these kind of operations (see Figure 8). 5 worker nodes of the cluster have been transfered between two infrastructures in both directions. Initial transfer experiments E3.1 - E3.3 (to cover all providers) were repeated 10 times. Follow up transfer experiments (E3.4 - E3.6) to cover all possible provider pairings were only repeated 5 times. In total 450 nodes were transfered between 4 providers.*

	AWS	GCE	Azure
OpenStack	**E3.1** 5 nodes, n=10 both directions	**E3.2** 5 nodes, n=10 both directions	**E3.3** 5 nodes, n=10 both directions
AWS	*see E1, E2*	**E3.4** 5 nodes, n=5 both directions	**E3.5** 5 nodes, n=5 both directions
GCE	*see E3.4*	*see E1, E2*	**E3.6** 5 nodes, n=5 both directions

To compare similar machine types it was decided to follow the approach presented in [22] to make use of machine types from different providers that show high similarities regarding processing, networking, I/O and memory performance. Table 5 shows the selection of machine types.

It turned out that most of runtimes are due to low level IaaS infrastructure operations and not due to elastic container platform operations. Figure 6 shows platform differences of *Kubernetes* and *Swarm* measured using the cloud service provider *AWS*. We see that the container platform *Swarm* can be installed approximately 10 s faster than *Kubernetes*. And the joining of a *Kubernetes* node is approximately 5 s slower than joining a *Swarm* node. Only the cluster initialization of *Kubernetes* is remarkable slower. However, that is an operation which is done only one time while bootstrapping the cluster. The reader should compare these platform runtimes with infrastructure specific runtimes presented in Fig. 5. Even on the fastest provider it took more than three minutes to launch a cluster. So, 15 s of installation and joining runtime differences between different elastic container platforms are negligible. So, only the data for *Kubernetes* is presented throughout this Chapter. The data for another elastic container platform like Swarm would be simply to similar to present. Instead of that, Fig. 7 can be used to identify much more severe and there more interesting time intensive

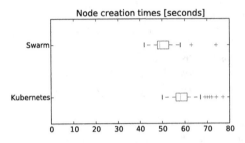
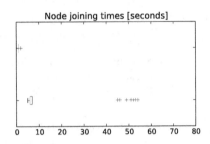

Fig. 6. Differences in platform specific timings: *differences in creation are due to slightly longer installation times of Kubernetes; differences in joining are due to a more complex join process of Kubernetes (especially for cluster initialization, initial join of approx. 50 s)*

infrastructure operations. Several interesting findings especially regarding software defined network aspects in multi-cloud scenarios and reactiveness of public cloud service infrastructures might be of interest for the reader.

Figure 5 shows the results of the experiments **E1** and **E2**. The reader might be surprised, that cloud infrastructure operations have a substantial variation in runtimes although similar resources were used for the presented experiments. Figure 5 shows that a cluster launch on AWS takes only 3 min but can take up to 15 min on Azure (median values). The termination is even more worse. A cluster can be terminated in approximately a minute on *AWS* or *OpenStack*, but it can take up 18 min to complete on *Azure*.

The question is why? Figure 7 presents runtimes of infrastructure operations to create/delete and adjust security groups and to create/terminate virtual cluster nodes (virtual machines) that have been measured while performing the mentioned experiments. Transfers are complex sequences of these IaaS operations and substantial differences for different IaaS infrastructures are observable for these operations. *AWS* and *OpenStack* infrastructures are much faster than *GCE* and *Azure* in creating security groups and nodes. The same is true for node terminations.

And because different providers (and their different runtime behaviors) can be combined in any combination this can result in astonishing runtime differences for node transfers. Figure 8 shows all E3 experiments and plots measured runtime differences of transfers between the analyzed infrastructures of *AWS*, *GCE*, *Azure* and *OpenStack*. In the best case (transfer from *OpenStack* to *AWS*) the transfer could be completed in 3 min, in the worst case (transfer from *Azure* to *GCE*) the transfer took more than 18 min (median values). Furthermore, a transfer from provider A to B did in no case take the same time as from B to A. A more in-depth analysis turned out that this is mainly due to different runtimes of create/terminate security groups and whether the APIs are triggering node terminations in a blocking or non-blocking way. The APIs used for the providers *GCE* and *Azure* are blocking operations (that means the call returns at the point in time when the infrastructure completed the termination operation). The behavior for *OpenStack* and *AWS* was non-blocking (that means, the calls returned immediately and just triggered the termination but did not wait until completion). The non-blocking behavior obviously leads to a more reactive behavior in case of node terminations (a complete node termination takes a minute and more). Figure 9 visualizes this by plotting how many nodes during a transfer are up at any point in time. A transfer from a "faster" provider (*AWS*) to a "slower" provider (*Azure*) can be done substantially faster than vice versa. **It turned out, that the runtime behavior of the slowest IaaS operation is dominating the overall runtime behavior of multi-cloud operations.** Taking all together, IaaS termination operations should be launched in a non-blocking manner (whenever possible) to improve the overall multi-cloud performance.

5.2   Critical Discussion

The proposed control loop is designed to be generic enough to adapt to each provider specific and non-standardized detail concepts which are likely to occur in a IaaS context. For instance, the control loop was even able to handle completely different timing behaviors. Intentionally, only very basic IaaS concepts

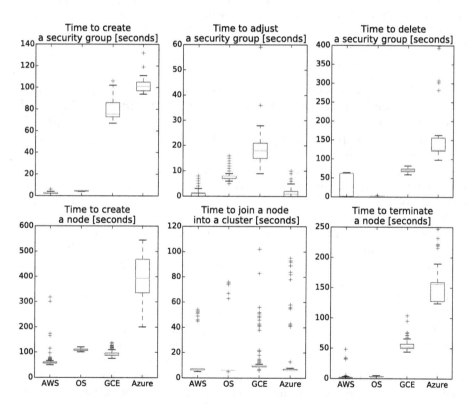

Fig. 7. Differences in infrastructure specific processing times: data is taken from experiments E1, E2 and E3.x and presented for the Kubernetes elastic container platform (AWS = Amazon Web Service EC2, OS = OpenStack, GCE = Google Compute Engine, Azure = Microsoft Azure).

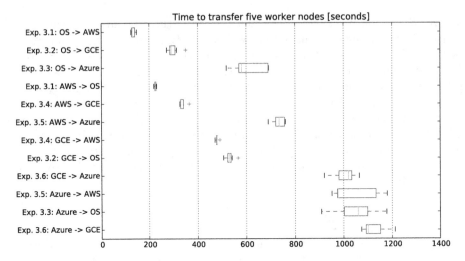

Fig. 8. Transfer times between different providers: data is taken from experiments E3.x and presented for the Kubernetes elastic container platform. The reader can deduce the effect of combining slow, medium and fast IaaS infrastructure providers on transfer durations. The slowest provider is dominating the overall runtime of an scaling operation. (AWS = Amazon Web Service EC2, OS = OpenStack, GCE = Google Compute Engine, Azure = Microsoft Azure).

are used in order to assure that the control loop can work with every public or private IaaS infrastructure providing concepts like virtual machines and IP-based network access control concepts. An IaaS infrastructure not providing these basic concepts is hardly imaginable and to the best of the author's knowledge not existing.

A migration from one infrastructure A to another infrastructure B could be expressed by setting all quantities of A to 0 and all quantities of B to the former quantities of A. The presented prototype keeps the cluster in an operational state under all circumstances. The current implementation of the execution pipeline executes simply a worst case scaling. The pipeline processes node creation steps before node termination steps. In consequence a migration increases the cluster to its double size in a first step. In a second step, the cluster will be shrinked down to its intended size in its intended infrastructure. This not very sophisticated and leaves obviously room for improvement. Figure 9 visualizes this behavior over time for different infrastructure transfers.

The execution pipeline is designed to be just the execution step of a higher order MAPE loop. That might lead to situations that an intended state is not reachable. In these cases, the execution loop may simply have no effect. For better understandability the reader might want to imagine a cluster under high load. If the intended state would be set to half of the nodes, the execution loop would not be able to reach this state. Why? Before a node is terminated the execution pipeline informs the scheduler of the elastic container platform to mark this node as unschedulable with the intent that the container platform will reschedule all load of this node to other nodes. A lot of elastic container platforms call this **"draining a node"**. For these kind of purposes elastic container platforms have operations to mark nodes as unschedulable (*Kubernetes* has the cordon command, *Docker* has a drain concept and so on). Only in the case that the container platform could successfully drain the node, the node will be deregistered and deleted. However, in high load scenarios the scheduler of the container platform will return an error due to the fact that draining is not possible. In consequence the execution pipeline will not terminate the node and will trigger to drain the next node on its list (which will not work as well). So, this cycle of the execution pipeline will be finished without substantially changing the current state. The analyzing step of the higher order MAPE loop will still identify a delta between the intended and the current state and will retrigger the execution pipeline. That is not perfect but at last the cluster is kept in an operational state.

5.3   Lessons Learned

By building, testing and evaluation the presented prototype several lessons learned have been derived from performed software engineering activities. These following lessons learned might be of interest for researchers or practitioners.

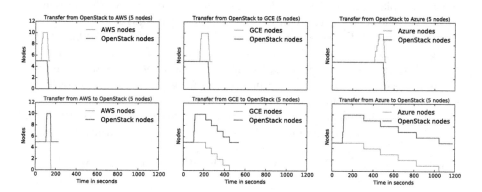

Fig. 9. Amount of nodes during a transfer: *These are randomly choosen transfers taken from experiments E3.1, E3.2 and E3.3 to visualize the pipeline behaviour of a transfer over time. For a longer or shorter amount of time (depending on the reactiveness of the provider) the cluster is doubled in its size. After that it is shrinked down to its intended size in the intended provider district. The transfer is completed when the lines end.*

1. **Secure Networking Should Be Considered from the Beginning.** If different IaaS cloud service providers shall be bridged, it is necessary to work with public IPs from the very beginning! According to made experiences this is not the default operation for most elastic platforms and may result in tricky details to consider[6]. A second essential aspect is, that the control and data plane encryption must be supported by the used overlay network of the elastic platform. If several overlay networks can be used by the elastic platform, encryption should be rated as a "showstopper" feature for overlay network selection.

2. **Do Not Rely on IaaS Infrastructure Elasticity Features** like auto-scaling, load-balancing and so on. Although these features are – from a high level point of view – very basic concepts, these features are in a lot of cases not 1:1 portable across providers. The elastic platform (and its supervising MAPE loop) has to cover this.

3. **Separate IaaS Support and Elastic Platform Support Concerns.** Both concerns can be solved independently from each other using two independent extension points. The proposed prototype introduced drivers for platforms like *Kubernetes* and *Swarm* and drivers for Infrastructures like *AWS, GCE, OpenStack, Azure*.

4. **To Describe an Intended State and Let a Control Process Take Care to Reach this Intended State is Less Complex.** To think in IaaS infrastructure specific workflows how to deploy, scale, migrate and terminate an elastic platform has the tendency to increase complexity. The presented prototype showed that this can be solved by a single control loop.

5. **Consider what Causes Stress to an Elastic Platform.** Adding nodes to a platform is less stressful than to remove nodes. To add a node has no immediate rescheduling involved, to deregister and remove a node has immediate rescheduling efforts in consequence. Knowing that, it seems a good and defensive strategy to add nodes in parallel but to shutdown nodes sequentially. However, this increases the runtime of the execution phase of a MAPE loop. To investigate time optimal execution strategies might be a fruitful research direction to make MAPE loops more reactive.

6. **Consider Varying Runtimes Of similar IaaS Infrastructure Operations Across Different Providers.** IaaS operations take often (several) minutes. Container platform operations just take seconds or even less. MAPE loops should consider this providing two adaption levels for auto-scaling. One slow reacting infrastructure-aware auto-scaling loop for the elastic container platform and one fast reacting infrastructure-agnostic auto-scaling loop for the applications operating on top of elastic container platforms. Furthermore, the infrastructure aware auto-scaling loop must be aware that different IaaS service providers might show substantial differing reaction times. The reader might want to recapitulate the really differing timing behaviours of the *AWS* and *Azure* IaaS infrastructures.

---

[6] To get *Kubernetes* running in a multi-cloud scenario it is necessary to assign an additional virtual network interface with the public IP address of the node. *Kubernetes* provides no config options for that mode of operation! However, even these kind of obstacles can be transparently handled by drivers.

7. **Respect Resilience Limitations of Elastic Platforms.** Never shutdown nodes before attaching compensating nodes (in case of transferability scaling actions) is an obvious solution! But it is likely not ressource efficient - especially if we consider different timing behaviours of public cloud service providers (see Figs. 5, 7, 8 and 9). To investigate resilient, resource and timing efficient execution strategies could be a fruitful research direction to optimize MAPE loops for transferability scenarios.

8. **Platform Roles Increase Avaidable Deployment Complexity.** Platform roles increase the inner complexity of platform drivers. Elastic container platforms should be more P2P-like and composed of homogeneous and equal nodes. This could be a fruitful research direction either and there exist first interesting ideas investigating this direction [23].

9. **Non-blocking APIs are Preferable.** This is especially true for terminating operations. In consequence elastic container platforms will show much more reactive behavior (and faster adaption cycles) if operated on IaaS infrastructures providing non-blocking terminating operations (see Figs. 8 and 9).

6   Related Work

Several promising approaches dealing with multi-cloud scenarios. There are some good survey papers on this [13–16]. But none of these surveys identified elastic container platforms as a viable option. Nevertheless, the need to "*adopt open-source platforms*" and "*mechanisms for real-time migration*" at run-time level is identified [14]. But to the best of author's knowledge there do not exist concrete and existing platforms or solutions based on container platforms. All surveys identified approaches fitting mainly in the following fields:

- **Volunteer federations** for groups of "*cloud providers collaborating voluntarily with each other to exchange resources*" [16].
- **Independent federations** (or multi-clouds) "*when multiple clouds are used in aggregation by an application or its broker. This approach is essentially independent of the cloud provider*" and focus the client-side of cloud computing [15].

This contribution intentionally did not proposed a broker-based solution [13] because cloud-brokers have the tendency just to shift the vendor lock-in problem to a broker. Instead of that mainly independent federations (multi-clouds) were focused by this Chapter. But if course there are similarities with other existing approaches.

Approaches like **OPTIMIS** [24], **ConTrail** [25] or **multi-cloud PaaS platforms** [26] enable dynamic provisioning of cloud services targeting multi-cloud architectures. These solutions have to provide a lot of plugins to support possible implementation languages. For instance, [26] mention at least 19 different plugins (just for a research prototype). Such solutions seem to come along with an increase of inner complexity. Container-based approaches seem to be a better fit handling this language complexity. **mOSAIC** [27] or **Cloud4SOA** [28] assume that an application can be divided into components according to a service oriented application architecture (SOA) and rely on the constraint that applications are bound to a specific run-time environment. This is true for the proposed approach as well. However, this paper proposes a solution where the run-time environment (elastic container platform) is up to a user decision as well.

The proposed deployment description format is based on JSON and shows similarities with other kind of deployment description languages like **TOSCA** [29], **CAMEL** [30] or **CloudML** [31]. In fact, some EC-funded projects like **PaaSage**[7] [32] combine such deployment specification languages with run-time environments. Nonetheless, the proposed prototype is focused on a more container-centric approach. Finally, several **libraries** have been developed in recent years like **JClouds, LibCloud, DeltaCloud, SimpleCloud, fog, Nuvem, CPIM** [33] to name a few. All these libraries unify differences in the management APIs of clouds and provide control over the provisioning of resources across geographical locations. And experiences with the **fog** library for the *Azure* and *OpenStack* driver show, that infrastructure specifics are not completely capsuled (even the (non-)blocking behavior can differ for the same operation in different infrastructures[8]).

Taking all together, the proposed approach leverages more up-to-date container technologies with the intend to be more "pragmatic", "lightweight" and complexity hiding. On the downside, it might be only applicable for container-based applications being on the cloud-native level of the maturity model shown in Table 2. But to use container platforms and corresponding microservice architectures gets more and more common in CNA engineering [2].

7   Conclusions

Elastic container platforms provide inherent – but often overlooked – multi-cloud support and are a viable and pragmatic option to support multi-cloud handling. But to operate elastic container platforms across different public and private IaaS cloud infrastructures can be a complex and challenging engineering task. Most manuals do not recommend to operate these kind of platforms in the proposed way due to operational complexity. In fact, to define an intended multi-cloud state of an elastic container platform and let a control process take care to reach this state is not less challenging. But it hides and manages complexity much better from the author's point of view. This Chapter showed that this complexity could be efficiently embedded in an execution pipeline of a control loop. This kind of resulting control process was able to migrate and operate elastic container platforms **at runtime** across different cloud-service providers. It was possible to transfer two of the currently most popular open-source container platforms *Swarm* and *Kubernetes* between *AWS*, *GCE*, *Azure* and *OpenStack*. These infrastructures cover three of the big five public cloud service providers

---

[7] http://www.paasage.eu/ (visited 15th Feb. 2017).

[8] In this case node termination (*Azure* blocking, *OpenStack* non-blocking).

that are responsible for almost 70% of the worldwide IaaS market share[9]. In other words, the presented solution can already be used for 70% of the most frequently used IaaS infrastructures. Due to its driver concept it can be extended with further IaaS infrastructures and further elastic container platforms.

However, there is work to do. It was astonishing to see, that the completion times of these transfers vary from 3 min to almost 20 min depending on the involved infrastructures (see Fig. 8). This should be considered for further thoughts how to implement a more time and resource efficient execution pipeline. Fruitful lessons learned about runtime behaviors of IaaS operations and promising research directions like more P2P-based and control-loop based designs of elastic container platforms could be derived for that purpose. The presented data can be used as reference for further research and development for these kind of ideas. However, even the worst transfer times are likely to be much faster than the engineering effort to port infrastructure-specific CNAs in a different cloud which is usually a very time consuming and complex one time exercise not being done in hours or minutes.

Acknowledgements. This research is funded by German Federal Ministry of Education and Research (13FH021PX4). I would like to thank Peter Quint, Christian Stüben, and Arne Salveter for their hard work and their contributions to the Project Cloud TRANSIT. Additionally I would like to thank the practitioners Mario-Leander Reimer and Josef Adersberger from QAWare for inspiring discussions and contributions concerning cloud-native application stacks.

Appendix

Cluster Definition File (Intended state)

This exemplary **cluster definition** file defines a *Swarm* cluster with the intended state to be deployed in two districts provided by two providers GCE and AWS. It defines three type of user defined node types (flavors): *small, med,* and *large*. 3 master and 3 worker nodes should be deployed on *small* virtual machine types in district *gce-europe*. 10 worker nodes should be deployed on *small* virtual machine types in district *aws-europe*. The flavors *small, med, large* are defined in Appendix 7.

---

[9] According to the *synergy 2016 Cloud Research Report* http://bit.ly/2f2FsGK (visited 12th Jul. 2017).

```
{
  "type": "cluster",
  "platform": "Swarm",
  // [...], Simplified for readability
  "flavors": ["small", "med", "large"],
  "deployments": [
    { "district": "gce-europe",
      "flavor": "med",
      "role": "master",
      "quantity": 3
    },
    { "district": "aws-europe",
      "flavor": "small",
      "role": "worker",
      "quantity": 10
    }
  ]
}
```

Listing 1.1. Cluster Definition (`cluster.json`).

Resources File (Current state)

This exemplary **resources** file describes provided resources for the operated cluster. This example describes a simple one node cluster (1 master) being operated in one district (OpenStack). A security group was requested. Some data is omitted for better readability.

```
[
  { "id": "36c76118-d8e4-4d2c-b14e-fd67387d35f5",
    "district_id": "openstack-nova",
    "os_external_network_id": "80de501b-e836-47ed-a413",
    "os_secgroup_name": "secgroup-a66817bd85e96c",
    "os_secgroup_id": "36c76118-d8e4-4d2c-b14e",
    "os_key_name": "sshkey-for-secgroup-a66817bd85e96c",
    "type": "secgroup"
  },
  { "id": "13c30642-b337-4963-94aa-60cef8db9bbf",
    "role": "master",
    "flavor": "medium",
    "public_ip": "212.201.22.189",
    "user": "ubuntu",
    "sshkey": "sshkey.pem",
    "district_id": "openstack-nova",
    "os_zone": "nova",
    "type": "node"
  }
]
```

Listing 1.2. Resources (`resources.json`).

District Definition File (JSON)

The following and exemplary **district definition** defines provider specific settings and mappings. The user defined district *gce-europe* should be realized using the provider specific GCE zones *europe-west1-b* and *europe-west1-c*. Necessary and provider specific access settings like project identifiers, regions, and credentials are provided as well. User defined flavors (see cluster definition format above) are mapped to concrete provider specific machine types.

```
[
  { "type": "district",
    "id": "gce-europe",
    "provider": "gce",
    "credential_id": "gce_default",
    "gce_project_id": "your-proj-id",
    "gce_region": "europe-west1",
    "gce_zones": ["europe-west1-b", "europe-west1-c"],
    "flavors": [
      { "flavor": "small", "machine_type": "n1-standard-1" },
      { "flavor": "med",   "machine_type": "n1-standard-2" },
      { "flavor": "large", "machine_type": "n1-standard-4" }
    ]
  }
]
```

Listing 1.3. District Definitions (`districts.json`).

Credentials File (JSON)

The following and exemplary **credential file** provides access credentials for customer specific GCE and AWS accounts as identified by the district definition file (*gce_default* and *aws_default*).

```
[ { "type": "credential",
    "id": "gce_default",
    "provider": "gce",
    "gce_key_file": "path-to-key.json"
  },
  { "type": "credential",
    "id": "aws_default",
    "provider": "aws",
    "aws_access_key_id": "AKID",
    "aws_secret_access_key": "SECRET"
  }
]
```

Listing 1.4. Credentials (`credentials.json`).

References

1. Kratzke, N.: Smuggling multi-cloud support into cloud-native applications using elastic container platforms. In: Proceedings of the 7th International Conference on Cloud Computing and Services Science (CLOSER 2017), pp. 29–42 (2017)
2. Kratzke, N., Quint, P.C.: Understanding Cloud-native applications after 10 years of Cloud Computing - a systematic mapping study. J. Syst. Softw. **126**, 1–16 (2017)
3. Quint, P.C., Kratzke, N.: Taming the complexity of elasticity, scalability and transferability in Cloud Computing - Cloud-Native applications for SMEs. Int. J. Adv. Netw. Serv. **9**, 389–400 (2016)
4. Kratzke, N., Peinl, R.: ClouNS - a Cloud-native applications reference model for enterprise architects. In: 8th Workshop on Service oriented Enterprise Architecture for Enterprise Engineering (SoEA4EE 2016) in Conjunction with the EDOC 2016 Conference (2016)
5. Qu, C., Calheiros, R.N., Buyya, R.: Auto-scaling Web applications in Clouds: a taxonomy and survey. CoRR abs/1609.09224 (2016)

6. Pahl, C., Jamshidi, P.: Software architecture for the Cloud – a roadmap towards control-theoretic, model-based cloud architecture. In: Weyns, D., Mirandola, R., Crnkovic, I. (eds.) ECSA 2015. LNCS, vol. 9278, pp. 212–220. Springer, Cham (2015). https://doi.org/10.1007/978-3-319-23727-5_17

7. Stine, M.: Migrating to Cloud-Native Application Architectures. O'Reilly, Sebastopol (2015)

8. Fehling, C., Leymann, F., Retter, R., Schupeck, W., Arbitter, P.: Cloud Computing Patterns: Fundamentals to Design, Build, and Manage Cloud Applications. Springer, Vienna (2014). https://doi.org/10.1007/978-3-7091-1568-8

9. Ashtikar, S., Barker, C., Clem, B., Fichadia, P., Krupin, V., Louie, K., Malhotra, G., Nielsen, D., Simpson, N., Spence, C.: Open data center alliance best practices: architecting Cloud-Aware applications Rev. 1.0 (2014)

10. Balalaie, A., Heydarnoori, A., Jamshidi, P.: Migrating to Cloud-Native architectures using microservices: an experience report. In: 1st International Workshop on Cloud Adoption and Migration (CloudWay), Taormina, Italy (2015)

11. Namiot, D., Sneps-Sneppe, M.: On micro-services architecture. Int. J. Open Inf. Technol. **2**(9), 24–27 (2014)

12. Newman, S.: Building Microservices. O'Reilly Media, Incorporated, Sebastopol (2015)

13. Barker, A., Varghese, B., Thai, L.: Cloud services brokerage: a survey and research roadmap. In: 2015 IEEE 8th International Conference on Cloud Computing, pp. 1029–1032. IEEE (2015)

14. Petcu, D., Vasilakos, A.V.: Portability in Clouds: approaches and research opportunities. Scalable Comput. Pract. Experience **15**, 251–270 (2014)

15. Toosi, A.N., Calheiros, R.N., Buyya, R.: Interconnected Cloud computing environments. ACM Comput. Surv. **47**, 1–47 (2014)

16. Grozev, N., Buyya, R.: Inter-Cloud architectures and application brokering: taxonomy and survey. Softw. Pract. Experience **44**, 369–390 (2014)

17. Hindman, B., Konwinski, A., Zaharia, M., Ghodsi, A., Joseph, A.D., Katz, R.H., Shenker, S., Stoica, I.: Mesos: a platform for fine-grained resource sharing in the data center. In: 8th USENIX Conference on Networked Systems Design and Implementation (NSDI 2011), vol. 11 (2011)

18. Peinl, R., Holzschuher, F.: The Docker ecosystem needs consolidation. In: 5th International Conference on Cloud Computing and Services Science (CLOSER 2015), pp. 535–542 (2015)

19. Kratzke, N., Quint, P.C.: How to operate container clusters more efficiently? Some insights concerning containers, software-defined-networks, and their sometimes counterintuitive impact on network performance. Int. J. Adv. Netw. Serv. **8**, 203–214 (2015)

20. Kratzke, N., Quint, P.-C.: Investigation of impacts on network performance in the advance of a microservice design. In: Helfert, M., Ferguson, D., Méndez Muñoz, V., Cardoso, J. (eds.) CLOSER 2016. CCIS, vol. 740, pp. 187–208. Springer, Cham (2017). https://doi.org/10.1007/978-3-319-62594-2_10

21. Aderaldo, C.M., Mendonça, N.C., Pahl, C., Jamshidi, P.: Benchmark requirements for microservices architecture research. In: Proceedings of the 1st International Workshop on Establishing the Community-Wide Infrastructure for Architecture-Based Software Engineering, ECASE 2017, Piscataway, NJ, USA, pp. 8–13. IEEE Press (2017)

22. Kratzke, N., Quint, P.C.: About automatic benchmarking of IaaS Cloud service providers for a world of container clusters. J. Cloud Comput. Res. **1**, 16–34 (2015)

23. Karwowski, W., Rusek, M., Dwornicki, G., Orłowski, A.: Swarm based system for management of containerized microservices in a Cloud consisting of heterogeneous servers. In: Borzemski, L., Świątek, J., Wilimowska, Z. (eds.) ISAT 2017. AISC, vol. 655, pp. 262–271. Springer, Cham (2018). https://doi.org/10.1007/978-3-319-67220-5_24

24. Ferrer, A.J., Hernandez, F., Tordsson, J., Elmroth, E., Ali-Eldin, A., Zsigri, C., Sirvent, R., Guitart, J., Badia, R.M., Djemame, K., Ziegler, W., Dimitrakos, T., Nair, S.K., Kousiouris, G., Konstanteli, K., Varvarigou, T., Hudzia, B., Kipp, A., Wesner, S., Corrales, M., Forgo, N., Sharif, T., Sheridan, C.: OPTIMIS: a holistic approach to Cloud service provisioning. Future Gener. Comput. Syst. **28**, 66–77 (2012)

25. Carlini, E., Coppola, M., Dazzi, P., Ricci, L., Righetti, G.: Cloud Federations in Contrail, pp. 159–168. Springer, Heidelberg (2012). https://doi.org/10.1007/978-3-642-29737-3_19

26. Paraiso, F., Haderer, N., Merle, P., Rouvoy, R., Seinturier, L.: A federated multi-cloud PaaS infrastructure. In: 2012 IEEE Fifth International Conference on Cloud Computing, pp. 392–399. IEEE (2012)

27. Petcu, D., Craciun, C., Neagul, M., Lazcanotegui, I., Rak, M.: Building an inter-operability API for Sky computing. In: 2011 International Conference on High Performance Computing & Simulation, pp. 405–411. IEEE (2011)

28. Kamateri, E., Loutas, N., Zeginis, D., Ahtes, J., D'Andria, F., Bocconi, S., Gouvas, P., Ledakis, G., Ravagli, F., Lobunets, O., Tarabanis, K.A.: Cloud4SOA: A Semantic-Interoperability PaaS Solution for Multi-cloud Platform Management and Portability, pp. 64–78. Springer, Heidelberg (2013). https://doi.org/10.1007/978-3-642-40651-5_6

29. Brogi, A., Soldani, J., Wang, P.W.: TOSCA in a Nutshell: promises and perspectives. In: Villari, M., Zimmermann, W., Lau, K.-K. (eds.) ESOCC 2014. LNCS, vol. 8745, pp. 171–186. Springer, Heidelberg (2014). https://doi.org/10.1007/978-3-662-44879-3_13

30. Rossini, A.: Cloud application modelling and execution language (CAMEL) and the PaaSage workflow. In: Advances in Service-Oriented and Cloud Computing - Workshops of ESOCC 2015, vol. 567, pp. 437–439 (2015)

31. Lushpenko, M., Ferry, N., Song, H., Chauvel, F., Solberg, A.: Using adaptation plans to control the behavior of Models@Runtime. In: Bencomo, N., Götz, S., Song, H. (eds.) MRT 2015: 10th International Workshop on Models@run.time, Co-located with MODELS 2015: 18th ACM/IEEE International Conference on Model Driven Engineering Languages and Systems, vol. 1474 of CEUR Workshop Proceedings. CEUR (2015)

32. Baur, D., Domaschka, J.: Experiences from building a cross-cloud orchestration tool. In: Proceedings of the 3rd Workshop on CrossCloud Infrastructures & Platforms, CrossCloud 2016, New York, NY, USA, pp. 4:1–4:6. ACM (2016)

33. Giove, F., Longoni, D., Yancheshmeh, M.S., Ardagna, D., Di Nitto, E.: An approach for the development of portable applications on PaaS Clouds. In: Proceedings of the 3rd International Conference on Cloud Computing and Services Science, pp. 591–601. SciTePress - Science and and Technology Publications (2013)

A Decentralized on Demand Cloud CPU Design with Instruction Level Virtualization

Erhan Gokcay[(✉)]

Software Engineering Department, Atilim University, Incek, Ankara, Turkey
erhan.gokcay@atilim.edu.tr

Abstract. Cloud technology provides many advantages and provides many services over traditional computational models. Although the provided virtual services increase resource sharing and cost effectiveness of the system, each node in the system is still centralized. Different CPU and OS versions bring interoperability problems in data exchange between nodes. In most cases less powerful units are left outside the service area. These units can only be considered as consumers of the cloud system. A new service called Cloud CPU is described elsewhere where the cloud provides the computational background for the components of a virtual CPU and the computation is distributed over internet. The design is using all units connected to the internet and it achieves a massively parallel operation. In this paper, the design of Cloud CPU will be extended and description of services needed with the new architecture will be discussed. One of the new services needed is a multi-language compiler where the target language is not fixed as well as the source language. The job of the compiler is not using the cloud for execution but to distribute the computation depending on the provided instruction sets published by each node. The computation makes sense only when all units work together and there is a need to synchronize and connect all nodes included in a particular computation. The need for synchronization will be gone when the computation is finished. Therefore an on demand Cloud-OS service is needed for bookkeeping and synchronization. The need for the Cloud-OS is temporary and the on demand initiated Cloud-OS will be terminated when the computation is ended.

Keywords: Cloud framework · Parallel computation · CPU on demand
Cloud CPU · Cloud Compiler · On demand configuration · Virtualization

1 Introduction

Advances in cloud systems are in-creasing rapidly as users are discovering cost and performance benefits of cloud systems. Some features can be listed as efficient resource sharing, security, flexibility and on-demand service. Available hardware and software resources can be shared among different users and/or systems with a higher granularity than before. This is important because most of the time the computing resources of a system is never utilized fully in standalone mode. There are different deployment models [1–4] like private, public, community and hybrid models. Almost anything is provided as a service.

© Springer International Publishing AG, part of Springer Nature 2018
D. Ferguson et al. (Eds.): CLOSER 2017, CCIS 864, pp. 46–60, 2018.
https://doi.org/10.1007/978-3-319-94959-8_3

The term cloud has different definitions. We could say that clouds are a large pool of virtual and easy to reach resources (hardware and/or software). These resources can be dynamically adjusted and assigned depending on the demand. Cloud computing is based on several old concepts like Service-oriented architecture (SOA), distributed and grid computing (utility computing) [5] and virtualization de-scribed in [1, 6, 7]. Security is always an issue in computing systems. With a distributed approach protection, security and privacy issues become more important and this issue is analyzed in [8–10].

There is a great deal of work to create a standard for the services provided such as Distributed Management Task Force (DMTF) which is an interoperable cloud infrastructure management standard focuses on interoperability [11]. Storage Networking Industry Association (SNIA) SNIA standards are used to manage the data, storage, information and also address the issues such as interoperability, usability, and complexity [12, 13]. OGF standards Open Virtual Machine Format (OVF) is a platform independent format which provides the features like efficiency, flexibility, security and mobility of virtual machines [13] in order to achieve interoperability.

One of the studies in this area is done in [14] where the focus is on the integration of Cloud and IoT. Although the integration is discussed in detail, still IoT devices are passive elements, not contributing to the computation power of Cloud.

The computational units are getting decentralized but the limit of this process needs to be answered. The growing IoT concept needs to be merged to Cloud systems and the interoperability problems need to be solved as well.

The main research question is that how small the computational units can get in a Cloud environment, how these small units can be configured; how IoT devices can contribute to the Cloud computation and how smaller devices will help to the interoperability problem.

Section 2 describes the basic challenges of cloud systems and the motivation of the paper. Section 3 describes the new decentralized extended service architecture. In Sect. 4, the basic building blocks of Cloud CPU architecture is explained. Section 5 describes Cloud CPU operations. Section 6 introduces the new level of virtualization. Finally, Sect. 7 discusses the Cloud CPU system.

2 Cloud Challenges

The cloud computing faces many challenges that are related to the data interoperability and portability, governance and management, metering and monitoring, security which are addressed by MOSAIC (Open source API and Platform for Multiple Clouds) [15]. There are interoperability problems between cloud systems and services because of different services depend on different operating systems and CPU types. Each vendor is providing a different service with a different set of tools. Most cloud computing systems in operation today are proprietary, rely upon infrastructure that is invisible to the research community, or are not explicitly designed to be instrumented and modified by systems researchers [16].

Although there are many open-source cloud systems for researchers as the development of cloud computing, they still are using a different Application Programming

Interface (API) from each other. For IaaS, there are some popular open-source cloud systems, such as Eucalyptus [16], Open Nebula [17], Nimbus [18], etc.

A different weakness of cloud computing is the exclusion of not-so-powerful units from the system as a source of the services provided. Smart devices and computational units with fewer resources are basically consumers in a cloud system as described in [19]. Those devices, although very high in terms of connected units, are using cloud systems but not providing any resource back.

3   Decentralized on Demand Service

The computational services provided by computers started with a centralized approach called mainframes. Although all computational and storage power is provided in a single environment, the centralized approach also created problems. The single point of failure problem and dependency on a single system and organization are the main disadvantages of mainframe systems. The workstation concept is introduced where high computational power can be obtained on desktop machines and the need for mainframes reduced drastically. Grid systems are introduced to increase parallel calculations. The computational power of systems are increased to such a level where the user cannot utilize current capacity anymore and the extra resources are made available to outside world by virtual services at different levels, which is called basically a Cloud System.

The user in a Cloud framework still depends on the service provider, since the service cannot be modified or changed by the user. The capability of a virtual service in a cloud system is decided by the service provider. In order to remove the dependency problem to the service provider, a new framework is needed in such a way that the consumer or user can configure the services needed, including functionality and computing power, from the cloud system. Instead of providing a high level service and computation, cloud systems will provide low level services or computations without any final computational goal and the user will combine these services to configure its own customized and dedicated service. The granularity of the service provided will be minimized and decentralized. A similar reduction is also introduced to a regular CPU design and it had faced a reduction in terms of complexity of the instruction set. The early designs include complex instructions (CISC), whereas later designs include very simple instructions (RISC) to execute a program with higher efficiency. The building blocks of RISC architecture can be designed with less complication and with higher efficiency.

The required computation is built on top of very basic cloud services which are very easy to implement by any unit attached to the cloud. Because of basic service requirement from each node, any smart device can contribute to the Cloud CPU. A simple device can provide a simple arithmetic operation whereas a complicated device or unit can provide a more sophisticated calculation.

The design is inspired from the design of a CPU, hence called Cloud CPU. The description and basic execution flow diagrams are given in [20]. In this paper the services required for Cloud CPU will be discussed in detail and extended.

4   Cloud CPU Architecture

The configurable service is called Cloud CPU and once it is created, it can be saved for future use. The instruction set represents minimized collection of sub-services or computations received from cloud units. Program counter represents a service that controls the flow of the execution. Register sets represent storage for the service. Process represents all the information that represents the created service or Cloud CPU. The CCPU basic architecture is given in Fig. 1.

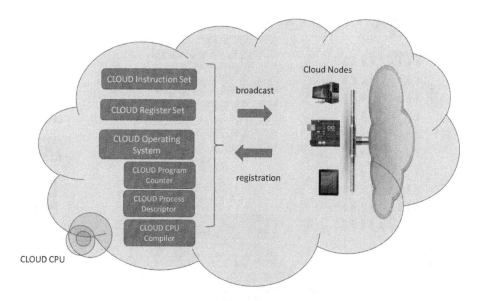

Fig. 1. Cloud CPU basic architecture and elements.

The instruction set of a CCPU is provided also as a service by each node where the total set will be called Cloud Instruction Set (CIS) for that particular CCPU. The number of instructions or services provided is limited by the capacity and number of the nodes connected to the cloud system.

For a given CCPU created in the cloud, nodes or resources connected to the cloud will register themselves to provide the required CCPU services. The node assignments may change with time due to failures or high load constraints where multiple resource assignments for each service will provide fault tolerance and protect the CCPU.

Since there are multiple CCPU's implemented, each node in the cloud may registers itself to more than one service, fully or partially. For example one node may have resources to execute two instructions from one CCPU and four instructions from another CCPU. Another node may register itself to store ten registers from one CCPU and four registers from another CCPU.

4.1   Cloud CPU Execution Flow

The main Cloud CPU execution flow is given in Fig. 2. The final collection of nodes and the sub-services provided as a whole creates the Cloud CPU for this particular application or service and it can be saved for future use. For another computation or service requirement, the same procedure will be repeated to create another Cloud CPU (CCPU).

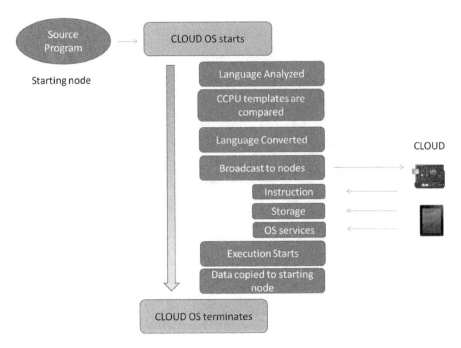

Fig. 2. Execution flow of Cloud CPU.

4.2   Cloud CPU ID (CCPUID)

The virtual CCPU created needs an id, so that it can be identified and referred later. During the creation of CCPU, several nodes in the cloud should register themselves. The instruction and register set of the CCPU, the set of nodes that registered themselves to implement Cloud Instruction Set (CIS) and Cloud Register Set (CRS) are also part of the information attached to CCPU ID.

4.3   Cloud Instruction Set (CIS)

The instruction set provided by the cloud for a particular CCPU is called Cloud-Instruction Set (CIS). Each node in the system registers itself to execute some or all of the CIS's of a CCPU. Since multiple nodes can provide this service, there is a great deal of fault tolerance and parallel execution in the system. Each node can serve to multiple CCPU's with a subset of CIS depending its capacity and load. For example in

Fig. 3, a sample configuration to implement instructions is given. Each node publishes possible instructions they can provide if needed. CELL-PHONE and LAPTOP nodes are registered themselves to CCPU1 and these nodes provide the corresponding instructions to CCPU1 configuration. The instruction of CELL-PHONE node is a simple instruction whereas the instructions provided by the LAPTOP node are high-level complicated ones. Each node can serve to multiple CCPU configurations like CCPU2 is using CELL-PHONE, LAPTOP and iPAD nodes as well. CELL-PHONE node is providing "inc" instruction to both CCPU configurations. Both CELL-PHONE and iPAD nodes can execute "inc" instruction which creates a fault tolerant system with multiple sources for the same instruction.

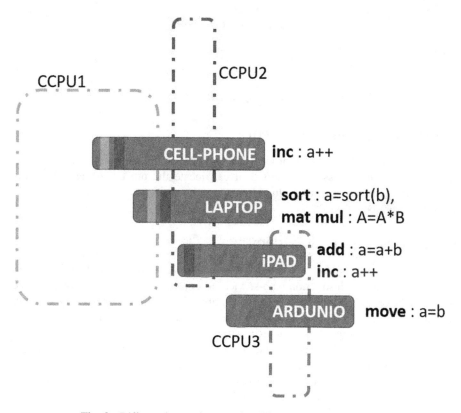

Fig. 3. Different instruction sets for different CCPU configure.

4.4   Cloud Register Set (CRS)

Each instruction may need temporary storage (i.e. registers). The register service provided by the cloud is called Cloud Register Set (CRS). CRS will be associated differently to each CCPU. High level register types can be created like queue types, arrays or any other high level storage types, since the register design seen by the CCPU configurations are virtual. A sample assignment of nodes to implement storage service is given in Fig. 4.

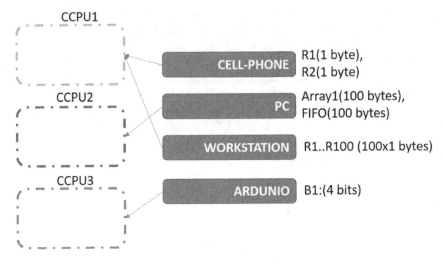

Fig. 4. Storage types and assignments.

4.5   Cloud Process Descriptor (CPD)

There is a need to identify each process that executes in the cloud. Also CPC should keep track of the process in the cloud. It can locate the process using CPD. This information again is saved in the cloud by nodes who registered themselves to provide the needed service.

4.6   Cloud Program Counter (CPC)

Each computation or process needs a cloud program counter (CPC), so that the system can calculate the next instruction (sub-service) to execute. CPC is created by the node that starts the execution initially. Using the distributed data storage service of the cloud, the Cloud Program Counter (CPC) is implemented easily. During the creation of the CCPU, nodes will register themselves to store and execute the CPC where the CPC created is associated with the process through a Cloud Process Descriptor (CPD). Since the CPC information is shared among the registered nodes for this service, it will provide the required fault tolerance. If one node fails, the other registered node will continue the execution. The structure of CPC is shown in Fig. 5.

4.7   Cloud Node

The nodes willing to participate in the Cloud CPU framework needs to perform several operations. The first decision is the service type(s) the node can contribute. Depending on the capability of the node more than one service type can be supported. The basic service types are storage and execution. Storage can be divided into storing Cloud program data or Cloud OS information like scheduling or program counter. Execution can also be

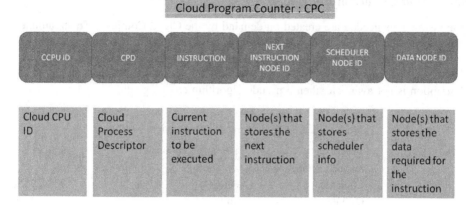

Fig. 5. CPC structure.

divided into two basic operations like executing Cloud CPU instructions or Cloud OS and Cloud Scheduler operations.

The role of the node can be decided by the administrator/user of the node or it can be decided by the node dynamically depending on the current load and capacity. The possible services for a node are shown in Fig. 6. The listener process will listen for the service calls and will respond to the corresponding calls related to its functionality. The configuration Manager holds all information regarding to registered services and nodes, implemented instructions, capacity and load.

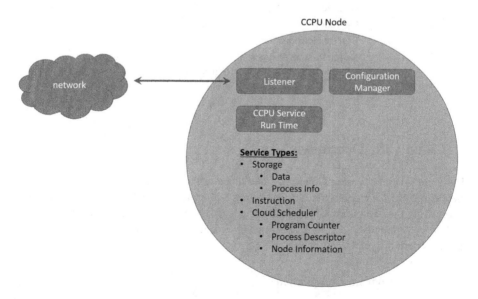

Fig. 6. Services of a Cloud CPU node.

4.8   Cloud Instruction Description

The instructions needed are created on demand by the Cloud Compiler. To streamline the process a detailed description of each instruction is needed. Two samples are shown in Tables 1 and 2 where details of each instruction, storage requirements, computational requirements, algorithm or description of the instruction are given. If a description is not available, then a pseudo algorithm can be given.

Table 1. Sample Cloud Instruction Description: sort(b).

Type	Statement, arithmetic
Instruction/function/class	a = sort(b)
Complexity	O(log(n))
Operation	Sort
Pseudo algorithm	N/A
Required storage types	Array: a Array: b
Input/output parameters	Input: b Parameter1: "ascending" Output: a

Table 2. Sample Cloud Instruction Description: a + b.

Type	Statement, arithmetic
Instruction/function/class	a = a + b
Complexity	O(1)
Operation	Addition
Pseudo algorithm	N/A
Required storage types	Register: a Register: b
Input/output parameters	Input: a, b Output: a

5   Cloud CPU Operations

There are several operations that may take place in the system. The user will decide to the desired service (represented by compiling a program) using a specific CCPU as the target using the compiler CCC and submit the program to the cloud as a Cloud Process (CPR). In the cloud, a CPC will be formed to execute the CPR. The operations required in the system are explained below.

5.1   Cloud Program Compilation

The difference in Cloud Process Compilation (CCC) is that the CPU hardware is not fixed anymore and the target CCPU, hence the target language, can be changed for each

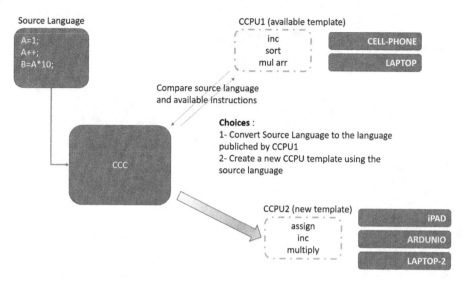

Fig. 7. Compiler instance.

compilation and most importantly it can be created from scratch. Several CCPU types can coexist and run in this system as shown as an instance in Fig. 7.

There are several choices for the compiler. The first decision is whether a new CCPU should be created for compilation or an existing one should be used. The user may also specify the target CCPU. In that case, the compiler will check if a conversion is possible or not. For example in Fig. 8, several choices a Cloud Compiler can face are shown. The source language needs to be executed. There are several choices for the compiler. CCPU1 and CCPU2 are two templates where the implemented instructions are not one-to-one match with the source language but it is possible to compile the compatible with the source language at all so it is dismissed. Depending on the source language with the available instructions. CCPU3 instruction set is not level of the similarity, either the compiler will use CCPU1 or CCPU2 templates and compiles the program for it, or it creates a new CCPU and the program is compiled for the new CCPU type created. The decision will be based on the programming language to be compiled, cloud capacity, complexity of the new CCPU needed, communication speed, execution speed of each node and the time for the compilation for an existing CCPU. The decision can change depending on a system from one instant to another and it is not hard-wired.

5.2 Cloud Instruction Set Creation

Determining the instruction list and storage types of the CCPU is a complicated process. There are almost infinitely many combinations of nodes. As a result the virtual hardware and available instructions are flexible and they can behave as you wish. The instructions are not limited by the hardware anymore. In addition to the number of combinations, there are other factors as the interconnection speed, storage capacity and

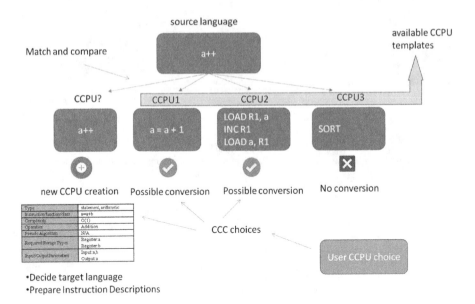

Fig. 8. Cloud compilation and choices.

processing speed of nodes. An exhaustive list and the decision process cannot be given here as it will be out of scope of this paper. The creation of the CCPU process can be initiated by the user to save it for future use but normally it will be initiated by the compiler when the user wants to run a program.

- The programming language is analyzed.
- A decision will be made if the language should be implemented as it is or it should be converted to a different language. For example we can have a microcontroller that can execute BASIC language directly. The second choice is to convert (compile) the BASIC language to a more basic RISC type language with few basic machine instructions. The decision depends on complexity of the source and target language.
- It is possible to have predefined templates for a language carefully designed by a user.
- The compiler will check the available templates if there is a close match to the current language. A close match means that although a one-to-one conversion is not possible, the source language can be converted to target language by using one or more in instructions. The compiler can decide to use one of the templates or create a new one.
- If a new template is needed by the compiler, the scope will be limited to the instructions in the current program. A new implementation may not cover all possible constructs of the target language, since the compiler scope is limited by the current program and it would be a waste of time and resources to implement instructions not needed. On the other hand, a user created template may cover the whole language elements.

- If the decision is to create a new instruction set, in that case the compiler will create a list of needed instructions using a Cloud Instruction Description (CID). Type can be class, function, statement, arithmetic or other constructs necessary. The description should give the required functionality as an operation or as a pseudo algorithm. Complexity can be given or can be calculated from the algorithm. Required storage types should also be listed. This information is needed so that each node in the cloud can respond to the request.

5.3   Cloud CPU Creation

Once the CCPU type is determined, the node performs two different actions depending on the state of the CCPU explained below and given in Fig. 9.

- Use an existing CCPU

Since there are many nodes involved in a CCPU, all these nodes should be checked before execution. The Cloud OS starting from the initiating node will check if all the nodes registered to execute this CCPU are still active or not. If not, a broadcast is sent to invite new nodes to join for the missing instructions and/or architecture. Once the CCPU is refreshed, all nodes are informed.

- Create a new CCPU

The instruction list created by the compiler for a new CPU is sent as a broadcast to the cloud to invite interesting nodes to implement the required instructions. Nodes with desired properties to implement the required functionality will respond and register themselves to execute a specific function. For example a system with high speed storage may respond to create the registers and/or queues, and another system with high

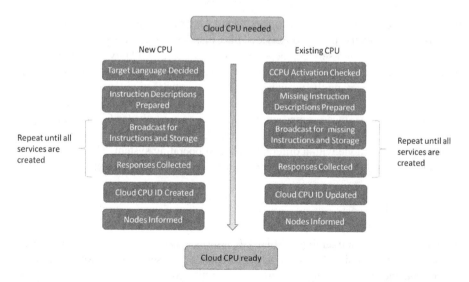

Fig. 9. Cloud CPU creation.

speed processing units may respond to implement a complicated instruction in the CCPU. The final decision is up to the Cloud Operating System.

5.4   Cloud OS

The operating system concept for the Cloud CPU is different than a regular one. In order to create and synchronize all operations of the CCPU, a Cloud OS is needed but since all nodes will have some kind of operating system or a similar controlling program, the need for a Cloud OS is temporary. The job of the Cloud OS is to create the CCPU, to communicate with all the nodes and to distribute the job and other information to registered nodes. Cloud OS works very closely with Cloud Compiler since most decisions are initiated by the compiler. In order to be compatible with the decentralized operation of Cloud CPU services, Cloud OS is also decentralized and executed by many nodes where each registered itself to be member of the Cloud OS. The Cloud Program Counter is passed from one node to another. During the execution, Cloud OS is informed by each node so that and the process is controlled and verified by Cloud OS. The information exchange is based on data that is small in terms of size and therefore will not create traffic congestion.

Cloud OS is a combination of all services created during the execution and it is initiated by the node that wants to execute a specific program using a Cloud CPU structure. When such a request is initiated by a node, a stub code executes and starts creating all needed services on demand. At the end of the requested execution, all created services terminates although the databases created are saved for a possible next execution.

6   Instruction Level Virtualization

When the virtualization layers of current Cloud systems are analyzed, it will be very easy to see that every provided service, like Platform as-a-Service, Software as-a-service, Hard-ware as-a-service, depends on a particular CPU type and operating system. The dependency of a program to the underlying hardware and software has not changed at all. By moving the virtualization layer to a instruction level granularity, the dependency to the underlying system is minimized. The dependency cannot be removed completely since current systems depend on a particular CPU and an operating system to run it properly. When the Cloud CPU is active, there is no need to get services from each node with a different CPU and operating system. The cloud system becomes an active platform where the program executes on it directly.

7   Conclusions

In this paper, the configurable Virtual CPU service using the cloud architecture is extended where the units of a CPU core represent nodes or services provided by a cloud system and the data transfer between them is replaced by a data transfer inside the cloud system. By pushing the CPU units to a cloud system, a giant virtual CPU is created where each unit of the CPU can have multiple implementations, support, and parallel execution and fault tolerance. The minimized functional block structure and implementation have many advantages like Fault Tolerance, Security, Scalability, Computational Requirements, Communication, Interoperability, Optimization, Heterogeneous CPU implementations, Hardware independent virtual CPU, Process and/or programming language specific virtual CPU, and Parallel Operation and these are discussed in detail in [20].

The Cloud CPU structure resembles the working principle of a living brain where simple structures (neurons) are connected to each other by many connections. The real power of a brain comes not from the speed of each neuron, but it comes from the high level of parallel connections. The calculations are not fast but highly parallelized which is also a reason for the fault tolerant structure. The Cloud CPU may not be the best choice for number crunching, but it will be very powerful in parallel operations. When you destroy some nodes from the Cloud CPU, it will stay running as high number of registered nodes provides the desired fault tolerance.

On the other hand, the Cloud CPU implementation will create a Global Unified on Demand Computational Software Platform. The compiler paradigm will change from compiling into a fixed language to compiling into an unconstrained flexible programming language. Cloud OS will select the best nodes for the current source language and execution and it will decide to the target language which is not fixed. Another change in computing paradigm is that the need for a particular CPU, real or virtual, becomes obsolete. The same is valid for a specific operating system, again real or virtual.

References

1. Vouk, M.: Cloud computing - issues, research and implementations. Comput. Inf. Technol. (CIT) **16**(4), 235–246 (2008)
2. Zhang, Q., Cheng, L., Boutaba, R.: Cloud computing: state of the art and research challenges. J. Internet Serv. Appl. **1**, 7–18 (2010)
3. Dillon, T., Wu, C., Chang, E.: Cloud computing: issues and challenges. In: 24th IEEE International Conference on Advanced Information Networking and Applications, pp. 27–33 (2010)
4. Sonisky, B.: Cloud computing bible, Chap. 1. Wiley Publishing Inc. (2011). https://doi.org/10.1002/9781118255674.ch1
5. Foster, I., Zhao, Y., Raicu, I., Lu, S.: Cloud computing and grid computing 360-degree compared. In: Grid Computing Environments Workshop, pp. 1–10 (2008)
6. Youseff, L., Butrico, M., Da Silva, D.: Toward a unified ontology of cloud computing. In: Grid Computing Environments Workshop (GCE 2008) (2008)
7. Vaquero, L., Rodero-Merino, L., Caceres, J., Lindner, M.: A break in the clouds: towards a cloud definition. SIGCOMM Comput. Commun. Rev. **39**(1), 50–55 (2009)
8. Hashizume, K., Rosado, D.G., Fernandez-Medina, E., Fernandez, E.B.: An analysis of security issues for cloud computing. J. Internet Serv. Appl. **4**, 1–13 (2013)
9. Liu, Y., Ma, Y., Zhang, H., Li, D., Chen, G.: A method for trust management in cloud computing: data coloring by Cloud watermarking. Int. J. Autom. Comput., 280–285 (2011). https://doi.org/10.1007/s11633-011-0583-3

10. Basu, A., Vaidya, J., Kikuchi, H., Dimitrakos, T., Nair, S.: Privacy preserving collaborative filtering for SaaS enabling PaaS clouds. J. Cloud Comput. Adv. Syst. Appl. **1**, 1–14 (2012)
11. Buyya, R., Shin Yeo, C., Venugopal, S., Broberg, J., Brandic, I.: Cloud computing and emerging IT platforms: vision, hype, and reality for delivering computing as the 5th utility. Future Gener. Comput. Syst. **25**, 599–616 (2009)
12. Popovic, K., Hocenski, Z.: Cloud computing security issues and challenges. In: MIPRO, Opatija, Croatia, 24–28 May 2010, pp. 344–349 (2010)
13. snia.org: Cloud Data Management Interface (CDMI). https://www.snia.org/cdmi. Accessed 19 Mar 2015
14. Botta, A., Donato, W., Persico, V., Pescapé, A.: Integration of cloud computing and internet of things: a survey, Future Gener. Comput. Syst. **56**, 684–700 (2016)
15. Petcu, D.Di, Martino, B., Venticinque, S., Rak, M., Mhr, T., Esnal Lopez, G., Brito, F., Cossu, R., Stopar, M.: Experiences in building a mOSAIC of clouds. J. Cloud Comput. Adv. Syst. Appl. **2**, 1–22 (2013)
16. Nurmi, D., Wolski, R., Grzegorczyk, C., Obertelli, S., So-man, G., Youseff, L., Zagorodnov, D.: The Eucalyptus open-source cloud-computing system. In: IEEE International Symposium on Cluster Computing and the Grid (CCGrid 2009) (2009)
17. opennebula.org: Open Nebular. http://www.opennebula.org
18. nimbusproject.org: Nimbus. http://nimbusproject.org
19. Khan, A., Othman, M., Madani, A., Khan, A.: A survey of mobile cloud computing application models. IEEE Commun. Surv. Tutor. **16**(1), 393–413 (2014)
20. Gokcay, E.: An on demand virtual CPU architecture based on Cloud infrastructure. In: Proceedings of the 7th International Conference on Cloud Computing and Services Science - Volume 1: CLOSER, Porto, Portugal, pp. 351–357 (2017)

Heterogeneous Resource Management and Orchestration in Cloud Environments

Dapeng Dong[✉], Huanhuan Xiong, Gabriel G. Castañé, Paul Stack, and John P. Morrison

Department of Computer Science, University College Cork, Cork T12 YN60, Ireland
{d.dong,h.xiong,g.castane,p.stack,j.morrison}@cs.ucc.ie

Abstract. The addition of heterogeneous resources to conventional homogeneous cloud environments has enabled clouds to embrace a wide variety of new applications that heretofore were traditionally confined to specialized computing environments. The enhanced and extended features offered by heterogeneous resources enable service offerings that pose challenges to traditional cloud management throughout the entire service delivery stack. The accelerated uptake of heterogeneous resources is exacerbating these challenges, which no longer can be efficiently addressed in an ad-hoc manner. Therefore, an integrated approach to heterogeneous resource management that is cognizant of the unique advantages of different hardware types is needed. In this paper, two candidate approaches, a platform-integration scheme and a server-integration scheme, are introduced to address this management challenge. The platform-integration scheme integrates and coordinates the management of various coexisting resource managers and associated environments each of which may be managing resources of different types using the most appropriate resource abstraction method. In contrast, the server-integration scheme provides a single, lower level, fine-grained management mechanism across all hardware resource types. Ultimately, the goal of each schemes is to provide a unified view of resources from a capability perspective to consumers.

Keywords: Architecture · Heterogeneous resource · Platform integration
Cloud · HPC

1 Introduction

The employment of various advanced technologies, such as virtualization and more recently, containerization, for managing and organizing resources in cloud environments has yielded several distinct system features, such as resource elasticity, system scalability, application load-balancing, configuration flexibility, cost-effective usage models and rapid deployment. Moreover, recent evidence shows an increased demand for support for High Performance Computing (HPC) applications in the cloud. For example, weather forecasting, medical imaging and computational fluid dynamics, that have traditionally been confined to cluster environments are now being migrated to the cloud. To effectively support applications of this type and to demonstrate that comparable performance can be achieved in the cloud, specialized hardware, such as, Graphical Processing Units (GPUs), Many-Integrated-Core processors (MICs) and Data-Flow

© Springer International Publishing AG, part of Springer Nature 2018
D. Ferguson et al. (Eds.): CLOSER 2017, CCIS 864, pp. 61–80, 2018.
https://doi.org/10.1007/978-3-319-94959-8_4

Engines (DFEs), and dedicated networking configurations, including 40 Gb/s Ethernet and InfiniBand, are being incorporated into the cloud infrastructure. Consequently, cloud service providers have begun to offer specialized services, for example, Amazon EC2 Cluster Compute, EC2 F1 Instances [1] and Microsoft FPGA-based cloud [2] are all designed to support these high-end applications. The introduction of a wide range of hardware and associated configurations to conventional homogeneous cloud environments is introducing heterogeneity and associated challenges for effectively integrating and efficiently managing heterogeneous resources and the heterogeneity arising from new hardware architectures, diverse computational abilities, diverse power usage patterns, mixed operating system architectures and specialized software libraries. This evolution is having a significant impact on the transitional cloud architectures, and a re-consideration of the organization of the physical hardware resources in the cloud infrastructure layer, the resource management and scheduling approaches in the cloud management layer, and the service orchestration and resource representation in service delivery layer is becoming necessary.

Several cloud management platforms exist for managing virtualized environments (e.g., OpenStack Nova [3]), container environments (e.g., Kubernetes [4], Mesos [5] and Docker Swarm [6,7]), containers in virtualized environments (e.g., Magnum [8]), bare metal servers (e.g., Ironic [9]). These platforms have sufficiently matured and have begun to find practical applications in many public and private clouds. Traditional clouds typically support only one of these platforms and this limits the structure of the cloud environment in terms of hardware diversity. For instance, in a virtualized environment, only certain models and types of computation accelerators (e.g., GPUs) can be accessed by virtual machines with additional configurations on both the underlying hardware (e.g., CPU and motherboard) and software (e.g., Hypervisor and host operating system). In contrast, containers can directly use many of the existing computation accelerators, but have limited features, especially for networking where advanced firewall and load-balancing are noticeably absent. Thus, having multiple abstraction methods simultaneously available in a single cloud deployment [10] is desirable. If a cloud provider supports more than one of these platforms simultaneously, each is provided in isolation from the rest in a manner that effectively partitions the cloud resources among them, thus, creating a situation where those resources can not be shared across platforms.

Without doubt, heterogeneity complicates resource management and resource allocation. In current homogeneous environments, resource allocation is typically formulated using multi-objective optimization equations involving resource availability (e.g., CPU cores, system memory and storage space) and system requirements (e.g., host-affinity and load-balancing). To make decisions in a timely fashion, relaxed algorithms (meta-heuristics or greedy algorithms) are often used. Since heterogeneity offers considerably more features, these calculations become consequently more complex. Improved organization at the system level offers a potential pathway for efficient resource allocation. However, this approach assumes the existence of a unified platform for managing heterogeneous resources. In this paper, two implementation schemes for such a unified platform are introduced. They are referred to as a platform-integration scheme and a server-integration scheme.

This paper is organized as follows. A brief introduction to the background of this work and a consideration of related work are presented in Sect. 2. The proposed unified platform schemes are outlined in Sect. 3, and a use case application demonstrating the platform-integration scheme is given in Sect. 4. Section 5 concludes the paper by highlighting the main ideas of this research and by indicating some potentially fruitful future directions.

2 Background and Related Work

The cloud computing paradigm has shifted the focus of data center management from providing bare-metal resources to providing virtual resources to the end user. These advantages have long been demonstrated in production cloud environments, such as the Amazon EC2, the Microsoft Azure, and the Google Cloud Platforms. Virtualization enhances cloud management by enabling flexible resource configuration and deployment, efficient use of resources, and by offering opportunities for reducing power consumption.

Virtualization and containerization are the two dominant technologies used for managing and abstracting computational resources. Virtualization is generally achieved through abstracting hardware components into logical objects. This abstraction can be realized by hardware emulation and/or by time sharing of a hardware component between multiple processes. A software component that provides virtualization functions is commonly referred to as a *hypervisor*, historically named as a Virtual Machine Manager (VMM). A hypervisor is responsible for providing instances of virtual environments identical to the underlying physical server with minimum performance cost, while retaining full control of the physical resources [11]. It allows for architecturally diverse operating systems to coexist and to simultaneously run on the same physical server. A complete operating system can be installed and run in a virtual environment exactly the same way that it runs on a physical server. This instance of the operating system is often known as a *guest* Virtual Machine (VM) [12]. All hardware resource related operations, which are initiated from guest VMs, are under the control of the hypervisor, and the hypervisor executes these operations on the actual hardware on behalf of each guest VM.

Containerization is another type of virtualization. Technically, containerization technology provides isolated application execution environments at the operating system level. It uses Linux native functions, mainly the control groups (*cgroups*) and the *namespace*, to isolate applications/processes. Because containers do not use hypervisor-like middleware, multiple container applications can share common libraries and hardware drivers installed on the host operating system. This also makes a container application lightweight and easier for it to access specialized hardware, such as GPUs and MICs. On the other hand, a container application is less secure because of its shared environment and offers less functionality; it is essentially an application wrapping mechanism. In practical deployments, selecting either virtualization or containerization technologies for managing a cloud environment depends on the business goals set out by Cloud Service Provider (CSP). From an architecture design perspective, containers are suitable for running applications, whereas VMs are suitable for building virtual Information Technology (IT) infrastructures.

In a cloud environment, each virtualization or containerization technology provides desired features such as elasticity, scalability and high-availability. This requires a hyper-level management framework that can coordinate virtual resources across physical servers at large scale. The following sections review the architectural design of several widely adopted Infrastructure-as-a-Service (IaaS) management frameworks focusing on computational resource management.

2.1   Virtualization Management Frameworks

OpenStack [3] is an open-source cloud platform focusing on the management of virtualized environments. In particular, for managing computational resources, OpenStack uses a front-end API server for receiving and responding to requests for resources. Allocating a computational resource will require various other components be associated with it, such as, networking, storage and security groups. This can be a very complex process when multiple simultaneous requests, with different configurations trying to acquire globally available resources are made. In order to reduce this complexity of this process, requests are forwarded to mediator service, known as the *nova-conductor*. The *nova-conductor* coordinates various components (e.g., networking, image, storage, and compute) for each request, and multiple instances of the *nova-conductor* can be created to deal with a high-volume of requests. The *nova-conductor* first uses a scheduler service (the *nova-scheduler*) to locate a group of potential physical server(s) that meet specified requirements, specified requirements, such as, the number of CPU cores, the size of memory, and the required storage space. Subsequently, those candidate physical servers are further filtered, in a iterative manner, based on the preferences and criteria (also know as *weights*) specified by the user and/or the CSP. The requested resources will subsequently be deployed by the *nova-compute* service (by calling Hypervisor specific APIs) on the most appropriate physical servers [13].

OpenNebula [14] provisions VMs in a similar manner to OpenStack. It uses a *front-end* service to deal with requests and resource management. A request for VMs is first formulated into a VM template, this template is forwarded to a *scheduler* service [15], which selects available resources based on the system requirements and/or user preferences, such as, Packing, Striping and Load-aware polices [16]. The *front-end* service coordinates VM deployment on the selected server(s) by calling Hypervisor specific APIs.

Nimbus [17] is another IaaS management framework for scientific users. It takes a simpler approach for managing resources than those mentioned above. Architecturally, Nimbus consists of three main core components including a *Nimbus IaaS central service*, a storage service (*Cumulus*) and *VMM control services*, running on each server basis. The *Nimbus IaaS central service* acts as a middleware between cloud end-users and cloud resources. From an end-user perspective, the central service is the server that deals with requests for resources; from a CSP point of view, the central service is a client that initiates requests for resource deployment to the *VMM control service(s)* on the selected server(s). Thus, Nimbus implements a client-server model. The client-server model greatly simplifies the Nimbus architecture and provides a robust platform. On the other hand, this model may limit scalability. Nevertheless, Nimbus supports cloud federations that can be formed by different cloud platforms and this is achieved through a centralized account management service [18].

2.2   Containerization Management Frameworks

Borg [19] is a former proprietary Google platform used for managing large-scale container environments. Borg manages tens of thousands of servers simultaneously. The Borg architecture consists of three main components including *Borg masters*, *job schedulers*, and *Borglet* agents. A typical Borg instance consists of a single *Borg master*, a single *job scheduler* and multiple *Borglet* agents. The *Borg master* is the central point for managing and scheduling jobs and requests. A *Borg master* and *job scheduler* are replicated in several copies for purposes of high-availability, however, only a single *Borg master* and a single *job scheduler* are active in the system at any one time. The *Borg master* is responsible for dealing with requests for deploying jobs and the *job scheduler* searches for suitable servers to host tasks. The actual deployment of the job is carried out by a *Borglet* agent on the selected server (multiple tasks on the same server are separated and distinguished by the Linux kernel functions *cgroups* and *namespace*).

Borg presents a centralized management approach. This also requires *Borg masters* and *job schedulers* (the original and all replicas used for high-availability) to be large enough to scale out as required. The Borg *job scheduler* may potentially manage a very high volume of jobs simultaneously, this has made Borg more suitable for long-running services and batch jobs, since those job profiles reduce the load on the job scheduler.

Omega [20] is an enhancement of Borg system's scheduler architecture. It employs multiple schedulers working in parallel to speed up resource allocation and job scheduling. Each scheduler maintains the complete state of all available resources and decisions are made by each scheduler, independently. Conflicting resource allocations will be determined in resource deployment phase, and one or both of the conflicting requests will be returned to their originating scheduler for rescheduling. Kubernetes [21,22] is the most recent evolution of Google's data center management technology. Architecturally, Kubernetes implements a master-worker model. The master runs an *API service* for dealing with requests, a cluster state maintenance service (*Etcd*) for tracking data center resource information, and a scheduler for locating resources. On each computational node, a local container management service (*kubelet*) is used for managing container life-cycles and a network proxy service (Proxy) is used for establishing inter- and intra-communications between containers and the Internet. Notably, containers are not managed individually. A collection of containers is organized together and managed as a single entity. This is commonly referred to as a *Pod*. The concepts of the *Pod* reflects the service management philosophy that a large cloud application should be decomposed into a set of self-contained services; each service carries a single function per container basis; and all services belonging to an application should be managed together. Additionally, the use of *Pods* also makes Kubernetes more scalable.

Docker Swarm [6,7] mimics *Pod* concept. It provides a flexible and easy way for building virtual clusters on demand in which cluster members can be distributed across physical servers. Members of a swarm cluster are connected through a designated overlay network. A *swarm* is conceptually a virtual cluster. Common services or services belong to the same application, can be managed and grouped into the same *swarm*.

Architecturally, a *swarm* consists of a *swarm master* and *swarm workers*. Any available computational nodes in a data center can freely join and leave a swarm, and provides the basis for application/service elasticity.

Mesos [5] is another management platform that is based on a master/worker architecture. Mesos enables multiple different scheduling frameworks to manage the same environment. This is achieved by employing a coordinator service that assigns controls on resources to a single scheduler during its decision making processes. This can potentially lead to an inefficient use of resources when the request is lightweight and available resources are significantly large.

Alibaba Inc. has created the Fuxi [23] platform for supporting its large scale worldwide *e*-commerce business. The Fuxi architecture design focuses on scalability and fault tolerance. It consists of three main components including a *FuxiMaster*, a *FuxiAgent* and an *ApplicationMaster* on each physical server. The *FuxiMaster* is responsible for receiving and responding to job requests and for locating a *FuxiAgent* suitable for each individual job. The designated *FuxiAgent* spawns an *ApplicationMaster* to handle the job and potentially split the job into smaller tasks depending on the job type. The *ApplicationMaster* then initiates requests to the *FuxiMaster* for resources. When the *FuxiMaster* returns a list of *FuxiAgents* that contain sufficient resources for the job, the *ApplicationMaster* starts issuing commands directly to the selected *FuxiAgents* to start the job. In comparison with common container technologies that use *cgroups* to control resource assignment and kernel *namespace* for isolating task execution environments, Fuxi continuous to use *cgroups* to control resource assignment, but makes use of independent *sandboxes* for isolating task execution environments.

2.3   Bare-Metal Management Frameworks

Although virtualization and containerization are the main technologies used for managing resources, in many situations, managing bare-metal resources are still important. For example, provisioning data center infrastructure and providing high-performance servers for heavily loaded database systems and specialized computation accelerators remain an important activity.

Bare-metal server management is technically different from managing containerized and virtualized environments. Since bare-metal servers do not have pre-installed operating systems, vendor-specific chip-level management modules such as, Intelligent Platform Management Interface (IPMI) and Preboot Execution Environment (PXE) must be used. In general, provisioning a new server requires the sending of a request to an API server, a controller service is then invoked to identify a target physical server by matching user specified criteria, such as, CPU architecture and system memory size. The controller service then prepares for the operating system images or *ramdisk* to be installed on the selected server and issues IPMI commands to the server for network booting and operating system image or *ramdisk* installation via PXE. After the image loading and installation processes, the status and access methods are handed to the end-user. Ironic [9], Razor [24], and Foreman [25] are several typical implementations of such a scheme.

In summary, modern data center management platforms still operate a client-server model and this model continuous to scales. Architecturally, those management platforms consist of three common components including a front-end facing API server, a coordinator service (e.g., schedulers and resource management), and back-end agents (e.g., Hypervisors, *Borglet* and *Kubelet*). To further improve on scalability, cloud federation can be used and is commonly implemented through centralized account management mechanisms incorporated with networking inter-routing schemes.

3   Heterogeneous Resource Integration

Existing data center management platforms typically employ a single resource abstraction method (such as, vitalization or containerization). These are efficient and effective for managing homogeneous resources. The increasing demand for supporting versatile high-performance accelerators and high-throughput network connections are changing the nature of a data center from a homogeneous environment to one that is more heterogeneous. This poses challenges to existing data center management platforms and how they accommodate various types of computational hardware resources. Orchestrating services and resources with complex configurations to meet user- and/or system-specific requirements is thus becoming increasingly more difficult. As system functions become more versatile, the complexity of the system is also increased. However, this complexity must be made transparent to end-users. Consequently this requires an adjustment the paradigms used for delivering services. In the following sections, a blueprint-oriented service delivery model and two integration schemes (a platform-integration scheme and a server-integration scheme) for managing and unifying heterogeneous resources in cloud environments are introduced.

3.1   Service Delivery Model

To fully exploit versatile service and resource options offered by heterogeneous resource, a careful and a considered approach to manage these resources is necessary. This can be challenging for both the service provider and for the service consumer, especially, when the components of a cloud application may require the deployment on different types of resources. Moreover, leaving aside the difficulties of working with heterogeneous hardware environment, expert knowledge related to the deployment of cloud application components is usually required to fully exploit these hardware resources and accelerators. Configuration complexity and deep domain-specific knowledge should be made transparent to end-users. Thus, an approach is taken that allows end-users to compose their tasks into a workflow of constituent service(s). Workflows of this kind are often referred to as *blueprints*.

An application blueprint can be visualized as a graph that expresses the business logic and intra-relationships of application components. Deploying an application blueprint effectively deploys the set of services that comprise the application. In an homogeneous cloud, deploying a set of services results in each being hosted by resources of a single type. This represented the state of the industry. However, in making the transition to an heterogeneous cloud a blueprint involves assigning services to the most appropriate heterogeneous resources. Depending on the nature of the application and/or user preferences, a service or a group of services can thus be assigned to the same resource or indeed to different resources of different types, when necessary. This advancement requires adjusting the resource provisioning models appropriately and is addressed in Sects. 3.3 and 3.4.

3.2 System Workflow

Given the blueprint-oriented service delivery model, the system workflow is shown in Fig. 1. An application blueprint is composed by end-users and first submitted to an API Server. The API Server is responsible for receiving and responding to end-user requests and forward the a blueprint to an instance of a Resource Coordinator. Many Resource Coordinators may potentially work in parallel to load-balance large volume of requests. Each application blueprint is processed by a single Resource Coordinator. The Resource Coordinator decomposes the blueprint into sub-groups of resource requests according to the resource abstraction types. For example, a complex blueprint may consists of many services and each of the service may require to be deployed on different types of hardware resources. For instance, a blueprint may be described as an application that requires front-end web servers to collect data which is subsequently processed using accelerators, thus, the resources required for this blueprint deployment may be a set of VMs running on CPUs, and a set of containers running on servers having Xeon Phi co-processors. After the blueprint decomposition process, the Resource Coordinator analyses the relationships between sub-groups of the resource requests and makes further amendments to the blueprint. The amendments are mainly made for realizing communications between sub-groups. The Resource Coordinator then forwards each sub-group of resource requests to designated Virtual Resource Partitions (VRPs) that are managed by corresponding management platforms. Details about VRPs and management platforms are given in Sects. 3.3, and 3.4.

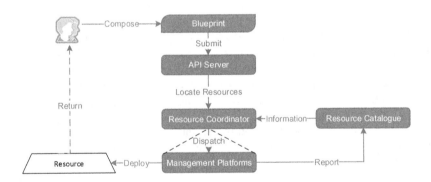

Fig. 1. System workflow.

3.3 The Platform-Integration Scheme

Different types of hardware resources require appropriate resource management techniques. The mechanisms for integration heterogeneous resources and their respective

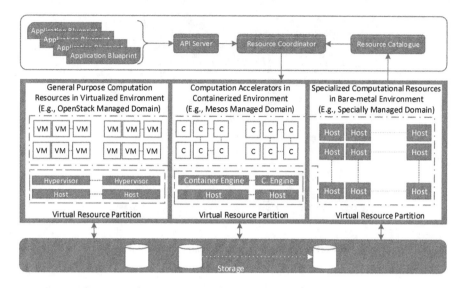

Fig. 2. Managing and accommodating heterogeneous hardware resources through multiple integrated platforms.

management techniques in a single unified scheme. An overview of the proposed platform-integration scheme is shown in Fig. 2. In this scheme, hardware resources are virtually partitioned based on the resource abstraction/access methods (virtualization, containerization and bare metal) most appropriate for the respective hardware type. A corresponding management framework is then adopted to manage groups of hardware of the same type. A central Resource Coordinator component is provided as an interface to be used by end-users to deploy applications on the underlining resources. More importantly, the Resource Coordinator component coordinates the deployment for the application blueprint components on, potentially, various types of resources across those virtual partitions.

Heterogeneous hardware resources are managed through the designated platforms. This may raise interoperability issues, however, as each platform manages a virtual resource partition, in the same management domain, the resulting interoperability issues reduced to a technical integration action and are not exacerbated by having to consider the interests of multiple entities. Figure 2 shows how the integration scheme may use OpenStack to manage virtual environment, Mesos to manage container environment, and Ironic [9] to manage bare-metal servers. Each platform offers a different set of Application Programming Interfaces (APIs) and utilities for similar resource management operations, such as, creating virtual machines and/or containers. The Resource Coordinator uses a Plug & Play Interface that defines a set of common operations for managing underlying resources, and these operations are then translated to platform-specific API calls or commands using the Plug & Play implementation modules to carry out service deployment processes. Additionally, storage systems are organized and managed independently. Processing units can be easily configured to use volume-based and/or network attached storage systems.

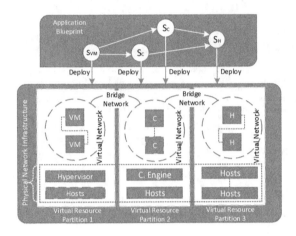

Fig. 3. Networking integration scheme using bringing network.

Networking Integration Strategy. Two schemes are available for networking integration. The first scheme is to treat networking in each VRP, independently, as shown in Fig. 3. Application components are deployed independently in their corresponding VRP and virtual networks are created accordingly within each VRP. At the same time, network bridges are created in order to establish communication channels across VRPs. The scheme does not require any modification to the respective resource management platforms. This gives the flexibility for integrating other resource management platforms, for example, Kubernetes and Docker Swarms, with existing environment. The concerns about this scheme arise from the differences associated with each of the networking approaches taken by each of the respective resource management platforms. Considering that different platforms offer different types of networking services at various level, for example, an OpenStack managed network uses the Neutron framework, which offers rich functionalities including firewalls, load-balancers, and security groups, etc., these may not be available in the container environment if it is managed by Mesos. As the available functional components are different from platform to platform, this will affect how an application blueprint can be created.

The second scheme employs the Neutron framework [26] for building and managing virtual network infrastructure. Figure 4 shows the simplified networking plan. All hardware resources are connected to the same physical networking infrastructure, but logically, they are managed by corresponding platforms, independently. From an end-user point of view, all resources are in a single resource pool. In the case that multiple components of a single application-blueprint need to be deployed on both VMs and containers, which are managed by different platforms, this requires a dedicated virtual network for the entire application-blueprint over the end-user (*tenant*) network. Thus, there is a need for a unified virtual network infrastructure management framework to be installed across all platforms, horizontally. In addition, the *tenant* networks must be managed in a seamless fashion. The second networking planning scheme adopts OpenStack Neutron for this purpose. In general, frameworks and services developed under the OpenStack *Big Tent Governance* natively support Neutron services. In contrast,

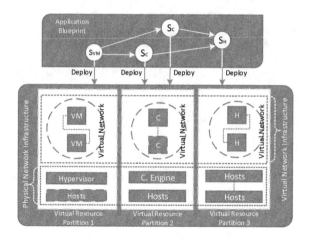

Fig. 4. Networking integration scheme using unified network framework across multiple platforms.

container technologies such as Kubernetes, Mesos, and Docker Swarm employ different networking models. For example, Kubernetes can use Flannel [27], Weave Net [28] frameworks operating in various modes; Docker uses libnetwork [29] by default. In the context of this work, the Kuryr network driver [30] is employed to link Neutron and container networks. Thus, end-users will experience seamless connections between all types of heterogeneous hardware resources.

3.4 The Server-Integration Scheme

In the second integration scheme, heterogeneous hardware is organized on a per server basis, as shown in Fig. 5. Each physical server is equipped with both general purpose processors and computation accelerators where they are applicable. Two types of networking interfaces, including high-speed interface(s) (e.g., InfiniBand or 40 Gb/s Ethernet) and standard-speed interface(s) (e.g., 1/10 Gb/s Ethernet) are also installed on a per server basis. Different types of networks are connected to their corresponding dedicated networking switches. In this configuration, a physical server is capable of offering high-performance computational resources for HPC applications as well as economical computational resources for general applications such as Web services.

The mixed hardware configuration also requires both container engine and hypervisor to coexist on the same physical server. This is because, in a virtualized environment, access to specialized computational accelerators (e.g., MICs, GPUs and DFEs), especially when dealing with various types and models of those accelerators, from a VM can be very problematic. It is generally requires both software (including operating system and hypervisor) and hardware (including CPU and motherboard) to support for passing through specialized accelerators to VMs. In contrast, a container application can directly use accelerators that have been already recognized by the underly host operating systems. Nevertheless, trade offs need to be taken into account when using different resource abstraction/access methods. For examples, VMs, as a complete operating

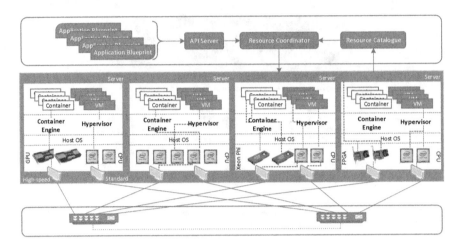

Fig. 5. Managing and accommodating heterogeneous hardware resources through hardware integration on a per server basis.

system, can provide all features that a standard operating system offers; a container provides a light-weight application execution environment which may result in better performance, but may be less flexible and secure. For applications to experience native performances or strict secure environment, for example heavily loaded database systems and banking transaction processing systems, the option for access to bare-metal servers is often needed. Thus, the coexistence of various resource abstraction methods on each individual server is desirable. Note that the coexistence of both container engine and hypervisor may affect the choices for selecting the types of hypervisor (Classic System VMs or Hosted VMs) [12].

At the management layer, all resources are registered with a Resource Catalogue and compatible computational resources are logically grouped together from an application perspective. Depending on the characteristics of an application blueprint to be deployed, the Resource Coordinator uses the information from the Resource Catalogue to make decisions on how and where to provision resources. One of the key features of the Server-Integration scheme is that it allows for various software and hardware components, including types of operating system, hypervisors, container engines, general purpose processors, computational accelerators, and different types of networking connections to be dynamically and flexibly combined together to meet application and system requirements.

3.5 Summary

The platform-integration scheme can provision heterogeneous resources through the integration of various existing platforms in which each platform manages a set of homogeneous hardware resources, independently. Globally, all types of resources are virtually presented in a unified resource pool to end-users. The use of existing management platforms provides a solution for rapid construction of a heterogeneous cloud. Most of the architectural components such as telemetry, fine-grained resource scheduling, and resource management, are reused. It is must be noted that, in some circumstances, for example, an orchestrated service that are deployed on various types of resources across different platforms, may encounter network congestion issues, especially for those high-throughput HPC alike applications. Additionally, as each management platforms (e.g., OpenStack and Mesos) have their built-in resource schedulers, the platform-integration scheme is limited on how they control and optimize resources at a coarse-grained level. In contrast, the server-integration scheme is more flexible. Multiple management platforms can be configured to simultaneously manage their corresponding resource types on the same server across the data center, provided no conflicts between them; or a customized platform to manage the system in a more dedicated manner, providing all necessary auxiliary services such as telemetry and resource manager. Additionally, as the coexistence of various types of resources on each server, more diverse applications and system requirements can be more easily met by *wiring* appropriate components.

4   Experiment

The initial implementation and the deployment of the proposed schemes have been realized in the context of CloudLightning project [31]. In this paper, a use case based on the Intel's Ray-Tracing application [32] is used to demonstrate the need for a unified platform to manage a cloud environment composed of heterogeneous resources.

4.1   Testbed Configuration

The experimental environment consists of an OpenStack managed virtualization environment (Newton release) which consists of eight Dell C6145 compute servers in total having 384 cores, 1.4 TB RAM, 12 TB storage and a Mesos managed Docker container environment (v17.04.0-ce) which consists of five IBM 326e servers in total having 10 cores, 40 GB RAM, 200 GB storage. In this deployment configuration, all physical servers have multiple dedicated network connections to three different networks including a *public*, a *private* and a *bridge* network. The *public* network connects to the Internet, the *private* networks are private to OpenStack or Mesos, respectively, the *bridge* network provides interconnections between virtual machines (managed by OpenStack) and containers (managed by Mesos). In the context of OpenStack, the *private* network is equivalent to the Neutron *Tenant* network, the *public* and *bridge* networks are the Neutron *Provider* networks. In the Mesos managed Docker environment, three Docker Bridge networks are created with each connecting to the *public*, *private* and *bridge* network, respectively. This deployment configuration is flexible to allow for future platforms, if needed, to be integrated with the existing environments. The detailed testbed layout and network configuration are shown in Fig. 6.

4.2   Use Case Blueprint

The Intel's Ray-Tracing application use case is composed of two parts, the first part is the Ray-Tracing engine and the second part is a Web interface. Both the engine and the Web interfaces should be respectively deployed on the most appropriate back-end

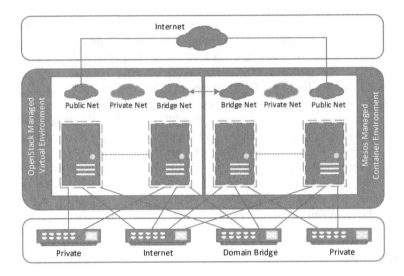

Fig. 6. Testbed layout and network configuration.

resources. For example, it has been demonstrated that the Ray-Tracing application can gain much better performance with MICs [33,34] comparing to general purpose CPUs. In order to use MICs, applications are generally required to be deployed in containers or directly on bare metal servers. And it is economically reasonable for deploying a Web server on a VM (providing more secured environment) that is configured with general purpose CPU processors. Thus, in the experiment, a blueprint is constructed which specifies that the Web interface should be deployed on VMs and the Ray-Tracing engine should be deployed in a container.

The graphical representation of the use case blueprint is shown in Fig. 7. The blueprint is also expressed in EXtensible Markup Language (XML) for machine interpretation. A blueprint consists of four main components:

1. *Execution Environments*, specifying the resource types such as virtual machines, containers, bare metal and so on,
2. *Service Element*, detailing the software component(s) to be deployed in an Execution Environment,
3. *Artifacts*, containing configurations for each Execution Environment or Service Element,
4. Connections, specifying the connectivity between Execution Environments and Service Elements.

The Resource Coordinator is responsible for parsing, decomposing and transforming blueprint components to a format, that can be understood by the underlying cloud management platforms, to facilitate application deployment.

The Resource Coordinator categorizes Execution Environments of the blueprint in to groups based on resource types (EE-Group), such as virtual machines, containers, or bare-metal. Within each EE-Group, Execution Environments are further partitioned

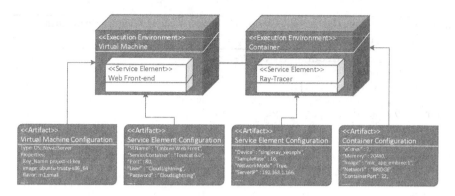

Fig. 7. Ray-Tracing application blueprint.

into sub-groups based on the connectivities (C-Group), for example, if another given blueprint consists of three virtual machines without specifying connections between them, then this blueprint will be partitioned into one EE-Group and three C-Group within that EE-Group. In the use case scenario described there, there are two EE-groups, and one C-Group within each EE-Group. This grouping can be determined by formulating the blueprint topology into a graph $G(V, E)$, then connectivities between Execution Environments can be identified using the Union-Find algorithm, as illustrated in Algorithm 1. Where V indicates the vertices in the graph corresponding to the Execution Environments in the blueprint, and E denotes the edges in the graph corresponding to the connections between Execution Environments.

The algorithm assumes the connections are symmetric (if Execution Environment A is connected to Execution Environment B, then B is connected to A) and transitive (if Execution Environment A is connected to B, B is connected to C, then A is connected to C). Additional constraints can be added to make blueprint connections asymmetric and/or non-transitive.

When the grouping process is completed, the Resource Coordinator seeks for connections between C-Groups within each EE-Group. A connection between a pair of Execution Environments in different C-Groups indicates that the both Execution Environments should be placed in a *bridge* network or need to be attached to a *bridge* network, to establish cross platform communications. Execution Environments in a completely isolated C-Group should be placed in a *private* network, if Internet access is desired, then each Execution Environment must be attached to the *public* network, independently. Once the networks are identified, Execution Environments with their corresponding configurations in each EE-Group are transformed into deployment templates that are compatible with the corresponding management platforms. The Resource Coordinator initiates the deployment process and subsequently manages the life-cycle of the application blueprint. Listing 1.1 shows the deployment template for the Intel Ray-tracing Web front-end, in YAML format. This template is converted from the use case blueprint (as shown in Fig. 7) to make it compatible with corresponding platforms. In this use case, the Ray-tracing Web front-end is configured to be deployed on a VM, and VMs are managed by OpenStack. Listing 1.2 shows the deployment template for

Algorithm 1. Identifying Connectivity Groups (C-Groups) in each Execution Environment (EE-Group) using Union-Find Algorithm.

```
/* Identify C-Groups in a EE-Group                              */
```
Data: EE-Group
Result: List{C-Group{v.idx}}
$G_{EE-Group}$(V, E); size ← V.size(); topology = new int[size];
for *i ← 0 to size-1* **do**
  | topology[i] = i;
end
foreach *Edge e(v_i, v_j) : E* **do**
  | **if** *connected(v_i, v_j)* **then**
  | | continue;
  | **end**
  | **else**
  | | idx_i = find(v_i); idx_j = find(v_j);
  | | **if** *idx_i == idx_j* **then**
  | | | **return**
  | | **end**
  | | **else**
  | | | **for** *q ← 0 to size-1* **do**
  | | | | **if** *topology[i] == idx_i* **then**
  | | | | | topology[i] = idx_j
  | | | | **end**
  | | | **end**
  | | **end**
  | **end**
end
```
/* Store topology to C-Groups                                   */
```
cgroupSize ← number of unique values in *topology*;
for *i ← 0 to cgroupSize-1* **do**
  | new cGroup$_i$()
end
for *i ← 0 to topology.lenght-2; i++* **do**
  | **if** *topology[i] == -1* **then**
  | | continue
  | **end**
  | cGroup$_k$.add(i);
  | **for** *j ← i+1 to topology.length-1; j++* **do**
  | | **if** *topology[j] == topology[i]* **then**
  | | | cGroup$_k$.add(j); topology[j] == -1
  | | **end**
  | **end**
  | topology[i] == -1; k++;
end
```
/* Determine which connectino group an Execution
   Environment belongs to                                       */
```
Function *find(v)*
  | **return** *topology[v.index]*
```
/* Detect whether two Execution Environments are connected
   */
```
Function *connected(v1, v2)*
  | **return** *find(v1) == find(v2)*

the Intel Ray-tracing back-end application, in JSON format. This templates is also converted from the use case blueprint, but the template is made compatible with Mesos/-Marathon for the application deployment in containers.

Listing 1.1. Intel Ray-tracing Web front-end deployment template in YALM format.

```
blueprint-id:  c97e718674c34adf815316ad4cec93cf
heat_template_version:  2016-10-14
resources:
    embree_web_frontend:
        type:  OS::Nova::Server
        properties:
            image:  Ubuntu14.04_LTS_svr_x86_64
            flavor:  ml.small
            key_name:  cl-project
            networks:
                - network:  bridge-provider
user_data:
    template:  |
        #!/bin/bash -v
        apt -y install httpd
......
```

Listing 1.2. Ray-Tracer in Mesos managed Docker containers using Marathon.

```
{
  "blueprint-id" : "c97e718674c34adf815316ad4cec93cf",
  curl -X POST -H "Content-type:_application/json"
  marathon:8080/v2/apps -d
  {
    "id" : "embree",
    "cpus" : 2,
    "mem" : 10240.0,
    "container" :
    {
      "type" : "DOCKER",
      "docker":
      {
        "image" : "mic-app-embree:1",
        "network": "BRIDGE",
        "portMappings":
        [
          {
            "containerPort":22,
            "hostPort":0
          }
        ]
      }
    }
  }
}
```

5 Conclusions

Conventional cloud environments typically consist of homogeneous resources. Driven by consumer needs and technological advances, this situation is gradually changing. Heterogeneity in resource types is being introduced, and this poses challenges to traditional resource management mechanisms which aspire to seamlessly deliver the advantages associated with novel heterogeneous architectures to the end user. In response to this transition, a platform-integration scheme and a server-integration scheme have been presented. The platform-integration scheme describes a hyper-level management approach by integrating, and coordinating various coexisting cloud management platforms. Each of these platforms manages hardware resources of a particular type, characteristics, and an abstraction method most appropriate for its management. A use case experiment was presented to demonstrate how an application blueprint can be deployed and managed in an heterogeneous environment implementing the platform-integration scheme. The experiment also illustrates the benefit of having a management framework providing a unified view of heterogeneous resources. In contrast, the server-integration scheme is employed at the lowest level in the service delivery stack and performs fine-grained resource optimization and flexible service orchestration. This is achieved by reorganizing the hardware components on each physical server and by resource grouping at data center infrastructure level. The development of a use case to illustrate the server-integration scheme requires specialized hardware capabilities including I/O virtualization. Moreover, specialized configurations and software libraries are required to support hardware accelerator pass-through technologies. This use case will be developed in future work.

The candidate heterogeneous cloud management solutions proposed here, while still in the early stage of the development, provide realistic solutions to the complex problem of heterogeneous resource management. The platform-integration scheme can more readily be exploited, since it integrates and manages a multiplicity of extant technologies. The server-integration scheme, being a lower-level solution, is more specialized in its requirements from both the hardware and software environments. Hence, it can be seen as more of a longer-term solution.

To efficiently and effectively manage an heterogeneous cloud as an holistic entity, re-consideration of physical server design (incl. on-board computation accelerator integration, a good balance between computation accelerator and general purpose processing capacity, and a redesign of the cooling system), heterogeneous environment management (incl. neural network based resource management and collective intelligence based autonomic computing), service delivery model and cloud application development methodology (incl. a unified view of heterogeneous resources and a script-less application development) should all be addressed in a coherent and integrated manner. This is the challenge for the designers of the emerging heterogeneous cloud.

Acknowledgment. This work is funded by the European Unions Horizon 2020 Research and Innovation Programme through the CloudLightning project under Grant Agreement Number 643946.

References

1. Barr, J.: Developer Preview-EC2 Instances (F1) with Programmable Hardware. Amazon Web Services (2016)
2. Russinovich, M.: Inside the Microsoft FPGA-based configurable cloud. Microsoft Developer Network (MSDN) (2017)
3. OpenStack, L.: The openstack project (2011)
4. Kubernetes (2017). http://kubernetes.io/
5. Hindman, B., Konwinski, A., Zaharia, M., Ghodsi, A., Joseph, A.D., Katz, R., Shenker, S., Stoica, I.: Mesos: a platform for fine-grained resource sharing in the data center. In: Proceedings of the 8th USENIX Conference on Networked Systems Design and Implementation, NSDI 2011, pp. 295–308. USENIX Association, Berkeley (2011)
6. Merkel, D.: Docker: lightweight Linux containers for consistent development and deployment. Linux J. **2014**, 2 (2014)
7. Turnbull, J.: The Docker Book. Lulu.com, Morrisville (2014)
8. OpenStack Magnum (2017). http://git.openstack.org/cgit/openstack/magnum
9. OpenStack Ironic (2016). https://docs.openstack.org/ironic/latest/
10. Dong, D., Stack, P., Xiong, H., Morrison, J.P.: Managing and unifying heterogeneous resources in cloud environments. In: Proceedings of the 7th International Conference on Cloud Computing and Services Science - Volume 1: CLOSER, pp. 143–150. INSTICC, ScitePress (2017)
11. Popek, G.J., Goldberg, R.P.: Formal requirements for virtualizable third generation architectures. Commun. ACM **17**, 412–421 (1974)
12. Smith, J.E., Nair, R.: The architecture of virtual machines. Computer **38**, 32–38 (2005)
13. OpenStack: Architecture design guide. Technical report 15.0.0 (2017)
14. Fontán, J., Vázquez, T., Gonzalez, L., Montero, R.S., Llorente, I.: OpenNebula: the open source virtual machine manager for cluster computing. In: Open Source Grid and Cluster Software Conference, vol. 86 (2008)
15. OpenNebula: OpenNebula 5.2 deployment guide. Technical report 5.2.1, OpenNebula Systems (2017)
16. OpenNebula: OpenNebula 5.2 operation guide. Technical report 5.2.1, OpenNebula Systems (2017)
17. Nimbus (2017). http://www.nimbusproject.org
18. Keahey, K., Armstrong, P., Bresnahan, J., LaBissoniere, D., Riteau, P.: Infrastructure outsourcing in multi-cloud environment. In: Proceedings of the 2012 Workshop on Cloud Services, Federation, and the 8th Open Cirrus Summit, FederatedClouds 2012, pp. 33–38. ACM, New York (2012)
19. Verma, A., Pedrosa, L., Korupolu, M., Oppenheimer, D., Tune, E., Wilkes, J.: Large-scale cluster management at Google with Borg. In: Proceedings of the Tenth European Conference on Computer Systems, EuroSys 2015, pp. 18:1–18:17. ACM, New York (2015)
20. Schwarzkopf, M., Konwinski, A., Abd-El-Malek, M., Wilkes, J.: Omega: flexible, scalable schedulers for large compute clusters. In: Proceedings of the 8th ACM European Conference on Computer Systems, EuroSys 2013, pp. 351–364. ACM, New York (2013)
21. Rensin, D.K.: Kubernetes - Scheduling the Future at Cloud Scale, 1005 Gravenstein Highway North Sebastopol, CA 95472 (2015)
22. Burns, B., Grant, B., Oppenheimer, D., Brewer, E., Wilkes, J.: Borg, Omega, and Kubernetes. Commun. ACM **59**, 50–57 (2016)
23. Zhang, Z., Li, C., Tao, Y., Yang, R., Tang, H., Xu, J.: Fuxi: a fault-tolerant resource management and job scheduling system at Internet scale. Proc. VLDB Endow. **7**, 1393–1404 (2014)

24. Razor Server (2017). https://github.com/puppetlabs/razor-server
25. Foreman (2017). https://theforeman.org
26. OpenStack Neutron (2017). https://github.com/openstack/neutron
27. Flannel (2017). https://github.com/coreos/flannel
28. Weaveworks WeaveNet (2017). https://www.weave.works/docs/net/latest/introducing-weave/
29. Libnetwork (2017). https://github.com/docker/libnetwork
30. Kuryr (2017). http://docs.openstack.org/developer/kuryr/
31. Lynn, T., Xiong, H., Dong, D., Momani, B., Gravvanis, G., Filelis-Papadopoulos, C., Elster, A., Khan, M.M.Z.M., Tzovaras, D., Giannoutakis, K., Petcu, D., Neagul, M., Dragon, I., Kuppudayar, P., Natarajan, S., McGrath, M., Gaydadjiev, G., Becker, T., Gourinovitch, A., Kenny, D., Morrison, J.: CloudLightning: a framework for a self-organising and self-managing heterogeneous cloud. In: Proceedings of the 6th International Conference on Cloud Computing and Services Science, pp. 333–338 (2016)
32. Intel Embree (2017). https://embree.github.io
33. Benthin, C., Wald, I., Woop, S., Ernst, M., Mark, W.R.: Combining single and packet-ray tracing for arbitrary ray distributions on the Intel MIC architecture. IEEE Trans. Visual Comput. Graph. **18**, 1438–1448 (2012)
34. Wald, I.: Fast construction of SAH BVHs on the intel many integrated core (MIC) architecture. IEEE Trans. Visual Comput. Graph. **18**, 47–57 (2012)

Using Docker Swarm with a User-Centric Decision-Making Framework for Cloud Application Migration

Esha Barlaskar[✉], Peter Kilpatrick, Ivor Spence,
and Dimitrios S. Nikolopoulos

The School of Electronics, Electrical Engineering and Computer Science,
Queen's University Belfast, Belfast BT7 1NN, UK
{ebarlaskar01,p.kilpatrick,i.Spence,d.nikolopoulos}@qub.ac.uk

Abstract. Vendor lock-in is a major obstacle for cloud users in performing multi-cloud deployment or inter-cloud migration, due to the lack of standardization. Current research efforts tackling the inter-cloud migration problem are commonly technology-oriented with significant performance overheads. Moreover, current studies do not provide adequate support for decision making such as why and when inter-cloud migration should take place. We propose the architecture and the problem formulation of a Multi-objective dYnamic MIgratioN Decision makER (MyMinder) framework that assists cloud users in achieving a stable QoS performance in the post-deployment phase by helping decide on actions to be taken as well as providing support to achieve such actions. Additionally, we demonstrate the migration capability of MyMinder by proposing an Automated Triggering Algorithm (ATA), which uses existing Docker Swarm technology for application migration.

Keywords: Cloud Computing · Dynamic decision making
QoS monitoring · Inter-cloud migration · Docker Swarm

1 Introduction

With the expansion of the range of Cloud Infrastructure-as-a-Service (IaaS) providers, efficient and accurate cloud provider (CP) selection based on user-specific requirements has become a significant challenge for cloud IaaS users. Cloud users have to engage in a number of complex decision-making processes which mainly stem from performance variability amongst the CPs and also from diversified pricing policies offered by different CPs. The reason for such variability is the heterogeneity prevailing amongst the CPs. In addition to this initial challenge in CP selection, there exist further challenges after the deployment of user applications in the form of monitoring the health of the acquired virtual machines (VMs) to verify whether the applications are performing in a stable manner with minimum or acceptable variations. In the post-deployment

© Springer International Publishing AG, part of Springer Nature 2018
D. Ferguson et al. (Eds.): CLOSER 2017, CCIS 864, pp. 81–101, 2018.
https://doi.org/10.1007/978-3-319-94959-8_5

phase the major cause for performance variability is multi-tenancy problems which arise because most of the computing resources (network and disk I/O) except for CPU cores are shared amongst several users' instances (from here on we will use the terms VM and instance interchangeably) running in a physical server [15,18,19]. Such variations due to performance degradation can be a serious problem for latency-sensitive and I/O-bound applications. Therefore, accurate monitoring and detection methods are required. Although cloud service monitoring tools are provided by CPs and third party companies [4,30,33], these monitoring tools do not provide any decision support on what steps a cloud user should follow if he/she realises that even their minimum performance requirements are not met by the selected instances in the current CP.

To meet the desired performance requirements cloud users may require to migrate their applications to new instance type with higher configuration from the same provider or with a similar configuration from a different provider. Apart from performance, cost can also be an important factor for certain budget-constrained users who may be interested to migrate to different instances if the price for the current cloud service rises or other providers offer a better price. Taking decisions on whether to migrate applications for better performance/cost poses further decision making and technical challenges for cloud users.

Although some researchers have tried to address the vendor lock-in issues by designing inter-cloud migration techniques, they have not provided any decision-making support. Others have focussed mainly on pre-deployment decision-making and there has been very limited work on post-deployment phase support, and these latter do not consider realistic migration overheads in the evaluation of their decision making framework. Therefore, naive cloud users should have an efficient dynamic decision making framework, which can help to provide guidance on the following:

1. How to detect if the current provider is not performing as required by user's application?
2. How to decide that the user's application needs to be migrated from the current provider?
3. Which alternative CP should be chosen to migrate the VM?
4. What instance type(s) will provide the best trade-off between cost and performance?
5. Whether the migration overhead will be more significant compared to the performance degradation in the current CP?

We envisage a system which can handle inter-cloud migration automatically along with a decision making framework, thus delivering the best of both the worlds. In previous work [1] we introduced a Multi-objective dYnamic MIgratioN Decision makER (MyMinder) framework designed to address the above issues. MyMinder offers a catalogue of metrics based on performance, cost and type of resources, from which cloud users can choose their requirement metrics depending on their application. Also, while choosing these metrics users can set some internal performance requirements and their maximum budget. MyMinder takes these requirements as inputs to carry out the monitoring and computes user satisfaction values based on their applications' performance requirements. In the event of any QoS violation or performance degradation MyMinder supports the user in finding alternative cloud services which can provide near-optimal performance, and efficiently migrate the application to that service provided by either the same or different CP. Our work in [1] presented the MyMinder architecture and problem formulation for selecting the most suitable CP to migrate the VM along with some initial experimental results that motivate the need for live VM migration from one CP to another. Although we presented the performance variability results from the bursting instance types of the selected public CPs, authors in [14,15] have experimentally proved that even dedicated instances show performance variability.

In this study we present MyMinder's migration module and demonstrate its use for performing user application migration across VMs within the same CP or across different CPs. We deploy user applications using Docker container technology [5]. Docker container is a lightweight virtualisation technology that relies on operating system virtualisation. Using operating system virtualisation, containers can be easily ported across multiple providers and can run smoothly on top of public cloud providers' virtual machines. These capabilities have made Docker container technology highly prevalent in the DevOps community [5]. All these features make containers a suitable lightweight option for cloud user applications that easily supports transferability/portability and interoperability across different CPs. Considering the benefits of Docker containers and Docker Swarm management facilities [8] (detailed discussion is in Sect. 2), the proposed MyMinder prototype adopts the widely accepted Docker Swarm technology in order to perform the multi-cloud deployment of user applications. However, Docker Swarm does not provide a facility for resource provisioning policies that are required by MyMinder. Therefore, we introduce an Automated Triggering Algorithm (ATA) that automates VM allocation and de-allocation in the Docker Swarm cluster and integrates the Swarm orchestration features as guided by the output generated by MyMinder's Decision-making process. We evaluate the performance of MyMinder's migration process by deploying it in an OpenStack testbed, where a cluster of Docker Swarm nodes are created using the VMs and application containers are transferred among these Swarm nodes. This evaluation is an attempt to verify the feasibility of MyMinder's migration process and does not include performance results from inter-cloud migration across public clouds.

The remainder of the paper is organised as follows. Section 2 presents background and related work in user centric live VM migration and decision making. Sections 3 and 4 provide detail of the problem formulation and the MyMinder architecture, respectively. Migration using Docker Swarm and ATA is explained in Sect. 5. MyMinder migration module prototype set-up and performance evaluation of ATA are discussed in Sect. 6. Section 7 concludes the paper and discusses future work.

2   Background and Related Work

With the proliferation of CPs it has become very difficult for cloud users to select the one that best meets their needs. Once they select the perceived optimal cloud service from a CP, cloud users encounter further challenges as they need to verify whether their applications are performing in a stable manner with minimum or acceptable variations after being deployed in the CP's instances. If the user realises that their desired QoS requirements are not met by the selected instances then they may require to migrate their applications to a new instance type from the same provider or to an instance with a similar configuration from a new provider. Apart from performance, cost can also be an important factor for certain budget-constrained users who may be interested in migrating to different instances if the price for the current cloud service rises or other providers offer better price. Taking decisions on whether to migrate applications for better QoS/cost poses further decision-making and technical challenges for the user. We discuss how current work in the literature addresses these challenges in the following sections.

2.1   Post-deployment Decision Making

Although researchers have proposed different decision making methods in the pre-deployment phase [3,11,16,24,26,32] decision making in the post-deployment phase has not received much attention, other than the works in [17,25].

The authors in [25] address decision making in the post-deployment phase by proposing a multi-stage decision-making approach. In the first stage, the available CP instances are shortlisted on the basis of the user's minimum QoS and cost criteria, and in the second stage, migration cost and time are evaluated. After completing these stages, they use the Technique for Order of Preference by Similarity to Ideal Solution (TOPSIS) [2] and ELimination Et Choix Traduisant la REalit (ELimination and Choice Expressing REality), commonly known as ELECTRE [28], to find the most appropriate migration suggestion. They demonstrate their approach using a case study example. However, in their evaluation, they consider the overhead of a manual migration process where they assume that the network throughput between the source and the destination hosts remains constant during the migration process, which is unlikely to be true in real scenarios.

In [17] a linear integer programming model for dynamic cloud scheduling via migration of VMs across multiple clouds is proposed in the context of a cloud brokerage system. The migration is triggered if a CP either offers a special discount or introduces a new instance type, and also if the user needs to increase the infrastructure capacity. They do not consider QoS violation or degradation in their migration decision. Moreover, they performed their experiments in a simulation based environment and the metrics that they considered for measuring migration overhead may not be feasible to obtain in real world scenarios.

2.2   User-Centric Inter-cloud Migration

Although cloud users should not be worried about the complexities involved in VM migration - which is the essence of the 'cloud philosophy', experienced cloud users may wish to have the flexibility that migration brings in the form of inter-cloud migration. However, there are complexities in migrating VMs from one CP to another CP due to vendor lock-in issues. Vendor lock-in makes a cloud customer dependent on a specific CP due to inherent dependencies on underlying cloud infrastructures. This makes it very difficult for the customers to transfer their applications to another CP without substantial migration costs. These dependencies are often subject to CPs specific (non-standardized) service APIs. For users to avail of the benefits of application migration independent of the CP's permission, recent studies proposed different inter-cloud migration techniques which use a second layer of hardware virtualisation called nested virtualisation [12,23,34]. Nested VMs are usually migrated by using an NFS-based solution or an iSCSI-based solution. In some cases such as that of [22] the focus is not on providing storage and network support for wide-area network (WAN) application but rather on providing an enclosed environment for distributed application development and debugging. In an NFS-based and iSCSI-based solution the WAN VM migration experiences increased latencies, low bandwidth, and high internet cost in accessing a shared disk image if the shared storage is located in a different data centre or region. To address this issue [31] proposed Supercloud using nested virtualisation with a geo-replicated image file storage that maintains the trade-off between performance and cost. They designed an image storage that tries to propagate only data which is frequently accessed and it proactively transmits data before migration is triggered. However, Supercloud have some performance overhead due to that fact that nested virtualization imposes additional performance overhead, I/O overhead and CPU scheduling delay and also they do not provide any decision-making framework.

Other state-of-the-art techniques which allow multi-cloud deployment are Docker [5] and Multibox containers [10]. Nowadays containers are widely used as an alternative solution to more traditional Virtual Machines (VMs) allowing the deployment of virtualised resources with comparatively limited performance impact. Unlike VMs which run a full OS on virtual hardware, containers provide operating system level virtualisation where the associated deployments are much smaller in size because the container-based applications share their underlying OS. Containers can easily package an application into a single file which makes the process of application delivery and orchestration very flexible for the developers. Docker offers an elastic container platform called Docker Swarm which integrates container hosts (also referred to as Docker nodes or Docker Engines) into one single and higher level cluster. The Docker SwarmKit performs the Docker Engine's cluster management and builds the orchestration features for the cloud user applications. These features include deployment, scale up/down, termination, and migration/transfer across Docker nodes. The author in [13] proposed a control loop which is able to scale and transfer elastic container platforms (i.e. Docker Swarm and Kubernates etc.) across different public and private cloud-service providers. However, this control loop is just one phase of a self-adaptive auto-scaling MAPE loops (monitoring, analysis, planning, execution) and does not include the monitoring, analysis and planning phases.

In an extensive discussion the author in [13] points out the four main benefits of using the elastic container platforms (like Docker Swarm, Google's Kubernetes, etc.), which are summarised below:

1. One logical cluster can be formed by integrating single container nodes (hosts), where the hosts are within a single CP in order to help in complexity management of the deployed application.
2. This logical cluster can be extended across different CPs.
3. Different CP container nodes can be accessed as one single cluster which will solve the vendor lock-in problem.
4. These elastic container platforms have self-healing capabilities as they are designed with failover mechanisms. Their auto-restart, auto-replication, and auto scaling features help in the event of node failure or any process failure.

Considering the benefits of lightweight virtualization and evaluating the complexities/performance overhead of the existing inter-cloud migration techniques like nested virtualisation [12], the proposed MyMinder prototype adopts the widely accepted Docker Swarm container technology [8] in order to perform the multi-cloud deployment of user applications. However, Docker Swarm does not provide the facility for resource provisioning policies that are required by MyMinder. Therefore, we introduce an Automated Triggering Algorithm (ATA) that automates Docker Swarm cluster management and orchestration features based on the output generated by MyMinder's Decision-making process.

3   Problem Formulation

As presented in [1] the MyMinder framework (Fig. 1) can assist cloud users in achieving a stable QoS performance in the post-deployment phase by helping decide on actions to be taken as well as providing support to achieve such actions. MyMinder can monitor the performance of the deployed users' applications and provide the required measurements to determine the satisfaction level of the user's requirements described in their requests. In the event of QoS violation or degradation in the current CP's service, MyMinder can trigger a migration decision after identifying a suitable CP to which the overhead of migration and the chances of QoS violation are the least. For performing these actions MyMinder needs to evaluate the satisfaction values based on the QoS/performance requirements specified in the user's requests. In the following subsections we illustrate user requirements, details of the CP instance type model, and the related measures [1].

3.1   User Requirements

A user sends a request describing his/her resource requirements and QoS/performance requirements. This request is represented by a requirement vector : $r = [r_1, r_2, ..., r_j]$ where r_j specifies the $jth(j = 1, 2, ...J)$ requirement of the user that has to be satisfied by the selected CP and these requirements may include the following information criteria [1]: (1) Resource criteria: amount of resources required for running user's application (e.g. memory, storage, CPU etc.). (2) Budget constraint: prices of the instances should be within the cost limit of the user. (3) QoS/performance criteria: Quality of service or performance requirements of user's application that has to be fulfilled (e.g. desired and maximum execution time, response time, throughput etc.) (4) Migration overhead constraint: cost of migration and performance overhead of migration should be acceptable.

Here, criteria 1 and 2 will be evaluated before deploying the application and only if these criteria are met then the application will be deployed and after deploying the application criteria 3 will be measured using a satisfaction value. The criteria 4 depends on the type of inter-cloud migration technology being used. The details of migration overhead measurement is discussed in Sect. 5

3.2   CP Instance Types Model

Instances of different CPs differ in performance depending on their characteristics such as VM instance size, hardware infrastructure, VM placement policies used for load balancing or power optimisation etc. Factors affecting the QoS obtained from a particular instance type of a CP are typically not known by the user and so the QoS data of a given CP are not available in advance. It is possible to measure the QoS parameters only after the instance is deployed and these measurements may be evaluated against the requirements specified in the user request by determining the runtime performances such as execution time of applications, instructions committed per second (IPS), throughput etc. These measurements constitute the evaluation of the extent to which the QoS/ performance requirements specified in the user's request r_j are satisfied. The satisfaction level of user requirement r_j is denoted by $s_j \in [0, 1]$, where $s_j = 1$ if the requirement r_j is fully satisfied, otherwise $0 \leqslant s_j < 1$ [1].

If a user provides the requirement vector r_i along with the desired QoS requirement and acceptable maximum variability in the QoS, then standard deviation (SD) is used as a measure of QoS performance variability. The closer the SD is to 0, the greater is the uniformity of performance data to the desired value $(r_{Qd(r_j)})$ and greater is the satisfaction value. The closer the SD is to 1, the greater is the variability of performance data to the desired value and smaller is the satisfaction value. Hence, the satisfaction value is given as follows [1]:

$$s_j \quad = 1 - SD \tag{1}$$

$$SD \quad = \sqrt{\frac{1}{N-1} \sum_{i=1}^{N} (Qa(r_j) - \overline{M(r_j)})^2} \tag{2}$$

$$M(r_j) \quad = \frac{1}{N-1} \sum_{i=1}^{N} (Qa(r_j)) \tag{3}$$

where,

$Qa(r_j)$ = Actual QoS value obtained after deploying the user's application (e.g. actual execution time, response time, etc.). These values are in normalised form.

$M(r_j)$ = The arithmetic mean of $Qa(r_j)$.

$r_{Qd(r_j)}$ = Desired QoS requirements of the user's applications (e.g. desired execution time, response time, etc.) for the QoS requirement r_j. This value is used as a standard value against which QoS variability is compared.

N = total number of measurements.

3.3 Utility Function

The utility function $f(r)$ for each user request r_j is a linear combination of the satisfaction value s_j and the associated weights w_j multiplied by an indicator function $\phi(r)$. The weight for each of the user requests indicates its importance to the user and the indicator function sets the satisfaction level to zero when the request is not satisfied. In the case of satisfied requests the value of the indicator function is selected such that: $\phi(r) = (\sum_j w_j)^{-1}$ normalizes the weight vector and limit the maximum possible value of $f(r)$ to 1 [1].

Thus, the utility function is defined as [1]:

$$f(r) = \phi(r) \sum_{n=1}^{J} w_j s_j \qquad (4)$$

where

$$\phi(r) = \begin{cases} 0, & \text{if } QoS \text{ not met.} \\ (\sum_j w_j)^{-1}, & \text{otherwise.} \end{cases} \qquad (5)$$

If all the requirements of a user are fully satisfied then $f(r) = 1$; otherwise if the requirements are partially satisfied then the value of $f(r)$ will vary with the amount of requirements being satisfied by a particular instance type of a CP. To demonstrate this lets consider one simple example [1]:

Let $r = [r_1, r_2, ..., r_j]$ be the user's requirement vector while making his/her initial request. The request contains the user's requirements constraints and the type of the requirement attributes are presented below:

(1) r_R: Requested amount of resources required for running the user's application (e.g. memory, storage, CPU etc.) where $r_R \in micro, small, medium, large, xlarge$.

(2) r_B: Prices of the instances specified in the user's budget where $r_B \in Max_{price}$

(3) r_{Qd}: Desired QoS requirements of the user's applications (e.g. desired execution time, response time, IPS, etc.) where $r_{Qd} \in D_{val}$.

(4) r_{Mo}: Maximum migration overhead a user can accept where $r_M \in Overhead\ of\ migration$.

The value of the satisfaction vector is calculated with the help of monitoring and detection modules (see Sect. 4) which is given by S_i^T (Eq. 1). We assume that for a user's request with a requirement vector $r_i = [\text{micro}, 200\,\text{s}, 400\,\text{s}, £5/\text{hr}, 30\%]$, the satisfaction vector is calculated as [1]:

$$S^T = [1, 0, 1, 1] \tag{6}$$

For simplifying the example we did not consider partial satisfaction values, and here 0 denotes fully satisfied and 1 denotes not satisfied. Therefore the utility value is calculated as follows if the weight vector is $W^T = [0.1, 0.1, 0.1, 0.3]$ [1]:

$$f(r) = \begin{cases} 0, & \text{if } QoS \text{ not met.} \\ \phi(r)W^T S^T = 0.5, & \text{otherwise.} \end{cases} \tag{7}$$

The induction function's value is considered to be 1 in this case and also the utility function's value did not exceed 0.5 even though more than half of the requirements were fully satisfied.

These utility values will be used to predict the QoS for each CP's instance types model [1].

4 MyMinder Architecture

In this section we describe the architecture of MyMinder [1] that will implement the problem formulation. Figure 1 [1] depicts the MyMinder architecture, which includes modules for: monitoring, detection, prediction, decision making and migration. We describe each of these modules in the following subsections:

4.1 Monitoring Module

The monitoring module is designed for monitoring the QoS performance of the user's application containers deployed in the VM. The performance data are collected by local monitoring agents deployed in each user's VM. The local monitoring agents send the collected data periodically to the global monitoring component in the monitoring module and then finally the data are stored in the QoS performance repository. Also, the monitoring module maintains another repository, which stores information regarding the list of available VMs from different CPs and their prices. This information is collected by CP profiling components.

4.2 Detection Module

The detection module is responsible for detecting any QoS violation or degradation in the performance. The performance data are retrieved from the QoS performance repository. It uses a window-based violation detection technique [20] to generate QoS violation or performance degradation alarms based on the user's QoS requirement constraints and the user can decide the size of the window.

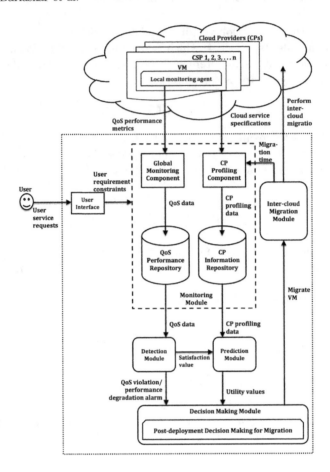

Fig. 1. MyMinder architecture.

This module generates QoS violation alarms if the current performance value falls outside the acceptable range as defined by the QoS statement. It also can be tuned to generate a degradation alarm if the performance moves to and stays within a defined distance of the QoS limits throughout a defined period. Degradation alarms may be used to predict likely breach of QoS and so may contribute to preventative migration. The module reports QoS violation and degradation alarms on a continuous basis by sending them to the decision making module.

4.3 Prediction Module

The objective of the prediction module is to help identify a suitable CP instance to which the user's application may be migrated. Based on the user's QoS satisfaction values (measured by the detection module) and the user's requirements, the prediction module calculates the utility function (see Eq. 4) for each of the available CP instances. The satisfaction values for the current as well as previously deployed CP instances by the same user or different users are stored with their corresponding utility values. These perceived utility values are used to train the prediction models for each of the CP instances using machine learning techniques. Thus, the prediction models are capable of predicting the QoS satisfaction values in the destination CP for the new user's instance which needs migration. Further, the prediction module predicts application migration/transfer time based on the analysis of the historical migration time data (stored in the monitoring module) factoring in similar type of applications and also the pair of CPs involved in the migration. The measurements of the migration time are previously obtained by ATA (see Sect. 5) in the migration module.

4.4   Decision-Making Module

The decision making module receives alarms from the detection module if any QoS violation or degradation is detected, and also it takes utility function values as input from the prediction module. It then checks with user requirement constraints to know whether the user wants to be informed before reaching the minimum requirement levels, i.e. performance degradation alert or to be informed if the minimum requirements are not met, i.e. QoS violation alert. After confirming user requirements, this module verifies whether the instances with different utility values provided by the prediction module are currently available for selection. If the instances are available then it evaluates the migration overhead of each of the instances and finally ranks the instances based on their utility value and migration overhead values. The instance with highest utility value and lowest migration overhead is chosen for migration. The migration overhead will depend on the type of inter-cloud migration technique being used. The migration overhead can be defined either in terms of monetary loss or performance loss and it usually denotes the service downtime penalty per time unit.

4.5   Migration Module

The migration module (Fig. 2) takes the decision generated by the decision-making module as its input for transferring/migrating user applications to the selected VM of the same CP or different CP. Once the migration module completes the task of application transfer/migration, it sends the migration overhead measurements to the monitoring module, which stores them as historical data for later use by the predication module. We adopt Docker containers to deploy user applications in the VMs of the selected CPs and Docker Swarm technology [8] to enable the transferability and portability features of Docker containers. We introduce an Automated Triggering Algorithm (ATA) that takes the output generated by the Decision-making module and makes use of the Docker Swarm cluster management and orchestration features (e.g. auto-placement, auto-restart, auto-replication and auto-scaling) in order to meet MyMinder's migration requirements. For example, if the decision making module takes a decision to migrate the user application from CP1 to CP2, ATA firstly adds the selected VMs of

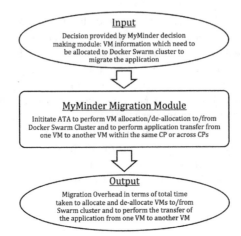

Fig. 2. MyMinder migration module.

CP2 to the Swarm cluster and secondly, ATA de-allocates the VMs of CP1. The Swarm cluster immediately identifies this de-allocation of VMs as node failures and then using its self-healing mechanism it auto-restarts the lost application containers in CP2. Although this action is just a rescheduling mechanism of the Docker Swarm platform due to the node failures, this appears to be a migration from CP1 to CP2 at real-time from a cloud user perspective. The following section explains the transferability/migration operations in details.

5   Migration Using Docker Swarm

As stated earlier, by proposing MyMinder we do not aim to design a new inter-cloud migration technique, but rather we aim to design a framework for cloud users which can take correct decisions on when and where to migrate their applications in case of QoS violations and degradations. In order to demonstrate the capability of MyMinder in performing migrations, we prototype the migration using the existing Docker Swarm technology in a lab-based OpenStack cloud.

In addition to using the Docker Swarm orchestration features we need to perform allocation and de-allocation of resources (VMs) to/from the Docker Swarm cluster in order to complete the migration operation. Specifically, we need to allocate new VMs (to which the applications need to be migrated) from the same CP or a different CP in the Swarm cluster and de-allocate current VMs (which failed to meet users's satisfaction) from the Swarm cluster. Figure 3 shows the migration scenario within a single CP, whereas Fig. 4 depicts inter-cloud migration scenario. However, adding VMs to a Swarm cluster from multiple CPs is challenging due to the different approaches followed by different CPs in providing access to their virtual resources. As reported in [13] the public CPs organize their IaaS by using mainly two approaches which are identified as project-based and

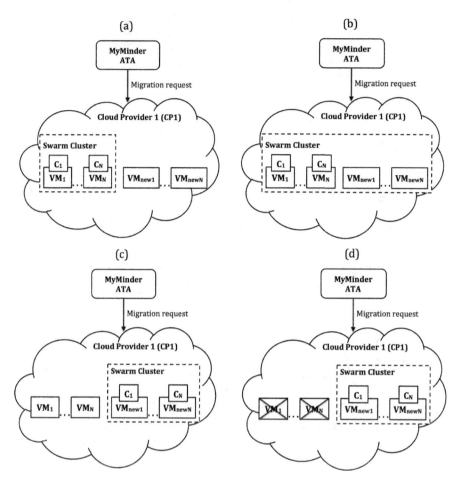

Fig. 3. MyMinder migration scenario 1 (migration within a single cloud provider (CP1)): (a) start new VMs, (b) allocate new VMs to Swarm Cluster, (c) de-allocate old VMs from Swarm cluster, (d) terminate the old VMs.

region-based service deliveries. Any multi-cloud deployment must consider the occurrence of both approaches in parallel. Therefore, we introduce an Automated Triggering Algorithm (ATA) to merge different approaches of different CPs and allocate/de-allocate VMs to Swarm cluster. To connect the Swarm cluster with a specific public CP it is required to have a configuration file for storing details used to communicate with the CPs. This can include authentication credentials and driver-specific configuration options. In this paper, the focus is on multiple VMs from a single private OpenStack cloud as depicted in Fig. 3, so the discussions on authentication credentials and driver-specific configurations are not included. Deployment in multiple public CPs will be considered in our future work once the decision-making module is functional; readers interested in details

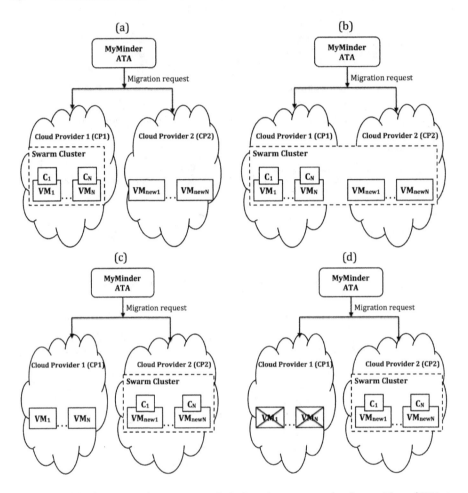

Fig. 4. MyMinder migration scenario 2 (migration across cloud providers (CP1 to CP2)): (a) start new VMs in CP2, (b) allocate new VMs to Swarm Cluster, (c) de-allocate old VMs from Swarm cluster, (d) terminate the old VMs from existing cloud provider (CP1).

of multi-cloud deployment can refer to [13]. We describe MyMinder's migration operation using ATA in the following subsection.

5.1   Automated Triggering Algorithm (ATA)

This section describes MyMinder's migration operation using ATA, which includes four stages. We present the pseudocode of the algorithm in Algorithm 1 and explain the stages as follows.

1. **Resource (VM) Provisioning:** ATA runs a configuration file for provisioning new VMs (as decided by the decision making module) either from the

---

Algorithm 1.

Automated Triggering Algorithm

VM_{new} : list of N new VMs (name and flavour of the VMs) to be allocated to Swarm cluster

VM_{old} : list of N old VMs (name and flavour of the VMs) to be de-allocated from

input: Swarm cluster

CP_{sel} : selected CP where the new VMs need to be allocated

$Cred$: credential file that includes the authentication credentials for the new VMs

$Driver$: IaaS driver for the selected CP

output: $M_{overhead}$ - total application migration overhead, which is calculated as the summation of VM allocation, VM de-allocation, and application transfer time.

explanation: *token = Swarm cluster joining token, one for master node and one for worker node,*

```
 1: for each VM_{new i} where i=1,...,N do
 2:     ssh to VM_{new i}
 3:     start_VM(VM_{new i}, Cred, Driver) in the CP_{sel}
 4: end for
 5: allocation_start_time = current_time()
 6: for each VM_{new i} where i=1,...,N do
 7:     if (VM_{new i} is INITIAL_VM) then
 8:         install_docker_engine()
 9:         token[master/worker] = swarm_init()
10:     else
11:         allocate_VM(token[master/worker])
12:     end if
13: end for
14: allocation_end_time = current_time()
15: allocation_time = allocation_end_time - allocation_start_time
16: de-allocation_start_time = current_time()
17: for each VM_{old i} where i=1,...,N do
18:     de-allocate_VM(SwarmLeave[master/worker])
19: end for
20: de-allocation_end_time = current_time()
21: de-allocation_time = de-allocation_end_time - de-allocation_start_time
22: transfer_start_time = current_time()
23: transfer_application (from VM_{old} to VM_{new})              ▷ this is performed by Swarm cluster's
    auto-restart feature
24: transfer_end_time = current_time()
25: transfer_time = transfer_end_time - transfer_start_time
26: for each VM_{old i} where i=1,...,N do
27:     terminate_VM(VM_{old i}, Cred, Driver) in the CP_{existing}
28: end for
29: M_{overhead} = allocation_time + de-allocation_time + transfer_time
30: return M_{overhead}
```

---

same CP (as shown in Fig. 3(a)) or from a different CP (as shown in Fig. 4(a)). This configuration file includes the detailed information about the VMs (e.g. flavor and name) along with the authentication credentials and IaaS drivers. In this stage all the requested VMs are started *(pseudocode lines 1–4)*. This installation is done by running SSH-based scripts. ATA starts the second stage only when all the requested VMs are running successfully and all the security groups are ready.

2. **VM Allocation to Swarm Cluster:** ATA installs Docker Engine in the VMs *(pseudocode line 8)* and allocates these VMs to the Swarm cluster (as shown in Figs. 3(b) and 4(b)) *(pseudocode line 11)*. During the allocation process their roles (master/ worker) are defined by calling the CP specific platform driver [6]. In Docker Swarm platform nodes acts as either masters

or workers. The master performs all scheduling tasks (auto-restart, auto-scale etc.) and the workers run the application containers. Therefore, the VMs which are master nodes are added first and then the worker nodes. If any of joining fails then ATA again runs the joining procedure until all the requested nodes are successfully added to the Swarm cluster.

3. **VM de-allocation from Swarm Cluster:** To reach the desired state (as given by the output of the decision-making module) the user application containers need to be rescheduled to the newly added Swarm nodes (new VMs). This is achieved by de-allocating the current Swarm nodes (old VMs) (as shown in Figs. 3(c) and 4(c)) *(pseudocode lines 17–19)* which in turn triggers the Swarm master to auto-restart the application containers in the available nodes (new VMs). Thus, in this stage all the old VMs are de-allocated from the Swarm cluster. After the de-allocation procedure, the Swarm scheduler recognises this as node failure and then using its auto-rescheduling features it automatically transfers all the application containers to the newly added Swarm nodes (new VMs) *(pseudocode line 23)*.

4. **Resource (VM) Termination:** After the containers are auto-restarted in the new Swarm nodes, ATA terminates the old VMs (as shown in Figs. 3(d) and 4(d)) and also deletes the old security groups *(pseudocode lines 26–28)*. Finally, the total application migration overhead is calculated by adding the time required for VM allocation, VM de-allocation, and application transfer *(pseudocode line 29)*.

6   Experimental Evaluation

In this section we evaluate the performance of MyMinder's migration operation while migrating user applications from one VM to another VM in a lab-based OpenStack cloud. As the decision making module is not yet fully functional, we trigger the migration module manually by requesting migration of a user application from one VM to another VM.

6.1   Experimental Set-Up

We built a multi-node Swarm cluster in an OpenStack cloud test-bed which consists of four compute nodes. All the compute nodes are Dell PowerEdge R420 servers which run CentOS 6.6 and have 6 cores, 2-way hyper-threaded, clocked at 2.20 GHz with 12 GB DRAM clocked at 1600 MHz. The nodes include two 7.2K RPM hard drives with 1 TB of SATA in RAID 0 and a single 1GBE port. KVM is the default hypervisor of the compute nodes.

To measure the application transfer time we run a simple voting application [29] from Docker [7] that is representative of real world microservice cloud applications. The application has several microservices. The voting application is composed of: (i) Python web app (vote-app) which allows users to vote between two options (cats or dogs), (ii) Redis queue which collects new votes, (iii) .NET worker which consumes votes and stores them in a database, (iv) Postgres database backed by a Docker volume (volume is created in the Swarm manager node), and (v) Node.js webapp (results-app) which shows the results of the voting. The services are deployed in the Swarm with certain constraints. The Python web app and the redis are deployed with two replicas and with a restart policy which restarts the containers on node failures. The Node.js webapp is also deployed with node failure restart policy and with one replica. But the Postgres database and the .NET worker are deployed with a placement constraint which starts them on the Swarm manager node only and without any restart policy. The database is stored in the host machine (Swarm manager node) which provides data persistence for the application. Therefore, in our experiments the Swarm manager node is not de-allocated (also referred to as drained) as the Docker volume is attached to this VM. We have put this placement constraint because if we deploy the Postgres container in one of the worker nodes which is drained later then losing the data of the Postgres container would cause the application to fail.

However, this approach does not allow migration of application containers with attached databases: to perform such migrations Docker Swarm requires additional storage plugins. Open-source container data volume orchestrators such as Flocker [9], Portworx [21] and REX-RAY [27] can be used for migrating stateful Dockerized applications. Unlike a Docker data volume which is tied to a single server, the data volume provided by these storage drivers is portable and can be used with any container in the Swarm cluster. Flocker can only be used within a single data centre whereas, Portworx and REX-RAY can migrate data across CPs. In our future work we will consider stateful application (databases) migration across CPs by using the storage drivers such as Portworx or REX-RAY.

6.2 Experimental Results and Discussion

MyMinder's migration operation is performed by Docker Swarm and with the help of ATA allocation and de-allocation of VMs (Swarm nodes) to/from Docker Swarm cluster. We examine the migration performance by measuring the allocation and de-allocation time of the Swarm nodes and the application transfer time taken by Docker Swarm node manager (scheduler). In order to collect these measurements we initially set the Swarm cluster with four VMs allocated as the Swarm nodes where one of the VMs acts as the Swarm master node and rest of the three VMs act as Swarm worker nodes. All four VMs are 'medium' flavour instances from OpenStack. Later we add three new 'large' flavour VMs (as Swarm worker nodes) to the Swarm cluster and remove the three 'medium' flavour VMs (Swarm worker nodes) one by one. The list of the VMs for addition and deletion are stored in a configuration file which is sent to the ATA to trigger the Swarm cluster's node allocation and de-allocation steps.

In the Fig. 5, we present the time taken to allocate new VMs (the new "large" flavour VMs as Swarm worker nodes) to the existing Swarm cluster, the time taken to de-allocate the existing VMs (the "medium" flavour VMs running as Swarm worker nodes) from the Swarm cluster, and the application transfer time from one VM to another VM which is performed by the Docker Swarm. We present the averaged values of the observed measurements, where the allocation, de-allocation, and transfer were performed 20 times. The allocation and de-allocation time are almost the same every time but the transfer time showed some variation in a 10 s range when we repeated the transfer procedure. As shown in Fig. 5 the time taken to allocate one Swarm worker node is less than 1 s and to allocate all the three worker nodes together is between 1 to 3 s. The de-allocation time is between 1 to 2 s to remove 1 worker node and between 3 to 6 s to remove all three worker nodes one by one. De-allocation takes longer than the allocation time because the nodes are removed sequentially to avoid over stressing the Swarm master in rescheduling the application containers, whereas allocation is done in parallel as the Swarm master does not assign any existing container on the newly allocated nodes until any new application is deployed or any existing node is failed [13]. Importantly, we observe that once the 'medium' flavour VMs are de-allocated from the Swarm cluster, the application containers running on those VMs are rescheduled to the new VMs (the 'large' flavour VMs). The application reschedule/transfer time is around 20 s for a single node and it is around 50 s for the three nodes, which is shown in the Fig. 5. The reschedule/transfer is performed using Docker Swarm's auto-restart feature. Since the de-allocation is performed sequentially, the Swarm scheduler performs the rescheduling of the application containers in the same order in which the their hosted nodes are de-allocated. We observe that during the transfer period when the Swarm node with the results-app (Node.js) containers is drained we are not able to browse the results of the poll until the container is rescheduled and restarted.

If we add up the time taken for allocation, de-allocation, and application reschedule/transfer, we get the overall migration time as observed in the Fig. 5, which is around 23 s if the migration requires a single node allocation/de-allocation and around 59 s if the migration requires multi-node allocation/de-allocation. These migration overhead results give us an understanding of the effectiveness of the proposed ATA in migrating applications across VMs in an

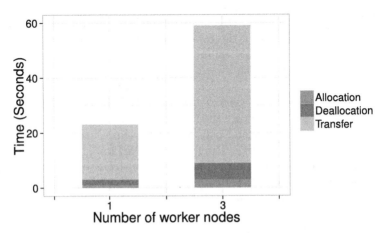

Fig. 5. Total application migration time as summation of VM allocation, de-allocation, and transfer time.

OpenStack cloud environment and we do not intend it to be compared with the inter-cloud migration performance across public clouds. We performed the migration in a private cloud environment in order to build the proof of concept of the migration functionality of MyMinder. In future, we will carry out further experiments on evaluating ATA in migrating cloud application across public CPs in order to build the proof of concept of the framework as a whole.

7   Conclusion and Future Work

In this paper we present the architecture of MyMinder [1], a post-deployment decision making framework, which can detect QoS violation and performance degradation and dynamically decide whether a user's VM requires migration from the current provider to another provider. Also, we present the problem formulation [1] for selecting the most suitable CP in the case that the VM requires migration from the current provider. As an extension, we present MyMinder's migration module and demonstrate its feasibility in performing user application migration across VMs from either the same CP or different CP. The MyMinder migration prototype adopts the widely accepted Docker Swarm technology. To merge and automate the migration steps, we propose an Automated Triggering Algorithm (ATA) that performs VM allocation and de-allocation to/from the Docker Swarm cluster in addition to the core Docker Swarm auto-rescheduling feature. We evaluate the performance of MyMinder's migration process by deploying it in a lab-based OpenStack testbed, where a cluster of Docker Swarm nodes is created using the VMs and application containers are transferred amongst the Swarm nodes. The experimental evaluation demonstrates that we can migrate user applications from one VM to another VM within a single CP without depending on the CP and with minimum migration overhead. This evaluation is an attempt to verify the feasibility of MyMinder's migration process and does not include performance results from inter-cloud migration across public clouds. In future, we consider to evaluate the performance of the proposed ATA in migrating applications across public CPs once the monitoring, detection, prediction, and decision-making modules are fully functional.

References

1. Barlaskar, E., Kilpatrick, P., Spence, I., Nikolopoulos, D.S.: MyMinder: a user-centric decision making framework for intercloud migration. In: Proceedings of the 7th International Conference on Cloud Computing and Services Science, pp. 588–595 (2017)
2. Behzadian, M., Khanmohammadi Otaghsara, S., Yazdani, M., Ignatius, J.: Review: a state-of the-art survey of topsis applications. Expert Syst. Appl. 39(17), 13051–13069 (2012). https://doi.org/10.1016/j.eswa.2012.05.056
3. Brock, M., Goscinski, A.: Toward ease of discovery, selection and use of clusters within a cloud. In: 2010 IEEE 3rd International Conference on Cloud Computing, pp. 289–296, July 2010

4. Ciuffoletti, A.: Application level interface for a cloud monitoring service. Comput. Stand. Interfaces **46**, 15–22 (2016). http://www.sciencedirect.com/science/article/pii/S0920548916000027
5. Docker: Docker Containers (2013). https://www.docker.com/. Accessed 25 Oct 2016
6. Docker: Docker Machine Drivers (2017). https://docs.docker.com/machine/drivers/. Accessed 1 Aug 2017
7. Docker: Try Swarm at scale (2017). https://docs.docker.com/swarm/swarm_at_scale/about/. Accessed 1 Aug 2017
8. Docker, S.: Docker Swarm (2017). https://docs.docker.com/engine/swarm/. Accessed 29 May 2017
9. Flocker: FLOCKER (2016). https://clusterhq.com/flocker/introduction/. Accessed 29 Dec 2016
10. Hadley, J., Elkhatib, Y., Blair, G., Roedig, U.: MultiBox: lightweight containers for vendor-independent multi-cloud deployments. In: Horne, R. (ed.) EGC 2015. CCIS, vol. 514, pp. 79–90. Springer, Cham (2015). https://doi.org/10.1007/978-3-319-25043-4_8
11. Han, S.M., Hassan, M.M., Yoon, C.W., Huh, E.N.: Efficient service recommendation system for cloud computing market. In: Proceedings of the 2nd International Conference on Interaction Sciences: Information Technology, Culture and Human, ICIS 2009, pp. 839–845. ACM, New York (2009). http://doi.acm.org/10.1145/1655925.1656078
12. Jia, Q., Shen, Z., Song, W., van Renesse, R., Weatherspoon, H.: Supercloud: opportunities and challenges. SIGOPS Oper. Syst. Rev. **49**(1), 137–141 (2015). http://doi.acm.org/10.1145/2723872.2723892
13. Kratzke, N.: Smuggling multi-cloud support into cloud-native applications using elastic container platforms. In: Proceedings of the 7th International Conference on Cloud Computing and Services Science - Volume 1: CLOSER, pp. 57–70. INSTICC, SciTePress (2017)
14. Kratzke, N., Quint, P.C.: About automatic benchmarking of IaaS cloud service providers for a world of container clusters. J. Cloud Comput. Res. **1**(1), 16–34 (2015)
15. Leitner, P., Cito, J.: Patterns in the chaos& mdash; a study of performance variation and predictability in public IaaS clouds. ACM Trans. Internet Technol. **16**(3), 15:1–15:23 (2016). http://doi.acm.org/10.1145/2885497
16. Li, A., Yang, X., Kandula, S., Zhang, M.: CloudCMP: comparing public cloud providers. In: Proceedings of the 10th ACM SIGCOMM Conference on Internet Measurement, IMC 2010, pp. 1–14. ACM, New York (2010). http://doi.acm.org/10.1145/1879141.1879143
17. Li, W., Tordsson, J., Elmroth, E.: Modeling for dynamic cloud scheduling via migration of virtual machines. In: Proceedings of the 2011 IEEE Third International Conference on Cloud Computing Technology and Science, CLOUDCOM 2011, pp. 163–171. IEEE Computer Society, Washington, DC (2011). https://doi.org/10.1109/CloudCom.2011.31
18. Li, Z., OBrien, L., Zhang, H.: CEEM: a practical methodology for cloud services evaluation. In: 2013 IEEE Ninth World Congress on Services, pp. 44–51, June 2013
19. Li, Z., O'Brien, L., Zhang, H., Cai, R.: On a catalogue of metrics for evaluating commercial cloud services. In: 2012 ACM/IEEE 13th International Conference on Grid Computing, pp. 164–173, September 2012
20. Meng, S., Liu, L.: Enhanced monitoring-as-a-service for effective cloud management. IEEE Trans. Comput. **62**(9), 1705–1720 (2013)

21. PORTWORX: The Solution for Stateful Containers in Production. Designed for DevOps (2017). https://portworx.com/. Accessed 16 Aug 2017
22. Ravello: Ravello Systems: Virtual Labs Using Nested Virtualization (2016). https://www.ravellosystems.com. Accessed 15 Nov 2016
23. Razavi, K., Ion, A., Tato, G., Jeong, K., Figueiredo, R., Pierre, G., Kielmann, T.: Kangaroo: a tenant-centric software-defined cloud infrastructure. In: 2015 IEEE International Conference on Cloud Engineering (IC2E), pp. 106–115, March 2015
24. ur Rehman, Z., Hussain, O.K., Hussain, F.K.: Multi-criteria IaaS service selection based on QoS history. In: 2013 IEEE 27th International Conference on Advanced Information Networking and Applications (AINA), pp. 1129–1135, March 2013
25. ur Rehman, Z., Hussain, O.K., Chang, E., Dillon, T.: Decision-making framework for user-based inter-cloud service migration. Electron. Commerce Res. Appl. **14**(6), 523–531 (2015). http://www.sciencedirect.com/science/article/pii/S1567422315000575
26. Rehman, Z.U., Hussain, O.K., Hussain, F.K.: Parallel cloud service selection and ranking based on QoS history. Int. J. Parallel Program. **42**(5), 820–852 (2014). https://doi.org/10.1007/s10766-013-0276-3
27. REX-RAY: Rex-ray container storage management (2017). http://rexray.readthedocs.io/en/stable/. Accessed 16 Aug 2017
28. Roy, B.: The outranking approach and the foundations of electre methods. Theory Decis. **31**(1), 49–73 (1991). https://doi.org/10.1007/BF00134132
29. Docker Samples: Voting Application (2017). https://github.com/dockersamples/example-voting-app. Accessed 12 Aug 2017
30. Scheuner, J., Leitner, P., Cito, J., Gall, H.C.: Cloud workbench - infrastructure-as-code based cloud benchmarking. CoRR abs/1408.4565 (2014). http://arxiv.org/abs/1408.4565
31. Shen, Z., Jia, Q., Sela, G.E., Rainero, B., Song, W., van Renesse, R., Weatherspoon, H.: Follow the sun through the clouds: application migration for geographically shifting workloads. In: Proceedings of the Seventh ACM Symposium on Cloud Computing, SoCC 2016, pp. 141–154. ACM, New York (2016). http://doi.acm.org/10.1145/2987550.2987561
32. Silas, S., Rajsingh, E.B., Ezra, K.: Efficient service selection middleware using electre methodology for cloud environments. Inf. Technol. J. **11**(7), 868 (2012)
33. Silva-Lepe, I., Subramanian, R., Rouvellou, I., Mikalsen, T., Diament, J., Iyengar, A.: SOAlive service catalog: a simplified approach to describing, discovering and composing situational enterprise services. In: Bouguettaya, A., Krueger, I., Margaria, T. (eds.) ICSOC 2008. LNCS, vol. 5364, pp. 422–437. Springer, Heidelberg (2008). https://doi.org/10.1007/978-3-540-89652-4_32
34. Williams, D., Jamjoom, H., Weatherspoon, H.: The xen-blanket: virtualize once, run everywhere. In: Proceedings of the 7th ACM European Conference on Computer Systems, EuroSys 2012, pp. 113–126. ACM, New York (2012). http://doi.acm.org/10.1145/2168836.2168849

A Decentralized Cloud Management Architecture Based on Application Autonomous Systems

Dapeng Dong$^{(\boxtimes)}$, Huanhuan Xiong, Gabriel G. Castañé, and John P. Morrison

Department of Computer Science, University College Cork, Cork T12 YN60, Ireland
{d.dong,h.xiong,g.castane,j.morrison}@cs.ucc.ie

Abstract. Driven by the successful business model, cloud computing is evolving rapidly from a moderate size data center consisting of homogeneous resources to a hyper-scale heterogeneous computing environment. The evolution has made the computing environment ever-increasingly complex, thus, raises challenges for the traditional approaches for managing a cloud environment in an efficient and effective manner. In response, a decentralized system architecture for cloud management is introduced. In this architecture, the management responsibility and resource organization in a conventional cloud environment are re-considered. The re-consideration results in composing a cloud environment into three entities including the Infrastructure, the Cloud Utility and Information Base, and Application Autonomous Systems. In this configuration, service providers focus on providing connected physical resources and introducing featured resources. Information related to the Infrastructure is stored and periodically updated in the Information Base. A consumer employs an Application Autonomous System for managing the life-cycle of a cloud application. An Application Autonomous System in the context of this paper is defined as a self-contained entity that encapsulates a cloud application, the associated resources and the management functions. An Application Autonomous System uses the Information Base and Cloud Utilities to locate and acquire desired resources, subsequently resources are deployed on the Infrastructure by invoking Cloud Utilities. Thereafter, the Application Autonomous System manages the life-cycle of both the application and the associated resources. Consumers are offered opportunities to employ preferred algorithms and strategies for this management. Thus, the responsibility of cloud application management and partially the resource management has shifted from service providers to the consumers in this decentralized system architecture.

Keywords: Cloud architecture · Decentralized management
Resource management · Service management

1 Introduction

The success of the business model and the service model of the utility computing have motivated service providers to build and expend their data centers to an

© Springer International Publishing AG, part of Springer Nature 2018
D. Ferguson et al. (Eds.): CLOSER 2017, CCIS 864, pp. 102–114, 2018.
https://doi.org/10.1007/978-3-319-94959-8_6

unprecedented size. It has been estimated that Google data centers may consist of one million servers in 2013 [1] and grew to ~2.5 million servers in 2016 [2]; Facebook data centers consist of ~60 K servers in 2010 [3]; and a more recent Microsoft data center has the capacity to host ~224 K servers on a single site [4]. At the same time, modern data center servers are built with tens of processing cores and hundreds of Gigabytes of system memory, the actual number of virtual machines and/or containers deployed in a data center can be several magnitude more than the physical servers. Along with the emerging trends for supporting High-Performance Computing (HPC) applications, a wide variety of heterogeneous hardware resources have been introduced to the cloud environments. The management of such large scale and diverse resources becomes increasingly challenging for cloud service providers.

Currently, the majority of existing cloud management platforms can be categorized by the cloud service models, namely Software-as-a-Service (SaaS), Platform-as-a-Service (PaaS) and Infrastructure-as-a-Service (IaaS), defined by the National Institute of Standards and Technology (NIST) [5]. The cloud platforms for managing IaaS, for example OpenStack [6], provide tools and utility libraries for managing physical and virtual resources. The main challenges for managing IaaS are on the resource allocation efficiency and infrastructure operational efficiency from a technical perspective. The IaaS management platforms also provide Application Programming Interfaces (APIs) and user interfaces to the resource consumers. Consumers use these interfaces for provisioning resources in a self-service mode. For instance, a consumer (either an user or a program) can acquire resources through the interfaces provided by the management platform. The resource scheduling and allocation components of the management platform decide where the resources (e.g., virtual machines or containers) should be allocated. This poses two concerns. First, resources are provisioned and allocated before the deployment of the actual cloud services. This process does not consider the characteristics of each individual service nor the inter-relationships between services that all together constitute as a complete cloud application. This can potentially be harmful to the overall performance of the cloud application, due to that the underlying virtual infrastructure/resources were not constructed/provisioned in an optimal configuration. Second, in response to the quantity and diversity of the underlying resources to be managed, the increasing complexity of resource acquisition requirements, the more restricted service level agreement, the volume of requests for resources and the dynamicity of the environment, novel management strategies for efficient and effective provisioning and managing the life-cycle of resources (physical and virtual) are needed, which determines a sustainable cloud environment.

The subscribers of IaaS services are responsible for configuring the leased resources and the subsequent deployment of the services/applications on the resources. Often, the configuration processes and the deployment of services/applications are time consuming and may require domain-specific knowledge and skills. To ease these processes, management frameworks and platforms for PaaS start gaining popularities, for example, OpenStack Solum [7] and Apache Brooklyn [8]. These PaaS management platforms provide facilities for consumers to express their needs and requirements in a blueprint alike style, articulated in domain-specific languages, for example, Topology and Orchestration Specification for Cloud Applications (TOSCA) [9] and Cloud Application Management for Platforms (CAMP) [10]. These languages are sufficiently flexible to express the details of the entire service and resource life-cycle management, and surely results in a blueprint that is complex and subject to error-prone.

Nevertheless, the service and resource deployment are still two separate processes. Resources are provisioned and deployed by invoking IaaS management functions, for example, in an OpenStack managed environment, an application and resource orchestration framework, such as Heat [11], invokes OpenStack Nova services (e.g., nova-api, nova-conductor, nova-scheduler and nova-compute) for provisioning and deployment of virtual machines [12], and uses OpenStack Neutron for creating virtual networking environment [13]. Given that the underlying resources are ready to use, the Heat deploys services/applications on the resources. This also implicitly allows cloud consumers to have full control over the management of applications as well as the underlying resources and subsequently narrows down the opportunities for cloud service providers to improve resource utilization, power efficiency and potentially the quality of services. Note that SaaS is often built on top of PaaS and IaaS. SaaS has the main focus on providing functions, utilities and services to consumers, directly. Thus, SaaS is outside of the context of this paper.

Additionally, the IaaS/PaaS resource allocation components typically do not take the characteristics of the services into account when provisioning resources. The optimizations are generally carried out afterwards during the service/application lifetime. Such optimizations are traditionally done through monitoring various aspects of resource usages, such as processor utilization, memory utilization, and network bandwidth consumption. But, this is often done for the interests of service provides, for instance, virtual machine consolidations for improving server utilizations. Certainly, more restrictions and requirements (for both consumers and service providers) can be expressed in a blueprint, provided that the service descriptionlanguages are capable of doing so. As the size of the data center increases and the number of services/applications hosted by the data center grows rapidly, the management overhead associated with such optimization becomes non-negligible. Shifting such overheads to cloud consumers may results in a more sustainable environment. In other words, shifting the management responsibility to consumers and splitting the centralized management overheads into distributed management on a per application basis. In the context of this paper, a cloud environment is virtually divided into Application Autonomous Systems (AASs). Each AAS presents a self-contained management domain and logically manages a cloud application. In this configuration, consumers need to bear the cost for the management processes (the underlying resources that are needed to host the management functions) and cloud service provides only need to provide resources and a set of common utilities that are essential for an AAS to function.

An AAS interprets and executes an application Blueprints consisting of many services and taking into account of the entire collection of services to determine an optimal set of resources, and subsequently controls the application and resource life-cycle management. It is also possible for an AAS to be reused for the similar type of applications. In this respect, it is imperative to maintain a separation between application life-cycle management and resource management. Thus, an AAS can address the potential conflicts between cloud service management and cloud resource management while maximizing user experience and cloud efficiency on each side, as well as making it is possible to implement continuous improvement on resource utilization and service delivery.

The remainder of this paper is organized as follows. Backgrounds and discussions on several related works are given in Sect. 2. The proposed solution is introduced in Sect. 3, Important concepts and detailed architecture are given in Sect. 4. Future directions and conclusions are drawn in Sect. 5.

2   Background and Related Work

Existing IaaS/PaaS management platforms manage the life-cycle of cloud applications together with their associated underlying resources. Three representative platforms are used in this section to highlight the mainstream approaches for managing a PaaS/IaaS cloud environment. Figure 1 shows the application/resource life-cycle management schemes employed by the OpenStack Solum [7], Apache Brooklyn [8], and OpenStack Heat [11]. These platforms provide tools for deploying and managing services/resources, and provide APIs to interface with cloud consumers and/or applications. Solum and Brooklyn are usually considered to be PaaS management platforms, while Heat is an service/resource orchestration framework for IaaS.

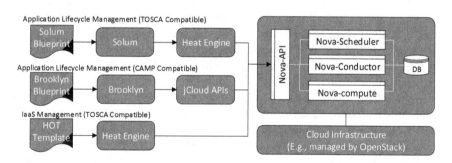

Fig. 1. An overview of cloud application/resource life-cycle management in OpenStack Solum, Apache Brooklyn and OpenStack Heat.

The Solum and Brooklyn frameworks allow cloud consumers to deploy and execute blueprints written in a service description language, particularly, TOSCA and CAMP. These languages are used to describe the characteristics of application components, deployment scripts, dependencies, locations, logging, policies, and so on. The Solum engine takes a blueprint as an input and converts it to a Heat Orchestration Template (HOT), this template can be understood by the application and resource management engine (Heat). The Heat engine, thereafter, carries out the application and resource deployment by invoking the corresponding service APIs that are provided by the underlying cloud infrastructure framework, for example, Nova and Neutron APIs.

In contrast, Brooklyn engine converts a blueprint into a series of jCloud [14] API calls that can be used to interact with the underlying cloud infrastructure management components. For example, a jCloud API call for creating an virtual machine in OpenStack is sent to the *nova-api* component. The *nova-api* component notifies the *nova-scheduler* component to determine where the requested virtual machine should be created. Once an suitable server is identified, the request is forwarded to the *nova-compute* component to carry our the actual deployment on the selected server. This *"Request and Response"* approach is simple, robust, and efficient. However, it should be noted that each request is processed independently, making it impossible to consider relative placement of virtual machines associated with multiple requests. Additionally, this *"Request and Response"* approach does not support the optimal deployment for a group of services that all together are considered as a complete cloud application. This limitation is not specific to virtual machine placement, but also applies to the deployment of containers, for example in a Kubernets [15,16] or Mesos [17] managed containerized environments.

3   Architecture Overview

Conventional clouds provide interfaces to consumers for consuming resources in a self-service manner. Either in an IaaS or a PaaS model, beneath the user interfaces, the underlying resource management typically take a centralized management approach. Recall from the discussions given in Sects. 1 and 2 that due to the ever-increasing size of the data center and resource heterogeneity, the centralized resource management systems are continuously being challenged. In response, a decentralized management architecture is introduced, as shown in Fig. 2. The main design principle is to divide a cloud environment into three entities including the Infrastructure, Cloud Utilities and Information Base, and Application Autonomous Systems. The Infrastructure provides interconnected physical resources. Information related to resources, such as server status and computational resource availabilities, are stored and periodically updated in the Information Base. An AAS is a self-contained entity that encapsulates a cloud application, the associated resources and the management functions. AASs use the Information Base and Cloud Utilities to locate and acquire resources, and resources are deployed on the Infrastructure by invoking the Cloud Utilities. Thereafter, the AAS manages the life-cycle of both the application and the associated resources.

In this design, the centralized resource management is divided by the number of AASs. Each AAS makes its own decisions on what resources to be used

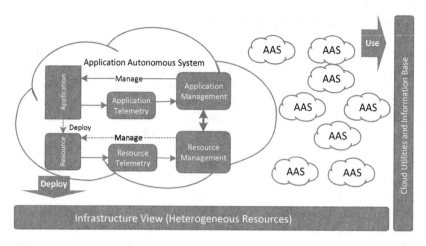

Fig. 2. Decentralized system architecture based on Application Autonomous Systems.

and where to provision the resources. This gives an opportunity to the consumers to employ preferred strategies for the management of their applications and resources. In addition, since each AAS manages a relatively small number of services, more sophisticated management strategies and optimization methods can be employed. All AASs indirectly compete with each others for the best of resources. This implicitly shifted the management costs and responsibilities from service providers to consumers. As all information about the resources are logged into the Information Base, an AAS can query the Information Base with desired features to locate appropriate resources. This also allows service providers to focus on providing better quality resources and makes the Infrastructure more *static*. When the number of AAS increases, it only makes AASs harder to compete with each others for resources. This has no effects on the underlying resources, the Cloud Utilities, and the Information Base that are organized by the service provider. At the same time, when adding more resources and/or introducing different types of resources to the Infrastructure, AASs are not affected. New features, such as computation accelerators, are advertised to AASs. It is the AASs' responsibility to locate the featured resources. Thus, a cloud environment that employs the decentralized management becomes more sustainable.

Since a cloud environment is logically divided into a number of Application Autonomous Systems, the answers to what defines a management domain for an AAS, how a management domain can be constructed, and how an AAS evolves internally and externally with the environment to achieve the designated goals, ensures the proposed decentralized management approach to function in an efficient and effective manner.

4 Application Autonomous System

An Application Autonomous System is an independent entity. An AAS manages a group of services that can be logically grouped together to form a complete cloud application. An AAS also manages the resources that are associated with the managed cloud application. AASs do not have direct intercommunications with each others. Each AAS reacts upon the changes in the cloud application and the environment. Conceptually, the environment is the Infrastructure. The changes in the environment is the changes of the status of the infrastructure, for example, the changes of the status on the computational resource availability of each server and/or the average networking traffic load on a particular link. The Resource Management component interacts with both the Application Management and the Infrastructure. Thus, the Resource Management must employ algorithms/strategies that can satisfy both the consumers' and service providers' interests. In contrast, the Application Management is an optional component for managing applications at various levels. In the absence of the application-specific interfaces, the Application Management manages the life-cycle of the application (e.g., deploy and decommission). With provided application-specific interfaces, more advanced optimizations can be carried out (e.g., load-balancing).

The AAS-based management approach provides PaaS services. It must be noted that the definition of the platform is a broad term. It can be a management framework, such as Apache Brooklyn, an application server, such as Google App Engine, or an analytic platform, such as Hadoop/Spark. The AAS-based management approach can be considered as an management framework, such as Apache Brooklyn. Application servers or analytic platforms can be seen as cloud applications in this context. However, the differences between AAS and the Brooklyn alike frameworks lie on the cloud application and resource management styles. More specifically, the cloud application and resource management in Brooklyn alike frameworks are tightly coupled. In other words, cloud applications

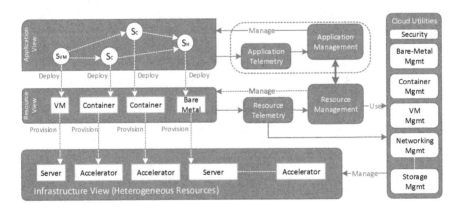

Fig. 3. The internal structures of an Application Autonomous System and its relationships to the cloud environment.

and the associated resources coexist. Decommission of a cloud applications implies freeing the underlying resources. In contrast, AAS is designed based on the concept of Separation of Concerns [18], i.e., cloud applications and the associated resources are manged independently, but they are also complementary to each other.

4.1   The Concept of Separation of Concerns

The main idea of the Separation of Concerns is to decouple the cloud application management from the associated resource management, while the *desires* (e.g., needing for more resources) from cloud application management actions can be forwarded asynchronously to the resource management functions, meaning that the resource management functions can decide whether to react upon receiving a *desire* based on the feasibility of doing so. Inversely, the outcomes from a resource management action (e.g., virtual machine migration to avoid resource contentions or server consolidation for improving power efficiency) can be fed back to the cloud application management functions in the same asynchronous manner. The separation yields several unique features. First, resources do not have to rely on the existences of cloud applications. When a cloud applications is at the end of its lifetime, the underlying resources can be kept by the AAS, so that the AAS can be reused as a pre-provisioned template for incoming cloud applications that have similar characteristics and requirements on resources, thus, it can accelerate the service delivery processes and improves user experiences. Second, the separation allows the cloud application and resource management functions to focus on their respective optimizations. Third, cloud application optimization and management generally require application-specific interfaces to interact with. More often, these interfaces are not available for many existing cloud deployable applications. In such a case, the absence of the application-specific interfaces does not affect the deployment and execution of the cloud application.

4.2   Resource Management in Application Autonomous Systems

A striking characteristic of traditional cloud management platforms is apparent, that global optimizations between multiple services are not generally available due to the way in which resource requests are individually processed. The Separation of Concerns provides direct architectural support for considering optimal resource requests from multiple interacting services simultaneously.

In order to separate the concerns of cloud application life-cycle management and resource life-cycle management, a cloud application, especially when a cloud application consists of several dependent services, need to be expressed in a service description language, for example, TOSCA and CAMP, in a *blueprint* style. In the context of AAS, a cloud application blueprint deployment starts by decomposing a blueprint into two parts: Resource Blueprint and Application Blueprint which can be used by the AAS resource/application management, respectively, as shown in Fig. 4 (label 1). The Resource Blueprint is first sent to the Resource

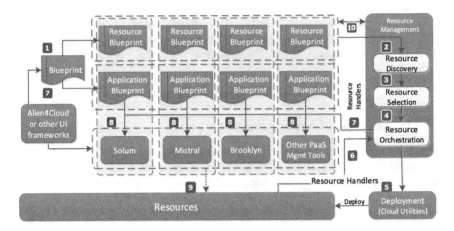

Fig. 4. Resource management in an Application Autonomous System.

Discovery and Resource Selection components to locate and acquire the most appropriate (defined by constrains, parameters, and preferences of both users and systems) resources for the cloud application, as indicated in Fig. 4 (label 2 & 3). The returned location information and the Resource Blueprint are then sent to the Resource Orchestration engine (e.g., a customized Heat Engine) to carry out the actual resource deployment on the infrastructure. The deployment processes are essentially invoking the Cloud Utilities, for example, in a Kernel-based Virtual Machine (KVM) [19] managed virtual environment, provisioning virtual machines on a designated server requires to invoke a series of *libvirt* API calls. These *libvirt* APIs thus must be included as a part of the Cloud Utilities. The resource deployment process results in the return of a number of resource handlers (A resource handler can be a login account includes, for example, user name, access key, and IP address to a virtual machine). These resource handlers are sent back to the Resource Orchestration engine, which, in turn, will use them to finalize the Application Blueprint. The Application Blueprint is then forwarded to the corresponding application life-cycle management component to carry out the application deployment on the pre-provisioned resources. This process is shown in Fig. 4 (label 6, 7, 8 and 9).

In contrast to existing frameworks, the proposed service delivery model will facilitate blueprint developers to specify comprehensive constraints and quality of service parameters for both services and resources. Based on the specified constraints and parameters, in contrast to existing solutions, can provide an initial optimal deployment of the resources. For example, creating and identifying resources on adjacent physical servers to minimize communication delay or provisioning containers with attached GPUs to balance performance and cost. During the life-cycle of the resources, optimizations (e.g., load-balance and elasticity) are done by the Resource Management functions, as shown in Fig. 4 (label 2, 3 and 4), in-conjunction with the resource telemetry services, as shown in Fig. 3, in a closed feedback-react loop.

4.3   Cloud Application Management in Application Autonomous Systems

The cloud application deployment is an incremental process. Depending on the different types of resources and the resource availabilities, each individual resource provisioning process may take different time to complete. For instance, given a blueprint that requires a virtual machine and a container resources, provisioning a virtual machine may take several tens of seconds, where as provisioning a container may only take several seconds. In order to improve the service delivery experiences, the resource handlers are returned asynchronously. Upon receiving a resource hander or a group of resource handlers, a temporary Application Blueprint is constructed, as shown in Fig. 4 (label 7 & 8). The temporary Application Blueprint is then sent to the Service Orchestration engine for deployment, as shown in Fig. 5. Subsequently, the Service Orchestration engine invokes the Cloud Utilities for the actual cloud application deployment. It must be noted that all deployment related information is embedded in the Application Blueprint, as shown in Fig. 5.

The Optimization component together with the Application Telemetry services (as shown in Fig. 3) attempt to perform continuous improvement over the life-time of the deployed blueprint. This is achieved by periodically reconstructing an Application Blueprint based on the information received from the Application Telemetry service, and re-submit the updated Application Blueprint to the Service Orchestration engine for the execution of the optimization actions, such as, load-balancing.

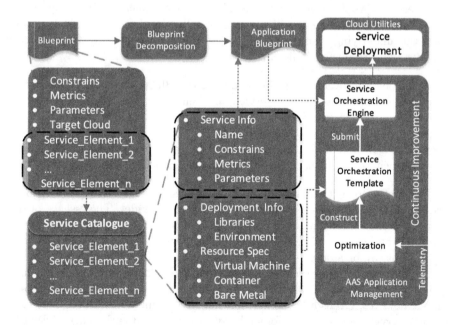

Fig. 5. Application management in an Application Autonomous System.

The concept of the Separation of Concerns has been realized in the Cloud-Lightning project [20]. In the service provider-consumer context, CloudLightning defines three actors including End-users (application/service consumers), Enterprise Application Operator/Enterprise Application Developer, and Resource Provider. These actors represent three distinct domains of concerns.

- For the end-users, the concerns are cloud application continuity, availability, performance, security, and business logic correctness.
- For the Enterprise Application Operators/Enterprise Application Developers, the concerns are cloud application configuration management, performance, load balancing, security, availability, and deployment environment.
- For the Resource Providers, the concerns are resource availability, operation costs such as power consumption, resource provisioning, resource organization and partitioning.

CloudLightning is built on the premise that there are significant advantages in separating these domains and the use of service description languages has been designed to facilitate this separation. Inevitability, there will always be concerns that overlap the interests of two or more actors. This may require a number of actors to act together, for example, an Enterprise Application Operator may need to configure a load-balancer and a Resource Provider may need to implement a complementary host-affinity policy to realize high-availability. These overlapping concerns are managed by each individual Application Autonomous Systems by providing vertical communications between the application life-cycle management and the resource life-cycle management.

Enterprise Application Operators/Enterprise Application Developers are responsible for managing the life-cycle of Application Blueprints. At the same time, the underlying resources are managed independently by the Resource Provider. As a result, the following advantages accrue:

- continuous improvement on the quality of the Blueprint services delivery;
- reducing the time to start a service and hence improve the user experience by reusing resources that have already been provisioned;
- resource optimizations and energy optimization;
- creating a flexible and extensible integration with other management frameworks such as the OpenStack Solum or Apache Brooklyn management system.

The first step in the CloudLightning is to establish a clear services interface between the service consumer and the service provider. The essence of this interface is the establishment of a separation of concerns between cloud service consumers and cloud service providers. In this view, various service implementation options can be assumed to already exist and consumers no longer have to be an expert creator of those service implementations. Consumers should not have to be aware of the actual physical resources being used to deliver their desired service, however, given the fact that multiple diverse implementations may exist for each service (each on a different hardware type, and each characterized by different price/performance attributes) consumers should be able to distinguish and choose between these options based on service delivery attributes alone. Service creation, in the approach proposed here, remains a highly specialized task that is undertaken by an expert.

5   Conclusion

The Application Autonomous System based on the decentralized cloud management tries to re-align the evolving cloud environment with the services-oriented architecture of conventional clouds. Application Autonomous Systems management uses a vertical management approach that implements the concept of Separation of Concerns. It is a more sophisticated management approach than current self-service models. The implementation allows the application management and the resource management to operate independently, consequently, it separates consumer concerns with optimizing cloud applications and service provider concerns with the efficient use of resources and the reduction of operational costs. Application Autonomous Systems virtually and logically divide a cloud environment in to a number of self-contained management domains, hence, it represents a decentralized system architecture. The application and resource decentralization shift the management responsibility from cloud service providers to consumers. This makes a cloud service provider focusing on providing resources, and consumers on taking responsibility for managing applications, thus, it results in a more sustainable computing environment.

Acknowledgment. This work is funded by the European Unions Horizon 2020 Research and Innovation Programme through the CloudLightning project under Grant Agreement Number 643946.

References

1. Ghiasi, A., Baca, R., Quantum, G., Commscope, L.: Overview of largest data centers. In: Proceedings of 802.3bs Task Force Interim Meeting (2014)
2. Data Center Knowledge: Google Data Center FAQ (2017). http://www.datacenterknowledge.com/archives/2017/03/16/google-data-center-faq/
3. Data Center Knowledge: The Facebook Data Center FAQ (2017). http://www.datacenterknowledge.com/the-facebook-data-center-faq/
4. Data Center Knowledge: Special Report: The Worlds Largest Data Centers (2017). http://www.datacenterknowledge.com/special-report-the-worlds-largest-data-centers/
5. Mell, P., Grance, T., et al.: The NIST Definition of Cloud Computing (2011)
6. OpenStack: The openstack project (2011). https://www.openstack.org
7. Solum (2017). https://github.com/openstack/solum
8. Apache Brooklyn (2017). https://brooklyn.apache.org/
9. Tosca, O.: Topology and Orchestration Specification for Cloud Applications (TOSCA) Primer Version 1.0 (2013)
10. Carlson, M., Chapman, M., Heneveld, A., Hinkelman, S., Johnston-Watt, D., Karmarkar, A., Kunze, T., Malhotra, A., Mischkinsky, J., Otto, A., et al.: Cloud application management for platforms. OASIS. Technical report (2012). http://cloudspecs.org/camp/CAMP-v1.0.pdf

11. Heat (2017). https://github.com/openstack/heat
12. Nova, O. (2017). http://docs.openstack.org/developer/nova/
13. OpenStack Neutron (2017). https://github.com/openstack/neutron
14. jCloud (2017). https://jclouds.apache.org
15. Burns, B., Grant, B., Oppenheimer, D., Brewer, E., Wilkes, J.: Borg, omega, and kubernetes. Commun. ACM **59**, 50–57 (2016)
16. Rensin, D.K.: Kubernetes - Scheduling the Future at Cloud Scale, 1005 Gravenstein Highway North Sebastopol, CA 95472 (2015)
17. Hindman, B., Konwinski, A., Zaharia, M., Ghodsi, A., Joseph, A.D., Katz, R., Shenker, S., Stoica, I.: Mesos: a platform for fine-grained resource sharing in the data center. In: Proceedings of the 8th USENIX Conference on Networked Systems Design and Implementation, NSDI 2011, pp. 295–308. USENIX Association, Berkeley (2011)
18. Dong, D., Xiong, H., Morrison, J.: Separation of concerns in heterogeneous cloud environments. In: Proceedings of the 7th International Conference on Cloud Computing and Services Science, CLOSER, vol. 1, pp. 775–780 (2017)
19. Kivity, A., Kamay, Y., Laor, D., Lublin, U., Liguori, A.: kvm: the linux virtual machine monitor. In: Proceedings of the Linux symposium, vol. 1, pp. 225–230 (2007)
20. Lynn, T., Xiong, H., Dong, D., Momani, B., Gravvanis, G.A., Filelis-Papadopoulos, C.K., Elster, A.C., Khan, M.M.Z.M., Tzovaras, D., Giannoutakis, K.M., et al.: Cloudlightning: a framework for a self-organising and self-managing heterogeneous cloud. In: CLOSER, vol. 1, pp. 333–338 (2016)

From Metadata Catalogs to Distributed Data Processing for Smart City Platforms and Services: A Study on the Interplay of CKAN and Hadoop

Robert Scholz[✉], Nikolay Tcholtchev, Philipp Lämmel, and Ina Schieferdecker

Fraunhofer Institute for Open Communication Systems (FOKUS),
Berlin, Germany
{robert.scholz,nikolay.tcholtchev,philipp.lammel,
ina.schieferdecker}@fokus.fraunhofer.de

Abstract. Smart Cities are emerging based on the idea of provisioning and processing large amounts of urban data for various use cases. Thereby, Urban Data Platforms are usually employed to accumulate and expose the large amounts of governmental (i.e. public sector), sensor, static and real-time data in order to enable the community to create valuable applications and services for future Smart Cities. Hitherto, the Open Data initiative was seen as the key driver to providing large amounts of data within a city. Open Data platforms employ so-called data registries in order to keep track of the available datasets at various sources spread throughout the city, with CKAN currently being among the most popular data catalog software worldwide. With the emergence of frameworks for large scale distributed computing and storage, such as Hadoop and the belonging distributed file systems (HDFS), there is an inherent need for bridging the worlds of metadata catalogs and distributed data processing towards the goal of providing sophisticated urban ICT services. The current paper constitutes a first attempt on this new field, by prototyping and evaluating components that enable the collaboration and interplay between CKAN and Hadoop/HDFS. This interplay is realized through extensions to CKAN and its harvesting process and its benefits are demonstrated by belonging case studies.

Keywords: Smart Cities · Open Data · Distributed processing
Hadoop · CKAN

1 Introduction

One pivotal concern for the creation of real Smart Cities is the establishment of a working data processing pipeline. Typical Smart City solutions require the integration of big and diverse data on (potentially) distributed systems. A first step towards this goal was and is the ongoing process of establishing city-wide metadata catalogs that index available datasets from all the different contributing stakeholders of the Smart City environment. This creates a single point of access for most of the available (open or specifically licensed) data for a particular city.

© Springer International Publishing AG, part of Springer Nature 2018
D. Ferguson et al. (Eds.): CLOSER 2017, CCIS 864, pp. 115–136, 2018.
https://doi.org/10.1007/978-3-319-94959-8_7

In a previous work [1], the authors highlighted a lack of research efforts concerning the seamless integration of the existing metadata hubs and the available data processing engines throughout a city. As of then, required data(-sets) needed to be manually collected, transferred onto the processing system and kept up-to-date, thereby forfeiting some of the potential advantages offered by the aforementioned cataloging systems. The authors therefore suggested a novel concept for integration of these two types of systems and consequently implemented an extension that closed this gap by providing the automated integration between the *Comprehensive Knowledge Archive Network* (CKAN) [2] and the Hadoop Distributed File System (HDFS) [3], serving as exemplary systems from each domain. This concept and its belonging prototype were denoted as *HdfsStorer* extension. The prototype builds on the CKAN platform and utilizes the core structure of a CKAN extension.

The current paper is a follow-up to this previous publication from the CLOSER 2017 proceedings [1]. The present update puts a stronger emphasis on the framework of projects in which the extension was developed and highlights some practicalities encountered during development of the presented extension. Additionally, the paper describes newly added functionalities that haven't been part of the previous publication.

The aforementioned extension was developed in the late stages of the German Governmental Data-Portal (GovData) project [4], whose main aim was the creation of a unified, country-wide metadata catalog for governmental data from municipalities, city councils and other federal and state entities. The project itself was part of a series of open government projects by the chief executive body of the German government (Bundesregierung) in cooperation with the IT-Planungsrat, which is responsible for the coordination of the collaboration of the federal government and federal states in the area of IT. As a key asset defined within the Open Data strategy of the German Government [5], the portal was launched in February 2013.

Such a metadata catalog holds only references to the data, along with other attributes, such as licensing, file size and -type or time of the last update. The actual data remains available only over the web portals of the belonging institutions. The aggregation of metadata accomplished either through manual addition of metadata entries or through "harvesting" of other metadata catalogs (e.g. separate catalogs of federal states or cities) or similar sources. CKAN is a major open source platform for metadata cataloging and was used to implement the GovData metadata engine. In CKAN, harvesting is realized through a dedicated extension [6], which provides harvesting plugins for specific standardized metadata formats. Additional plugins may be developed to enable the harvesting of sources that provide their metadata in a different format.

The previously developed extension established a means for integrating CKAN as a metadata store with the powerful capabilities of Hadoop [7], in order to enable the efficient handling of large (open) datasets in urban environments. This first extension allowed for the entirety of all harvested datasets by intercepting resource addition and update events. This is now extended by a CKAN harvester plugin that provides a means for selecting the desired type of datasets for each harvested source (i.e. other metadata catalogs) in order to allow for the realization of more dedicated use cases and resource (storage space and bandwidth) usage optimization.

The HDFS was chosen as the system for data storage for a range of reasons. As integral part of the Hadoop framework for big data processing, it enables parallel data-local processing of data distributed over a cluster of machines. Efficient replication of datasets, aside of bestowing failure resistance, allows for the dynamical addition and removal of (virtual) machines during runtime and thus provides the scalability necessary for the creation of different applications that make use of ever growing datasets and serve a continuously growing user base. This can be facilitated by cluster coordinators such as Zookeeper [8]. The stored data can be processed by a multitude of HDFS-compatible software solutions, such as batch processing engines (MapReduce [9]), in-memory solutions (Flink [10], Spark [11]), integrated with stream processing (Spark Streaming, Storm [12]) or used within graph processing frameworks (Giraph [13]) as well as data base/warehousing systems (HIVE [14], Impala [15], HBase [16]). This allows for the development of small to large scale applications within Smart Cities or other environments. Hadoop-based machine learning systems may additionally benefit from the ease of creation of homogenous big datasets – ensured through restricted harvesting of many data sources - that are usually required for their initial training phase.

The remainder of this paper is divided as follows: The next section presents already existing relevant work from the fields introduced above. Sections 3 and 4 describe the envisioned solutions, namely the *HdfsStorer* and the CKAN harvester plugin for filtering. Thereupon, the implementations of both extensions are described in detail (Sects. 5 and 6, respectively). A realized proto-use case is given in Sect. 7. In complement to that, Sect. 8 outlines a possible real-world application of said extensions within an aspiring Smart City. Lastly, the authors provide a discussion of aspects presented hitherto and summarize the contributions of the paper.

2 Related Work

A multitude of projects worldwide – such as the Open Data portal of Japan [17] or the municipal data hub in Rio de Janeiro [18] - use CKAN for metadata cataloging. Its major competitor is Socrata [19]. Proprietary solutions such as Konema [20] exist as well. CKAN instances find their application on all levels of geographical and administrative granularity, ranging from the regional (i.e. in Berlin Open Data Portal [21]), over the federal level (GovData [4]) to multinational communities (such as the European Data Portal [22]). Fraunhofer FOKUS has played a major role in the conceptualization and development of these latter three Open Data portals. These portals aim to provide a single point of access to predominantly governmental data, whereby the data itself remains on the web portals of the belonging institutions (also denoted as data providers). GovData indexes data from a multitude of providers i.e. municipalities, city councils, or federal institutions such as the Federal Statistical Office of Germany, which are either directly publishing the data (i.e. via custom Application Programming Interfaces [APIs]) or providing access to it through their own metadata catalogs. The European Data portal is one position downstream and itself harvests the metadata hubs of the individual countries, such as those of Germany (GovData.de), Portugal (dados.gov.pt) or Estonia (opendata.riik.ee). Private entities such as companies also

Fig. 1. Schematic overview of the metadata accumulation for the European Open Data Portal. Regional catalogs receive exclusively direct input (not shown). Direct Data Provider may either provide their data in a harvestable format (akin to the regional catalogs) or their data can be manually registered in the corresponding catalog (dotted arrow).

provide their data to some of the harvested data hubs upstream. This harvesting pipeline is shown in Fig. 1.

To enable the efficient integration of metadata from different data hubs and data sources, a set of specifications and standards pertaining harvesting protocols, interfaces and metadata schemes have been developed. These include the Open Archives Initiative Protocol for Metadata Harvesting (OAI-PMH) [23] and Object Exchange and Reuse (OAI-ORE) standards [24], the open government data (ODG) metadata scheme [25], the Infrastructure for Spatial Information in the European Community (INSPIRE) specification [26] for geospatial data and the Dublin-Core [27] and Machine-Readable Cataloging (MARC) [28] metadata vocabularies. Harvest sources usually provide their data in one of those standardized formats and different harvester types or plugins are needed for automated metadata import.

GovData supports harvesting of three types of sources. Firstly, a large number of CKAN based platforms are harvested over the belonging CKAN-Representational State Transfer (REST) interfaces by a standard CKAN-Harvester. Geospatial data compliant with the INSPIRE specification is captured via CSW interfaces by a dedicated harvester. The inclusion of such geospatial data requires the CKAN spatial extension. Lastly, a number of data providers come up with own metadata representations provided over REST services that output JavaScript Object Notation (JSON) strings. Those are imported through custom harvester plugins. The harvested metadata is then transformed into OGD metadata scheme, which constitutes the base for capturing metadata within GovData.

The OAI-PMH standard was originally developed in the context of publication retrieval and later on taken up by further institutions, such as the Internet Archive [29], to serve different purposes. It can make use of the Dublin-Core metadata vocabulary for object and document description, but also supports further formats such as MARC. The OAI-ORE standard builds on the OAI-PMH stack and adds the possibility of defining links between different documents and associated alternative formats and version in a so-called resource map, akin to the package description of CKAN. The CKAN harvester implementation for the OAI-PMH [30] allows for selective harvesting of only a subset of datasets based on certain *spec* attributes, which may be comparable to tags. These *specs* have to be set by the data source for each dataset individually. As only a few harvest sources are compliant with this standard – i.e. none of the harvest sources from GovData - and out of those that are compliant not all come with a complete set of specs, a more general way for filtering or selection is desirable.

The HDFS was preferred over other available distributed storage systems, because they are either focused on a specific type of data (i.e. wide-columnar databases such as Apache Cassandra [31] or document stores such as Open Stack Cinder [32]), proprietary (Amazon S3 cloud [33] and the Ceph File System [34]) or appeared to be to a lesser degree in focus of the developer community (OpenStack Swift [35]). Furthermore, data stored on either of these other sub-systems can be readily made available to multitude of Hadoop solutions [36, 37]. More efficient transfer of big data files between repositories can be achieved through usage of the Remote Direct Memory Access protocol over Converged Ethernet (RoCE) [38] that overcomes a weakness of the Transmission Control Protocol (TCP) regarding resource consumption that becomes apparent when transferring big amounts of data.

Streaming data - i.e. coming in real-time from various sensors in the city - can be already readily persisted on the HDFS through tools such as Kafka [39] or integrated later on in-memory at the level of processing engines (such as Spark or Flink) with static data that has been previously imported to the HDFS. Static data so far had to be manually transferred onto the file system, even if it was already cataloged within the corresponding metadata engine. The *HdfsStorer* – proposed by the authors - closed this gap by enabling the automated data import of indexed resources/files in those metadata catalogs to the HDFS. Filtering of the imported data allows for resource economization and benefits the topicality of the imported data as it allows for more frequent harvesting cycles.

The following sections will give an overview about the structure of these two extensions and highlight their possible utilization through both a realization of a proto-use case, as well as a description of a potential real-world application in a Smart City context.

3   Requirements for the HdfsStorer and the Filter Plugin

Various requirements have to be met by the data import procedure in order to be used sensibly in future Smart City as well as for Big Data applications. These are motivated by the nature of the different environments - determined by the diversity of use cases and infrastructure deployments within different Smart Cities - in which systems like CKAN and Hadoop operate:

Req. 1: Smooth Interplay and Integration between the *HdfsStorer* and CKAN. User experience and established operational perception should not be affected by the emerging *HdfsStorer* extension running in the background.

Req. 2: Tracking and Being Up-to-Date with Resource Changes. Given that a new resource was created, or an existing one was changed or deleted, the belonging updates should then be transferred directly to the employed distributed file system (HDFS).

Req. 3: Network Bandwidth Optimization. HDFS entries (i.e. files) should only be updated in case the original resources have changed, such that the network utilization is kept minimal.

Req. 4: Handling Large Data Files. The HDFS extension should be able to import files to the HDFS, irrespective of their size and format. Size limitations - as in the case of the CKAN-internal FileStore - should not be present.

Req. 5: Import of Datasets, which are Already Registered with CKAN. Given that the *HdfsStorer* is activated after a number of datasets have already been cataloged within the belonging CKAN, it should be possible to automatically import the data resources for those already registered datasets.

Req. 6: Filtering. It should be possible to set specific exclusion as well as inclusion filters to restrict the range of datasets imported through the harvesting procedure.

Req. 7: Flexibility of Filters. It should be possible to define a separate set of filters for each harvest source.

Based on these key requirements, the next sections proceed with devising the architecture of the *HdfsStorer* extension and the *Harvester Filter Plugin*, evaluating it based on a prototype, as well presenting the belonging case study and measurements.

4   Internal Architecture of the CKAN HdfsStorer and TheHarvester Filter Plugin

The CKAN platform provides different integration points for extension development. These integration points constitute a set of programming interfaces, which are to be utilized by Python extensions running on top. In general, the programming interfaces are event triggered and are related to the lifecycle of a data resource, encompassing (1) the initial creation of a data resource, (2) its updates, and at the end (3) its deletion/removal. A belonging Python interface is provided, which encompasses hooks to catch and process these events on top of the CKAN harvesting platform. The relevant interface for resource updates is denoted as *IResourceController* and the main hooks of interest are called *after_create*, *after_update* and *before_delete*.

When working with the CKAN metadata catalog, a number of special features related to the metadata and the belonging process of dataset registration should be taken into account. Within CKAN, the concept of a *package* captures the metadata descriptions of a particular dataset along with all its attributes and a list of belonging data resources. The resources stand for single files or data dumps, but can also point to service endpoints on the Internet. Irrespective of the presence of a service, file or a data dump, the resources are referenced by an URL and are accessible over the Internet. In case resources and packages are removed from CKAN, these are not really deleted but rather marked as hidden within the corresponding PostgreSQL [40] database, i.e. a single attribute is changed preventing the datasets from being visible on the belonging portals/platforms and being searchable over the CKAN platform interfaces. Indeed, datasets that are marked for deletion are only visible for administrator users with appropriate authorization. In order to fully remove the corresponding *packages* from the system, a *purging* process needs to be initiated, either through the CKAN portal graphical user interface or by directly accessing the database underneath, in order to delete resource and package metadata entries. It has to be noted that there is no possibility to purge "deleted" metadata over an API. Similarly, there is no possibility to intercept a purge even – i.e. a hook called "after_purge" does not exist. Hence, a design decision was made to completely remove a dataset from the HDFS storage every time the *before_delete* function of the *IResourceController* is triggered. This leads to a construction where each *package* deletion (i.e. marking of a *package* as pending for deletion) leads to removing the belonging data from the HFDS storage.

Datasets come from a range of sources that each have different quality standards and most importantly index very diverse data, from which only a subgroup may be required for a particular use case. Therefore, it should be possible to create separate sets of filters for each data source (see **Requirement (6)**). This ensures a maximum degree of flexibility and does not restrict the range of potential future use cases. In order to harvest a specific data source, a separate harvest job has to be created and data source specific parameters can be set. The CKAN harvesting extension allows for the development of specific harvester plugins. Those plugins are derived from the *HarvesterBase* class and override or extend certain provided methods, corresponding to different harvest stages. Usually such plugins are developed to enable the harvesting of a different kind of data source. We can use this capability to introduce a means for filtering of imported datasets.

Based on the above generic considerations, the next two sections proceed with introducing the internal components of the emerging *HdfsStorer* extension and *Harvest Filter Plugin*.

4.1 Components and Dynamic Aspects

Figure 2 depicts the general architecture of the extensions including the flow of information (as sequence operations) in an enumerated manner. In this scope, it is clearly described which components are accommodated within the CKAN platform and which are to be viewed as related to the HDFS.

Filtering takes place within the harvesting procedure (more specifically during the *gather stage*) shortly before step (1b). The harvesting procedure is subdivided into three main stages: During the first stage - the *gather stage* - a list of available datasets is retrieved from the harvest source. This is followed by the *fetch stage*, wherein the corresponding metadata packages to these datasets are accumulated to be then - during the *import stage* - integrated into the local catalog (triggering e.g. resource creation or update events). Each of these methods can be altered independently in each harvester plugin implementation. Practically, the *gather and fetch stage* are often regarded as a single process, with all the functionality implemented in the *gather_stage* method. Filtering should take place as early as possible to reduce the load on the entire system. The required attributes for filtering are part of the metadata packages and filtering can thus already take place during the *gather and fetch stage*. Because a multitude of specific harvester plugin implementations override the original *HarvesterBase* class gather method entirely, the authors decided to alter the *gather stage* method of a specific harvester implementation (the general CKAN harvester) instead of altering the method of the base class.

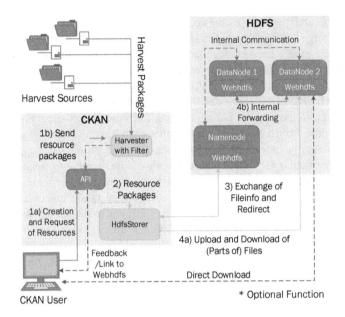

Fig. 2. Extension and Plugin Architecture (highlighted). Figure modified from [1].

Provided that a resource is imported and created or updated with respect to its metadata in CKAN, through either manual interaction or the harvesting procedure – operations (1a) and (1b), all included resource files need to be newly uploaded or refreshed within the HDFS. This flow is given by operations (2), (3) and (4a-b) in Fig. 2.

Furthermore, in case a package or single resources are marked for "deletion" from CKAN, the belonging data files have to be removed again from the HFDS. The identification of the files to delete is performed over the resource IDs, given that for each ID a directory on the HDFS is maintained. Indeed, the CKAN platform generates deletion events and triggers corresponding API calls for the methods implemented by *HdfsStorer* extension based on the *IResourceController* interface. After each CKAN data handling event – such as creation, update and deletion - the corresponding ID and a reference to the latest version of the resource are passed as parameters to the *HdfsStorer*. During the deletion of CKAN-packages, the corresponding ID is given, which leads to a database lookup for obtaining and identifying the resources for removal from the HDFS.

Various communication and data exchanges between the HdfsStorer extension and the HDFS (in the upper right part of Fig. 2) are realized using the WebHDFS protocol [41], which is a REST-API for Hypertext Transfer Protocol/TCP based manipulation of resources kept within the HDFS. The belonging WebHDFS operations are provided in Table 1, including functions such as (1) checking whether a file or directory exist, (2) download and access to resources/files or parts (i.e. chunks) of files/resources, (3) the creation of directories, (4) obtaining a resource/file handle for overwriting an existing resource/file, (5) appending data to an existing resource file and (6) the removal of resource files and directories from the HDFS.

Table 1. List of WebHDFS Operations as described in [1].

Method	Operation	Fields	HTTP return type
GET	liststatus		200 (OK) + JSON
GET	open		200 (OK) + FILE
PUT	mkdirs		200 (OK) + JSON
PUT	createfile	data = ' '	203 (redirect)
POST	append	data; content-type	200 (OK)
DELETE	delete		200 (OK) + JSON

5   CKAN-Based Extension Implementation

The following paragraphs elucidate in detail the *HdfsStorer* extension implementation, starting with the procedure for resource creation and update.

5.1   Creation and Update of Resources

When a new resource is created within CKAN, the *before_create* method is invoked for CKAN extensions that have registered over the corresponding hooks of the *IResourceController* interface. A new resource can be either created manually (e.g. through a Command Line Interface or through the CKAN portal interface) or can be the result of a data harvesting procedure. Thereby, the available implementations of the *before_create* method are invoked with the appropriate data (dictionary) structure filled with information for the new resource as a main parameter. Subsequently, the resource is internally cataloged (i.e. added to the database) and the corresponding *after_create* method is invoked. Similar procedures are followed in the course of resource updates and removals.

Figure 3 details the overall procedure within the *HdfsStorer* extension. The call of the *after_create* method - provided by the *IResourceController* interface and implemented by the extension – results in the creation of an HDFS directory named after the ID of the resource. This directory is located on the resource storage folder, which is prepared in advance on the HDFS and passed to the overall system via a CKAN configuration parameter. Furthermore, the mirroring of the remote resource is prepared by creating an empty file carrying an identical name as the name of the remote resource. In order to enable the subsequent appending of data, a redirect is provided to the HDFS DataNode hosting the newly created empty file. On this basis, the original data resource is read chunk-by-chunk and the chunks are appended to the previously created empty file. This continuous piecewise process of chunking and appending allows for transferring large (larger than the machine's memory) amounts of data from their original locations to the HDFS – during the experimentations the authors managed to transfer files of roughly 30 GB in size. Hence, it can be claimed that **Requirement (4)** is fulfilled. In case the resource size is larger than the block size specified by HDFS, then the remaining data is automatically redirected to a different DataNode where a new block is created. In all cases, data replication is automatically conducted in the background.

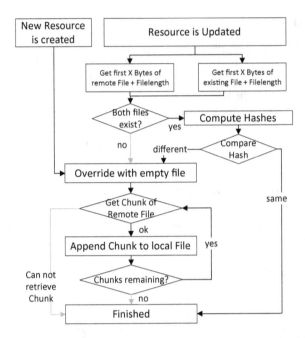

Fig. 3. Resource Addition and Update onto the HDFS as described in [1].

Some very important aspects of the current processes – as described here – are tackled through the usage of hashing concepts. Given that only such resource files should be harvested (i.e. transferred to HDFS) which have changed since the last harvesting processes, a hash check was put in place as visualized on the right in Fig. 3, thereby addressing **Requirement (3)**. A typical approach would be to calculate the checksum (i.e. hash) using the entire file in question. In order to conduct such a checksum computation, the complete files need to be locally in place, i.e. on one single machine. Since it cannot be assumed that data providers will provide appropriate checksums for their data resources, this circumstance would require the files to be additionally downloaded to a single machine in order to compute the hashes and compare the resulting checksums. Unfortunately, this would lead to additional network traffic and contradict **Requirements (3)** and **(4)**, as all files would be downloaded irrespective of their novelty and single machines may not accommodate enough storage space for very big data files. The optimization of this process is a potential topic for further research. However, a first proposition on how to deal with this challenge is given in the following paragraph.

Based on the files' characteristic according to the various contexts of application, two possible approaches can be considered: (1) the comparison procedure is completely omitted and each resource is always harvested and uploaded to the HDFS, or (2) the comparison of the resources is conducted thereby using a partial checksum. Within the (CKAN-)*HdfsStorer* extension the second approach was considered, given that the HDFS and the *HdfsStorer* are meant to be utilized in Big Data generating urban environments. A side remark: the name of a resource (including a checksum based on it) is not considered as an indicator for a resource update given that a simple renaming of a file does not necessarily imply a change in the belonging contents. Another good indicator for changes in large resources is provided by changes in the file size for a resource. Hence, the file sizes can serve as one constituent for the hash key. However, there are also cases where the size doesn't hold as a good indicator. For example, log files – constituting a big share of the resources to be processed by big data engines – are usually changed on a *log-rotate* principle, which means that the file size remains constant, whilst the oldest data is removed and the newest is appended. By selecting a number of bytes at either the beginning or the end of a file (or both), and including these bytes as further parameters for the hash key, changes to such files would be reliably detected and taken into account. If the number of bytes is of a large enough amount, then for smaller files (e.g. configuration files or images) the entire checksum is computed within the presented approach. The downside is that resources which do not differ in file size after update and are larger than the defined chunk size, with static header (beginning of the file) and footer (last bytes of the file) will be omitted as resources that have changed and need to be harvested anew. Such files are not very suitable for distributed computing and processing, given that they are normally hard to split. In addition, the (rare) case of data with only minor differences in a large splittable, identically sized resource will be omitted. Given the large size of the expected datasets, individual items should be only of minor importance to the final result (after processing the entire dataset) and the more single items are updated, the higher is the probability that a difference in file size can be detected. Hence, the above described drawback can be considered acceptable for the majority of scenarios.

5.2 Parallel Upload of Data

In order to avoid negative influence on the performance of the CKAN system - thus addressing **Requirement (1)** - the design decision was made to avoid parallel running data uploads to the HDFS, since - based on the specific setting - many parallel data upload processes may use up the entire network bandwidth to the server. This should be considered when setting the repetition period for data/metadata harvesting, because a single harvesting job might be significantly slowed down and might result in an ever-increasing queue of harvesting jobs leading to outdated and invalid data. Provisioning of a second CKAN server only for the purpose of harvesting is a possible solution, thereby establishing a periodical synchronization of its database with the main CKAN server. This is expected to enable parallel data upload without influencing **Requirement (1)** in a negative way.

5.3 Deletion of Resources

The process of resource and package deletion is visualized in Fig. 4. The removal of a single resource from CKAN leads to the call of the *before_delete* function of the *IResourceController* interface, which is implemented and utilized by the *HdfsStorer* extension. As previously explained, package removal in CKAN does not lead to the deletion of the respective resources, and hence does not result in the call of any additional functions from the *IResourceController* interface. Correspondingly, package removal has to be intercepted and handled by the (CKAN-) *HdfsStorer* extension, which is done by implementing the *after_delete* function from the *IPackageController* interface (depicted in Fig. 4). It is required to retrieve all corresponding resource IDs in both of these two functions and initiate the deletion of the specific directories on the HDFS and their contents by utilizing the belonging WebHDFS API. This fulfills **Requirement (2)**.

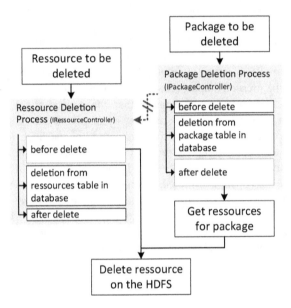

Fig. 4. Deletion of a Package or a Resource. Package deletion does not usually result in resource deletion and hence had to be explicitly implemented.

5.4   Backwards Compatibility

Given the need to address **Requirement (5)** - referring to handling existing CKAN entries - another module was designed and implemented. This module is mainly responsible for reading the internal CKAN database and the transfer of the referenced files to the HDFS, whilst ensuring in parallel the consistency of the data. The belonging process flow is demonstrated in Fig. 5. The information for each resource registered within CKAN is obtained from the PostgreSQL-database in the backend and subsequently uploaded to the HDFS DataNodes. Packages and resources which have been marked as deleted (i.e. they wait to be purged) are excluded from uploading to the HDFS.

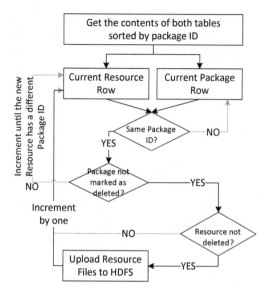

Fig. 5. Resource Import from the CKAN-internal Database as described in [1].

6   Implementation of the Harvester Filter Plugin

A way of filtering datasets has been implemented through extending one of the available harvest plugins of the CKAN harvest extension. In order to satisfy **Requirements (6)** and **(7)**, a means for the definition of the set of filters for specific harvest sources and the actual application of the filters - within the harvesting proce-dure – were realized.

6.1   Initialization of Filters

In order to harvest a specific data source, a *harvest job* has to be defined in the CKAN backend by a user with the appropriate privileges. This definition includes the URL under which the harvest source is reachable, the harvester plugin to be used (which depends on the type of the data source), the periodicity of harvest iterations and an optional dictionary including further configuration settings. We can pass therein the desired filter settings that are then available to the harvester plugin. In order to ensure a required degree of quality, these settings are validated upon creation of the harvesting job and an error can be thrown in case faulty or conflicting parameters were provided.

Mainly two types of filters can be used: (1) *Inclusion filters* define certain criteria that have to be met by an item, in order to successfully pass the selection process. In contrast to that stand (2) *exclusion filters* that pass all items that do not meet the filter criteria. The filter type can be set through the *filter* attribute of the harvest job con-figuration dictionary.

Possible filtering criteria include restrictions on file formats, file size or string matching within the file name. Similar to the filter type, these criteria are also defined in the harvest job configuration dictionary. For instance, to harvest only images exceeding a file size of 3 MB, the following configuration would have to be used: *{filter: 'inclusion', size: ' > 3mb', file_type: 'jpg,png,gif'}*. Disjunction of multiple attributes for inclusion filtering can be achieved by the creation of multiple harvest jobs working in a pipeline, each of which would be configured with one of the disjunct inclusion criteria as filtering settings.

6.2   Application of Filters

During the *gather stage*, the configuration dictionary that has been passed during the creation of the harvest job is parsed and the different filtering parameters extracted and compared against the "to-be-gathered" datasets. Resources and packages that do not belong to the group specified by the filters are excluded from further harvesting stages and thus are not imported. This process is illustrated in Fig. 6.

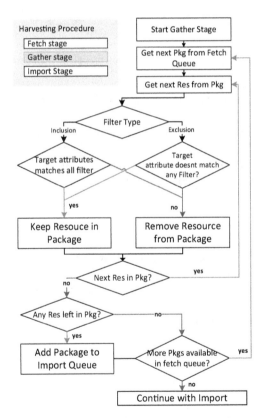

Fig. 6. The Filtering Procedure implemented in the Harvester Plugin. Res: Resources, Pkg: Package.

In order to realize the logic from the previous paragraph, the list of available packages is iterated through. For each of the resources, it is then ascertained that they either do - in case of inclusion filters - or do not - in case of exclusion filters - match the defined filter criteria. Shouldn't this be the case, the resource is removed from the current package. The package – given that some resources remain contained within – is then put onto a stack that is later handed over to the *import stage* of the *HdfsStorer*. Empty packages are discarded.

7 Proof of Concept

In order to demonstrate the feasibility and the processes around the *HdfsStorer* extension, a scenario was worked out making use of an established technique from the field of Machine Learning. Thereby, the techniques are employed on top of two different processing engines for classification of multi-dimensional data. The utilization of two different processing engines demonstrates the variety of further utilization the data can be used for (e.g. based on the free choice of processing engines), once it has been imported to the HDFS. In this scope, the *HdfsStorer* is the key element for such analyses by enabling large scale Big Data and Open Data to be integrated and efficiently re-used in the scope of urban data platforms. Creating an application that has as input datasets, which are linked in the belonging CKAN-registry, essentially consists of three major steps described in the following.

7.1 Import of the Dataset(S) to the HDFS by Means of the Hdfsstorer

The utilized dataset [42] contains descriptions of phoneme properties (such as place of articulation) and the belonging classification (i.e. classification tags) of those into phoneme classes. It was necessary to split the data into training and a test subset for evaluation purposes. Both subsets were stored in different files. Once the files are cataloged within CKAN, either through manual addition or file type-specific harvesting of a data source, they are automatically imported to the HDFS by the *HdfsStorer*.

7.2 Selection of the Appropriate Processing Engine and Program Logics

Both Standard Hadoop Mapreduce and Its in-Memory Counterpart Spark Were Used to Separately Train an Artificial Neural Networks (ANN) on The Training Subset. Thereby, a Standard Backpropagation Algorithm Was Used to Perform The Training Procedure. The Details of The Employed Back Propagation Algorithm Can Be Found in [43]. The Trained Anns Were Subsequently Used as Data Point Classifiers for The Evaluation Set.

7.3 Job Execution and Result Retrieval

The executed jobs were triggered over the command line. The belonging data classification results - based on the *HdfsStorer* data imports - can be in turn retrieved from the HDFS filesystem. As the goal of this work is not given by the evaluation of the classification quality of different ANN implementations, only the training step is considered in the following text, with the goal to look into the performance of two key Big data technologies (Hadoop MapReduce and Spark) on top of the *HdfsStorer* results, i.e. the imported datasets.

The performed execution time measurements are provided in Fig. 7. The execution time was obtained as the time difference between job application submission (be it a Spark or a Hadoop job) and job termination. The Spark and Hadoop execution times in Fig. 7 show that for the dataset in question - which was imported over CKAN and the *HdfsStorer* extension - not only Spark execution times are by far shorter (based on experiments with various number of ANN iterations), but also rise more slowly than Hadoop execution times. This can be attributed to the much lower Spark overhead for each iteration.

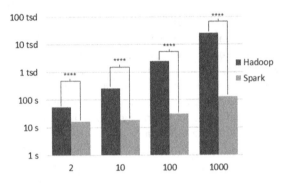

Fig. 7. Execution times of Spark and Hadoop compared. Stars indicate the level of significance (p < 0.0001) as described in [1].

In addition, Fig. 8 describes the average memory utilization of both Hadoop and Spark during idle time and job execution with 100 iterations on top of the open dataset that has been imported to HDFS over the *HdfsStorer* extension and CKAN. The vertical axis displays the memory usage in Mega-Bytes. Because of the comparably small size of the dataset, expected characteristics (e.g. the much higher expected memory utilization of Spark) in the absolute statistics have not been evident. The difference between idle time and work intensive job execution periods is greater for both slaves in the Spark deployment than that of the slaves in the Hadoop deployment. This is a clear sign for the stronger memory dependence of Spark during data processing.

The above evaluation gives an idea of how important it is to choose the right processing engine for the overall efficiency of a Big Data driven Smart City service. The usage of the HDFS thereby facilitates the free choice of the processing engine, given that HDFS is a common platform for distributed processing in modern data centres. The processing engine evaluation can be done on a broader basis or can be targeting specific datasets within particular Smart City scenarios. Overall, this constellation is made possible by the *HdfsStorer* extension, which has been specified and prototyped in the current work.

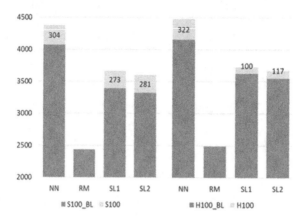

Fig. 8. Comparison of ANN Training Memory Usage of Hadoop (H) and Spark (S) Memory Usage between idle ("Baseline", BL) and work intensive Periods for 100 Training Iterations as described in [1]. NN: NameNode/MasterServer, RM: ResourceManager, SL1/2: Slaves.

8 A Smart City Scenario Using Hadoop and CKAN

Having shown the general architecture and process flows of the extension, and having evaluated its principal applicability, a natural next step is to apply the *HdfsStorer* for the purpose of realizing a more complex scenario. We target a use case relating to the public transport system of a forthcoming Smart City, which requires to be streamlined and optimized. This includes various aspects such as schedule improvements based on the dynamic identification of peak traffic hours combined with delay and occupancy prediction integrated with trip planning [1]. The ultimate goal is to provide a better travel experience to passengers.

The data needed for the above scenario is given by two different types: static and real-time. The transport schedule and history of occupancy and punctuality statistics together with the belonging history of road and weather condition records are distributed over different data stores as static data. Correspondingly, these datasets would be indexed in a CKAN-catalog. Periodical harvesting based on CKAN mechanisms would guarantee that this catalog is up-to-date and the *Harvester Filter Plugin* would ensure that only relevant data is indexed by the local catalog and consequently transferred to the Hadoop cluster. Data regarding the current weather, road and traffic conditions as well as the amount of passengers — e.g. measured by sensors inside the transport vehicle - are provided as streaming data. The interplay between these two types of data within Hadoop is sketched in Fig. 9. The *HdfsStorer* extension takes the role of the key component responsible for importing static data to the HDFS according to metadata provided within the CKAN-catalog (e.g. URL of the original dataset). Consequently, various processing engines - that can make use of the files stored on the HDFS and of data streams provided through message brokers - integrate the data and enable the envisioned correlation and data integration towards sophisticated urban services.

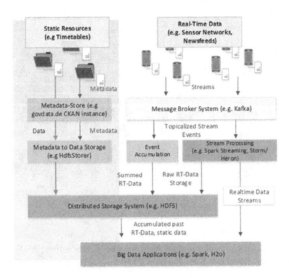

Fig. 9. Integration of both static and streaming Data coming from different Sources on the Level of distributed Storage and Processing Engines, as described in [1].

A realization of a similar process can be found on the H2O.ai github-page [44]. Thereby, Spark is utilized in combination with an H2O extension (=Sparkling water) to create a prediction system for flight delays based on historical data and current weather information. As compared to our use case, the dataset in question is presumed to be in place on the HDFS right from the beginning, e.g. through a manual upload. The current work enhances such traditional solutions by a more convenient way for data import to HDFS, thereby making use of a widely applied data cataloging system (i.e. CKAN) for Open Data in the Smart City context.

9   Discussion

In this paper, the authors described the implementation of two extensions to the CKAN metadata storage system. The first allowed for the automated transfer of the actual data files that are described by the cataloged metadata entries to a designated data storage and processing hub, exemplified by the HDFS. The second extension allows to restrict the range of datasets imported to CKAN through its harvesting procedure. In combination, these two extensions enable the rapid import of (only) relevant data, which has been referenced in various metadata catalogs, onto a scalable distributed file system. This imported data can then be directly used as the basis for a diverse range of Smart City as well as general data science applications.

The creation of applications on the basis of Open Data and the possibly resulting informational and economic gain is one of the main motivations for making previously closed data available to the public [45]. However, making data available to the public remains a heavy burden for the required institutions. Normally this comes at the cost of having to invest additional labour and exposing their inner workings to the scrutinizing eye of the general public. This results in the current situation, where even though the European Commission has issued corresponding regulations years ago (European PSI directive 2003 [46]), the amount of available Open Data across Europe remains far behind the identified potentials. A further factor that may contribute to the currently apparent shortcomings of Open Data, in both the private as well as the governmental sector, could be the lack of quality assurance mechanisms. To ensure the quality of the publicized data, providers are required to go through a process of continuously updating these datasets and belonging metadata. Currently, they are not obliged to this commitment. This has the consequence that, after an initial dataset is published, it very often is not continuously updated since it requires an additional effort from the data provider's side. Potential users thus may find incomplete, outdated or erroneous data and refrain from using it altogether for the development of new applications or as a reliable source of information. This interactive but manual procedure could be complemented by automated periodic quality checks on the basis of either actual data or metadata, addressing issues such as completeness, accuracy, timeliness, as well as privacy concerns and other quality parameters. The frequency of these checks could be coupled to the harvesting frequency or run independently at regular intervals, possibly defined separately for each type of dataset or data source, or estimated by analysis of the time course of previous dataset and version changes. The described data import extension could additionally empower such automated quality checks, as these could make use of the already imported data on the distributed file system without the additional overhead of having to download (parts of) the data files a second time and furthermore run in parallel by virtue of the distributed nature of the HDFS and associated processing engines.

Also, other fields outside the scope of Smart Cities may benefit from the outlined extensions, especially those that require the accumulation of big corpora of textual or other data files. These include computational linguistics and other data/machine learning-heavy disciplines. The reduction or corpora reuse - through enabling also small research and development groups to create their own corpora – and the introduction of more diverse sources may enable better generalization of applications such as speech generation and translation engines [46]. Dedicated corpora that can be accumulated from multiple data sources through more filtered selection (i.e. by language, text type or image/video resolution) of datasets could furthermore enable more detailed insights - i.e. into situative or group-specific media and language usage or geographically and time-restricted phenomena and interactions - as well as the creation of more dedicated applications. Certain types of advanced filtering may imply the necessity for downloading parts of the actual data files and possibly the need for conducting expensive (non-distributed) computations. Thus, it may be more reasonable in some use cases to carry out such second step filtering after data import.

The insights gained during the development of both extensions, and the above considerations regarding the success of Open Data initiatives and application development, will be taken up as input for emerging and running national and international projects on *Urban Data Platforms*.

10 Summary and Conclusions

Smart City projects are currently on the rise, as major and minor municipalities strive to be on the forefront of state-of-the-art technologies and smart solutions in areas such as mobility, energy and ICT. Correspondingly, ample funding is available. In parallel, initial expectations on the impact of Open Data remained unmet and have been dampened. The current work described a possibility of re-establishing and strengthening the link between these two fields – Smart Cities and Open Data - by means of integrating metadata hubs with data processing engines. Thereby each aspect represents a key component in its corresponding field. The authors hope that this link may have some contribution in transferring the momentum that Smart City concepts currently enjoy also to the field of Open Data and furthermore also highlight how Smart Cities may benefit from the continued publication of freely useable data.

References

1. Scholz, R., Tcholtchev, N.,Lämmel, P., Schieferdecker, I.: A CKAN plugin for data harvesting to the Hadoop distributed file system. In: 7th International Conference on Cloud Computing and Services Science (CLOSER) (2017). http://dx.doi.org/10.5220/0006230200470056
2. CKAN Association: CKAN Overview. http://ckan.org
3. Shvachko, K., Kuang, H., Radia, S., Chansler, R.: The Hadoop distributed file system. In: 2010 IEEE 26th Symposium on Mass Storage Systems and Technologies, MSST2010 (2010). http://dx.doi.org/10.1109/MSST.2010.5496972
4. Helene, M.: GovData - Das Datenportal für Deutschland. In: Hill, H., Martini, M., Wagner, E. (eds.) Transparenz, Partizipation, Kollaboration: Die digitale Verwaltung neu denken, pp. 109–116. Nomos Verlagsgesellschaft mbH & Co. KG, Baden-Baden (2014)
5. Bundesministerium des Innern: Nationaler Aktionsplan der Bundesregierung zur Umsetzung der Open-Data-Charta der G8. https://www.bmi.bund.de/SharedDocs/Downloads/DE/Broschueren/2014/aktionsplan-open-data.pdf (2014)
6. Mercader, A., et al.: ckanext-harvest - remote harvesting extension (2012). https://github.com/ckan/ckanext-harvest
7. The Apache Software Foundation: Hadoop Project Webpage. http://hadoop.apache.org/
8. Hunt, P., Konar, M., Junqueira, F.P., Reed, B.: ZooKeeper: wait-free Coordination for Internet-scale systems. In: USENIX Annual Technical Conference, Boston, MA, USA, p. 9 (2010)
9. Dittrich, J., Quiané-Ruiz, J.-A.: Efficient big data processing in Hadoop MapReduce. Proc. VLDB Endow. **5**, 2014–2015 (2012). https://doi.org/10.14778/2367502.2367562
10. The Apache Software Foundation: Apache Flink: Scalable Stream and Batch Data Processing. https://flink.apache.org/
11. The Apache Software Foundation: Apache Spark - Lightning-Fast Cluster Computing. https://spark.apache.org/
12. Iqbal, M., Soomro, T.: Big Data Analysis: Apache Storm Perspective (2015). https://doi.org/10.14445/22312803/ijctt-v19p103
13. Avery, C.: Giraph: large-scale graph processing infrastructure on hadoop. Proc. Hadoop Summit. St. Cl. **11**, 5–9 (2011)

14. Thusoo, A., Sarma, J.S., Jain, N., Shao, Z., Chakka, P., Anthony, S., Liu, H., Wyckoff, P., Murthy, R.: Hive: a warehousing solution over a Map-Reduce framework. Proc. VLDB Endow. **2**, 1626–1629 (2009). https://doi.org/10.14778/1687553.1687609
15. Bittorf, M., Bobrovytsky, T., Erickson, C.C.A.C.J., Hecht, M.G.D., Kuff, M.J.I.J.L., Leblang, D.K.A., Robinson, N.L.I.P.H., Rus, D.R.S., Wanderman, J.R.D.T.S., Yoder, M.M.: Impala: A modern, open-source SQL engine for Hadoop. In: Proceedings of the 7th Biennial Conference on Innovative Data Systems Research (2015)
16. Vora, M.N.: Hadoop-HBase for large-scale data (2011). http://dx.doi.org/10.1109/ICCSNT.2011.6182030
17. National Strategy Office of Information and Communications Technology in Cabinet Secretariat: data.go.jp. http://www.data.go.jp/?lang=english
18. Matheus, R., Vaz, J., Maia Ribeiro, M.: Open Government Data and the Data Usage for Improvement of Public Services in the Rio de Janeiro City (2014). http://dx.doi.org/10.1145/2691195.2691240
19. Socrata: Socrata - The Data Platform for 21st Century Digital Government. https://www.socrata.com/
20. Knoema: knoema.com Webpage. https://knoema.com/
21. Senatsverwaltung für Wirtschaft, E. und B.: Offene Daten Berlin. https://daten.berlin.de/
22. European Commission Directorate-General Communication: European Data Portal. https://www.europeandataportal.eu/en/
23. Lagoze, C., Van de Sompel, H., Nelson, M., Warner, S.: Open Archives Initiative Protocol for Metadata Harvesting (2015)
24. Open Archives Initiative: Object Reuse and Exchange Specifications and User Guides. https://www.openarchives.org/ore/1.0/toc
25. Marienfeld, F.: Open Government Data (OGD) - Die Metadaten-Struktur für Open Government Data in Deutschland. http://open-data.fokus.fraunhofer.de/die-metadaten-struktur-fur-open-government-data-in-deutschland/
26. Bartha, G., Kocsis, S.: Standardization of geographic data: the european inspire directive. Eur. J. Geogr. **2**, 79–89 (2011)
27. Weibel, S., Kunze, J., Lagoze, C., Wolf, M.: Dublin core metadata for resource discovery (1998). https://doi.org/10.17487/rfc2413
28. Coyle, K.: MARC21 as data: a start. Code4Lib J. **14**, 1–10 (2011)
29. Liu, Xiaoming, Balakireva, Lyudmila, Hochstenbach, Patrick, Van de Sompel, Herbert: File-based storage of digital objects and constituent datastreams: XMLtapes and Internet Archive ARC files. In: Rauber, Andreas, Christodoulakis, Stavros, Tjoa, A.Min (eds.) ECDL 2005. LNCS, vol. 3652, pp. 254–265. Springer, Heidelberg (2005). https://doi.org/10.1007/11551362_23
30. Open science and research initiative: OAI-PMH harvester for CKAN. https://github.com/kata-csc/ckanext-oaipmh
31. Lakshman, A., Malik, P.: Cassandra: a decentralized structured storage system. SIGOPS Oper. Syst. Rev. **44**, 35–40 (2010). https://doi.org/10.1145/1773912.1773922
32. McGninnis, S., et al.: OpenStack Block Storage Cinder. https://wiki.openstack.org/wiki/Cinder
33. Amazon.com, In.: Amazon Web Services S3 - Simple Cloud Storage Service
34. Watkins, N., Sevilla, M., Jimenez, I., Maltzahn, C.: Ceph: An Open-Source Software-Defined Storage Stack
35. Dickinson, J., et al.: OpenStack Object Storage. https://wiki.openstack.org/wiki/Swift
36. Nóbrega, T.: OpenStack Sahara. https://wiki.openstack.org/wiki/Sahara
37. Red Hat Inc.: Using Hadoop with CephFS. http://docs.ceph.com/docs/master/cephfs/hadoop/

38. Tierney, B., Kissel, E., Swany, M., Pouyoul, E.: Efficient data transfer protocols for big data (2012). http://dx.doi.org/10.1109/eScience.2012.6404462
39. Kreps, J., Narkhede, N., Rao, J.: Kafka: a distributed messaging system for log processing. In: Proceedings of the NetDB, pp. 1–7 (2011)
40. Momjian, B.: PostgreSQL: Introduction and Concepts. Addison-Wesley, New York (2001)
41. The Apache Software Foundation: WebHDFS REST API. http://hadoop.apache.org/docs/%0Ar1.0.4/webhdfs.html
42. Alinat, P., Pierrel, J.M.: Esprit II project 5516 Roars: robust analytic speech recognition system (1993)
43. Liu, Z., Li, H., Miao, G.: MapReduce-based Backpropagation Neural Network over large scale mobile data (2010). http://dx.doi.org/10.1109/ICNC.2010.5584323
44. H2O.ai: AirlinesWithWeatherDemo. https://github.com/h2oai/sparkling-water/tree/master/examples/
45. Klessmann, J., Denker, P., Schieferdecker, I., Schulz, S.: Open government data Deutschland. Eine Studie zu Open Government in Deutschland im Auftrag des Bundesministerium des Innern. Deutschland <Bundesrepublik>/Bundesministerium (2012)
46. Wuebker, J., Ney, H., Zens, R.: Fast and scalable decoding with language model look-ahead for phrase-based statistical machine translation. In: Proceedings of the 50th Annual Meeting of the Association for Computational Linguistics: Short Papers, vol. 2, pp. 28–32. Association for Computational Linguistics, Stroudsburg (2012)

An Optimization Model to Reduce Energy Consumption in Software-Defined Data Centers

Claudia Canali[1], Riccardo Lancellotti[1(✉)], and Mohammad Shojafar[2]

[1] Department of Engineering "Enzo Ferrari", University of Modena
and Reggio Emilia, Modena, Italy
{claudia.canali,riccardo.lancellotti}@unimore.it
[2] Italian National Consortium for Telecommunications (CNIT), Rome, Italy
mshojafar@cnit.it

Abstract. The increasing popularity of Software-Defined Network technologies is shaping the characteristics of present and future data centers. This trend, leading to the advent of Software-Defined Data Centers, will have a major impact on the solutions to address the issue of reducing energy consumption in cloud systems. As we move towards a scenario where network is more flexible and supports virtualization and softwarization of its functions, energy management must take into account not just computation requirements but also network related effects, and must explicitly consider migrations throughout the infrastructure of Virtual Elements (VEs), that can be both Virtual Machines and Virtual Routers. Failing to do so is likely to result in a sub-optimal energy management in current cloud data centers, that will be even more evident in future SDDCs. In this chapter, we propose a joint computation-plus-communication model for VEs allocation that minimizes energy consumption in a cloud data center. The model contains a threefold contribution. First, we consider the data exchanged between VEs and we capture the different connections within the data center network. Second, we model the energy consumption due to VEs migrations considering both data transfer and computational overhead. Third, we propose a VEs allocation process that does not need to introduce and tune weight parameters to combine the two (often conflicting) goals of minimizing the number of powered-on servers and of avoiding too many VE migrations. A case study is presented to validate our proposal. We apply our model considering both computation and communication energy contributions even in the migration process, and we demonstrate that our proposal outperforms the existing alternatives for VEs allocation in terms of energy reduction.

Keywords: Cloud computing · Software-defined networks
Software-defined data center · Energy consumption
Optimization model

© Springer International Publishing AG, part of Springer Nature 2018
D. Ferguson et al. (Eds.): CLOSER 2017, CCIS 864, pp. 137–156, 2018.
https://doi.org/10.1007/978-3-319-94959-8_8

1   Introduction

The fast deployment of new services involving more and more intense data traffic exchange and complex QoS demands require the underlying infrastructure of a cloud data center to be highly flexible and adaptable. This scenario motivates the paradigm shift towards the adoption of techniques such as Software-Defined Network applied to data centers, giving origin to Software-Defined Data Centers (SDDCs), where virtualization is extended to network elements and functionalities. This change will have a major impact on the solutions to address the issue of reducing energy consumption in cloud systems, since SDDCs realize a more seamless integration of the network within the data center IT processes, opening up to the possibility of novel energy-efficient resource strategies for the cloud infrastructures integrating complex and adaptive network management.

Most of the existing solutions to reduce energy consumption in cloud data centers mainly focus on server consolidation, which aims at minimizing the number of turned on physical servers while satisfying the resource demands of the active Virtual Machines (VMs) [1–4]. However, an effective management of SDDCs must be network-aware, meaning the need to consider the impact of data traffic exchange between the Virtual Elements (VEs) of the cloud infrastructure, that may be both Virtual Machines and Virtual Routers. Failing to do so is likely to result in a sub-optimal energy management, because networks in modern data centers tend to consume about 10%–20% of energy in normal usage, and may account for up to 50% energy during low loads [5]. Furthermore, few studies proposing solutions for VEs allocation consider the contribution of VEs migration to energy consumption, both in terms of computational and network costs. On the other hand, when taking into account the costs for migration, this is carried out in a quite straightforward (e.g., [6]): the allocation model considers just the number of VEs migrations, and introduces weight parameters to address the trade-off of minimizing the number of turned on physical servers while reducing expensive VMs migrations required for the server consolidation. These limitations are clearly visible in modern data centers, but will be even more critical in future SDDCs, where the support for more flexible network reconfiguration allows the migration of both virtual machine and communication channels and virtualized network apparatus [7]. Hence, we believe that traditional allocation policies, that are network blind or adopt simplified models for migration, will be inadequate to support future SDDC infrastructures.

This chapter, which extends a previous study of the authors [8], presents a joint computation-plus-communication model for Virtual Elements (VEs) allocation that minimizes energy consumption in a SDDC scenario. The proposed optimization model for VMs allocation aims not only to reduce as much as possible the number of turned on servers, but also to minimize the energy consumption due to the exchange of data traffic between VMs over the data center infrastructure. The main contribution of our proposal is threefold. First, the model is aware of the heterogeneous connections existing within the data center and considers the data traffic exchanges occurring between VEs. Second, the energy contribution of VEs migration takes into account both the data transfer and the computational overhead. Third, the objective function of the proposed optimization model does not need to add weight parameters to merge the often conflicting goals of avoiding a high number of VEs migrations while guaranteeing the optimal VEs allocation.

We evaluate the performance of the proposed model by considering a case study based on traces from a real data center. The results confirms the validity of our model, showing that the proposed solution outperforms approaches for VEs allocation in terms of energy reduction. Moreover, we show that our optimization model allows to limit the number of VM migrations, thus achieving more stable energy consumption over time and leading to major global energy saving if compared with other existing approaches.

The remainder of this paper is organized as follows. Section 2 presents the reference scenario for our proposal, while Sect. 3 describes the main requirements for an energy model in SDDCs. Section 4 describes the proposed model for solving the VEs allocation problem. Section 5 describes the case study based on traces from a real data center. Finally, Sect. 6 concludes the paper with some final remarks and outlines open research problems.

2   Reference Scenario

In this section we describe the reference scenario for our proposal, comparing the characteristics of a Software-Defined Data Center (SDDC) with a more traditional cloud data center. Starting from this scenario, we illustrate how the characteristics of a SDDC impact on the model used to ensure the energy-efficient management of a cloud data center, with special focus on the operations that decide the allocation of the VMs over the physical servers of the infrastructure.

Figure 1 presents the general schema of a traditional cloud data center.

The considered data center is based on the Infrastructure as a Service (IaaS) paradigm, where VMs can be deployed and destroyed at any time by cloud customers. This explains the system view at a virtual level, where we simply have the VMs that are the object of the cloud customer attention. The cloud provider must map these VMs over the physical infrastructure, defining the data center management strategies. The VMs are hosted on physical servers, which are grouped into pods (roughly corresponding in a set of interconnected racks housing the servers). The data center is based on a two-level network architecture, with *Top-of-Rack (ToR) switches* connecting the servers of the same pod, and an upper layer of networking (*data center core network*) that manages the communication among multiple racks of servers. This structure implies two different costs for transferring data between servers belonging to the same pod (passing through the ToR switch) and to different pods (passing through the data center core network).

The figure also presents the logical blocks of the system implementing the data center management logic (in the right part of Fig. 1). The input of such task is the data about the resource utilization of the VMs and the information about the network traffic over the data center. Two main components are involved in

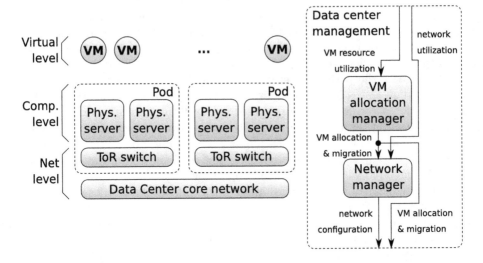

Fig. 1. Traditional cloud data center.

the management of the data center. The *VM allocation manager* (on the top-right side of Fig. 1) is the data center component responsible for running the model for VMs allocation that determines the optimal allocation of VMs on the physical servers to minimize the global energy consumption. After achieving a solution, the allocation manager notifies the servers of the VMs migrations that need to be applied. The VM allocation and migration decisions are then used as the input for a second block: the *Network manager* that, considering the current network utilization level, issues commands for re-configuring routing tables, firewalling rules and to turn on or off some network links to cope with the network traffic patterns changes resulting from the VM allocation manger decisions.

The VMs allocation manager operates mainly by planning VMs migrations across the infrastructure to accomplish the goal of minimizing the energy consumption of the cloud data center in terms of both computational and network contributions. It is worth to note that many solutions for energy-aware VMs allocation are based on reactive approaches, which rely on events to trigger the VM migrations [1,4,6]. On the other hand, in a SDDC scenario an approach based on time intervals, where a control of the optimality of the VMs allocation on the physical servers is periodically performed, could be preferable. The main reason is that, while for CPU utilization it is feasible and easy to define events (typically based on thresholds) to trigger migrations, for network-related energy costs it is much more difficult to define similar triggers. The details of the optimization model proposed to reduce energy consumption in the networked cloud data center are described in Sect. 4.

Figure 2 presents an example of a newer generation of infrastructure, called Software-Defined Data Center (SDDC), which is a data center where

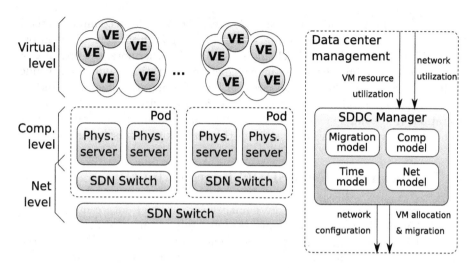

Fig. 2. Software-defined data center.

virtualization is much more pervasive within the system. A first significant difference with a traditional data center is evident if we compare the virtual level of Figs. 1 and 2: while a traditional data center considers just VMs, in a SDDC we focus on virtual networks composed of *Virtual Elements (VE)* that can be either Virtual Machines (VMs) or Virtual Routers (VRs). A virtual router can be both implemented as a VM running a routing software, or as a set of rules and actions for a SDN appliance. This paradigm shift explains why there is a partial overlap between the computational and network layers in Fig. 2. The need to take into account the interaction between virtual elements in a virtual network and the inherent programmability of the network layer have a major impact on the data center management (right part of Fig. 2): in a SDDC the management is an integrated process that combines different models for the multiple elements of the data center. In particular, we evidence four models that must be taken into account for the SDDC management: a *computational model*, a *network model*, a *migration model* for VMs and VRs, and a *time model*. These models (that we will discuss in more detail in the following section) take as input the data on computation and networking usage from the data center and produce an integrated decision about VMs/VRs allocation and migrations, and re-configuration of the network policies.

It is worth to note that considering the data center management as a single process is important to cope with the double nature of VRs and is the only viable choice to support the vision of virtual networks at the level of the virtual layer that characterize this scenario. It is also worth to note that a model that fully leverages the potential of SDN and router virtualization simplifies the adoption of common standards, such as the OpenFlow protocol[1], that can be

---

[1] http://archive.openflow.org/wp/learnmore/.

used both in physical and virtual SDN devices, and provides a common method to define heterogeneous network functionalities, ranging from network monitoring, to IP routing, and up to NAT and firewalling. Furthermore, the presence of virtualization simplifies both the management of migration (supporting traffic engineering techniques [9] to make sure that live VEs migration does not interfere with network operations) configuration savings and device status checkpointing operations (for example using VM snapshots), thus making faster and less error prone the recovery form a faulty state of the networking infrastructure.

3   Requirements for a SDDC Energy Model

The approaches for efficient energy management in cloud data centers can be classified according to how they model the four main components already underlined in the previous section: (1) computation, (2) network, (3) VEs migration, and (4) time, as shown in Fig. 3 (and anticipated in the internal representation of the SDDC management in Fig. 1).

Existing solutions typically adopt simplified models not considering all the above components. Most of the studies just consider the energy consumption related to computational processes, not taking into account networking aspects in their proposed model [10,11]. In this case, the main mechanism for optimizing energy consumption in the cloud data center is to operate a VEs allocation that minimizes the number of active physical hosts through server consolidation techniques [10,12,13]. However, this vision does not capture the challenges of SDDC with the increasing amount of data-intensive applications. Few studies consider the energy consumption related to the data transfer among VEs, and they typically focus only on optimizing the network infrastructure in terms of links reconfiguration or reallocating VEs based only on their traffic exchanges [14]. The rest of this section details the possible options in modeling the different contributions to energy consumption in a SDDC.

Computation Model. Three main approaches are typically adopted to model computation-related energy. A possibility is to focus on a detailed model of CPU utilization that includes frequency scaling features (e.g., DVFS). These models typically introduce a *non-linear dependency* (e.g., quadratic, cubic or

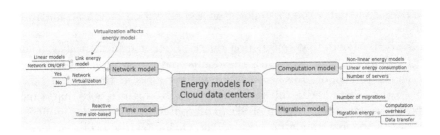

Fig. 3. Models for energy contributions in SDDC.

exponential) of energy consumption on the CPU frequency [12,15]. However, this approach would lead to very complex models when a high level of virtualization is applied to computational tasks (through VMs or containers) as in large size cloud data centers. Moreover, it does not capture the fact that power consumption of several sub-systems, such as disks and memory, is not related to the actual CPU frequency. Hence, the most widespread option is to model the energy consumption at the level of physical host, considering the energy consumption starting from a minimum (idle) value and increasing with a *linear dependency* on the host utilization [1,11]. The final option is the simplest approach, that just considers the *number of physical hosts* [13]. However, this latter model is hardly applicable in a SDDC, because of the inherent complexity of the data center (possibly composed of heterogeneous physical hosts) and of the difficulty of combining possible energy contributions expressed through different units of measurements (e.g., number of hosts and energy due to data transfers).

Network Model. When network-related energy consumption is taken into account, multiple choices may affect the resulting model. The energy consumption due to traffic exchange on data links may be modeled following two main approaches. The first approach considers the energy consumption as mainly related to the *status ON or OFF* of the network link [16]: this is appropriate when the link has a fixed data rate or when the main energy expenditure is due to features, such as Power-over-Ethernet, that are not affected by the volume of data exchanged over the link. Recent proposals suggest a second more realistic approach where energy is modeled as the sum of a fixed value, related to the status of the network interfaces, plus a variable contribution that depends on the actual link activity. This model has been proposed both to model the impact of energy consumption of data center network appliances [17] and to model the actual consumption of network link interfaces in the presence of *Adaptive Link Rate (ALR)* systems [14]. Another important consideration regards should be done about the presence of *Network Virtualization*. In this case, all or part of networking is implemented through virtual devices: for example, exploiting the added flexibility of Software-Defined Network elements [7], or running multiple virtual routers on a single physical router with virtualization capabilities [14], or using VMs to run the IP routing software [18]. In this case, the energy consumption of networking elements virtualized over highly programmable or general purpose hardware should be considered linearly proportional to the network utilization [15,19] (similarly to virtualized computation over a general-purpose hardware).

Migration Model. A migration process occurs when a virtual element (a VM or a VR) is moved from one host to another one. We should consider that migration is not a cost-free operation from an energy point of view: developing an energy model able to reduce the amount of migrations is a critical goal to achieve. Several optimization models simply consider the *number of VM migrations* in the objective function to minimize the data center energy consumption [6,12]. However, this approach presents two main limitations: first, the assumption of identical virtual elements from a migration energy point of view; second, the need to use weight parameters to include the number of migrations in the energy budget of the data center. More sophisticate approaches have been recently proposed that consider two possible energy contributions of the migration process. The first contribution is the energy associated with the *data transfer* of the VE memory from one host to the another, possibly including also the management of dirty memory pages during a live migration. The second contribution is related to the *computational overhead* caused by the virtual element migration at the level of hypervisor, that may reach up to 10% for the duration of the migration process [11].

Time Model. As regards time modeling, we have two main approaches: *reactive* and *time slot-based* models. In the reactive model, any action aiming to reduce energy consumption is triggered by some events. This model is suitable to cope with critical situations, such as overload of the physical hosts, while keeping a minimum level of reconfiguration operations carried out only when strictly required [1,4,11,12]. On the other hand, the time slot-based model carries out a continuous optimization effort, where reconfigurations of the data center are periodically evaluated [10]. This approach is useful in situations where sub-optimal configurations of the data center would not trigger any reconfiguration in a reactive model but, over long period of time, cause significant energy waste. A reactive model is the most common choice when the energy optimization considers mainly computational resources. However, optimization of network traffic across the data center is more often associated to a time slot-based approach for the difficulty to define network-related thresholds that trigger events. This motivates the preference towards the time slot-based model when features of the SDDC are taken into account (e.g., use of virtual routers).

As a concluding remark, we observe that none of the previously cited energy models, considered by itself, is suitable to fully exploit the opportunities and to capture the inherent complexity of a SDDC. Indeed, to achieve this goal the energy model needs to include all the four previously aspects with an adequate level of accuracy. On the other hand, each of the above considered models includes some oversimplification that makes it not completely suitable for SDDC case. This motivates our proposal of an example model that is explicitly tailored to this type of scenario.

4   Problem Model

This section describes the proposed model to address the problem of optimizing the VEs allocation on the physical servers of the data center with the goal to reduce the energy consumption. Specifically, we take into account the contributions of computational and networking tasks as well as of VEs migrations. The energy model used for the contribution of VEs migration is a qualifying and original point of the proposed solution.

4.1   Model Overview

The model considers a set of servers $\mathcal{M}$, where each server i hosts multiple VEs. For each VE $j \in \mathcal{N}$, we consider requirements expressed in terms of CPU power c_j, memory m_j and network traffic, that is described by the data traffic passing between two VEs d_{j_1,j_2}. In this model, we made the assumption that a SLA is respected if and only if the VE actually has the specified CPU, memory, and network resources (same approach in [1], where the SLA is based only the CPU resource). This assumption for the SLA is consistent with the Infrastructure as a Service (IaaS) paradigm.

As for the time model adopted in our proposal, we assume that time is modeled through a discrete succession of intervals, where each interval has the same length $\mathcal{T}$. It is worth to note that, differently from our approach, many other studies rely on a reactive model based on events: for example, an event is triggered when the CPU utilization exceeds a certain threshold [1,4,6]. We assume that the VEs resource demands refer to a generic time interval t, and that the VEs allocation over the physical servers of the data center is known from the previous time interval $t - 1$. The knowledge of the previous VEs allocation is a necessary condition to exploit an approach based on dynamic programming. On the other hand, the knowledge of the future VEs requirements in terms of CPU, memory and network traffic may be predicted on the basis of recurring resource demand patterns, such as diurnal patterns that are typical of the network traffic exchange among VEs within a data centers [10].

For a new VE entering the system at time interval t, we consider the nominal values of the resource requirements in terms of CPU and memory, and we discard inter-VEs communication costs since we cannot assume to have information about it. As the new VE enters, it is placed in the system using the Modified Best Fit Decreasing (MBFD) algorithm presented in [1].

The optimization model is now described. The list of the main decision variables, model parameters and internal variables used in the formal description is presented in Table 1 (the table has been used also in a previous work of the authors [8]).

We recall that in our model the VEs migration is not only necessary for server consolidation, but it also allows us to reduce the energy contribution related to the data transfer between couples of VEs. The VEs migrations are modeled by means of two matrices, whose elements $g_{i,j}^-(t)$ and $g_{i,j}^+(t)$ represent the source and destination of a migration (with i being the server and j the VE), similarly to [6].

The decision variables of the problem are: an allocation binary matrix, whose elements $x_{i,j}(t)$ determine the allocation of the VE j on the server i, and a binary vector, where the elements $O_i(t)$ represents the status of the physical server i, that can be ON ($O_i(t) = 1$) or OFF ($O_i(t) = 0$). Finally, the allocation matrix at time $t - 1$ represents the system status at the *end* of the interval $t - 1$: this means that the VEs that left and joined the system in the interval $t - 1$ have been removed and added in the allocation matrix.

Table 1. Notation.

Symbol	Meaning/Role
Decision variables	
$x_{i,j}(t)$	Allocation of VE j on server i at time t
$O_i(t)$	Status (ON or OFF) of server i
Model parameters	
$x_{i,j}(t-1)$	Allocation of VE j on server i at time $t-1$
$\mathcal{T}$	Duration of a time interval
$\mathcal{N}$	Set of existing VEs to deploy $|\mathcal{N}| = N$
$\mathcal{M}$	Set of on servers in the data center $|\mathcal{M}| = M$
$c_j(t)$	Computational demand of VE j at time t
$d_{j_1,j_2}(t)$	Data transfer rate between VE j_1 and j_2 at time t
$m_j(t)$	Memory requirement demand of VE j at time t
c_i^m	Maximum computational resources of server i
d_i^m	Maximum data rate manageable by server i
$\mathcal{E}_{d_{i_1,i_2}}$	Energy consumption for transferring 1 data unit from i_1 to i_2
m_i^m	Maximum memory of server i
P_i^m	Maximum power consumption of server i
P_i^d	Power consumption related to the "on" status of network connection of server i
K_{C_i}	Ratio between maximum and idle power consumption of server i
K_{M_i}	Computational overhead when server i is involved in a migration
Model variables	
i	Index of a server
j	Index of a VE
$\mathcal{E}_{C_i}(t)$	Energy for server i at time t
$\mathcal{E}_D(t)$	Energy for data transfer for server i at time t
$\mathcal{E}_{M_j}(t)$	Energy for migration of VE j time t
$g_{i,j}^-(t)$	1 if VE j migrates *from* server i time t
$g_{i,j}^+(t)$	1 if VE j migrates *to* server i at time t

We now detail the optimization problem defining the VEs allocation for the time interval t.

4.2   Optimization Model for VEs Allocation

In this section we formally describe the considered optimization problem. The objective function (1.1) of the optimization model aims to minimize the main three contributions to the energy consumption: *Computational demand*, *Data transfer*, and *VE migration*. The optimization model is now discussed in details, analyzing each of the three components. We recall that the objective function and the model constraints comes from the previous work of the authors [8].

$$\min \sum_{i \in \mathcal{M}} \mathcal{E}_{C_i}(t) + \mathcal{E}_D(t) + \sum_{j \in \mathcal{N}} \mathcal{E}_{M_j}(t) \tag{1.1}$$

subject to:

$$\sum_{j \in \mathcal{N}} x_{i,j}(t)c_j(t) \leq c_i^m O_i(t) \quad \forall i \in \mathcal{M}, \tag{1.2}$$

$$\sum_{j_1 \in \mathcal{N}} \sum_{j_2 \in \mathcal{N}} \left(x_{i,j_1}(t) + x_{i,j_2}(t) - 2x_{i,j_1}(t)x_{i,j_2}(t)\right)d_{j_1,j_2}(t)$$
$$\leq d_i^m O_i(t), \quad \forall i \in \mathcal{M}, \tag{1.3}$$

$$\sum_{j \in \mathcal{N}} x_{i,j}(t)m_j(t) \leq m_i^m O_i(t), \quad \forall i \in \mathcal{M}, \tag{1.4}$$

$$\sum_{i \in \mathcal{M}} x_{i,j}(t) = 1, \quad \forall j \in \mathcal{N}, \tag{1.5}$$

$$\sum_{i \in \mathcal{M}} g_{i,j}^+(t) = \sum_{i \in \mathcal{M}} g_{i,j}^-(t) \leq 1, \quad \forall j \in \mathcal{N}, \tag{1.6}$$

$$g_{i,j}^-(t) \leq x_{i,j}(t-1), \quad \forall j \in \mathcal{N}, i \in \mathcal{M}, \tag{1.7}$$

$$g_{i,j}^+(t) \leq x_{i,j}(t), \quad \forall j \in \mathcal{N}, i \in \mathcal{M}, \tag{1.8}$$

$$x_{i,j}(t) = x_{i,j}(t-1) - g_{i,j}^-(t) + g_{i,j}^+(t), \quad \forall j \in \mathcal{N}, i \in \mathcal{M}, \tag{1.9}$$

$$x_{i,j}(t), g_{i,j}^+(t), g_{i,j}^-(t), O_i(t) = \{0,1\}, \quad \forall j \in \mathcal{N}, i \in \mathcal{M}, \tag{1.10}$$

We model the *Computational demand* energy consumption of a generic server i as the sum of two components (as in [1]): first, a fixed energy cost for a server in the ON status ($P_i^m K_{C_i}$ is the power consumption for an idle server); second, a variable cost which is linearly proportional to the server utilization (P_i^m is the power consumption of a fully utilized server). The server utilization is computed based on the computational demands of each VE hosted on the server $c_j(t)$ and the maximum server capacity (c_i^m). The computational demand component is expressed as follows:

$$\mathcal{E}_{C_i}(t) = O_i(t)T P_i^m \left(K_{C_i} + (1 - K_{C_i})\frac{\sum_{j \in \mathcal{N}} x_{i,j}(t)c_j(t)}{c_i^m}\right)$$

As regards the *Data transfer* component, it represents a data center-wise value that we model again as the sum of two elements: the first component is represented by the power consumption of the server network interfaces when they are in an idle but turned on status (P_i^d for server i); the second component is proportional to the amount of data exchanged and is based on the parameter d_{j_1,j_2} describing the data exchange between two VEs j_1 and j_2. This approach is consist with the proposal presented in [19]. According to [1,10,19], we assume a linear energy model for the network data transfer: this model is realistic for current data centers and will be even more viable for modeling future data centers exploiting software-defined and virtualized network functions, where the network functions can be considered as abstract computation elements [7]. It is worth to note that the square matrix $\mathcal{E}_{d_{i_1,i_2}}$, representing the cost to transfer a data unit between two different servers, can capture the characteristics of any topology of a data center network. Hence, the global energy cost of the data exchange is described as follows:

$$\mathcal{E}_D(t) = \sum_{i \in \mathcal{M}} O_i(t)\mathcal{T}P_i^d + \sum_{j_1 \in \mathcal{N}} \sum_{j_2 \in \mathcal{N}} \sum_{i_1 \in \mathcal{M}} \sum_{i_2 \in \mathcal{M}} x_{i_1,j_1}(t)x_{i_2,j_2}(t)d_{j_1,j_2}(t)\mathcal{T}\mathcal{E}_{d_{i_1,i_2}}$$

The third component is the *VEs migration* cost, which represents a per-VE value modeling the energy consumption for the migration process. The energy contribution caused by the migration of a generic VE j depends on two main elements. First, the whole memory m_j of the migrating VE is transferred from a source to a destination server (note that the amount of data actually transferred is slightly higher than the nominal one because it is necessary to retransmit the dirty memory pages, but the typical small size of the active pages with respect to the VE global memory space allows us to neglect this effect). Second, we need to take into account the performance degradation occurring during the memory copy between two servers: we model the performance degradation through the parameter $K_{M,j}$ for the server i hosting the VE j. The degradation is typically in the order of 10% of the performance [20] and takes typically a few tens of seconds, which is significantly lower with respect to the length of the time slot $\mathcal{T}$. The energy cost for the migration VE j can be described as:

$$\mathcal{E}_{M_j}(t) = \sum_{i_1 \in \mathcal{M}} \sum_{i_2 \in \mathcal{M}} g_{i_1,j}^-(t)g_{i_2,j}^+(t)\left(m_j(t)\mathcal{E}_{d_{i_1,i_2}} \right.$$
$$\left. + (1 - K_{C_{i_1}})P_{i_1}^m K_{M_{i_1}}\mathcal{T} + (1 - K_{C_{i_2}})P_{i_2}^m K_{M_{i_2}}\mathcal{T} \right)$$

It is important to note that the proposed model is significantly more complex with respect to state-of-the-art models considering only the number of VEs migrations, as done in [6]. The model complexity is motivated by the need to consider a complete network model assuming that a VE migration should be triggered in the system only if the energy savings due to the better VE allocation in the future time slot will compensate the cost of the migration.

Let us now describe the constraints of our optimization problem. The capacity limit of the bin-packing problem of VEs allocation is expressed through the first group of constraints. The constraint 1.2 indicates that the sum of the CPU demands $c_j(t)$ of the VEs allocated on each server must not exceed the server maximum capacity c_i^m. The quadratic constraint 1.3 means that the link capacity of each server (defined as d_i^m) should not be exceeded by the data exchanged between the VEs on that servers and the ones on other servers. d_{j_1,j_2} indicates the data exchanged between the VEs j_1 and j_2, while the formula $x_{i,j_1}(t) + x_{i,j_2}(t) - 2x_{i,j_1}(t)x_{i,j_2}(t)$ corresponds to the binary operator based formulation $x_{i,j_1}(t) \oplus x_{i,j_2}(t)$: since VEs that are places on the same physical server do not use network links to exchange data, our model only takes into account the VEs located on different servers. The constraint 1.4 requires that the available memory on each servers m_i^m is not exceeded by the sum of memory demands $m_j(t)$ of the VEs allocated on that server. The constraint 1.5 indicates that each VE must be allocated on one and only one server (classic bin-packing problem constraint). The following constraints concern the VEs migration process. The short notation used in constraint 1.6 actually combines two different constraints: first, each VE cannot be involved in more than one migration (inequality constraint); second, a VE involved in a migration must appear in both the matrices $g_{i,j}^-(t)$ and $g_{i,j}^+(t)$. The constraint 1.7 indicates that a VE migration must start from the server where the VE was allocated at the previous time slot $(t-1)$, while the constraint 1.8 requires that a VE migrates only toward a server where the VE is allocated at time t (we add this constraint for the clarity of the model even if it is actually redundant, because satisfied by constraint 1.9). The constraint 1.9 means that the VEs allocation at time t must be the result of the allocation at the previous time $t - 1$ plus the VEs migrations. Finally, the constraint 1.10 expresses the boolean nature of $x_{i,j}(t)$, $g_{i,j}^+(t)$, $g_{i,j}^-(t)$, and $O_i(t)$.

5   Case Study

We now introduce a case study showing how the proposed model can be applied to a SDDC with Virtual Machines (VMs) and Virtual Routers (VRs), in short referred to as Virtual Elements (VEs). The present section starts with a a description of the considered case study; next, we provide a performance comparison between the proposed VEs allocation model and other alternatives presented in literature. A qualifying point of our analysis is considering the contribution of VEs migration on the overall energy consumption of the data center. Furthermore, we discuss how the size of the data center impacts on the optimization model performance.

5.1   Experimental Setup

Let us start with the experimental setup of the considered case study. We consider a time slot with a duration $\mathcal{T} = 15$ min for the migration of VEs among the infrastructure. Each VE is implemented as a Virtual Machine (that my host routing software in the case of a VR) that requires 4 cores and 40 GB of RAM. For the server we rely on the data provided by the the the energystar datasheets[2] that are freely available. In particular, we focus on a Dell R410 server with a 2×6 cores Xeon X5670 2.93 MHz and 128 GB of RAM, so that each server can host up to three VMs. For the considered servers, the power consumption ranges form from 197.6 W to 328.2 W.

For the data center network, we recall that its architecture is based on a two-level topology as described in Fig. 2. In our case study we assume communication

---

[2] https://www.energystar.gov/index.cfm?c=archives.enterprise_servers.

between VEs not involving data exchange across different Pods consumes half energy with respect to a communication passing both levels of the data center network. Clearly, communication between VEs on the same server has no cost associated. The model for network communication energy cost is obtained by combining multiple sources. On one hand, the switching infrastructure energy cost is based on the Cisco Catalyst 2960 series data sheet[3]. On the other hand, we rely on technical blogs[4] to infer the power consumption when a link can take advantage from *idle mode* and other advanced energy saving features. In the case study we consider that the per-port network power is 4.2 W, while the energy cost for transferring one byte of data is 3 or 6 mJ in the case communication occurs within one Pod or across multiple pods, respectively. It is worth to note that, even if in our case study we consider an homogeneous data center, the model can capture much more complex and heterogeneous scenarios.

Finally, we use the IBM ILOG CPLEX 12.6[5] solver that implements solution algorithms that can cope with the non-convex and quadratic nature of our problem.

In our case study we rely on time series describing the resource (CPU, memory, and network) utilization of VMs in a private cloud data center hosting a e-health application. We also assume that VRs, implemented through Additional VMs, are part of the virtual networks hosted in the data center and we consider the resource consumption on these VRs as proportional to the network traffic. All the VEs show resource utilization characterized by regular daily patterns. In our case study we consider, by default, 80 VEs, resulting in 20–30 servers being powered on. While this scenario is small compared to large public cloud data centers, we consider that for our goal, that is the validation of the optimization model proposed in the present chapter, the case study is significant. Furthermore, we consider that the scalability of the VEs allocation process may be improved integrating a Class-based approach as described in [3,21], where the solution of a small allocation problems can be replicated as a building block of a larger solution.

In our case study we compare three different models for VEs allocation. The first model, namely *Migration-Aware (MA)*, is the model proposed in our study and detailed in Sect. 4. The second model, namely *No Migration-Aware (NMA)*, differs from our proposal because it does not consider the cost for VEs migration. For the sake of our model, this means that we consider $\mathcal{E}_{M_j}(t) = 0 \ \forall j \in \mathcal{N}$ in the objective function Eq. 1.1. The NMA model is consistent with other proposals in literature, such as [22]. The third and last model, namely *No Network-Aware (NNA)*, does not consider neither migration nor network-related energy costs. The model just minimize the number of powered-on servers, as in [2]. The last model (NNA) and, to a lesser degree, the second one (NMA) are more suitable for the traditional data centers, where network and management are considered

[3] http://www.cisco.com/c/en/us/products/collateral/switches/catalyst-2960-x-series-switches/data_sheet_c78-728232.html.

[4] http://blogs.cisco.com/enterprise/reduce-switch-power-consumption-by-up-to-80.

[5] www.ibm.com/software/commerce/optimization/cplex-optimizer/.

as less important issues, while most focus is devoted to the management of computational demands of VEs (in a traditional scenario, VEs consist only in VMs).

A critical point in the traces for network traffic available to us is that we do not have a full description of the data exchange between each couple of VEs and we limit our knowledge to the total amount of data coming in/out form each single VE. To cope with this limit, we reconstruct the data exchange between each couple of VEs creating two different scenarios: *Network 1* and *Network 2*. In the Network 1 scenario we randomly distribute among the VEs the incoming/outgoing traffic to/from each VEs making sure that the total traffic still matches. In the Network 2 scenario we consider in the traffic distribution the presence of a Pareto Law, so that 80% of the traffic of each VE goes to just 20% of the remaining VEs. Furthermore, we make sure that the set of VEs with the highest data exchange shifts over time.

In our analysis we consider mainly the total energy $\mathcal{E}_{tot}$ consumed in the data center. However, we also measure the single energy contributions related to computational demand ($\mathcal{E}_C$), data transfer ($\mathcal{E}_D$), and VE migrations ($\mathcal{E}_M$) to provide additional insight on the model performance.

5.2 Model Comparison

As a first comparison between the three considered models, we analyze the total energy consumption and its components for the *Network 1* and *Network 2* scenarios. The results are shown in Fig. 4 (results in Fig. 4(a) were already presented in [8]).

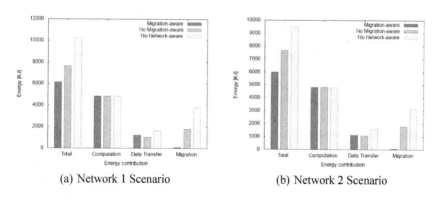

(a) Network 1 Scenario   (b) Network 2 Scenario

Fig. 4. Energy consumption comparison.

A first general result is evident from the leftmost column of Fig. 4(a) and concerns the total energy consumption. The proposed MA model clearly outperforms the alternatives with an energy saving of 20% over the NMA model and up to 40% with respect to the NNA alternative. To clarify this result, we can compare the contributions to the total energy consumption in the other columns of the figure. From the point of view of energy for computation, all three solution achieve the same results because every approach can consolidate the VEs in the same number of physical servers. The second component of the total energy is related to data transfer. In this case the NMA model provides the best performance due to its objective function that consider just computation and data transfer. As a clarification, it is worth to recall that data transfer does not include the bytes transferred to migrate VEs across the infrastructure. The energy for data transfer in the MA model is 20% higher and the NNA model has an even higher 60% more energy for data transfer. The poor performance of the NNA model is intuitive. However, to understand why the NMA model outperforms the MA alternative we can refer to the last columns of the graphs that is the energy consumed for VEs migration. Specifically, we see that the lower network-related energy consumption of the NMA model comes at the price of a number of migrations that far overweight the benefits of optimized network data exchange. We can thus conclude that not considering the cost of migrations results in an higher than necessary number of migration that, in the end, increase the total energy consumption.

The results for the *Network 2* scenario are shown in Fig. 4(b) and confirm the message previously explained for the *Network 1* scenario. Indeed, we observe that the behavior of the different considered models have similar results also under different different network traffic conditions. Furthermore, comparing Fig. 4(a) and 4(b), we observer that even the ratio in energy savings are similar: in the *Network 2* the MA model uses 37% and 22% less energy with respect to the NNA and NMA alternatives, respectively (compared with the 40% and 20% of the *Network 1* scenario).

5.3   Impact of Migration

We can conclude, from the previous set of experiments that the network-aware models (MA and NMA) clearly outperform the NNA alternative in reducing the energy consumption in a modern data center. It is then interesting to delve into a more detailed comparison of MA and NMA models to understand the impact of migration awareness.

Figures 5 and 6 provide a per-time slot breakdown of the energy consumption of the MA and NMA models for the two network scenarios, respectively. Starting with the Network 1 scenario, a comparison of Figs. 5(a) and (b), provides a further confirmation that the MA model outperforms the NMA alternative not just in terms of global energy consumption over time, but also for almost every time slot, as shown by the total energy consumption (lines with empty squares). We have also a confirmation that the different results in total energy consumption is mainly related to the energy consumption due to VEs migrations, as testified by the similar behavior of the total energy line (empty squares) and migration energy (filled circles). This finding is even more clear if we refer to the Network 2 scenario. Looking at Fig. 6(b) (presented also in [8]) we observe that in the NMA model the minimization of data transfer costs (line with empty circles)

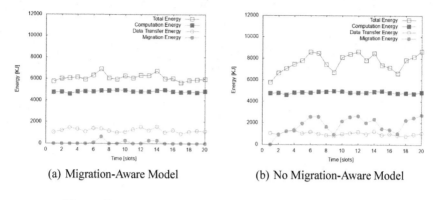

(a) Migration-Aware Model   (b) No Migration-Aware Model

Fig. 5. Energy consumption over time, Network 1 scenario.

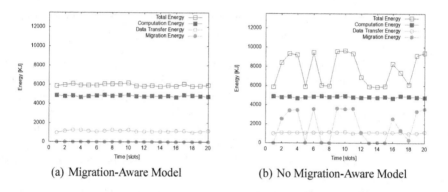

(a) Migration-Aware Model   (b) No Migration-Aware Model

Fig. 6. Energy consumption over time, Network 2 scenario.

comes at the cost of a herding effect with burst of migrations that dominates
the energy consumption of the data center. Looking at the MA alternative in
Fig. 6(a) it is clear that the MA model accepts a sub-optimal energy consumption
for data transfer, but achieves a major energy saving by reducing significantly
the number of migrations and the associated energy cost compared with the
NMA alternative.

5.4   Result Stability

The last analysis focuses on the stability of the energy savings with respect to
the problem size in terms of VEs.

Figure 7 shows the per-VE energy consumption for the MA model as a function of the data center size with the number of VEs ranging from 20 to 140.
We present the analysis for both the Network 1 (Fig. 7(a), already presented
in [8]) and for the Network 2 scenarios (Fig. 7(b)). The graphs for both scenarios, demonstrate that the per-VE data transfer and migration energy are quite

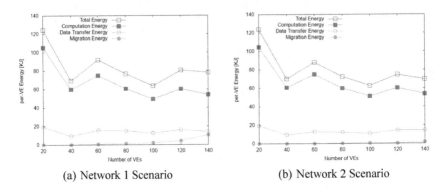

(a) Network 1 Scenario   (b) Network 2 Scenario

Fig. 7. Energy consumption *vs.* problem size.

stable with respect to the data center size. On the other hand, the computation energy presents more variability, accounting for the fluctuations in the total
energy.

The variability in the computation energy is explained by the impact of
fragmentation on the server consolidation process. Especially for small problem
sizes, we may have servers not fully utilized and, due to the small problem size the
cost for a marginally utilized server (dominated by the idle power of the server)
is spread over a limited number of VEs, thus determining a low efficiency in
the server consolidation. The fragmentation effect is amplified by adopting the
Class-based consolidation model [3], that trade the possibility of sub-optimal
allocations for scalability in the VEs allocation. However, as the data center
grows the fraction of servers under-utilized due to fragmentation in the VEs
allocation is reduced, resulting in more stable performance with problem size.

6   Conclusions and Future Work

In this chapter we discussed the problem of energy-wise optimization of VEs
allocation in cloud data centers. This discussion may be applied to existing data
centers, but it is mainly focused to a new generation of infrastructures which
follow the paradigm of a Software-Defined Data Center, leveraging technologies
such as network virtualization and software-defined networks.

Our main contribution is to point out the key differences of these new type of
data centers with respect to traditional scenarios and to propose an optimization
model to determine VEs allocation in order to combine three goals. The first goal
is the reduction of the number of powered-on physical servers achieving what
is called *server consolidation*. The second goal is the reduction of the power
consumption for data transfer; as we model the energy cost of data exchange
between VEs in the infrastructure, we can reduce this energy component by
placing VEs with significant amount of data exchange close to each other (ideally
on the same server). The third and last goal is to reduce energy consumption due
to VEs migration, where this energy contribution is modeled considering both

data transfer and CPU overhead due to migration. The model is designed to automatically evaluate if the cost of migrating a VE is balanced by the benefits of reducing the number of turned on servers and optimizing the data transfer over the data center infrastructure. A qualifying point of our proposal is that the components of the objective function considered in our optimization problem measures directly the energy consumption. As a consequence, we do not need to introduce and tune weight parameters to merge the often conflicting goals of optimal VEs allocation and of avoiding a high number of VEs migrations, because the components of the objective function can be immediately combined together.

We consider a case study based on traces from a real data center, that confirms the validity of our model. The results show that we can reduce the energy consumption from 60% to 37% with respect to a solution which is not aware of network-related energy consumption, and from 22% to 20% with respect to a model that does not take into account the cost of migrations.

Acknowledgement. The authors acknowledge the support of the University of Modena and Reggio Emilia through the project S^2C: *Secure, Software-defined Clouds*.

References

1. Beloglazov, A., Abawajy, J., Buyya, R.: Energy-aware resource allocation heuristics for efficient management of data centers for cloud computing. Future Gener. Comput. Syst. **28**(5), 755–768 (2012)
2. Beloglazov, A., Buyya, R.: Optimal online deterministic algorithms and adaptive heuristics for energy and performance efficient dynamic consolidation of virtual machines in cloud data centers. Concurrency Comput. Pract. Exp. **24**(13), 1397–1420 (2012)
3. Canali, C., Lancellotti, R.: Exploiting classes of virtual machines for scalable IaaS cloud management. In: Proceedings of the 4th Symposium on Network Cloud Computing and Applications (NCCA), June 2015
4. Mastroianni, C., Meo, M., Papuzzo, G.: Probabilistic consolidation of virtual machines in self-organizing cloud data centers. IEEE Trans. Cloud Comput. **1**(2), 215–228 (2013)
5. Greenberg, A., Hamilton, J., Maltz, D.A., Patel, P.: The cost of a cloud: research problems in data center networks. ACM SIGCOMM Comput. Commun. Rev. **39**(1), 68–73 (2008)
6. Marotta, A., Avallone, S.: A simulated annealing based approach for power efficient virtual machines consolidation. In: Proceedings of 8th International Conference on Cloud Computing (CLOUD). IEEE (2015)
7. Drutskoy, D., Keller, E., Rexford, J.: Scalable network virtualization in software-defined networks. IEEE Internet Comput. **17**(2), 20–27 (2013)
8. Shojafar, M., Canali, C., Lancellotti, R.: A computation- and network-aware energy optimization model for virtual machines allocation. In: Proceedings of International Conference on Cloud Computing and Services Science (CLOSER 2017), Porto, Portugal, April 2017
9. Akyildiz, I.F., Lee, A., Wang, P., Luo, M., Chou, W.: Research challenges for traffic engineering in software defined networks. IEEE Network **30**(3), 52–58 (2016)

10. Eramo, V., Miucci, E., Ammar, M.: Study of reconfiguration cost and energy aware vne policies in cycle-stationary traffic scenarios. IEEE J. Sel. Areas Commun. **34**(5), 1281–1297 (2016)
11. Verma, A., Ahuja, P., Neogi, A.: pmapper: power and migration cost aware application placement in virtualized systems. In: Issarny, V., Schantz, R. (eds.) Middleware 2008. LNCS, vol. 5346, pp. 243–264. Springer, Heidelberg (2008). https://doi.org/10.1007/978-3-540-89856-6_13
12. Cao, Z., Dong, S.: An energy-aware heuristic framework for virtual machine consolidation in cloud computing. J. Supercomputing **69**(1), 429–451 (2014)
13. Gu, L., Zeng, D., Guo, S., Ye, B.: Joint optimization of VM placement and request distribution for electricity cost cut in geo-distributed data centers. In: 2015 International Conference on Computing, Networking and Communications (ICNC), pp. 717–721. IEEE (2015)
14. Eramo, V., Cianfrani, A., Miucci, E., Listanti, M., Carletti, D., Gentilini, L.: Virtualization and virtual router migration: application and experimental validation. In: Proceedings of International Teletraffic Congress (ITC), pp. 1–6. IEEE (2014)
15. Boru, D., Kliazovich, D., Granelli, F., Bouvry, P., Zomaya, A.Y.: Energy-efficient data replication in cloud computing datacenters. Cluster Comput. **18**(1), 385–402 (2015)
16. Yi, Q., Singh, S.: Minimizing energy consumption of fattree data center networks. SIGMETRICS Perform. Eval. Rev. **42**(3), 67–72 (2014)
17. Mandal, U., Habib, M.F., Zhang, S., Mukherjee, B., Tornatore, M.: Greening the cloud using renewable-energy-aware service migration. IEEE Netw. **27**(6), 36–43 (2013)
18. Wood, T., Ramakrishnan, K., Hwang, J., Liu, G., Zhang, W.: Toward a software-based network: integrating software defined networking and network function virtualization. IEEE Netw. **29**(3), 36–41 (2015)
19. Chiaraviglio, L., Ciullo, D., Mellia, M., Meo, M.: Modeling sleep mode gains in energy-aware networks. Comput. Netw. **57**(15), 3051–3066 (2013)
20. Clark, C., Fraser, K., Hand, S., Hansen, J.G., Jul, E., Limpach, C., Pratt, I., Warfield, A.: Live migration of virtual machines. In: Proceedings of 2nd conference on Symposium on Networked Systems Design & Implementation-Volume 2. USENIX Association (2005)
21. Canali, C., Lancellotti, R.: Scalable and automatic virtual machines placement based on behavioral similarities. Computing **99**(6), 575–595 (2017)
22. Huang, D., Yang, D., Zhang, H., Wu, L.: Energy-aware virtual machine placement in data centers. In: Proceedings of Global Communications Conference (GLOBECOM). IEEE, Anaheim, December 2012

The Benefits of Using Experimental Exploration for Cloud Migration Analysis and Planning

Frank Fowley[1], Divyaa Manimaran Elango[1], Hany Magar[1], and Claus Pahl[2(✉)]

[1] IC4, Dublin City University, Dublin 9, Ireland
[2] SwSE, Free University of Bozen-Bolzano, Bolzano, Italy
claus.pahl@unibz.it

Abstract. Migration software systems to the cloud causes challenges. This applies especially for companies that do not have sufficient cloud expertise. In many of these companies there is a clear ideas about expected benefits. There is also an awareness of some potential problems. However, this is often not sufficient to assess the risks before starting on a full cloud migration of a legacy system.

Technical and conceptual analyses can only help to identify risks in the migration process with from a cost and a quality perspective to a limited extent. So, we investigate here the suitability of feasibility studies with a focus on experimental exploration. These studies would generally only cost 5% of the overall costs of a migration project, but can strongly support a reliable risk assessment. These can determine how much of the expectations and intentions can achieved in a cloud deployment. The cost of the migration, but also the cost of operating an IT system in the cloud can be estimated in the context of quality expectations. Using a feasibility study with an experimental core based on a partial prototype delivers much more reliable figures regarding configurations, quality-of-service and costing than a theoretical analysis could deliver.

We will embed our feasibility study approach into a pattern-based migration method. We report on a number of case studies to validate the expected benefits of feasibility-driven migration.

Keywords: Cloud migration · Experiment · Prototyping · Migration patterns
Cloud architecture · Cloud cost model · Performance · Scalability

1 Introduction

Today, cloud computing is a widely used form of operating software. However, the migration of software systems to the cloud [2] is still a problem for many, especially small and medium-sized enterprises and organisations without sufficient cloud expertise [12]. These companies generally need to rely on support from consultants and solution providers. Expected benefits are known and an awareness of potential problems exists. However, this is often not sufficient to confidently embark on a full migration of a software system, which requires estimates of the migration costs as well as costs of operating software within the limits of required quality in the cloud.

© Springer International Publishing AG, part of Springer Nature 2018
D. Ferguson et al. (Eds.): CLOSER 2017, CCIS 864, pp. 157–176, 2018.
https://doi.org/10.1007/978-3-319-94959-8_9

Technical and cost-oriented discussions can help to some extent, but many assumptions rely on expert knowledge from similar cases, but might not always be fully reliable. We investigate here feasibility studies with a focus on experiments to assess risk through quality and cost analyses. These studies cost typically be five percent of the overall migration cost. They can consequently be considered a worthwhile investment.

Apart from legacy-to-cloud migration, our solution can also be used for migrations to another cloud architectures. So, rather than cloud-onboarding, the source architecture is already cloud-based. An IaaS to PaaS migration from a basic, virtualized on-premise system into a fully cloud-native architecture could serve as an example here.

An adequate project scoping for any cloud migration is a problem [4], because of misconceptions and unclear technical expectations that significantly increase the risk. Migration frameworks and case studies have been reported in the literature by academics and practitioners from industry [2,3,18], but how to reliably estimate a 'right-scaling' of a cloud deployment remains unclear if cost and quality concerns need to be aligned.

Feasibility studies can support risk assessment. It can clarify how much of the expectations and intentions can be achieved. The cost of the migration [5] and also the cost of operating a software system in the cloud can be better estimated [6]. It also helps to better understand technical cloud architecture concerns. Another question is a re-engineering one. What is migratable and what is the extent of refactoring necessary to make migration work are questions. Often, re-engineering software in order to modernise and adapt to cloud constraints is needed. Prototyping in the cloud can help to address scalability requirements, i.e., to align performance and cost concerns. Using a feasibility study with an experimental core based on a partial prototype of the proposed cloud software system [13] delivers much more reliable figures regarding configurations, quality-of-service and costing than a theoretical analysis could delivery.

In this investigation, we report on case studies that we carried out as independent consultants with small and medium-sized enterprises in the software sector. These case studies serve to validate the benefits of the approach towards a more reliable risk analysis by integrating cost and quality.

The paper is structured as follows. We introduce a migration feasibility framework in Sect. 2. The, in Sect. 3, we define our architecture assessment and risk framework that links to known architecture analysis methods. We investigate the goals of feasibility studies and practical concerns of feasibility studies in a migration project in Sect. 4. We focus on the experimentation process in Sect. 5. In Sect. 6, we discuss a selected use case in more detail. In Sect. 7, we discuss our observations. Related work is discussed in Sect. 8, before ending with conclusions and a discussion of future work.

2   A Pattern-Based Migration Planning Framework

Our migration approach starts with a pattern-based architecture description. These are used to define an initial migration plan.

2.1   Pattern-Based Cloud Architecture Migration

Our proposed pattern-based architecture migration method considers the following components: (i) the source architecture of the system, (ii) the target architecture options in the cloud, and (iii) the high-level architectural transformations for the different target architectures [7]. This is formalised through a catalogue of migration patterns which each describe simple architectural transformations for specific scenarios (e.g. for simple cloudification in an IaaS solution). This defines a staged process based on a migration path which in the individual steps are driven by selection criteria (e.g., time to market or introduction of new capabilities). A sample pattern is Multi-Cloud Relocation [6], see Fig. 1, which simply replaces on-premise by cloud-based components.

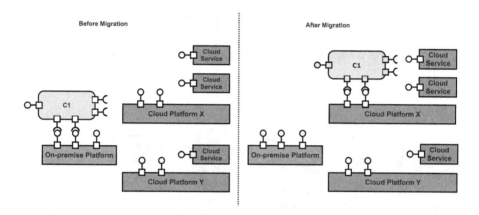

Fig. 1. Cloud migration pattern: multi-cloud relocation.

Several migration patterns are sequenced together to form an incremental migration path, see Fig. 2 which gives a path with options included. Usually, a cloud migration is an incremental activity, which is reflected in the path.

A concrete application shall also be introduced. A sample migration from a legacy system's architecture to a cloud-based one is displayed in Figs. 3 and 4. In this case, the migration of a classical enterprise application, an expense system, is migrated into the cloud, ultimately using several cloud-native services (here Azure storage services), but also other external services (such as the Payment component).

Of key importance in a migration are:

– the expected quality-of-service;
– the resources needed;
– the architecture patterns meant to be preserved or employed;
– the platforms chosen to host the application in the cloud.

These need to be mapped to patterns.

A migration pattern is represented by an architecture diagram of the service architecture deployment before and after migration, i.e., a migration pattern is a transformation triple based on source and target architecture combined with the applied pattern

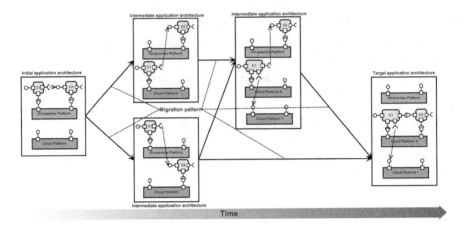

Fig. 2. Migration path based on several pattern applications.

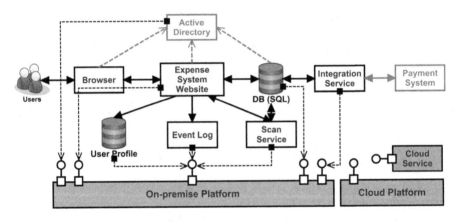

Fig. 3. Sample migrated architecture – before migration.

as the transformation specification. Each source or target architecture is represented by architectural elements such as services and connectors, deployment platforms (on-premise and cloud-based) and cloud services. The notation here is somewhat aligned with UML component diagrams. We have specific component types color-coded.

A service component can either be atomic or contain internal components allowing for hierarchical decomposition. For example, the migration pattern MP1 in Fig. 1 consists of a coarse-grained component that consumes services of an on-premise deployment platform. These can be coordination services that orchestrate different components in larger compartments or simply configurable IaaS resources providing required operating system or storage features. After migration, this component, instead of using on-premise platforms, uses services offered by a public cloud platform. Thus, the application component is re-deployed as-is on a cloud platform.

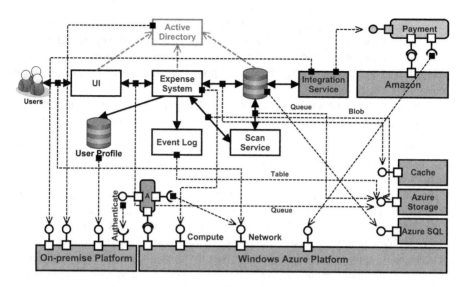

Fig. 4. Sample migrated architecture – after migration.

To identify a suitable pattern, the patterns are specified by pattern descriptions that focus on quality and resources/patterns to guide the selection process:

- Definition: A component re-hosted (or relocated) on a cloud platform is enhanced by using the environmental services of the other cloud platforms.
- Problem: Availability of an application needs to be enhanced without architecture change, and without capital expenditure for hardware.
- Solution: Leverage cloud platform environment services to improve availability, e.g., live migration from existing platform to target platform in case of outage.
- Benefits: As component re-hosting in multiple cloud platforms and improve availability and avoid vendor lock-in.
- Risks: Cloud providers do not provide the necessary services for applications to run in cloud platforms without re-architecting or rewriting code.

Our migration patterns are meant to be aligned sequences of architectural changes in the application, through which the current application is gradually refactored and modernized. For each migration pattern, an architectural migration schema has to be defined.

Our migration pattern catalogue comprises of 15 individual patterns. We have identified these 15 patterns through an empirical extraction process. To make the selection easier, these 15 patterns can be categorised into a number of Core Patterns and derived Pattern Variants. Full descriptions of core patterns and variants for the following core patterns can be found in detail in [26]. The categorisation is as follows:

- Re-deployment (core pattern MP1): variant pattern MP2 (for re-deployment in public cloud)
- Relocation (core pattern MP3): variant pattern MP4 (relocation for multi-clouds)

- Multi-Cloud Refactoring (core pattern MP5): variant patterns MP6 (hybrid refactoring), MP7 (hybrid refactoring with on-premise adaptation), MP8 (hybrid refactoring with cloud adaptation), MP9 (hybrid refactoring with hybrid adaptation)
- Multi-Cloud Rebinding (core pattern MP10): variant pattern MP11 (rebinding with cloud brokerage [23])
- Replacement (core pattern MP12): variant patterns MP13 (replacement with on-premise adaptation), MP14 (replacement with cloud adaptation)

Further variants can be added, but there is a sufficient completeness of the given set to model common PaaS migration scenarios, which we have demonstrated through past case study evaluations.

The core pattern and variants guides the migration pattern selection. Architecture aspects (from the application and platform profiles) and the technical quality constraints are the initial selection criteria. The pattern selection can be seen as a variability management problem that distinguishes internal (provider-based deployment) and external (application and application access) perspectives. To make this more clear, we can look at different applications. Some applications are integrated and support core business processes and services, but many of them support utility needs, are certainly non-core applications and are independent. The latter category may be obvious candidates for direct re-deployment. For the former integrated core ones, refactoring (re-architecting or redesigning) is more appropriate.

Migration paths emerge as sequential compositions of these patterns on a source architecture, see Fig. 1. These paths are defined based on discussions with the company about their existing architecture and a high-level specification of technical and business targets. Migration paths define decision points where typically several architectural options emerge, e.g., different data storage options [7–9]. For (a subset of) these options, an experimental evaluation can be considered.

2.2 Experimental Evaluation of Migration Options

The current architecture is ported into the cloud, but can there take advantage of virtualization to not only reduce operational expenditure, but also to create multiple instances of the application to improve scalability and failover without increasing capital expenditure. A risk is that underlying architecture concerns are not sufficiently addressed. A monolithic legacy application in the cloud is still monolithic including the previous limitations such as a lack of scalability. Scalability cannot easily be achieved if, e.g., the architecture does not allow the database to be updated by multiple instances.

We can used the pattern-based migration paths (including options) to investigate quality and cost concerns.

Based on the identified migration paths, a plan focusing on a subset of components is identified for experimental evaluation: Firstly, define source and possible target architectures. Secondly, select critical components, e.g., high volume data process to test scalability of storage (DB) or communications infrastructure to test integration and communications scalability. The benefit of the patterns is that they link architecture configuration to quality. We use this link to select components for the feasibility exploration based on the most relevant quality concern to be explored.

3   Architecture Assessment and Risk

This cloud migration process can be seen as an incarnation of a wider architecture modifiability method. We can benefit from a scenario-based approach to frame this, in particular one supporting the evaluation of modifiability. The migration patterns we introduced actually reflect different migration scenarios. An architecture analysis can inform the decision how migrateable (i.e., modifiable in a certain way) a system is and whether to migrate this. ATAM (Architecture Tradeoff Analysis Method) and ALMA (Architecture-Level Modifiability Analysis) are two widely used methods for architecture analysis [15]. Using these can help assessing the migration risk and identifying possible quality concerns that need to be further explored.

ATAM is not specifically positioned for migration evaluation, but it does more generally target the trade-offs between different quality concerns. However, a scenario-based approach as followed by ATAM is useful and can be complemented by architecture-level metrics that we use specifically for the migration evaluation.

ALMA is another scenario-based method, which is more specific to modifiability [15] and thus applies better in the migration context. ALMA is proposed for software architecture modifiability assessment by using a number of indicators: maintenance cost prediction, risk assessment. In case of assessing and comparing different system, the modifiability analysis performed with ALMA supports software architecture selection as well. ALMA is based on five steps, which we actually implement as part of the migration pattern method:

- Step 1: Goal definition using pattern properties.
- Step 2: Target architecture description using a pattern-based migration path.
- Step 3: Define (elicit) change scenarios. This means in our context to define migration plans, possibly involving different architectural alternatives (represented as alternative paths in a transition graph). The use of patterns allows us then to assemble alternatives from basic building blocks.
- Step 4: Evaluate scenarios, analyse expected and unexpected changes on a number of qualities. Examples of assessment criteria are cost and workload or performance to be experimentally evaluated. This is supported by properties attached to patterns.
- Step 5: Interpret results (pattern-based migration paths, annotated with quality properties).

The ALMA method allows us to consider maintenance cost and carry out in this way a form of risk assessment for a migration decision, which are the relevant concerns at the interaction of technical and business sustainability. Risks are clarified here through an experimental feasibility study, see Fig. 5.

We use the migration pattern to define a draft plan, to which we add here a risk assessment model of the target architecture options, driven by a selected architecture assessment method, such as ATAM or ALMA. The risk assessment introduces quality and cost metrics that can be integrated with the target architecture. The metrics include factors such as complexity and amount of changes on both of the architecture and source code, code efficiency and security. Those metrics change depending upon the existing software. However, the metrics also may change when correlated with business objectives and services costing model [25,29]. In order to answer those risk-based migration

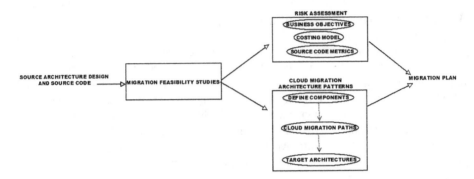

Fig. 5. Architecture and risk framework.

questions, a survey has been conducted by us about the business needs and costs. The risk assessment aims to address the issues that could occur in the migration process, as well as designing more reliable plan in terms of resources and time.

- Defining the metrics: defining what we aim by each factor since those factors could be utilized in different way:
  - Efficiency metrics: indicate how many methods, modules will be called and executed that are included in scaling cycle iterations, e.g., how far the application scales, how many times it was used.
  - Complexity metrics: indicate the amount of effort needed to develop and maintain the code. The more difficult code, the more effort and time needed to develop and maintain this code. The code metrics calculates: Maintainability Index, Cyclomatic Complexity, Depth of Inheritance, Class Coupling and Lines of Code.
  - Security metrics: security requirements that indicate vulnerability, violations, and threats with perspectives of Authentication, Authorisation and Storage Security. However, security practices and related metrics is beyond the scope here.
- During experimentation: we apply the new metrics approach on our use cases, such as performance and scalability concerns.
- Understanding the new architecture components: a way to improve the scalability and efficiency of the existing software is to refactor the software architecture to have more decoupled and separated service components.

From the different metrics listed here, we will largely focus on efficiency aspects in the use cases that will be introduced later.

4   Experimentally-Oriented Migration Feasibility Studies

Experimentation is the most important activity in the proposed feasibility study approach. We will look into objectives and the role of experiments to determine feasibility. Some use cases will illustrate the concerns.

4.1 Quality Requirements and Possible Cost Implications

The feasibility studies are driven by the following goals:

- Quality and Cost: This concerns the quantification of quality and cost aspects. Often, scalability is an important concern, driven by the business objective to expand. In this case, an experimental feasibility study can validate a proposed architecture scalability. Another motivation is a cost-vs-performance experiment, i.e., to consider different options and compare them technically (e.g., scalability of different target architecture options), but rank them considering the costs that they would incur [14, 22].
- Usage and Cost: By looking at the usage, we change the focus to the potential user. Usage exploration through experiments is a suitable tool to explore usage patterns and predict potential income based on this. This can then directly be related to the resources (and their costs) to facilitate user requests.
- Process and Platform Understanding: Experimentation allows to achieve a better understanding of technical constraints and operational activities in the cloud. What experimentation can shows is the difference between PaaS/IaaS/SaaS solutions (as consumer and provider) and integration and interoperation problems. It also clarifies how to structure and cost a staged migration (plan derivation).

The problem that emerges in the migration decision and planning process that links quality, usage and costs to the architectural configuration, can be phrased in the following question: *How many processes can be hosted on a fixed cloud compute resource with a pre-defined latency performance target for a forecasted number of users of a particular application with a forecasted mix of application operation usage.*

4.2 Experimental Studies as a Solution for Quality and Cost Estimation

Experimental studies can play an important role in the determination of migration feasibility. Experimentation often results in a prototype evaluation of a partly cloud-native architecture. Rather than just cloudifying a system in a virtual machine, we often selected a component such as data storage and have experimented with different cloud-native storage options, including for instance a mix of traditional RDBM and other table/blob storage formats. Partial experimentation with cloud-native prototypes allows to consider a fully cloud-native architecture to be discussed with realistic technical (e.g., scalability) and cost assumptions (storage, access) [10]. Only realistic costs for cloud operation allows a charging model to be developed and validated that fits their own product.

4.3 Use Cases

We discuss the migration concerns and how they are documented. When looking at concrete use cases, we distinguish what is expected and understood on the one hand and misconceptions and lack of knowledge on the other.

- Clarity of expectations and objectives: Business reasons to go to cloud are often clear, e.g., a planned internationalisation or expecting an increase in company value (in the cloud). Technical reasons for a cloud migration are at a high level clear, for instance scalability, but often lack deeper understanding of cost and quality.
- Understanding of cloud concerns (having an impact on architecture and process selection) is often limited. Technically, the difference between provision models/layers is unclear. This includes the management effort at I/P/SaaS level in comparison. Another problem is a possible vendor lock-in. In business terms, e.g., possibly required revenue model changes remain very unclear. Legal/Governance concerns such as data location are known, but without reliable knowledge.

We have conducted a number of case studies in the following application domains. We highlight the specific needs for a feasibility study that has emerged in each of the cases.

The central case study, which we will also use later for further illustration is *document management*: the application is document image processing to allow more efficient processing in the cloud, but also to enable the company to extend into new markets.

The other relevant use cases are:

- *Banking solution:* an integrated solution (account management plus ATM operations) – provided in Africa and Asia, raising uncertainty concerns from security to legal,
- *Insurance:* a solution for multi-product management in multiple countries – uncertainty arise from the need for variability management of a single product across different regions/jurisdiction,
- *Food sector ERP:* an ERP solution for food production and sales – where a stable in-house solution is prepared for launch as a product into different markets. Food safety regulations impact on the architecture a cloud-based solution,
- *Business Registry:* enterprise repositories – scalable internationalisation is the driver, allowing clients to access their services through the cloud.

5   Structured Experimentation in Migration Feasibility Studies

We now explore the proposed feasibility studies based on experimentation in more detail. Experimentation aims to allow to establish a link between technical feasibility and quality (e.g., performance) and costs [7]. The pattern-approach helps to guide the select the components for exploration based on the most relevant quality concern. This can range from performance to security to integration and interoperability, as indicated for the use cases.

Furthermore, in many development approaches, quality testing is an integral component, in particular if the software is directly used by end-users. Load testing is difficult if prior testing has been done in-house and no expertise in testing in the cloud exists. The feasibility study thus also addresses load testing.

5.1   A Process for Migration Feasibility Studies

We frame our experimental approach in a process for migration feasibility studies:

1. Definition of the source architectures and a number of possible target architectures,
2. Selection of critical components, e.g., a high volume data process to test scalability of storage (DB) or a communications infrastructure to test integration or communications scalability.

This is a critical challenges for the migration expert and the company architects. They have to understand the existing architecture and to select the most suited component for the experimental studies (ranges from individual component to full virtualisation as VM). The feasibility process is based on architecture determination, prototype component selection, and construction of realistic use case application for further analysis: (i) setup of services and data (real or dummy) and monitoring, (ii) experiment specification, (iii) experiment execution, (iv) data collection and analysis.

5.2   Benefits of Experimentatal Studies

Some of the experiments that we carried out targeted for instance data storage for image processing in the 'Document Management' use case. What experimentation shows are a number of concerns that would normally not always be identified and clarified in discussions and non-experimental analyses:

- Difference between PaaS/IaaS/SaaS solutions (as consumer and provider). Based on the migration architecture it allows to practically demonstrate configuration and operation of different scenarios.
- Scalability of the solutions, as exemplified in Figs. 6 and 7 for response time behaviour based on different retrieval and update loads.

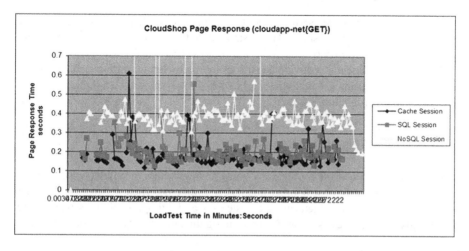

Fig. 6. Comparison of storage options (technical quality). Three DB configurations (Cache, SQL, NoSQL) are compared in terms of the page response time (in sec) [1] for given load test times.

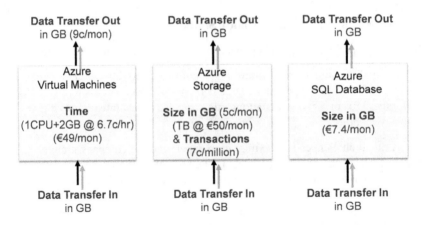

Fig. 7. Comparison of storage options (data consumption versus cost) [1].

– Identification of integration and interoperation problems that emerge in the prototype implementation when on-premise components are migrated.
– How to structure and cost a staged migration (plan derivation) can be estimated on
  the prototype component migration that typical involves the migration of existing
  components. In order to experiment, data and traffic needs to be available, again
  either imported or generated. In all cases, a realistic prediction of software and data
  migration tasks and related costs is possible.

Figure 6 shows the performance results for different storage options for a Web application. Figure 7 maps the architectural options onto costs.

5.3   Costs of the Experimental Effort

Cost is a key factor in the decision whether to conduct a feasibility study, i.e., does it pay
off to carry out a feasibility study. The costs include the cloud platform to experiment
with and the migration expert.

The total experimental costs are 5–10% of the predicted migration costs based on
our case study experience – including architectural analysis, draft migration plan and
security and data protection analysis[1].

6   A Selected Migration Use Case

In the migration process, the problem is costing an application on a public cloud within
the given performance and scalability quality requirements. The total costs include the
implementation costs of refactoring the system as a cloud application, as well as the
operational cloud charges associated with running the new system on a cloud provider.

---

[1] Please note, these costs were part-funded for the given use cases documented here by governmental business innovation schemes.

This use case – the document management use case – focuses on the migration of a legacy client-server on-premise single-tenant enterprise application to the cloud by re-designing, re-engineering and recoding the system as a cloud application. The company in question is an independent software vendor (ISV) that has over 1,000 existing client installs and this case study is to estimate the costs in migrating a part of these to a cloud platform. The application is Document Management, which enables scanning documents and save them as electronic images. Documents can be classified and meta-data templates are used to store searchable tagged data for the documents for retrieval and reporting. Additional services such as image processing, which allows for example Optical Character Recognition (OCR) and barcode reading can be added. The application is a multi-process system that consists of a web server (a compute resource) and a separate image processing component (another compute resource). However, the functional dependency between these does not need to be considered in any cost analysis as image processing VMs work independently from the web server, which operates regardless of the state of the image processor. Therefore, we can calculate VM configuration requirements based on a linear multiplication of the CPU load per tenant.

For the experimental part of this use case, we have considered the following architecture components:

- A cloud data store – made up of Azure-based NoSQL Table structure (Azure Table service) and an object store (Azure Blob Storage service). The former service stores metadata associated with the documents. The latter service stores the corresponding document image files.
- A cloud compute architecture made up of a separate compute resource for the web server of the web application (Web Role Virtual Machine), and a separate compute component for carrying out the image processing functions, such as barcode reading (Worker Role Virtual Machine);

The following data sources of data were used for an estimated technical configuration and cost calculation of a suitable full system.

- Prediction of the usage of storage resources when applications and their tenant are migrated: if available, we can use actual historical data from an existing average-sized tenant with a typical application usage pattern. The historical storage information, available from experiments or related sources, namely, the images, metadata and template files saved by a user of the application a given period in an on-premise context, provided a reference data store usage profile for a typical average user of data stored on the cloud.
- Prediction of the cloud compute resources required: we can monitor the usage and performance during an experimental period of the operational use of the application, again by a typical user as above. Monitoring includes here the application functions called and the number of document images/metadata stored and modified.
- In order to support the configuration to select the optimal VM type, we can carry out a benchmark study of the performance of the different VMs as part of the experimentation.

For the given use case, an experimental benchmarking and performance analysis has identified that the VM CPU load is the driving factor that determines the compute resource required. Therefore, this parameter is used as the main driver in the calculation of cloud costs in relation to performance requirements.

As an observation on the experiments carried out, there is an important difference between storage and compute resources in the cost calculation.

- When the cloud provider provides automatic scaling of the available storage capacity so that it appears to be effectively infinite from the application perspective. The application or cloud orchestration do not need to consider scaling storage capacity.
- The same is not the case for the compute resources. The auto-scaling of Virtual Machines (VM) must be configured and monitored by the administrator and set according to changing tenant numbers and sizes and application usage patterns and operational profiles. It must be carried out by taking Quality-Of-Service (QoS) parameters and Service Level Agreement (SLA) targets into account.

As a consequence, we monitored the usage and performance of the application over a test period during which a user carried out some typical operations of the application. We measured VM CPU and Memory utilisation as well as web application page response times and storage access end-to-end latency times. In the use case, the measured response times have demonstrated that the performance for file searching and scanning are within acceptable limits. Note that storage latency times are outside the control of the application and are a quality issue with the cloud provider, such as Microsoft Azure in the given case. The Memory and CPU usage indicated that the dedicated image processing VM is constant. This was expected since the processing was managed by an Azure Queue service which spreads the workload suitably. The memory utilisation of the server is equally constant, which can also be expected for a web server running web applications such as this.

While these observation are helpful in the configuration and cost calculation, we need to note some caveats. The calculations carried out in the experimental phases were to some extent rudimentary, because they were carried out before more comprehensive performance tuning could have been performed on the full application and the platform it was put on. The following aspects of the application and cloud platform could be further assessed during full operation of the application, e.g., in order to improve and optimise the deployment of the application.

- The existing deployment does not include any data caching, which would likely significantly reduce the CPU overhead as well as data storage access costs.
- The platform can be re-engineered to make use of newer platform services which allow for code to be run on demand rather than on compute role services – cf., recent lambda functions available by some major cloud service providers that should significantly reduce compute costs.
- The CPU load can be further optimised by looking at the queries to the table service through the use of indexing tables or schema denormalisation. This could be carried out once the more heavily used operational queries have been identified.

It should also be noted that a simple linear multiplier has been used here to estimate the tenant load for the forecasted tenant numbers. This, as explained does not take into account of the smoothing effect of multiple tenants sharing the same application compute resources. It therefore represents a conservative estimate of compute VMs required.

Detailed results on the effectiveness of the experimental feasibility studies will be reported in the next section.

7   Observations on Use Cases and Evaluation

The benefits of feasibility studies in the proposed format are experimentation results and documentation:

- a proper documentation of scenarios and plans needed at a high level, which allow detailed migration plans for a full migration to be developed,
- experiments help to clarify options, address misconceptions, and identify open problems.

They help to scope a full migration project. We have evaluated our feasibility approach to cloud migration analysis and planning based on the following criteria:

- Clarification of architectural options ans concerns.
- Reliable quality prediction & cost prediction.
- Cost effectiveness as an instrument.

7.1   Clarification of Architectural Concerns

A clarification of architectural options for organisations planning to migrate through architectural prototyping using a pattern approach allows to use patterns that link quality to structure [16, 19]. A survey has been carried out with architects involved in the migration studies – with at least 3 architects for each participating use case. This includes architects both within the company in question and also consulting software architects.

The key results of the survey we carried out are:

- All participants surveyed (100%) agree or strongly agree that the method is suitable as an analysis tool to identify options and concerns.
- Almost all (88% of the participants) agree that the migration method is suitable to analyse and discuss functional and non-functional architecture requirements for migration.

However, there has been one limitation that has been flagged by the survey participants. While 55% strongly agree that the method is suitable for SMEs and that is also suitable for multi-cloud migration (80% positive), there are also 43% that have concerns with its applicability for large-scale migration. This remains a concern for future work.

7.2   Prediction of Software Quality and Cost

We have already talked about the link between quality and cost. We can distinguish quality and cost observations in an attempt to obtain reliable estimations:

– Reliable Quality Prediction: experimental quality assessment results in trustworthy, reliable input to predict full system behaviour. This has been discussed and analysed with the customer companies in question. In the case of successful migrations at a later stage, we have not found any major deviations from the predictions when using the configurations experimented with.
– Reliable Cost Prediction: experimental cost assessment provides a low-to-high demand cost range, allowing to predict to system costs on a reliable basis [11]. These have been discussed with the customer company and, where possible, evaluated through a later full implementation.

Only an empirical evaluation of the two quality items is currently possible due to the lack of suitable quality and cost mapping models. Cloud computing is here, however, highly suitable as monitoring of technical details can be set to be detailed for the experiments and billing for the resources used is equally detailed with typically metered usage for different resources used. For instance, for the 'Document Management' use case, the factors considered for storage only were: *region, replication options, data size stored, transaction number, data transfer*.

7.3 Cost Effectiveness of Migration Feasibility Studies

Cost effectiveness as an instrument is a key aim of our approach. We looked at the actual costs of feasibility studies relative to full migration costs. We also considered how successful feasibility studies were in terms of determining a decision for the actual migration.

– Cost per project: For the 5 migration cases that we have carried out, the average cost was around 5% of the total budget for a full migration. The full migration budget was determined after the feasibility study concluded. The 5% cost was considered adequate. Please note that the overall budget for the migrations ranged between 100,000 and 250,000 Euros, including substantial re-architecting in some cases.
– Decisions taken: Concrete results from the use cases are as follows: 1 full migration (document management) has started and is currently being finalised, 1 full migration (insurance) has started, 1 decision against due to quality grounds (banking), 2 decision have at this stage not yet been taken (food, registry). In the all finalised cases, the companies in questions have based their decision on the outcome of the feasibility studies.

For the discussion with the companies in question, readiness to make a decision to embark on a full migration is considered a success. The experimental feasibility study is also considered successful if a decision against migration is taken on the grounds of an unfavourable quality or cost result.

7.4 Discussion of the Effectiveness of Migration Feasibility Studies

The limitations of the approach are related to the delay it might cause. In many circumstances this might not be an issue, but in some situations an approval to embark on a full migration is necessary, possibly depending on a successful outcome of the study. The format of this approval is typically one of the following:

- External private investment in a cloud
- Public support, e.g. through innovation schemes
- Internal approval for further funding

While there might be a delay particularly if an approval process is included, any full migration decision can be based on reliable input data. Please note that in the use cases where a decision has not been taken yet, this was not due to the study results.

In the context of the whole migration costs and generally some risk involved, the low feasibility study cost are a valuable investment.

Another limitation at the moment is that we have only carried out migration studies for small to medium sized applications with SMEs as customers. Data for large-scale experimentation with a possibly more complex setup does not exist yet.

8   Related Work

We distinguish related work in terms of three concerns – architecture migration, general cloud costing and quality-linked costing and pricing.

Architecture Migration. A number of cloud migration approaches exist. Authors like Jamshidi et al. [2] survey the literature on cloud migration. Fahmideh et al. [18] provide a comparison framework for cloud migration methods. We target specifically an experimental framework that goes beyond the surveyed process models for migration. However, we assume here a pattern-based migration method, into which a number of existing methods fall. To the best of our knowledge, the role of feasibility studies has not been explored yet in the context of cloud migration.

Costing in Migration. Costing models for cloud are important for organisations to understand their own costs and expenses. In [5], an overview of pricing models for the cloud for operational costs is provided. On the expenses side, e.g., at IaaS level, resources are priced often like commodities [11]. At the income side for an ISV operating through the cloud, the product is typically provided as a SaaS with possibly a mix of model from pay-per-use to pay-per-user and flat-fee models. Our solution is meant to bridge between the two perspectives.

Another direction would be the consideration of the total cost of ownership (TCO) and the Return-On-Investment (ROI) [32]. TCO in a cloud context would include the migration costs as well as the operational costs of running an application in the cloud. We were primarily interested in the operational costs for given quality requirements. Thus, actual migration costs for re-engineering and adaptation have been ignored in this investigation. Our work could be extended by determining the TCO for an SLA-compliant configuration.

Architecture and Pricing. Quality in the cloud is manageable for quality factors as performance by configuring and adapting the virtual resources used appropriately. We propose a manual experimentation approach for cloud prototype implementation. In [4] a system to support automated resource selection is suggested. Although this is not generally applicable, the ideas could help to automate our approach further. The automation of cloud experimentation is also addressed in [20] through a tool suite for the OpenStack platform.

9   Conclusions

The decision whether to run software in the cloud is both a cost and a quality question. For instance, fior a cloud-based software provider, quality and cost need to be reconciled in a cloud-based system architecture. This architecture needs to map software hosted using IaaS or PaaS services onto a SaaS delivery model. In this context, the reliability of relevant data and an understanding of the processes of migration and operating in the cloud and their impact are important elements for taking a decisions [17].

Our proposal here is to support this process through feasibility studies. These can help the companies in question to determine or at least confidently estimate the costs of the cloud migration, but also the operation of a software product in the cloud. Feasibility studies provide decision support. The key questions are whether and how a software product can be deployed and delivered cost-effectively in the cloud while at the same time maintaining desired quality. The benefit is increased reliability of data/assumptions, rather than relying on experience or guesses. We put experiments at the core of these feasibility studies. Testing and experimentation is often not don until a much later stage around systems deployments. Performance is the focus of these experiments. Load tests are normally not done a performance testing stage. In our proposal, load testing is an experimental technique that allows to reduce technical risks before the actual migration starts.

We have demonstrated the costs of conducting a feasibility study are moderate given the risks of failure during a full migration or during the operation of the software in question.

The experimental part relies currently on the manual setup by an experienced consultant. This could be improved through an automation of the experiments. What could help is automated test case generation for performance and scalability. The test configuration could also consider alternative configurations, such as an automated storage service selection and configuration. Also relevant is the consideration of large-scale application migration. For instance, it is currently unclear if migration costs scale up linearly based on the application size or if normal development cost heuristics can be applied. A further possible direction is to focus on prevalent architectural trends such as cloud-native microservice [24,30,31] or container-based architectures [27]. These architectures can be reflected in the patterns themselves, for instance more clearly identifying cloud-native architectures in terms of a microservices style [21]. This would allow to fine-tune settings in terms of performance [28].

Acknowledgements. This work was partly supported by IC4 (the Irish Centre for Cloud Computing and Commerce), funded by EI and IDA.

References

1. Fowley, F., Elango, D.M., Magar, H., Pahl, C.: The role of experimental exploration in cloud migration for SMEs. In: International Conference on Cloud Computing and Services Science, CLOSER 2017 (2017)
2. Jamshidi, P., Ahmad, A., Pahl, C.: Cloud migration research: a systematic review. IEEE Trans. Cloud Comput. 1(2), 142–157 (2013)

3. Jamshidi, P., Pahl, C., Mendonca, N.C.: Pattern-based multi-cloud architecture migration. Softw. Pract. Experience **47**(9), 1159–1184 (2016)
4. Son, J.: Automated Decision System for Efficient Resource Selection and Allocation in Inter-Clouds. The University of Melbourne (2013)
5. Arshad, S., Ullah, S., Khan, S.A., Awan, M.D. and Khayal, M.: A survey of Cloud computing variable pricing models. In: Evaluation of Novel Approaches to Software Engineering (2015)
6. Jamshidi, P., Pahl, C., Chinenyeze, S., Liu, X.: Cloud migration patterns: a multi-cloud service architecture perspective. In: Toumani, F., Pernici, B., Grigori, D., Benslimane, D., Mendling, J., Ben Hadj-Alouane, N., Blake, B., Perrin, O., Saleh, I., Bhiri, S. (eds.) ICSOC 2014. LNCS, vol. 8954, pp. 6–19. Springer, Cham (2015). https://doi.org/10.1007/978-3-319-22885-3_2
7. Xiong, H., Fowley, F., Pahl, C., Moran, N.: Scalable architectures for platform-as-a-service clouds: performance and cost analysis. In: Avgeriou, P., Zdun, U. (eds.) ECSA 2014. LNCS, vol. 8627, pp. 226–233. Springer, Cham (2014). https://doi.org/10.1007/978-3-319-09970-5_21
8. Pahl, C., Xiong, H.: Migration to PaaS clouds - migration process and architectural concerns. In: MESOCA Symposium (2013)
9. Pahl, C., Xiong, H., Walshe, R.: A comparison of on-premise to cloud migration approaches. In: Lau, K.-K., Lamersdorf, W., Pimentel, E. (eds.) ESOCC 2013. LNCS, vol. 8135, pp. 212–226. Springer, Heidelberg (2013). https://doi.org/10.1007/978-3-642-40651-5_18
10. Al-Roomi, M., Al-Ebrahim, A., Buqrais, S., Ahmad, I.: Cloud computing pricing models: a survey. Int. J. Grid Distr. Comp. **6**(5), 93–106 (2013). https://doi.org/10.14257/ijgdc.2013.6.5.09
11. Wang, W., Zhang, P., Lan, L., Aggarwal, V.: Datacenter net profit optimization with deadline dependent pricing. In: Conference on Information Sciences and Systems (2012)
12. Giardino, C., Bajwa, S.S., Wang, X., Abrahamsson, P.: Key challenges in early-stage software startups. In: Lassenius, C., Dingsøyr, T., Paasivaara, M. (eds.) XP 2015. LNBIP, vol. 212, pp. 52–63. Springer, Cham (2015). https://doi.org/10.1007/978-3-319-18612-2_5
13. Li, H., Zhong, L., Liu, J., Li, B., Xu, K.: Cost-effective partial migration of VoD services to content clouds. In: Cloud Computing (2011)
14. Pahl, C., Jamshidi, P., Weyns, D.: Cloud architecture continuity: change models and change rules for sustainable cloud software architectures. In: Proceedings IEEE 4th International Conference on Cloud Computing, pp. 203–210 (2011). https://doi.org/10.1109/CLOUD.2011.41
15. Koziolek, H.: Sustainability evaluation of software architectures: a systematic review. In: Joint ACM Symposium on Quality of Software Architectures QoSA and Architecting Critical Systems ISARCS, pp. 3–12 (2011)
16. Pahl, C.: Layered ontological modelling for web service-oriented model-driven architecture. In: Hartman, A., Kreische, D. (eds.) ECMDA-FA 2005. LNCS, vol. 3748, pp. 88–102. Springer, Heidelberg (2005). https://doi.org/10.1007/11581741_8
17. Chappell, D.: Cloud Computing White Papers (2016). http://www.davidchappell.com/writing/white_papers.php
18. Gholami, M.F., Daneshgar, F., Rabhi, F.: Cloud migration methodologies: preliminary findings. In: CloudWays Workshop (2016)
19. Pahl, C., Lee, B.: Containers and clusters for edge cloud architectures - a technology review. In: International Conference on Future Internet of Things and Cloud (2015)
20. Affetti, L., Bresciani, G., Guinea, S.: aDock: a cloud infrastructure experimentation environment based on open stack and docker. In: International Conference Cloud Computing (2015)
21. Pahl, C. Jamshidi, P., Zimmermann, O.: Architectural principles for cloud software. ACM Trans. Internet Technol. **18** (2017). Article no. 17

22. Fowley, F., Pahl, C., Zhang, L.: A comparison framework and review of service brokerage solutions for cloud architectures. In: Lomuscio, A.R., Nepal, S., Patrizi, F., Benatallah, B., Brandić, I. (eds.) ICSOC 2013. LNCS, vol. 8377, pp. 137–149. Springer, Cham (2014). https://doi.org/10.1007/978-3-319-06859-6_13

23. Fowley, F., Pahl, C., Jamshidi, P., Fang, D., Liu, X.: A Classification and Comparison Framework for Cloud Service Brokerage Architectures. IEEE Trans. Cloud Comput. **6**(2), 358–371 (2018). https://doi.org/10.1109/TCC.2016.2537333

24. Taibi, D., Lenarduzzi, V., Pahl, C.: Processes, motivations and issues for migrating to microservices architectures: an empirical investigation. IEEE Cloud Comput. **4**(5), 22–32 (2017)

25. Pahl, C., Giesecke, S., Hasselbring, W.: Ontology-based modelling of architectural styles. Inf. Softw. Technol. (IST) **51**(12), 1739–1749 (2009)

26. Jamshidi, P., Pahl, C., Mendonca, N.C.: Pattern-based multi-cloud architecture migration. Softw. Pract. Experience **47**(9), 1159–1184 (2017)

27. Pahl, C., Brogi, A., Soldani, J., Jamshidi, P.: Cloud container technologies: a state-of-the-art review. IEEE Trans. Cloud Comput. (2017). https://ieeexplore.ieee.org/document/7922500/

28. Heinrich, R., van Hoorn, A., Knoche, H., Li, F., Lwakatare, L.E., Pahl, C., Schulte, S., Wettinger, J.: Performance engineering for microservices: research challenges and directions. In: Proceedings of the 8th ACM/SPEC on International Conference on Performance Engineering Companion (2017)

29. Javed, M., Abgaz, Y.M., Pahl, C.: Ontology change management and identification of change patterns. J. Data Semant. **2**(2–3), 119–143 (2013)

30. Pahl, C., Jamshidi, P.: Microservices: a systematic mapping study. In: Proceedings CLOSER Conference, pp. 137–146 (2016)

31. Aderaldo, C.M., Mendonca, N.C., Pahl, C., Jamshidi, P.: Benchmark requirements for microservices architecture research. In: Proceedings of the 1st International Workshop on Establishing the Community-Wide Infrastructure for Architecture-Based Software Engineering. IEEE (2017)

32. ISACA. Calculating Cloud ROI: From the Customer Perspective (2012). https://www.isaca.org/knowledge-center/research/researchdeliverables/pages/calculating-cloud-roi-from-the-customer-perspective.aspx

Dynamic Reconfiguration of Computer Platforms at the Hardware Device Level for High Performance Computing Infrastructure as a Service

Akihiro Misawa[1](✉), Susumu Date[1], Keichi Takahashi[1],
Takashi Yoshikawa[1,2], Masahiko Takahashi[2], Masaki Kan[2],
Yasuhiro Watashiba[1,3], Yoshiyuki Kido[1], Chonho Lee[1],
and Shinji Shimojo[1]

[1] Cybermedia Center, Osaka University,
5-1 Mihogaoka, Ibaraki, Osaka 567-0047, Japan
{misawa.akihiro,
takahashi.keichi}@ais.cmc.osaka-u.ac.jp,
{date,tyoshikawa,kido,leech,
shimojo}@cmc.osaka-u.ac.jp, watashiba@is.naist.jp
[2] System Platform Research Laboratories, NEC,
1753 Shimonumabe, Nakahara, Kawasaki, Kanagawa 211-8666, Japan
m-takahashi@ex.jp.nec.com, kn.mski@gmail.com
[3] Information of Science, Nara Institute of Science and Technology,
8916-5, Takayama, Ikoma, Nara 630-0192, Japan

Abstract. Users' needs and requirements for high performance computing (HPC) has become increasingly diversified. As user needs become increasingly diverse, it becomes increasingly difficult to own high-performance computing platforms themselves and the HPC platform provider are required to provide computing platforms to execute diverse applications. In this paper, we propose a computer architecture for providing HPC infrastructure dynamically and promptly as a cloud computing service in response to users' request for computing platforms. In order to gain flexibility to accommodate various HPC jobs with application specific computing platforms, the proposed system reconfigures a software and hardware platform by utilizing the synergy of Open Grid Scheduler/Grid Engine and OpenStack. The experimental system developed in this research shows the high flexibility of hardware platform reconfiguration and the high performance of Spark's benchmark application. In addition, our simulation evaluation shows that dynamic reconfigurable hardware cluster system can improve hardware resource utility rate, and also eliminating the worst case of resource congestion in the real-world operational record of our university's computer center during the first half of 2016.

Keywords: Cloud computing · Disaggregation · Resource pool
GPU/FPGA accelerator · Hetero computer · Distributed storage
Job scheduling · Resource management · PCI Express · OpenStack
Software defined system

© Springer International Publishing AG, part of Springer Nature 2018
D. Ferguson et al. (Eds.): CLOSER 2017, CCIS 864, pp. 177–199, 2018.
https://doi.org/10.1007/978-3-319-94959-8_10

1   Introduction

High performance computing (HPC) systems have increasingly delivered a wide variety of functions and been difficult for HPC system users to own a variety function of HPC systems for themselves. Besides HPC systems have been used for conventional scientific simulations, they have been used for some applications analyzing a lot of streaming data coming from such as many sensors (IoT/BigData) and getting an Artificial Intelligence (AI) to learn a function from these data. Future HPC systems are required to perform a wider range of functions and provide higher performance than today. However, the HPC systems tend to require application specific configuration, and it is becoming increasingly difficult for users to own such HPC systems. For example, a server of a HPC system for graphics processing unit (GPU) computing must have a high electrical power supply, a large slot space, and a cooling mechanism to install a high-power GPU accelerator. Generally, MPI (Message Passing Interface) is installed in the cluster computing system, and introduction of InfiniBand's high-speed and expensive host bus adapter (HBA) is considered for high performance. As a result, these HPC systems are far more expensive and consume more electrical power than conventional computing systems.

For such the users, advanced cloud services are a way to obtain HPC systems such as a GPU computing platform [1, 2] and a distributed cluster system using an MPI [3]. However, each system configuration of these HPC systems is unique and fixed in that it uses specific devices, network topologies, and protocols (see Fig. 1).

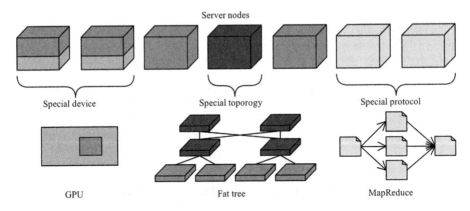

Fig. 1. HPC systems need special configuration.

For this reason, the computing resources in the cloud must be reserved only for prepared usage and cannot be flexibly used for other usages. For example, even if one GPU of server nodes that installed two GPUs is used, the remaining one GPU cannot be used for another application. In order to provide the best performance for each system, it is necessary to configure a cluster system consisting of multiple server nodes with carefully designed networks in advance. For example, a MPI application may require a mesh or fat tree topology, whereas a Hadoop/Spark application may necessitate a topology for map and reduce tasks.

This rigidness causes problems against the users and the cloud service providers. From the users' point of view, they cannot obtain the most appropriate computing resources in a cloud for their applications because computing resources must be chosen from a fixed configuration menu. This menu may not be the optimal configuration for their usage because the menu items may be under or over the predicted specifications. In addition, conflicts of resource requests between users may occur. This happens because the cloud's HPC resources are less than the traditional server of the general cloud service. From the perspective of cloud service providers, providers need to prepare various HPC platforms to meet the diversified needs of HPC users. This shortens the time that each platform is used to execute jobs. As a result, although HPC platforms have high installation and maintenance costs, the utility rate of each HPC platform is low.

Our goal is to flexibly provide HPC resources that meet the needs of diverse users from the cloud. We call the concept High performance computing Infrastructure as a Service (Hi-IaaS). Providing HPC resources as a cloud service encounters the above-mentioned problems caused by the rigidness of the HPC systems. Therefore, a system for Hi-IaaS needs a flexibility to cover diversified HPC applications and different platforms for each application.

In addition to the scientific simulation of the major applications of HPC, Hi-IaaS needs to provide a computer platform that runs recently emerging applications such as IoT/BigData and AI. In other words, Hi-IaaS must provide computing platforms for both high performance data analytics (HPDA) and HPC from a cloud. The key to cover a variety of application specific computing platforms is software and hardware reconfigurability.

In this paper, we present the architecture of Hi-IaaS and describe key technologies mainly focusing on the hardware reconfigurability. The hardware platform reconfigurability of the Hi-IaaS system includes important functions from hardware reconfiguration to job execution according to the user's job and request submission.

2   Concept and Architecture of Hi-IaaS

Hi-IaaS provides a computing platform for various HPDA and HPC applications flexibly according to user's request as a cloud service. This section explains Hi-IaaS concept and architecture.

2.1   Architecture

From the background mentioned in Sect. 1, the requirements for Hi-IaaS system are summarized as follows.

a. Covering diversified HPDA and HPC applications.
b. Providing optimal hardware for each user's job.
c. Minimizing users' job waiting time.

d. Minimizing hardware and software cost.
e. Increasing resource utility rate.

In a conventional cloud computing system, a graphics processing unit (GPU), a field programmable gate array (FPGA) accelerator, a high-speed storage, and an interconnection network are prepared in order to execute various applications with high performance. In addition, from the perspective of the cloud service provider, computing platforms must be provided quickly without conflicts among users. The simplest solution is to prepare sufficient quantity and quality of hardware to execute all diverse applications at high performance. However, this solution does not solve problems of high initial cost and operating costs including electrical power consumption and low resource utility rate. Therefore, this solution does not satisfy requirements (d) and (e).

Hi-IaaS system architecture is shown in Fig. 2. the system has three functional blocks, reconfigurable hardware, reconfigurable software, and a job resource cross-management system. With these functions, the system has the following three features and then these tree features can satisfy the five requirements.

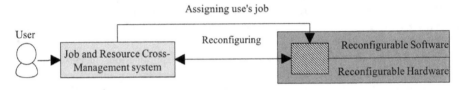

Fig. 2. Proposed system architecture.

a. A computing platform is reconfigured dynamically.
b. Application specific software framework can be used.
c. Hardware resources are shared among different jobs.

In terms of requirement (d), the platform must be implemented on the basis of open standard hardware and software because utilizing open source resources effectively reduces the capital cost and operational cost for a big system like a cloud.

2.2   Reconfigurable Hardware

The solution we present in this paper is based on a highly reconfigurable hardware with a software defined management method. A reconfiguring hardware process can be executed dynamically along with each user's job with the method. Therefore, an optimum number and type of hardware resources can be allocated to each user's job and hardware cost become minimum and resource utility rate increases by sharing them among different user jobs.

Reconfigurable hardware can be reconfigured at the level of each device. This means that each user can specify the number and type of hardware devices required for the job. For example, if the user wishes to execute a deep learning job with GPUs, the user can specify the number of GPUs required for that job. In addition, when the job is completed, the GPUs are detached and assigned to other jobs. This hardware device level reconfigurability is the key to execute various applications at high performance by preparing the optimum hardware for each application.

2.3 Reconfigurable Software

In order to execute applications with high performance, application specific software frameworks should be installed for each user's job before processing. For example, most recently-emerged high performance applications such as high performance data analytics are executed on a distributed system by using software framework such as Hadoop [4] and Spark [5]. These software frameworks provide users with distributed data storage and scaling out methods and can increase the throughput of HPDA applications. On the other hand, if a user's job utilizes GPUs or FPGA accelerators in a system with heterogeneous processing units, the system needs a mechanism to allocate a set of processors and accelerators to execute the user's job from multiple central processing units (CPUs). Therefore, the system needs to install a software framework for heterogeneous processing.

The proposed system needs to provide optimum computing resources by installing the required software framework in cooperation with reconfigurable hardware. Reconfigurable software platform is important and essential for the reconfigurable hardware because the number of processors, accelerators and storages devices might change after the reconfiguration sequence. According to a user's job and reconfiguring hardware sequence, reconfigurable software platform uninstalls and installs application specific software frameworks in the hardware platform provided to the user.

2.4 Job and Resource Cross-Management

In order for the proposed system to realize reduction of job waiting time and improvement of resource utilization rate, it is necessary to accept requests from users and cooperate with reconfigurable computer platforms according to the requests. In other words, the proposed system avoids conflicts of resource requests among users, which occurred in a system with a predefined configuration, by dynamically reconfiguring the computer platform according to the user's request. It is possible to eliminate waiting time of jobs and resources not used due to the conflict.

For this purpose, we introduce the job and resource cross-management system (JRMS) in the proposed system. the JRMS has two functions of allocating computer resources to jobs and working with reconfigurable computer platforms. When a user's job is submitted, the JRMS's job scheduler enqueues the job and makes a list of necessary hardware and software frameworks as a resource recipe. Then the JRMS asks for reconfigurable hardware and software platform to configure hardware and software for the job in accordance with the resource recipe. After that, the scheduler gives the dynamically configured computer platform to the job.

3 Dynamic Reconfigurable Hardware

The Hi-IaaS system proposed in Sect. 2 provides a computer platform reconfigured in response to user's request. In terms of hardware platform, even after system introduction, the proposed system must be able to change the hardware configuration such as the number of servers, network connection, data storage and so on. In addition, hardware devices (GPU accelerator, solid state drive (SSD) storage, InfiniBand HBA, etc.) that make up each platform need to be easily connected and disconnected by resource management software. We realize such dynamic hardware reconfiguration with the cooperative operation of the function enabling reconfiguration at device level and the function of accepting user's job and resource request.

3.1 Software Defined Reconfigurable Hardware Platform

The first key component is a software defined reconfigurable hardware platform. One way to realize a reconfigurable hardware platform is a resource pool system (or dis-aggregated computer system) [6–8]. It has pools of hardware devices such as a set of CPU and memory (compute) pool, a GPU pool, FPGA accelerator pool, a storage pool, and a network interface pool. Interconnect technology is one of the most important in such disaggregated computer systems. In order to attach hardware devices such as accelerators, storages, and network interfaces at the same point in the computer architecture, peripheral component interconnect express (PCI Express) is known as the most common open standard of an I/O interface today.

However, PCI Express is a bus technology with limited link distance and number of connected devices. Due to the scalability performance of PCI Express switch chips, most PCI Express bus technologies limit the number of devices that can be connected to less than 10. The link distance is also limited by the conventional basic input/output system (BIOS). Cascading PCI Express switches creates a complex and deep PCI bridge forest, where traditional BIOS cannot complete all detection and enumeration processes for buses and endpoint devices. In addition, PCI Express has a single root tree topology implemented by switch chips so that only one computing can exist in a PCI Express based fabric network.

As a technique to reduce these limitations of PCI Express, Express Ether (ExpEther) [9] is available. ExpEther is a PCI Express switch over the Ethernet as shown in Fig. 3, which enables creation of multiple single-hop PCI Express switches on the Ethernet network. ExpEther has advantages as an interconnect network of highly reconfigurable disaggregated computer hardware [10]. The distributed PCI Express switch architecture of ExpEther [9] creates multiple single-hop PCI Express trees, even though the Ethernet network consists of multiple switches. Each ExpEther device has a ExpEther chip with group ID and PCI Express logical connections are controlled by setting the same group ID. That is, ExpEther chips with the same group ID connected through the Ethernet are logically equivalent to a PCI Express switch. With this architecture, the required number of computes and devices can be connected to a single Ethernet network without distance limitations, then multiple single-hop PCI Express trees can be created on that network. In addition, ExpEther's internal Ethernet network is transparent to OS and software. From the OS and software, all devices are recognized

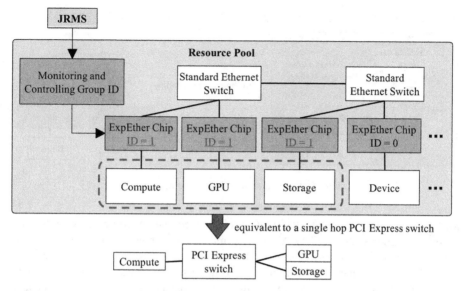

Fig. 3. PCI Express over Ethernet.

as local devices as if they were in the local chassis. Therefore, by controlling the group ID with a management software, software defined reconfiguration of hardware platforms becomes possible. Note that all ExpEther functions are implemented on a hardware chip, and the chip latency is 1 μs or less. Therefore, hardware devices have performance equivalent to that installed in the local slot in the computer's chassis.

In consideration of these features, we adopt ExpEther as an interconnection fabric of reconfigurable computer hardware platforms. The simplest implementation of a resource pool is using a pair of an ExpEther HBA card and an IO Expansion box connected directly or via an Ethernet switch. The IO Expansion box contains multiple PCI Express slots with an ExpEther chip on the motherboard. By using ExpEther when creating a resource pool, we can use conventional servers as a compute, and use a PCI Express device without modification. we also can use software including OS and device driver without modification. In addition, ExpEther chips have congestion control and a retry mechanism. Therefore, a standard Ethernet switch that does not support the converged Ethernet specification can be used.

In order to flexibly provide hardware platform in accordance with users' requests by using ExpEther, all the devices and PCI Express device connections in a resource pool need to be remotely controlled (software defined). As mentioned above, PCI Express devices can be attached and detached logically by controlling the group ID of ExpEther chips. Controlling the group ID is realized by sending a control packet to an ExpEther chip in ExpEther technology. In addition, if the PCI Express device does not support the PCI-compliant hot-plug process, the (re)boot process is necessary for computes to recognize these PCI Express devices.

We have developed the Resource Manager based on the OpenStack framework [11] as shown Fig. 4. The resource manager is a software which monitors and controls all

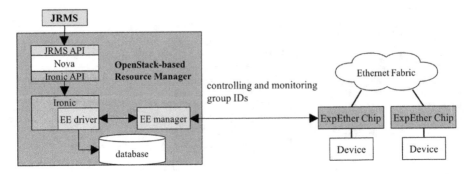

Fig. 4. OpenStack-based resource manager.

the computes, devices and PCI Express level connections in the resource pool. One version of OpenStack (MITAKA) has no management methods for disaggregated computers and devices. The Openstack framework mainly controls virtual machines, but it also has the function of bare metal (physical) server control (Ironic). The Ironic has the advantage of controlling (re)booting of bare metal server required to attach and detach PCI Express devices. Therefore, we modified Ironic's functionality to support ExpEther's device level management.

The monitor and controller functions of the ExpEther system are implemented as EE managers. The EE manager is a simple module that monitors and sends ExpEther's control packets. The monitored information is recorded in the database through Ironic. When reconfiguring the system, the EE manager sends control packets containing the new group ID to the ExpEther chips of the specified computes and devices via Ethernet. ExpEther-specific management method is implemented as Ironic's EE driver. By separating management methods, modified Ironic can also accommodate other distributed computer systems using interconnect fabrics other than ExpEther.

The resource manager has a control application program interface (API) for Job Resource cross-Management System (JRMS). The resource manager controls the group IDs of computes and devices that need to be connected according to the hardware reconfiguration specified in the JRMS described below. In addition, the resource manager has a graphical user interface (GUI) and a command line interface (CLI) for direct user control. The Horizon GUI has been extended to include PCI Express device level monitors and their connection control interface. Other functions (Heat: Orchestration, Ceilometer: Telemetry, Nova: Scheduler, Keystone: Authentication etc.) necessary for managing bare metal servers are implemented together without changing from the original OpenStack framework.

3.2   Job and Resource Cross-Management System

The second key component is job and resource cross-management system (JRMS). The JRMS realizes that application specific hardware platforms are dynamically allocated to users' job in accordance with users' requests. The JRMS has two major function blocks; accepting users' jobs with their requests about application specific hardware platforms, allocating reconfigured resources to users' jobs. As shown in Fig. 5, one function block is a job management system (JMS) based on Open Grid Scheduler [12]. JMS receives users' jobs and requests, then the jobs are scheduled and the requests are sent to another functional block. Another functional block is a policy based resource assignment controller (Brain). The Brain has an interface between the Resource Manager. The flow of instructions for accepting a request for each user and allocating the reconfigured hardware platform to a job for each user is as follows:

a. User submits a job with resource request.
b. JMS makes a list of resources.
c. Brain asks the resource manager to configure computing platform.
d. Resource manager controls the group IDs and (re)boot processes.
e. JMS executes the job on reconfigured computing platform.

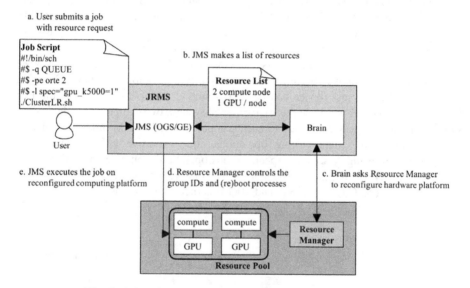

Fig. 5. Job and Resource Cross Management System (JRMS).

The JMS receives a user's job with resource requests. The requests are described in a job script as a standard style of Open Grid Engine's job script (It is a kind of a special comment sentence starting with "#$"). Then, the JMS makes a resource recipe used for reconfiguration. The number of server nodes and devices the user requests are described in a resource recipe. In addition, the JMS sends it to the Brain and waits for completion of reconfiguration.

Brain receives the resource recipe from JMS and current hardware resource utilization from the resource manager. If a resource pool has sufficient resources to execute the user's job, Brain asks for the resource manager to reconfigure hardware platform in accordance with the resource recipe. After the reconfiguration, the resource manager notifies the Brain of the resource status. Then Brain tells the JMS the address of reconfigured resources.

4   Experimental System

We have built an experimental system and confirmed the feasibility of our proposed system architecture. In this experiment, we confirmed whether the experiment system could execute the job after reconfiguring the computer platform according to user's resource requirements. In addition, we confirmed whether using GPU via ExpEther does not prevent acceleration of job execution by using one Spark benchmark job.

4.1   Implementation

The experiment system consists of a resource pool, a resource manager, and a job and resource cross-management system as shown in Fig. 6. The resource pool has two computes, two GPUs and one non-volatile memory express (NVMe) storage. These computes are commercially available compact workstations which attached an ExpEther chip (NEC Express 5800 52Xa: CPU: E3-1200v3, Memory: DDR3-1600 SDRAM). These I/O devices (two GPUs and one NVMe storage) are connected to PCI Express slot of ExpEther I/O expansion box. These GPUs are commercially available (NVIDIA K-5000) and the NVMe storage card is a laboratory-level prototype. It supports NVMe 1.1 specification including single-root input/output virtualization (SR-IOV). By using ExpEther, a PCI Express device can be shared among multiple computes at the PCI Express level. In other words, in this experimental system, two computes use the NVMe storage card as if it was connected to each compute's local slot. In order to avoid the conflict between two data writing operations, the "exclusive write" operation is implemented by using NVMe 1.1 specifications operation "compare and write". Two computes, two GPUs and the NVMe storage are connected by ExpEther via a standard Ethernet switch (NEC QX-S5828T) and 10G-Ethernet with two paths.

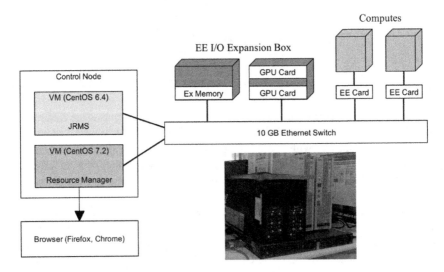

Fig. 6. Experimental system.

The resource manager and JRMS are installed on separate virtual machines (VMs) on the same machine using VirtualBox. The operating system (OS) for the resource manager is CentOS 7.2, and the JRMS is CentOS 6.4. The version of the OpenStack is Kilo. The resource manager is connected to the ExpEther network (Ethernet), and JRMS is connected to each compute via an Internet protocol (IP) network.

In this implementation, the software platform including the OS installed on each compute is static. Apache Spark, storage software and computational accelerator utilization management software are pre-installed on each compute. It is possible to install these software on each compute after hardware platform reconfiguration by using Ironic's function. Reconfiguration of the software platform is out of the scope of this paper and it is a topic to be addressed in the future.

4.2 Operation

We Confirmed Whether the Experiment System Could Execute the Job after Reconfiguring the Computer Platform According to User's Resource Requirements. In This Experimental System, Two Computes, Two Gpus and an Nvme Storage Card Are in the Resource Pool. The Software Platforms on Each Compute Node Are Static as Mentioned in Sect. 4.1.

We Set an Experimental Operation Scenario as Shown in Fig. 7. In This Scenario, the Group Ids of Expether Are Assigned for Each Device in Resource Pool in an Example Scenario. The Group Ids Are Assigned as #1 and #2 for Each Compute Node in Advance. These Computes Share an External Nvme Storage Card in the Pool by using the Software Storage Engine We Have Developed. The Group Ids of Other Devices (Two Gpus) in the Resource Pool Are Assigned as #0 Which Mean That These Devices Are Logically Unconnected to Any Compute. The Flow of Operation Is as Follows:

a. JMS makes a resource recipe (two computes, a GPU attached to each node).
b. Brain tells the resource manager to attach a GPU to each node.
c. Resource Manager sets two GPUs' group IDs to #1 and #2.
d. Resource Manager monitors configuration status of the resource pool.
e. Brain get an information of completion of the reconfiguration.

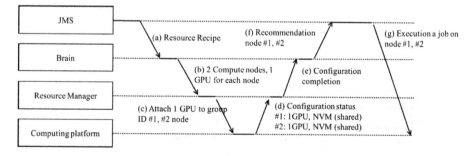

Fig. 7. Sequence of reconfiguration and job execution.

f. Brain tells JMS to assign the job to compute #1 and #2.

g. JMS executes the job on compute #1 and #2.

First, a job request is submitted to the JRMS. It contains a user's requirements for the computing platform. In this scenario, the user requests two computes both installed with one GPU (K-5000). Both computes share the same external NVMe storage regarded as a local storage from the software view of each compute.

The JRMS puts the job into the queue. Then JRMS makes a list of the resources that can be used to satisfy the request described in the job script. Brain always gathers the information of the resource pool from the Resource Manager and puts it in the database. When Brain receives the resource list, Brain determines the devices (GPU in this scenario) for each compute by referring to the database.

Then the Resource Manager indicates to attach a GPU to each compute node. In order to manage the PCI Express connection, the group ID of each ExpEther chip connected to the compute and IO device is recorded in the device list. In this scenario, the group IDs of each GPU are assigned #1 and #2. Then the GPUs are attached to each compute node and each OS of compute node recognize attached GPU. We set the waiting time for completion of the hot-plug process in OS to 20 s. This waiting time is longer than the time for the hot-plug process, but the time for the hot-plug process differs depending on the computing platform environment. It should be shortened by investigating the hot-plug process in future work.

In the end, the Brain tells the JRMS to executed the job on a two-node cluster (compute #1 and #2) in which both nodes are installed with a GPU in accordance with the user's request.

The hot-plug process of the GPUs can be seen by the horizon GUI of OpenStack framework as shown in Fig. 8. The GUI is modified to show the PCI Express tree just like "lspci –t" command in LINUX. Figure 8 shows the server-view that displays the PCI Express connections from a compute node to endpoint devices.

The device tree before the job execution is shown in the left part of Fig. 8. PCI Express trees of two computes with group IDs of #1 and #2 are shown here. The red mark of the NVMe storage cards indicates that the device shared among other computes. No GPU was seen in either PCI Express tree because both are in the resource pool with a group ID set as #0.

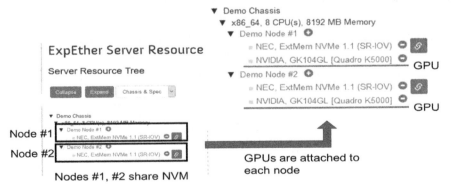

Fig. 8. Hot plug process on OpenStack management window (cited from [17]).

When the job is submitted with a request for using GPUs, the Resource Manager connects them to each compute by setting group IDs of each GPU as #1 and #2. After the reconfiguration, GPUs are seen in both PCI Express trees as shown in the right part of Fig. 8. Then, the job is executed on compute node #1 and #2. Through this experimental scenario, we found that our proposed system architecture can execute the expected operation dynamically reconfiguring a computer hardware platform before job execution.

4.3   Performance

We have used the experiment setup described in the previous section to verify that the system can function as an HPC system. The main performance concerns are the interconnect latency to form a resource pool, ExpEther chip, cable, and switch latency.

It is about 700 ns for the ExpEther chip and 5 ns/m for the cable. Switch single hop is about 500 ns. This means a roundtrip takes about 3 µs.

The performance degradation due to this latency varies widely depending on the application. The group of Amano evaluated in detail by examining the performance scale up according to the number of GPUs [13, 14]. In this experiment, we investigated whether the logarithmic regression, Spark benchmark software, is accelerated by connected GPUs from the resource pool. Figure 9 shows the time to run a spark benchmark job with different configurations. In this verification, we found that degradation of I/O performance by ExpEther does not prevent accelerated by GPU.

It should be noted that the computer used in this experiment was too compact to install the GPU internally so it was not possible to compare the performance with the system where the GPU was directly installed in the computer. Therefore, we cannot investigate to what degree ExpEther's latency worsens performance compared to HPC system and should investigate in the future. However, this research focuses on the use of HPC in the cloud, and most cloud users understand that the computer resources in

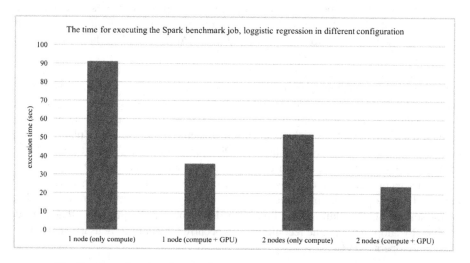

Fig. 9. Execution time for one Spark benchmark in different configuration.

the cloud are executed worse than specially designed HPC systems. Therefore, we conclude that GPU computing can be provided by using this reconfigurable mechanism, even for traditional 1-U machines deployed in the cloud that cannot connect GPUs. This increases the probability of obtaining a computer platform matching the user's request from the cloud.

4.4   Reconfiguring Time

Another performance impact to consider is the time for reconfiguring computer platforms. If a reboot process is required during a reconfiguration process, the reconfiguration lasts as long as the OS restarts. Currently, there is no technology to shorten the startup time of OS that takes more than tens of seconds, it is much longer than any other process of reconfiguration. Rebooting the OS occurs, for example, when connecting a device that cannot be hot-plugged, adding special drivers for devices that the OS does not support, allocating memory, etc.

On the other hand, if it is not necessary to restart the OS, changing the PCI Express setting with ExpEther only takes a few μsec to send a control packet to change the group ID of the ExpEther chip to the target device. However, before using a device which support hot-plug process in software, a hot plug handler that manage the attach and detach process in the OS needs to recognize the device. Depending on the computing device and status, it may take about 10 s to recognize the device. Therefore, we set the hardware reconfiguration waiting time to 20 s in this experimental setup. Currently this waiting time dominates the reconfiguration time in non-reboot case. In the future, it is necessary to investigate to accurately evaluate the hot-plug processing time and speed up hardware reconfiguration with minimal hot-plug processing time.

5   Evaluation in Cloud Usecase

Our organization, the Cybermedia Center, provides computer resources to researchers and students of Osaka University as well as other universities. It has three major computing systems; a vector super computer (SXAce), a scalar cluster computer (HCC), and a scalar cluster computer with GPU (VCC) [15].

VCC consists of 65 servers with IO extensions by using ExpEther. However, in the current operation, the configuration of the computer platform is not dynamically changed. A reconfiguration is done semi-annually by investigating the user's plans on the utilization of the computing platform. For example, the computer platform configuration for the next six months is determined according to the user's plan, such as using the four computing nodes with two GPUs for 200 h, using 16 nodes with PCI-SSD for 100 h. That is, the system configuration has been fixed for half a year.

In this section, we evaluate how resource utilization and job waiting time can be improved by adopting the proposed dynamic reconfiguration by using resource allocating simulation. In addition, we investigated whether or not problems that can be resolved by adopting dynamic reconfiguration occurred, by collecting usage status data of actually operated VCC.

5.1   Resource Utilization Simulation

We have been evaluating how resource utilization and job waiting time are improved by proposed dynamic reconfiguration by simulating resource allocation to jobs. We have developed a resource allocation simulator for jobs simulating a dynamically reconfigurable cluster based on the job scheduling simulator ALEA [16].

ALEA can deal with common problems of job scheduling in clusters and grids, like heterogeneity of jobs and resources and dynamic runtime changes, and provide a handful of features including a large set of various scheduling algorithms, several standard workload parsers, and a set of typical fairness-related job ordering policies.

Determining the best job and resource scheduling algorithm for a dynamically reconfigurable computer system is too complicated to address in this paper. This is because the system is very flexible and the simulation conditions to consider are very diverse. Therefore, we fixed some conditions to simplify the simulation and estimated the dependency of utility rate on hardware reconfiguration and job workload.

Firstly, we simulated five types of GPU cluster system to investigate the difference how our proposed system improves GPU utility rate [17]. We have investigated GPU utility rate in two cases about cluster configuration; dynamic reconfigurable hardware and static. The five static cluster configurations in Table 1 and simulation conditions are as follows:

a. All GPU cluster systems are composed of 64 GPUs and 64 compute nodes.
b. Job scheduling algorithm is FIFO.
c. Reconfiguration is applied only for the number of nodes and GPUs.
d. All job execution time is fixed and same.
e. A node can accept only a single job at a time.
f. Number of nodes each job request is fixed to 8 or 16.
g. Number of GPUs on each compute node each job request is fixed to 0 or 1.

Table 1. Cluster system configuration (cited from [17]).

Cluster set	Number of GPU/node set		
#1	1/64	-	-
#2	2/8	1/48	0/8
#3	2/16	1/32	0/16
#4	4/8	2/16	0/40
#5	4/10	2/12	0/42

Average GPU utility rate of all the static cluster configuration is plotted in Fig. 10. In addition, average GPU utility rate of hardware reconfigurable cluster is also plotted in the figure as a dotted line because it is independent from the static cluster configuration. The numbers of GPUs for each compute node jobs requests are well balanced to execute jobs in cluster sets #1 to #3. However, because the total number of GPUs is limited to 64, #4 and #5 that include four-GPU machines, the number of nodes without

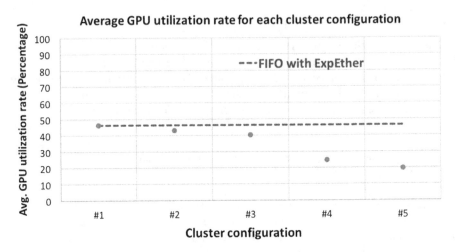

Fig. 10. Utility rate depending on cluster configuration (cited from [17]).

GPUs becomes dominant. Thus, more jobs that request GPUs have to wait for GPU nodes to be released and then average GPU utility rate become low.

The GPU utility rate of cluster set #5 is shown in Fig. 11 as an example. When a job cannot be assigned on its requested computer resources in terms of the number of nodes or GPUs, the job stays in a queue waiting for finished other jobs to release the resources. This happens even if some resources are available. For example, if the job requests four-GPU nodes, it cannot be executed even if two-GPU nodes are available. Then the GPUs on the two-GPU nodes are left unused until a job with two-GPU nodes is submitted. By using a reconfigurable hardware platform, unused GPUs are returned into the resource pool, then four-GPU nodes are configured by using them, and thus, the four-GPU job can be executed without waiting time. This results in decreasing the

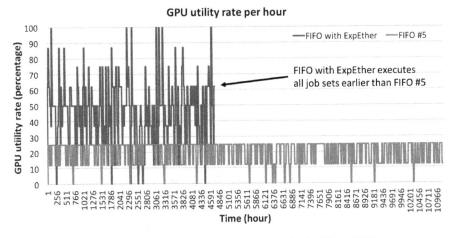

Fig. 11. Utility rate of GPU of cluster set #5 (cited from [17]).

time for executing all jobs by about 42% that of the rigid system, in addition to increasing the average GPU utility rate from 20% to 47% in the example use case shown in Fig. 11.

Secondly, we simulated the GPU cluster system which models VCC and the situation in which number of GPUs each job request is diversified to investigate how our proposed system improves GPU utility rate. The static cluster configuration is described in Table 2 and simulation conditions are as follows:

a. Job scheduling algorithm is FIFO.
b. Reconfiguration is applied only for the number of nodes and GPUs.
c. All job execution time is fixed and same.
d. A node can accept only a single job at a time.
e. Number of GPUs on each compute node each job request is randomly chosen from 0 to 4.

Table 2. Cluster configurations of VCC in 2016 (cited from [17]).

Node number #	GPUs per node
#0 to #4	4
#5 to #10	3
#11 to #21	2
#22 to #64	0

Generally, static cluster configuration is announced to users in advance and users of the cluster request computing resources within the limits of static configuration. Thus, we assumed that a job request compute nodes and GPUs as executable on a cluster in this simulation. For example, VCC users must request four-GPU machines less than five. If a VCC user submit a job which request six four-GPU machines, the user's job dose not be executed on VCC because of lack of four-GPU machine. Therefore, in this hypothesis, the number of compute nodes and the number of GPUs per node are limited by static cluster configuration. When the number of compute nodes (GPUs per node) is randomly chosen within the limits of static configuration, the number of GPUs per node (compute nodes) has biased distribution. In this simulation, we focus on diversified number of GPUs a job request. Therefore, we randomly changed the number of GPUs per node a job request in range of zero to four and histograms about requested the number of compute nodes and GPUs per node are shown in Fig. 12.

The average GPU utility rate and the time for executing all jobs of the static cluster configuration and dynamic reconfigurable hardware are shown in Fig. 13. Dynamic reconfigurable hardware cluster decreases 50% the time for executing all jobs and improves from 39% to 78% the average GPU utility rate. Our proposed system can improve average GPU utility rate in the situation in which the number of GPUs per node requested is diversified.

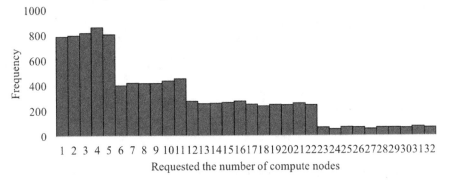

Fig. 12. Histograms of requested the number of GPUs per node and compute nodes.

5.2 Job Waiting Time Estimation with Real Operation

In order to investigate whether Hi-IaaS can increase resource utility, we investigated actual usage record of VCC system. Table 2 shows the cluster configuration in the first half of 2016. In this static configuration, some users' jobs were congested.

Figure 14 shows the worst case of 2Q–3Q in 2016. For simplicity of explanation, only nodes #19–#23 are shown in this figure. On September 28, a blue job was executed on nodes #22 and #23. Then at 15:00, a yellow job was enqueued. Although the yellow job did not request any GPUs, because computer nodes without GPU are occupied by the blue job (#22, #23), the yellow job was executed on the GPU machine (#19, #20, #21). At 20:00, a purple job that requested two nodes with a GPU was enqueued. However, since all the GPU machines (#19, #20, #21) were occupied at that time, the purple job had to wait for resources to be released. At 20:00 on September 29th, the yellow job was completed. After that, a purple GPU job was executed. Purple job waiting time was 25.1 h.

In this case, when a purple job with GPU request was enqueued, the compute nodes were free (#22, #23). At the same time, GPUs of #19 to #21 were not used. Therefore, if the system can be dynamically reconfigured by returning the unused GPUs of the #

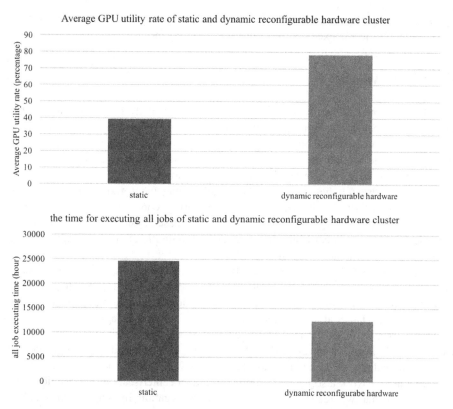

Fig. 13. Average GPU utility rate and all job execution time of static and dynamic reconfigurable hardware configuration.

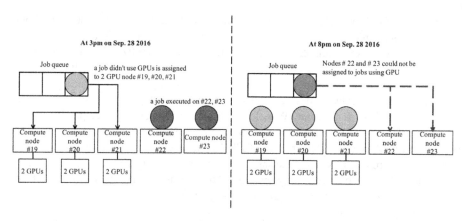

Fig. 14. Stacked jobs can be executed by using this platform.

19 to #21 to the resource pool and connecting it flexibly to the computing nodes (#22, #23), the purple job is executed without long waiting time.

6   Related Works

Our research aims to realize disaggregated computing platform which can flexibly provide resources to more users at the hardware device level by using ExpEther. Although previous research on distributed computing using ExpEther [10, 18] has been focused on scale up and device sharing in multiple servers, this research focuses on providing a reconfigurable HPC platform from the cloud.

A lot of research has done on the cloud management frameworks including OpenStack [19, 20] which can realize reconfiguring computing platforms. These research focus on reconfiguration of virtual machine based system. On the other hand, our research focuses on hardware device level reconfiguration aiming at improving the performance of computer platform provided to users.

Interest in Intel Rack Scale Architecture [6] and OpenComputeProject [7] have been growing as a research aimed at realizing a disaggregated computing system. However, these works mainly focus on the distribution of computing resources within the server rack. Han et al. considered the computing resource disaggregation of a data center focusing mainly on performance degradation of memory disaggregation caused by the interconnection network [8]. Katrinis et al. also published a research plan for cloud data center scale disaggregation [21] but it was a vision level at the time of publication. Our work also has been aiming at a data center scale disaggregation. The difference is that we realized the resource disaggregation by pure open standard interface PCI Express and Ethernet. In terms of the performance consideration of disaggregated computing system with ExpEther, Amano's team has investigated performance in detail and found the performance scalability according to the number of GPUs [13, 14].

In terms of computing resource allocation scheduling, G. Lee et al. studied about computing jobs which is executed in a hetero computing platform in a cloud [22]. In this study, as with the current cloud, the allocated resources are fixed instances selected from the menu. Considering the reconfiguration of the computer platform at the hardware device level realized by our research, there is a possibility of more flexible job scheduling by hardware device level scheduling algorithm.

In terms of HPC as a service, Wheeler et al. made a framework to dispatch a user's job over different HPC system including BlueGene [23]. This framework can provide HPC resource to more users than current HPC system without long waiting time. The purpose of this research is partly the same as the purpose of our research. This research takes the approach of connecting external HPC systems and providing a lot of resources. Our research takes an approach to provide resources to many people by using resources efficiently.

7   Conclusions

We introduced the concept of High performance computing Infrastructure as a Service (Hi-IaaS) and proposed a system architecture which can meet Hi-IaaS's requirements. The Hi-IaaS system has three key functional blocks; reconfigurable hardware, reconfigurable software, and job and resource cross-management system (JRMS). Reconfigurable hardware can flexibly be reconfigured in device level in accordance with a user's request. Reconfigurable software can make a middleware and software platform in accordance with user's requests after reconfiguration of hardware platform. Reconfigurable software provides application specific software sets to conventional high performance computing application and recently-emerged applications such as high performance data analysis. JRMS realize dynamic allocation optimal computing resources to users' job. JRMS accepts users' job and users' computing resource requests then allocates optimal computing resource in cooperation with reconfigurable hardware and software platform.

In this paper, we focused on the reconfigurable hardware of Hi-IaaS. The reconfigurable hardware can be realized by adopting the technology of peripheral component interconnect express (PCI Express) over Ethernet. By attaching and detaching computes and devices in the resource pool, the reconfigurable hardware can be reconfigured at the PCI Express device level. We have developed a small experimental implementation of the proposed system with two computes, two graphics processing units (GPUs), and a shared non-volatile memory express standard storage card. By running one Spark benchmark application on the experimental system, we confirmed whether the proposed system could perform and whether using GPU via ExpEther does not prevent acceleration of job execution.

In addition, the simulation results showed the effectiveness of reconfigurable platform for the resource utility rate increased from 39% to 78% and job execution time reduced by 50% in the system which models our university's cloud system. Finally, we found our system can eliminate the 25-h waiting time recorded as the worst case in the half-year real job operational record of our university's computing center.

8   Future Work

We have investigated the effectiveness of our proposed system in terms of fixed conditions about job workloads and system configurations. Next, in order to reveal the effectiveness of the system, we will simulate the time for hardware reconfiguration process and think about distribution of job execution time. Especially, the time for hardware reconfiguration process causes decreasing resource utility rate.

In addition, we will investigate suitable algorithms for the reconfiguration that fit these job workloads and system configuration variations. We will also try to investigate the dynamic reconfiguration process and performance in a real-world big system by using a VCC system when it can be utilized for experimental usage that does not conflict with ordinary HPC services.

References

1. Linux Accelerated Computing Instances of Amazon Web Service. http://docs.aws.amazon.com/AWSEC2/latest/UserGuide/accelerated-computing-instances.html. Accessed 31 Aug 2017
2. Azure GPU Instance. https://azure.microsoft.com/en-us/blog/azure-n-series-preview-availability/. Accessed 31 Aug 2017
3. A Set of Scripts to Create Simplest MPI Cluster on SoftLayer. https://github.com/irifed/softlayer-mpicluster. Accessed 31 Aug 2017
4. Apache Hadoop Homepage. http://hadoop.apache.org/. Accessed 31 Aug 2017
5. Apche Spark Homepage. http://spark.apache.org/. Accessed 31 Aug 2017
6. Intel Rack Scale Architecture Overview. http://goo.gl/ATtRR5. Accessed 31 Aug 2017
7. Open Compute Project. http://www.opencompute.org/. Accessed 31 Aug 2017
8. Han, S., Egi, N., Panda, A., et al.: Network support for resource disaggregation in next-generation datacenters. In: 12th International Proceedings on ACM Workshop on Hot Topics in Networks (HotNets), pp. 10:1–10:7. ACM, New York (2013)
9. Suzuki, J., Hidaka, Y., Higuchi, J., et al.: Expressether - Ethernet-based virtualization technology for reconfigurable hardware platform. In: 14th International Proceedings on IEEE Symposium on High-Performance Interconnects, Stanford, CA, USA, pp. 45–51. IEEE (2006)
10. Yoshikawa, T., Suzuki, J., Hidaka, Y., et al.: Bridge chip composing a PCIe switch over Ethernet to make a seamless disaggregated computer in data-center scale. In: 26th International Proceedings on IEEE Hot Chips 26 Symposium (HC26), Cupertino, CA, USA, p. 1. IEEE (2014)
11. OpenStack framework Homepage. https://www.openstack.org/software/. Accessed 31 Aug 2017
12. Open Grid Scheduler Homepage. http://gridscheduler.sourceforge.net/. Accessed 31 Aug 2017
13. Nomura, S., Mitsuishi, T., Suzuki, J., et al.: Performance analysis of the multi-GPU system with ExpEther. In: ACM SIGARCH Computer Architecture News - HEART 2014, vol. 42, issue 4, pp. 9–14. ACM, New York (2014)
14. Mitsuishi, T., Suzuki, J., Hayashi, Y., et al.: Breadth first search on cost-efficient multi-GPU systems. In: ACM SIGARCH Computer Architecture News - HEART 2015, vol. 43, issue 4, pp. 58–63. ACM, New York (2015)
15. Cybermedia Center. http://www.hpc.cmc.osaka-u.ac.jp/en/. Accessed 31 Aug 2017
16. Klusáček, D., Rudová, H.: Alea 2 - job scheduling simulator. In: 3rd Proceedings on ICST Conference on Simulation Tools and Techniques, Brussels, Belgium, Belgium, pp. 61:1–61:10. ICST (2010)
17. Misawa, A., Date, S., Takahashi, K., et al.: Highly reconfigurable computing platform for high performance computing infrastructure as a service: Hi-IaaS. In 7th International Proceedings on Cloud Computing and Services Science (CLOSER 2017), Setúbal, Portugal, pp. 135–146. Science and Technology Publications, Lda (SciTePress) (2017)
18. Suzuki, J., Hidaka, Y., Higuchi, J., et al.: Disaggregation and sharing of I/O devices in cloud data centers. IEEE Trans. Comput. 65(10), 3013–3026 (2016)
19. Sefraoui, O., Aissaoui, M., Ekeuldj, M.: Dynamic reconfigurable component for cloud computing resources. Int. J. Comput. Appl. 88(7), 1–5 (2014)
20. Xu, F., Liu, F., Jin, H., et al.: Managing performance overhead of virtual machines in cloud computing: a survey, state of the art, and future directions. Proc. IEEE 102(1), 11–31 (2014)

21. Katrinis, K., Syrivelis, D., Pnevmatikatos, D., et al.: Rack-scale disaggregated cloud data centers: the dReDBox project vision. In: 20th International Proceedings on Design, Automation and Test in Europe Conference and Exhibition (DATE), Cupertino, CA, USA, pp. 690–695. IEEE (2016)

22. Lee, G., Chun, B., Katz, R.H.: Heterogeneity-aware resource allocation and scheduling in the cloud. In: 3rd International Proceedings on USENIX conference on Hot topics in cloud computing (HotCloud 2011), p. 4. USENIX Association, Berkley (2011)

23. Wheeler, M.F., Pencheva, G., Tavakoli, R., et al.: Enabling high-performance computing as a service. Computer **45**, 72–80 (2012)

Controlling Cloud-Based Systems for Elasticity Test Reproduction

Michel Albonico[1]([✉]), Jean-Marie Mottu[2], Gerson Sunyé[2],
and Frederico Alvares[3]

[1] Federal University of Technology - Paraná, Francisco Beltrão, Brazil
`michelalbonico@utfpr.edu.br`
[2] Inria/IMT-Atlantique/LS2N, AtlanModels, Nantes, France
`{jean-marie.mottu,gerson.sunye}@inria.fr`
[3] Inria/IMT-Atlantique/LS2N, Ascola Teams, Nantes, France
`frederico.alvares@inria.fr`

Abstract. Systems deployed on elastic infrastructures deal with
resource variations by adapting themselves, which is error-prone. Therefore, we must test Cloud-Based Systems (CBS) throughout elasticity.
Such tests may be re-executed regularly to diagnose and fix CBS bugs,
which requires to design tests to execute in a deterministic manner.
In this paper, we identify three main challenges that testers face when
reproducing elasticity tests: to control the elasticity behaviour, to select
specific resources to be deallocated, and to coordinate events parallel
to elasticity. Since elasticity tests can last long, we consider the test
execution time as a secondary challenge. In this paper, we propose an
approach that meets such challenges. Experimental results show that the
proposed approach successfully reproduces elasticity-related bugs that
face the listed challenges while reducing the execution time.

Keywords: Cloud computing · Elasticity · Elasticity testing
Test reproduction · Speediness

1 Introduction

Elasticity is one of the main reasons that make cloud computing an emerging
trend. It allows to allocate or deallocate system resources according to demand
[1,2]. Therefore, *Cloud-Based Systems* (CBS) must adapt themselves according
to resource variations. These adaptations are not trivial and may affect the CBS
execution. According to Bersani et al. [2]:

> "Scaling resources may incur in non-trivial operations inside the system.
> Component synchronization, registration, and data migration and data
> replication are just the most widely known examples[...], which may
> degrade system QoS."

© Springer International Publishing AG, part of Springer Nature 2018
D. Ferguson et al. (Eds.): CLOSER 2017, CCIS 864, pp. 200–222, 2018.
https://doi.org/10.1007/978-3-319-94959-8_11

Therefore, to guarantee their quality, we must test CBSs in the presence of elasticity, i.e., *elasticity testing.*

During CBSs development, tests may be regularly re-executed [3] to detect, diagnose, and correct bugs, where each execution must reproduce the same behaviour. This requires to design elasticity tests to be deterministic, which raises four challenges that we have identified: three functional and one non-functional. The *first challenge* (functional) is to repeat the CBS elastic behaviour by managing sequences of resource allocations and deallocations. In this case, the same elastic behaviour leads the CBS to repeat its adaptations over the multiple test executions. As a consequence, this reproduces the issues related to those adaptations, in case such issues have not been corrected. Looking into two CBSs bug tracking, i.e., MongoDB[1] and ZooKeeper[2], we measure that as soon as bugs are related to elasticity, all of them require to be able to repeat the CBS elastic behaviour.

By analysing further MongoDB and ZooKeeper bug tracking, we realize that other elasticity-related bug reproductions require to combine the elastic behaviour along with two further conditions, which we consider as second and third challenges. At least one of them is required 70% and 67% of the MongoDB and ZooKeeper bugs respectively.

The *second challenge* (functional) is to repeat time-based events, where elasticity tests may require to repeat an elastic behaviour, and to synchronize time-based events with specific CBS states. This is required when testing ≈40% of MongoDB and ≈33% of ZooKeeper elasticity-related bugs. An example is the MongoDB NoSQL database bug 7974 [4], where two time-based events are required to reproduce the bug: (1) to create a unique index before one of the MongoDB nodes is removed by a resource deallocation, and (2) to upload a document after a new node is added by a resource allocation.

The *third challenge* (functional) is to repeat a specific CBS components variation, what we call *selective elasticity*. Elasticity tests may require repeat an elastic behaviour, and to remove a specific CBS component during a resource deallocation. This is the case when testing ≈44% of both MongoDB and ZooKeeper elasticity-related bugs. An example is the Apache ZooKeeper bug 2164 [5], which only occurs when the ZooKeeper leader component is removed by a resource deallocation.

Finally, reproducing elasticity tests has a *fourth challenge* (non-functional), to reduce elasticity test execution time. Reducing the execution time can also save money since in cloud computing the billing model is pay-as-you-go, where customers are charged by the time they use resources. One way to do this is to anticipate the reaction to resource demands. Indeed, driving CBSs is time consuming since elastic controllers take a while (at least 60 s) to react to a resource demand. This, summed to the time to allocate or deallocated a resource, result in test executions that last hours, or even days, depending on the length of the elasticity states sequence.

---

[1] https://www.mongodb.com/.
[2] https://zookeeper.apache.org/.

In this paper, we present an approach and a prototype to address the three functional listed challenges in reproducing elasticity tests: *the reproduction of an elastic behaviour, the scheduling of time-based events,* and *the reproduction of CBS components variation.* The approach also addresses the non-functional challenge by anticipating the reaction to resource demand, and as a consequence, accelerating the test reproduction.

To support our claims, we conduct five experiments with two different CBS case studies. The first two experiments aim at measuring the test execution time reduction when using the proposed approach. The other three experiments aim at reproducing three existing elasticity-related bugs by controlling the test reproduction with the proposed approach.

The remainder of this paper is organized as follows. In the next section, we remind the major aspects of cloud computing elasticity, and a previous work of part of the authors in driving CBSs throughout elasticity. Section 3 details the challenges in elasticity test reproduction and introduces the proposed approach. The experiments and their results are described in Sect. 4. Section 5 discusses the related work. Finally, Sect. 6 concludes.

2   Cloud Computing Elasticity

This section defines the main concepts related to Cloud Computing Elasticity, which will help the understanding of our approach.

2.1   Typical Elastic Behavior

Figure 1 presents the typical behavior of elastic cloud computing applications.

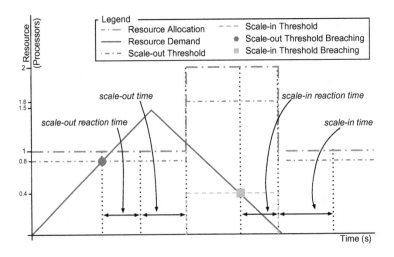

Fig. 1. Typical elastic behavior [6].

In this figure, the *resource demand* (continuous line) varies over time, increasing from 0 to 1.5 then decreasing back to 0. A resource demand of 1.5 means that the application demands 50% more resources than the current allocated ones.

When the resource demand exceeds the *scale-out threshold* and remains higher during the *scale-out reaction time*, the cloud elasticity controller assigns a new resource. The new resource becomes available after a *scale-out time*, the time the cloud infrastructure spends to allocate it. Once the resource is available, the threshold values are updated accordingly. This behavior is similar when considering a resource *scale-in*, respectively. Except that, as soon as the scale-in begins, the threshold values are updated and the resource is becomes unavailable. Nonetheless, the infrastructure needs a *scale-in time* to release the resource.

2.2   Elasticity States

Workload fluctuations lead to resource variations (elasticity) that drive the CBS throughout elasticity-related states. Figure 2 depicts the possible transitions between elasticity states.

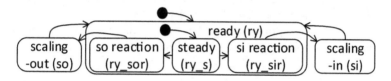

Fig. 2. Elasticity states [6].

At the beginning the CBS is at the *ready* state (*ry*), when the resource configuration is steady (*ry_s* substate). Then, if the CBS is exposed for a certain time (*scale-out reaction time*, *ry_sor* substate) to a pressure that breaches the scale-out threshold, the cloud elasticity controller starts adding a new resource. At this point, the CBS moves to the *scaling-out* state (*so*) and remains in this state while the resource is added. After a *scaling-out*, the CBS returns to the *ready* state, and can move either back to a *scaling-out* state or to a *scaling-in* state (*si*).

2.3   Elasticity Control

When testing CBSs throughout elasticity, testers should be able to drive the CBS in a deterministic way, controlling its elastic behaviour. Thus, they can be more specific and model situations they judge as critical. Furthermore, this can also reduce testing execution time since the elasticity behaviour is specific. In cloud computing, this also means reduction of cost since most of cloud providers use the policy of *pay-as-you-go*, where consumers pay for the time they use resources.

We can categorize *CBS driving* into two groups: (i) direct resource management, and (ii) generation of adequate workload. The first and simplest one
(i) interacts directly with the cloud infrastructure, asking for resource allocation
and deallocation. The second one (ii) consists in generating adequate workload
variations that drive CBS throughout elasticity states, as previously explained
in Sect. 1, which reproduces a realistic scenario. The second group is more complex since requires a preliminary step for profiling the CBS resource usage, and
calculating the workload variations that trigger the elasticity states.

In a previous work [7], we propose a CBS driving approach that fits in the
second group. That approach is based in the assumption that elasticity state
transitions occur due to workload variations that eventually breach the thresholds, as illustrated in Fig. 1. We provide further details about this approach in
the following paragraphs.

An input workload has three characteristics [8]: *workload type*, *request mix*,
and *request intensity*. The *workload type* is the type of requests sent to the CBS,
such as *read* and *write* operations. The *mix of requests* is the set of requests
associated to a *workload type*. Finally, the *request intensity* is the amount of
requests sent to the CBS in a period. Then, given a workload type, the CBS
driving approach calculates the *requests intensity variation* that should drive
the CBS throughout a pre-set list of elasticity states.

Figure 3 depicts the approach workflow, which has three execution phases:
workload profiling, *workload calculation*, and *application leading*.

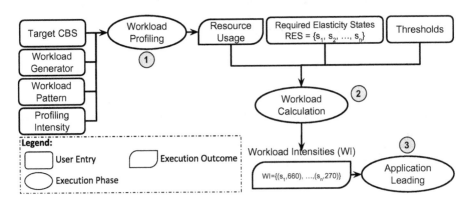

Fig. 3. CBS driving procedure workflow [7].

The *workload profiling* phase has four parameters: the *target CBS*, the *workload generator*, the *workload type*, and the Profiling Intensity (PI). The *target
CBS* is the CBS driven throughout elasticity. The *workload generator* is the
tool that generates the workload. The *workload type* describes the type or set
of requests sent to the CBS. Finally, the PI defines the number of requests per
second sent to the CBS during the *workload profiling* phase.

To profile the effect of the *workload* on the CBS, the approach generates the workload according to the workload profiling parameters. Then, it calculates the Average Resource Usage (ARU) for the period, which is the input of the *workload calculation* phase.

In the *workload calculation* phase, the CBS driving approach calculates the *request intensity(ies)* that drive the CBS throughout the *Required Elasticity States (RES)*, which we call *workload intensity(ies)*.

Therefore, to drive a CBS throughout elasticity states we must know which are the workload intensities that breach the scale-out, and the scale-in thresholds, which we call *multipliers*. The scale-out multiplier, denoted by M_{so}, is the workload intensity that breaches the scale-out threshold. The scale-in multiplier, denoted by M_{si}, is the workload intensity that breaches the scale-in threshold.

After discovering the multipliers, the CBS driving approach calculates the workload intensities for each elasticity state in the RES. For scaling states, i.e., scaling-out and scaling-in, the workload intensity must breach a threshold, while for the ready state it must not breach any threshold. However, since scaling states change the amount of resources over time, the amount of allocated resource (AR) is a key parameter. The approach calculates the workload intensities by multiplying it by M_{so} and M_{si}. We call the product of this multiplication as *current multiplier (CM)*, where $CM_{so} = M_{so} \cdot AR$ and $CM_{si} = M_{si} \cdot AR$. Such multipliers correspond to the workload intensities that drive the CBS through the scaling-out and the scaling-in states, denoted by WI^{so} and WI^{si}. The workload intensity for ready states ($WI^{ry\text{-}s}$) is calculated as ι percent of CM_{so} ($WI^{ry\text{-}s} = \frac{\iota}{100} \cdot CM_{so}$), where ι is a configurable parameter. Such intensity must lead the resource usage to a level close to CM_{so}, a significant amount of work, but without breaching any threshold.

In the *application leading* phase, we lead the CBS using the calculated workload intensities (WI), which is presented in Algorithm 1. We expose the CBS to each workload intensity until the related elasticity state ends. To identify the elasticity state transitions, the approach monitors the cloud infrastructure periodically.

Algorithm 1. Application Leading.

Data: workload intensities WI
monitorElasticity();
foreach $p < s, i > \ \in \ WI$ **do**
   while $s.isUp$ **do**
      generateWorkload(i);
   end
end

---

3   Elasticity Testing Approach

In this section, we first present the challenges in elasticity test reproduction, then we present the overall architecture of our approach and aspects of the prototype implementation.

3.1   Challenges in Elasticity Test Reproduction

Elasticity test reproduction consists in exposing the CBS to the same conditions as previous executions, which should stimulate it to repeat the same behaviour. Then, testers can find CBS bugs, correct them, and then check whether they have been fixed, requiring several runs of failed tests. Another use is to check if changes in the CBS, such as new features, affect its behaviour, or introduce bugs.

To discover which are the conditions that CBSs face, we analyse elasticity-related bugs reported in the bug tracking of two popular CBSs: MongoDB and ZooKeeper. Bug reports have rich information since developers use them to implement tests reproducing bugs. Therefore, these reports reveal the conditions necessary to reproduce elasticity-related bugs, and as a consequence, elasticity tests. The search for elasticity-related bugs has two steps:

1. Select bug reports that contain in their description words that may refer to elasticity, such as: *elasticity, scaling, adding, removing, node, sync* (for synchronization), and *replic* (for replication).
2. Gather the bug reports whose description refers to resource changes, excluding bug reports where the resource changes do not reflect an elastic behaviour, such as the ones that restart a Virtual Machine (VM) rather than remove or add one.

The two CBS projects use *JIRA*[3] issue tracking to report their bugs. Therefore, for the Step 1, we use the query in Listing 1 to select bug reports related to elasticity. In the query, we change $PROJECT by the project name that corresponds to the CBS, where for MongoDB the project name is *SERVER*, while for ZooKeeper, it is *ZOOKEEPER*. We exclude bug reports whose resolution is *Cannot Reproduce* or *Duplicate*. The first resolution refers to bugs that developers could not reproduce due to either wrong or insufficient information, while the second resolution refers to duplicate bug reports.

Listing 1. Query Used at Step 1.

```
project = "$PROJECT" AND issuetype = Bug AND resolution not
in ("Cannot Reproduce","Duplicate") AND (description ~ "elasticity"
OR description ~ "scaling" OR description ~ "adding"
OR description ~ "removing" OR description ~ "node"
OR description ~ "sync" OR description ~ "replic")
```

Table 1 lists the number of bugs selected at each searching step. MongoDB has 25,780 bugs reported on its bug tracking system, where we find 316 in the first step, and 43 in the second step. ZooKeeper has 2677 bugs reported, where we find 188 bugs in the first step, and 9 in the second step.

The selected bugs reveal three main challenges in reproducing elasticity-related bug, which we consider as elasticity tests reproduction challenges: *elasticity control, selective elasticity,* and *event scheduling*. These challenges are functional since the tests cannot be reproduced and the bugs corrected without

---

[3] https://jira.atlassian.com.

Table 1. Selected bugs in the systematic search.

	Total of bugs	Bugs at step 1	Bugs at step 2
MongoDB	25.780	316	43
ZooKeeper	2.677	188	9

solving them. As usual non-functional challenge of the *speediness* is a concern. It is a requirement to be able to run the numerous tests of such systems. Moreover, since cloud computing's billing model is pay-as-you-go, speediness is a cost concern.

- *Elasticity Control* is the ability to reproduce a specific elastic behaviour. All the selected Elasticity-related bugs occur after a specific sequence of resource allocations and deallocations. Therefore, the challenge is to repeat the CBS elastic behaviour by managing sequences of resource allocations and deallocations.
- *Event Scheduling* is the ability to synchronize events to elasticity states. An event is any interaction with or stimulus to CBS, such as forcing a data increment or to simulate infrastructure failures. The challenge is to identify elasticity states at CBS runtime, and to switch among events according to the elasticity state they are associated.
- *Selective Elasticity* is the ability to remove a specific CBS component. The challenge is to identify and to deallocate the resource that hosts the CBS component that must be removed.
- *Speediness* is the ability of reproducing elasticity tests faster than relying on native cloud computing elasticity controllers. The challenge is to repeat the CBS elastic behaviour anticipating the resource changes.

Table 2 shows the quantity of challenges faced by each CBS bug reproduction. As previously mentioned, all the selected bugs face the elasticity control, where 13 MongoDB (30%) and 3 ZooKeeper (33%) do not face the other challenges for their reproductions. Out of MongoDB bugs, 30 bugs (70%) also face challenges rather than elasticity control, within which 6 (14%) bugs face all the challenges. Out of ZooKeeper bugs, 6 bugs (66%) face further challenges, and 5 (55%) of them face all the challenges.

Table 2. Challenges in bug reproduction.

	Bugs considered	Elasticity control	Selective elasticity	Event scheduling	All	Only elasticity control
MongoDB	43	43	19	17	6	13
ZooKeeper	9	9	4	3	5	3

3.2   Architecture Overview

Figure 4 depicts the overall architecture of our approach. The architecture has four main components, which aim at meeting the elasticity test reproduction challenges: *Elasticity Controller Mock* (ECM), *Workload Generator* (WG), *Event Scheduler* (ES), and *Cloud Monitor* (CM).

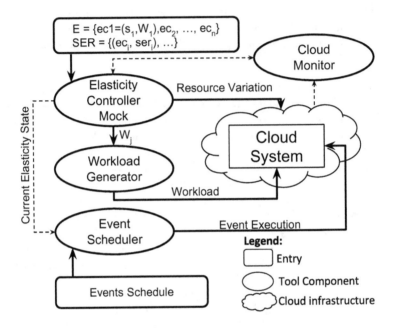

Fig. 4. Overall architecture [6].

The *ECM* simulates the behaviour of the cloud provider elasticity controller, allocating and deallocating determined resources, according to testing needs. It also asks the *WG* to generate the workload accordingly. The role of the *ES* is to schedule and execute a sequence of events in parallel with the other components. Finally, the *CM* monitors the cloud system, gathering information that helps orchestrating the behaviour of the three other components, ensuring the sequence of elasticity states, and their synchronization with the events.

Table 3 summarizes the challenges that each component meets, as we detail in this section.

Elasticity Controller Mock. The ECM is designed to reproduce the elastic behavior. By default, ECM requires as input a sequence of *elasticity changes*, denoted by $E = \{ec_1, ec_2, ..., ec_n\}$, where each ec is a pair that corresponds to an elasticity change. Elasticity change pairs are composed of a required elasticity state (s_i) and a workload (W_i), $ec_i = \langle s_i, W_i \rangle$ where $1 \leq i \leq n$. A workload

Table 3. Challenges met by the architecture components.

Component	Elasticity control	Selective elasticity	Event scheduling	Speediness
ECM	Yes	Yes	Yes	Yes
WG	Yes	No	No	No
ES	No	No	Yes	No
CM	Yes	Yes	No	No

is characterized by an intensity (i.e., amount of operations per second), and a workload type (i.e., set of transactions sent to the cloud system).

ECM reads elasticity change pairs sequentially. For each pair, ECM requests resource changes to meet elasticity state s_i and requests the Workload Generator to apply the workload W_i. Indeed, we have to send the corresponding workload to prevent cloud infrastructure to provoke unexpected resource variations. In particular, it could deallocate a resource that ECM just allocated, because the workload has remained low and under the scale-in threshold.

Rather than waiting for the cloud computing infrastructures for elasticity changes, the ECM directly requests to change the resource allocation (*elasticity control*). Based on both, required elasticity state and workload (elasticity change pair), ECM anticipates the resource changes. To be sure CBS enters the expected elasticity state, ECM queries the CM, which periodically monitors the cloud infrastructure.

The ECM may also lead to a precise resource deallocation (*selective elasticity*). Typically, elasticity changes are transparent to the tester, managed by the cloud provider. To set up the *selective elasticity*, ECM requires a secondary input, i.e., Selective Elasticity Requests (*SER*). *SER* is denoted by $SER = \{(ec_1, ser_1), ..., (ec_n, ser_n)\}$, where $ec_i \in E$, and ser_i refers to a *selective elasticity request*. A *selective elasticity request* is a reference to an algorithm (freely written by tester) that gets a resource's ID. When ec_i is performed by ECM, the algorithm referred by ser_i is executed, and the resource with the returned ID is deallocated by ECM.

ECM helps in meeting all of elasticity testing challenges. As earlier explained in this section, it deterministically requests resource variations (*elasticity control* and *selective elasticity*), and helps in ensuring the *event scheduling* providing information of the current elasticity state to the Event Scheduler. As earlier explained in this section, the ECM deterministically requests resource variations (*elasticity control* and *selective elasticity*). In addition, the ECM helps in ensuring the *event scheduling* by providing information of the current elasticity state to the Event Scheduler, and in meeting the speediness by anticipating resource changes.

Workload Generator. The Workload Generator is responsible for generating the workload (W). We base it on our previous work [7], which takes into account a threshold-based elasticity (see Fig. 1), where resource change demand occurs when a threshold is breached for a while (*reaction time*). Therefore, a workload should result in either threshold breached (for scaling states) or not breached (for ready state), during the necessary time. To ensure this, the Workload Generator keeps the workload constant, either breaching a threshold or not, until a new request arrives.

Considering a scale-out threshold set at 60% of CPU usage, the workload should result in a CPU usage higher than 60% to request a scale-out. In that case, if 1 operation A hypothetically uses 1% of CPU, it would be necessary at least 61 operations A to request the scale-out. On the other hand, less than 61 operations would not breach the scale-out threshold, keeping the resource steady.

The Workload Generator contributes with the Elasticity Controller Mock to meet the *elasticity control* challenge.

Event Scheduler. The ES input is a map associating sets of events to elasticity changes (ec_i), i.e., the set of events that should be sent to the cloud system when a given elasticity change is managed by the ECM. Table 4 abstracts an input where four events are associated to two elasticity changes.

Table 4. Events schedule.

Elasticity change	Event ID	Execution order	Wait time
ec_1	$e1$	1	0 s
	$e2$	2	10 s
	$e3$	2	0 s
ec_2	$e2$	1	0 s
	$e4$	2	0 s

Periodically, the ES polls the ECM for the current elasticity change, executing the events associated to it. For instance, when the ECM manages the elasticity change ec_1, it executes the events e_1, e_2, and e_3. Events have execution orders, which define priorities among events associated to the same state: event e_1 is executed before events e_2 and e_3. Events with the same *execution order* are executed in parallel (e.g., e_2 and e_3). Events are also associated to a *wait time*, used to delay the beginning of an event. In Table 4, event e_2 has a wait time of 10 s (starting 10 s after e_3, but nonetheless executed in parallel). This delay may be useful, for instance, to add a server to the server list a few seconds after the ready state begins, waiting for data synchronization to be finished. The ES meets the *event scheduling* challenge.

Cloud Monitor. The CM helps ECM to ensure *elasticity control* and *selective elasticity*. It periodically requests current elasticity state and stores it in order to respond to the ECM queries, necessary for elasticity control. It also executes the selective elasticity algorithm of SER, responding to ECM with the ID of the found resources.

3.3   Prototype Implementation

Each component of the testing approach architecture is implemented in Java and communicate with each other through Java RMI. Currently, we only support Amazon EC2 interactions, though one could adapt our prototype to interact with other cloud providers.

Elasticity Controller Mock. The elasticity changes are described in a property file. The entries are set as $\langle key, value \rangle$ pairs, as presented in Listing 2. The key corresponds to the elasticity change name, while the value corresponds to the elasticity change pair. The first part of the value is the elasticity state, and the second part is the workload, divided into intensity and type.

Listing 2. Example of Elasticity Controller Mock Input File (Elasticity Changes).

```
ec1=ready, (1000,write)
ec2=scaling-out, (2000,read/write)
...
ec4=scaling-in, (1500,read)
```

As previously explained, for each entry, the ECM sends the workload parameters to the Workload Generator and deterministically requests the specified resource change. Resource changes are requested through the cloud provider API, which enables resource allocation and deallocation, general infrastructure settings, and monitoring tasks. Before performing an elasticity change, the ECM asks the CM whether the previous elasticity state was reached. The CM uses the Selenium[4] automated browser to gather pertinent information from cloud provider's dashboard Web page.

We use Java annotations to set up selective elasticity requests (SER), as illustrated in Listing 3. A Java method implements the code that identifies a specific resource and returns its identifier as a String type. This method is annotated with metadata that specifies its name and associated elasticity change.

Listing 3. Selective Elasticity Input File.

```
@Selection{name="ser1", elasticity_change="ec4"}
public String select1() {
        ... //code to find a resource ID
        return resourceID;    }
```

Workload Generator. The WG generates the workload according to the parameters received from the ECM (i.e., *workload type* and *intensity*), whereas the workload is cyclically generated until new parameters arrive. It uses existing benchmark tools, setting the workload parameters in the command line.

---

[4] http://www.seleniumhq.org/.

For instance, YCSB benchmark tool allows three parameters related to the workload: the preset workload profile, the number of operations, and the number of threads. The preset workload profile refers to the workload type, while the multiplication of the two last parameters results in the workload intensity.

Event Scheduler. Event schedules is set in a Java file, where each event is an annotated method, such as the example illustrated in Listing 4. Java methods are annotated with the event identifier, the related elasticity change, the order, and the waiting time. EC periodically polls the ECM to obtain the current elasticity change. Then, it uses Java Reflection to execute the Java methods related to it.

Listing 4. Example of Event Scheduler Input File.

```
@Event{id="e1",elasticity_change="ec1",order="1", wait="0"}
public void event1() { ... }
```

3.4 Prototype Execution

Figure 5 illustrates the prototype execution sequence. This execution starts by the CM component, which interacts with the cloud infrastructure (*Cloud*) to get information that identifies the current elasticity state. Then, the prototype executes the $ec \subset EC$ in parallel to the elasticity states identification. For each $ec \subset EC$, the ECM sends a message to WG, which generates the workload W_i until the ECM sends a message to stop this process. The ECM sends this message when the CM identifies that the current elasticity state has ended. During the workload generation, if es_i is different from *ready*, the ECM changes the resource. Otherwise, it only waits for a given time-frame before moving to the next *ec*. When a new elasticity state begins, the ECM sends a message to the EVs, which leads the execution of all the events related to this state. The prototype repeats this process until the last *ec* ends.

4   Experiments

In this section, we present five experiments. The first two experiments aim at demonstrating the test execution time reduction when using the Elasticity Controller Mock (ECM). The other three experiments aim at controlling the test reproduction of three existing elasticity-related bugs. We conduct all the experiments in the environment described in the next section.

4.1 Experimental Environment

CBS Case Studies. In the experiments, we use two CBS case studies, MongoDB[5] and Apache ZooKeeper[6] (or simply ZooKeeper).

---

[5] https://www.mongodb.org/.
[6] https://zookeeper.apache.org/.

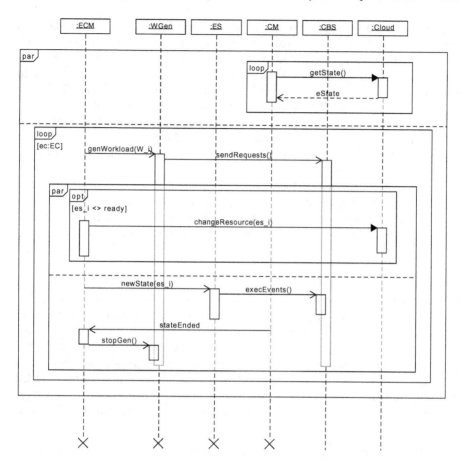

Fig. 5. Prototype execution sequence.

MongoDB is a NoSQL document database. It has three different components: configuration server, MongoS, and MongoD. The configuration server stores meta-data and configuration settings. The MongoS instance is a query router, which ensures load balance, while MongoD instances store and process data.

ZooKeeper is a coordination service for distributed systems. ZooKeeper coordination is intended to be replicated over a set of nodes, called as an *ensemble*. Requests from ZooKeeper clients are forwarded to a single node, the *leader* (which is *elected* using a distributed algorithm). The leader works as a proxy, distributing the request among other nodes called as *followers*. The *followers* keep a local copy of the configuration data to respond to requests.

To generate the workload in the experiments with MongoDB, we use the Yahoo Cloud Serving Benchmark (YCSB) [9], while in the experiments with ZooKeeper, we use an open-source benchmark tool [10].

Cloud Computing Infrastructure. All the experiments are conducted on the commercial cloud provider Amazon Elastic Cloud Compute (EC2), where we set *scale-out* and *scale-in* thresholds as 60% and 30% of CPU usage, respectively. Since the threshold values are not critical for the experiment goals, we set them in an arbitrary manner. We choose a scale-out threshold value as 60% of CPU since it should not result in CBS stress. This threshold value also makes it possible to reduce the execution cost since the workload generation can be executed on a single medium machine (*m3.medium*[7], with a 2.6 GHz vCPU, 3.75 MB of memory, and 4 GB of disk). We set the scale-in threshold value as half of the scale-out threshold value.

In the experiment with MongoDB, the MongoS instance is deployed on a large machine (*m3.large*, with 2 vCPUs of 2.6 GHz, 7.5 MB of memory, and 32 GB of disk), while the other instances are deployed on medium machines. In the experiments with ZooKeeper, every node is deployed on a medium machine.

4.2   Speediness Experiment

In this second set of experiments, we verify whether the Elasticity Controller Mock (ECM) reduces test execution time. In the experiment we lead two CBS case studies, MongoDB and ZooKeeper, through an elasticity states sequence that covers all the possible elasticity state transitions. This is the elasticity states sequence: *ready*, *scaling-out*, *ready*, *scaling-in*, and *ready*. This leading is done in two ways, by using the Elasticity Controller Mock, and by using the Amazon EC2 elasticity controller. The workload pattern used in this experiment is only read operations, which keeps the data size unchanged along the experiment execution.

Speediness Considering ZooKeeper. For the ZooKeeper, we consider the following elasticity changes sequence:

$$E = \langle ry\_sor, \langle 5800, r \rangle \rangle, \langle so, \langle 5800, r \rangle \rangle, \langle ry\_sir, \langle 5000, r \rangle \rangle,$$
$$\langle si, \langle 5000, r \rangle \rangle, \langle ry, \langle 5000, r \rangle \rangle$$

Aiming at accelerating the elasticity changes sequence execution, the first two ready states correspond to ry_sor and ry_sir sub-states (see Fig. 2), according to the next scaling state in the sequence. Thus, as soon as the CBS enters a ready state, there is a threshold breaching that triggers the next scaling state. The last ready state corresponds to a ry_s sub-state, where none of thresholds is breached. When executing the sequence by using the native Amazon EC2 elasticity controller, we set the scale-out and scale-in reaction times (see Fig. 1) as the minimum allowed, i.e., 60 s. In the ECM, we set this as 30 s, half of the minimum allowed by the Amazon EC2 elasticity controller. In both cases, the last ready state lasts 30 s.

Figures 6(a) and (b) present ZooKeeper performance results when using Amazon EC2 and the ECM.

---

[7] https://aws.amazon.com/fr/ec2/itype/.

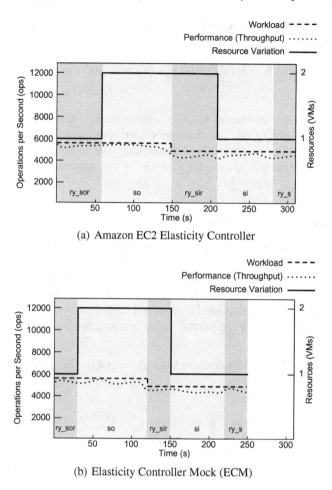

(a) Amazon EC2 Elasticity Controller

(b) Elasticity Controller Mock (ECM)

Fig. 6. ZooKeeper performance.

The execution by using the ECM lasts ≈250 s, while with Amazon EC2 the execution lasts ≈310 s. This difference of (2×30) s is due to our shortest reaction time after the threshold breaching. Both executions show a similar performance variation (doted line), which corresponds to the applied workload (dashed line): it starts by ≈5800 ops and keeps at this level until the end of the scaling-out state, goes down to ≈5000 ops from the second ready state until the end of the execution. When using the ECM, the average performance varies less than 1% compared the execution by using the Amazon EC2 elasticity controller. This value is insignificant, and can be associated to external factors, such as network latencies.

Speediness Considering MongoDB. For the MongoDB, we consider the following elasticity changes sequence:

$$E = \langle ry\_sor, \langle 1500, r \rangle \rangle, \langle so, \langle 1500, r \rangle \rangle, \langle ry\_sir, \langle 1000, r \rangle \rangle,$$
$$\langle si, \langle 1000, r \rangle \rangle, \langle ry, \langle 1000, r \rangle \rangle$$

The test sequence execution time is ≈ 330 s when using Amazon EC2 and ≈ 270 s when using the ECM. The difference corresponds to the (2×30) s shortest reaction time after the threshold breaching. We measured a performance difference of less than 2% comparing the use of our approach with the default Amazon EC2.

4.3 Test Reproduction Experiment

In this section, we describe the use of our approach to reproduce the three bugs, and compare the results to reproduction attempts without our approach. We do not explain in details the setup of reproductions without the proposed approach, though in such executions the *elasticity control* is managed. Indeed, reproducing elasticity is a native feature of cloud computing infrastructures, and we just drive CBS through required elastic behavior using our approach [7].

Selected Bugs. Table 5 summarizes the challenges in the reproduction of the three selected bugs.

Table 5. Challenges in reproducing the three selected bugs.

Bug	Feature		
	Elasticity control	Selective elasticity	Event scheduling
MongoDB − 7974	Yes	Yes	Yes
ZooKeeper − 2164	Yes	Yes	No
ZooKeeper − 2172	Yes	No	Yes

The selected bugs cover all the possible combinations of challenges, constrained by the mandatory presence of *elasticity control*, and the need of at least one of the other challenges. We do not attempt to reproduce any bug that only faces *elasticity control* challenge since one could reproduce the required elastic behavior using our elastic control approach [7].

MongoDB Bug 7974. This bug affects the MongoDB versions 2.2.0 and 2.2.2, when a secondary component of a MongoDB replica set[8] is deallocated. Indeed, in a MongoDB replica set, one of the components is elected as primary member, which works as a coordinator, while the others remain as secondary members.

---
[8] https://docs.mongodb.com/replica-set.

To reproduce this bug, we must follow a specific elastic behavior: initialization of a replica set with three members, deallocation of a secondary member, and allocation of a new secondary member. Therefore, the second step of the elastic behavior requires the deallocation of a precise resource, one of the secondary members. The bug reproduction also requires two events synchronized to elasticity changes. Right after the secondary member deallocation, we must create a unique index, and after the last step of the elastic behavior, we must add a document in the replica set.

In conclusion, the reproduction of this bug faces all the challenges that we consider in this paper: *elasticity control*, *selective elasticity*, and *event scheduling*.

ZooKeeper Bug . This bug is related to ZooKeeper version 3.4.5 and concerns the leader election. According to the bug report[9], in an ensemble with three nodes, when the node running the leader shuts down, a new leader election starts and never ends.

The reproduction of this bug must follow a precise sequence: initialization (allocation of the first node), followed by the allocation of two nodes and the deallocation of the leader node. The main difficulty of reproducing this bug is that when ZooKeeper is deployed on three nodes, the deallocated node is not necessarily the leader. The problem is that during a scale-in, Amazon EC2 removes either the newest or the oldest node and cannot reproduce the bug straightforwardly. In conclusion, the reproduction of this bug faces two challenges: *elasticity control* and *selective elasticity*.

ZooKeeper Bug 2172. This bug is related to ZooKeeper version 3.5.0. According to the bug report[10], when a third node is added to a ZooKeeper ensemble, the system enters an unstable state and cannot recover.

After a thorough analysis of the available logs, we understand that the bug occurs when a leader election starts right after the allocation of a third node. More precisely, when a new node joins the ensemble, there is a data synchronization with the leader. Then, if the data is not already synchronized at the moment of the leader election, the bug occurs.

The reproduction of this bug requires a simple elastic behaviour: the allocation of one initial node, and then the allocation of two more nodes. However, this sequence alone does not reproduce the bug: we need to be sure that the leader election starts before the end of the data synchronization process. We can force this by increasing the data amount through an event synchronized with the completion of the third node allocation.

The reproduction of this bug faces two challenges: *elasticity control* and *event scheduling*.

---

[9] https://issues.apache.org/jira/ZK2164.

[10] https://issues.apache.org/jira/ZK2172.

4.4   Bug Reproductions

MongoDB-7974 Bug Reproduction. This bug reproduction has been already described in our previous paper [6]. To reproduce MongoDB bug 7974 using our approach, we first manually create the MongoDB replica set, composed of three nodes. Then, we set up the following sequence of elasticity changes, which should drive MongoDB through the required elastic behavior:

$$E = \langle ry_1, \langle 4500, r \rangle \rangle, \langle si_1, \langle 1500, r \rangle \rangle,$$
$$\langle ry_2, \langle 3000, r \rangle \rangle, \langle so_1, \langle 4500, r \rangle \rangle, \langle ry_3, \langle 4500, r \rangle \rangle$$

Since we must deallocate a secondary member of MongoDB replica set at elasticity change ec_2, it is associated to a selective elasticity request (SER). The SER queries MongoDB replica set's members, using MongoDB shell method *db.isMaster*, until finding a member that is secondary.

In parallel to the elasticity changes, we set up two events, $e1$ and $e2$, which respectively create a unique index, and insert a new document in the replica set. The $e1$ is associated to elasticity change ec_3, a ready state that follows the scaling-in state where a secondary member is deallocated. The $e2$ is associated to elasticity change ec_5, the last ready state. Both events are scheduled without waiting time (Table 6).

Table 6. MongoDB-7974 event schedule [6].

Elasticity change	Event ID	Execution sequence	Wait time
ec_3	$e1$	1	0 s
ec_5	$e2$	1	0 s

We repeat the bug reproduction for three times. After each execution, we look for the expression *"duplicate key error index"* in the log files. If the expression is found, we consider the bug is reproduced.

Table 7 shows the result of all the three executions, either using our approach or not. All the attempts using our approach reproduce the bug, while none of the attempts without our approach do it.

Table 7. MongoDB-7974 bug reproduction results [6].

Reproduction	Reproduced	Not Reproduced
With our approach	3	0
Without our approach	0	3

For the executions without our approach, we force MongoDB to elect the intermediate node (in the order of allocation) as primary member[11], what can

---

[11] https://docs.mongodb.com/force-primary.

occur in a real situation. In this scenario, independent of scale-in settings, cloud computing elasticity controllers always deallocate a secondary member, since Amazon EC2 only allows to deallocated the oldest or newest nodes. This is because we want to see the effect of event synchronization. Therefore, we assure the elastic behaviour is the required to reproduce the bug. Even though we force the reproduction of the required elastic behaviour, this bug still needs the event executions, which must be correctly synchronized. This is the reason the bug is not reproduced without our approach.

ZooKeeper-2164 Bug Reproduction. To reproduce this bug, we translate and complete the scenario (Sect. 4.3) into the following sequence of elasticity changes:

$$E = \langle ry_1, \langle 3000, r \rangle \rangle, \langle so_1, \langle 5000, r \rangle \rangle, \langle ry_2, \langle 5000, r \rangle \rangle,$$
$$\langle so_2, \langle 10\,000, r \rangle \rangle, \langle ry_3, \langle 10\,000, r \rangle \rangle, \langle si_1, \langle 5000, r \rangle \rangle$$

The sequence of elasticity changes first initializes the cloud system with one node, then it requests two scale-out. Once the three nodes are running, the sequence requests a scale-in.

To discover the leader node, we write a SER that is associated to the last elasticity change $e6$ ($\langle si_1, \langle 5000, r \rangle \rangle$). The SER method connects to every Zookeeper node and executes ZooKeeper command named `stat`. This command describes, among other information, the node execution mode: leader or follower.

The sequence of elasticity states, including a selective elasticity, is supposed to reproduce the bug. To verify whether the failure occurs, we write a test oracle, which is implemented in JUnit [11]. It is run after the last elasticity change ($\langle si_1, \langle 5000, r \rangle \rangle$), and repetitively searches for a leader until it is found or the timeout is reached. In the first case, the verdict is *pass*, what means the bug is reproduced and observed. Otherwise, the verdict is *fail*.

As well as in the first experiment, we use two different setups to execute this experiment: with our approach, and without our approach. We repeat the experiment three times for each setup.

Since the selective elasticity is one of the challenges for this bug reproduction, when executing without our approach, we try to reproduce a real scenario, where every node can be elected as a leader. Therefore, we force ZooKeeper to elect a different node as the leader at each execution: the newest, the oldest, then the intermediate node. Then, we use Amazon EC2 to deallocate a node. Its policy is to deallocate either the newest or the oldest node, it is not possible to deallocate the intermediate node. Hence, during two executions we can ask Amazon EC2 to deallocate the leader, but not during the third one.

Table 8 summarizes the results. When using our approach, all the three test executions pass, demonstrating the ability of our testing approach to deterministically reproduce the bug. In contrast, only two executions without our approach pass, the ones where the leader is the newest or the oldest node. Therefore, without our approach the bug was not reproduced deterministically.

Table 8. ZooKeeper-2164 bug reproduction results.

Reproduction	Pass verdicts	Fail verdicts
With our approach	3	0
Without our approach	2	1

ZooKeeper-2172 Bug Reproduction. We create the following sequence of elasticity changes to reproduce this bug (Sect. 4.3):

$$E = \langle ry_1, \langle 3000, r \rangle \rangle, \langle so_1, \langle 5000, r \rangle \rangle,$$
$$\langle ry_2, \langle 5000, r \rangle \rangle, \langle so_2, \langle 10\ 000, r \rangle \rangle, \langle ry_3, \langle 10\ 000, r \rangle \rangle$$

According to the bug log files, the bug occurs when the leader election starts before the end of the data synchronization between the third node and the previous leader. Thus, the test sequence must ensure that the data synchronization process is longer than the delay needed to start a new election, which is about 10 s according to the log files. Forcing the data synchronization to take long enough, we create an event schedule to associate an event $e1$ to the state so_2, as described in Table 9. The $e1$ requests a data increasing to an amount that should take longer than 10 s to synchronize. Since this experiment uses Amazon $m3.large$ machines, which have a bandwidth of 62.5 MB/s, the data amount must be ≈625 MB of data.

Table 9. ZooKeeper-2172 event schedule.

Elasticity change	Event ID	Execution sequence	Wait time
ec_4	$e1$	1	0 s

We use the test oracle as for the bug 2164, which is associated to the last *ready* elasticity state which is not supposed to be able to elect a leader before the timeout. Table 10 summarizes the experiment execution. In all three executions, the test verdict is *pass*, meaning that the testing approach reproduces the bug successfully. Since Amazon EC2 cannot manage natively the scheduling of events synchronized with elasticity states, it cannot reproduce the bug deterministically.

Table 10. ZooKeeper-2172 bug reproduction results.

Reproduction	Pass verdicts	Fail verdicts
With our approach	3	0
Without our approach	0	3

5   Related Work

Several research efforts are related to our approach in terms of elasticity control, selective elasticity, and events scheduling. The work of Gambi et al. [8,12] addresses elasticity testing. The authors predict elasticity state transition based on workload variations and test whether cloud infrastructures react accordingly. However, they do not focus on controlling elasticity and cannot drive cloud application throughout different elasticity states.

Banzai et al. [13] propose D-Cloud, a virtual machine environment specialized in fault injection. Like our approach, D-Cloud is able to control the test environment and allows testers to specify test scenarios. Test scenarios are specified in terms of fault injection and not on elasticity and events, as in our approach.

Yin et al. [14] propose CTPV, a Cloud Testing Platform Based on Virtualization. The core of CTPV is the private virtualization resource pool. The resource pool mimics cloud infrastructures environments, which in part is similar to our elasticity controller. CTPV differs from our approach in two points: (i) it does not use real cloud infrastructures and (ii) it uses an elasticity controller that does not anticipate resource demand reaction.

Vasar et al. [15] propose a framework to monitor and test cloud computing web applications. Their framework replaces the cloud elasticity controller, predicting the resource demand based on past workload. Contrary to our approach, they do not allow to control a specific sequence of elasticity states or events.

Li et al. [16] propose Reprolite, a tool that reproduces cloud system bugs quickly. Similarly to our approach, Reprolite allows the execution of parallel events on the cloud system and on the environment, but it does not focus on elasticity, one of our main contributions.

6   Conclusion

In this paper, we proposed an approach to reproduce elasticity tests in a deterministic manner. This approach meets four challenges: elasticity control, selective elasticity, event scheduling, and execution time reduction.

We used this approach to reduce the execution time when driving two CBSs, ZooKeeper and MongoDB, throughout an elasticity state sequence that covers all the elasticity state transitions. We compare these executions to the ones without the proposed approach by measuring the CBS performance throughout the executions. The performance in both executions does not present a significant variation, which indicates that the approach reduces the execution time without compromising the CBS behaviour.

We also used the approach to control the reproduction of three bugs of those two CBSs. Indeed, the bugs cannot be deterministically reproduced with state-of-the-art approaches. This also indicates that execution time reduction does not hamper such bug reproductions.

As testing is not only about reproducing existing bugs, but also diagnosing them. An evolution for the proposed approach is to generate different test scenarios combining elasticity state transitions, workload variations, selective elasticity, and event scheduling. Another perspective could be to further investigate the impacts of speediness. In fact, in this paper, we proposed a way to accelerate elasticity test executions, but it lacks a deeper investigation on how fast we can reproduce elasticity tests without compromising them.

References

1. Herbst, N.R., Kounev, S., Reussner, R.: Elasticity in Cloud Computing: what it is, and what it is not. In: ICAC (2013)
2. Bersani, M.M., Bianculli, D., Dustdar, S., Gambi, A., Ghezzi, C., Krstić, S.: Towards the formalization of properties of Cloud-based elastic systems. In: Proceedings of PESOS 2014, New York, NY, USA. ACM (2014)
3. Engstrom, E., Runeson, P., Skoglund, M.: A systematic review on regression test selection techniques. Inf. Softw. Technol. **52**, 14–30 (2010)
4. Mongodb bug 7974: Suppress stack trace on replication errors. (https://jira. mongodb.org/browse/SERVER-7974). Accessed 29 May 2017
5. Zookeeper bug 2164: Fast leader election keeps failing. (https://issues.apache.org/ jira/browse/ZOOKEEPER-2164). Accessed 08 Feb 2017
6. Albonico, M., Mottu, J.M., Sunyé, G., Alvares, F.: Making Cloud-based systems elasticity testing reproducible. In: Proceedings of the 7th International Conference on Cloud Computing and Services Science, CLOSER 2017, pp. 495–502, Porto, Portugal, 24–26 April 2017
7. Albonico, M., Mottu, J.M., Sunyé, G.: Controlling the elasticity of web applications on Cloud Computing. In: Proceedings of the 31st SAC. ACM (2016)
8. Gambi, A., Hummer, W., Truong, H.L., Dustdar, S.: Testing elastic computing systems. IEEE Internet Comput. **17**, 76–82 (2013)
9. Cooper, B.F., Silberstein, A., Tam, E., Ramakrishnan, R., Sears, R.: Benchmarking Cloud serving systems with YCSB. In: Proceedings of SoCC 2010, New York, NY, USA. ACM (2010)
10. Hunt, P., Konar, M., Junqueira, F.P., Reed, B.: Zookeeper: wait-free coordination for internet-scale systems. In: 2010 USENIX, Boston, MA, USA (2010)
11. Gamma, E., Beck, K.: Junit: a cook's tour. Java report (1999)
12. Gambi, A., Hummer, W., Dustdar, S.: 2013 28th IEEE/ACM International Conference on Automated Software Engineering (ASE). IEEE (2013)
13. Banzai, T., Koizumi, H., Kanbayashi, R., Imada, T., Hanawa, T., Sato, M.: D-Cloud: design of a software testing environment for reliable distributed systems using cloud computing technology. In: Proceedings of CCGRID 2010, Washington, USA (2010)
14. Yin, L., Zeng, J., Liu, F., Li, B.: CTPV: a Cloud testing platform based on virtualization. In: The Proceedings of SOSE 2013 (2013)
15. Vasar, M., Srirama, S.N., Dumas, M.: Framework for monitoring and testing web application scalability on the Cloud. In: Proceedings of WICSA/ECSA Companion, NY, USA (2012)
16. Li, K., Joshi, P., Gupta, A., Ganai, M.K.: ReproLite: a lightweight tool to quickly reproduce hard system bugs. In: Proceedings of SOCC 2014, New York, NY, USA (2014)

Cost Analysis for Big Geospatial Data Processing in Public Cloud Providers

João Bachiega Jr.[✉], Marco Sousa Reis[✉], Aletéia P. F. Araújo[✉],
and Maristela Holanda[✉]

Department of Computer Science, University of Brasilia, Brasilia/DF, Brazil
joao.bachiega.jr@gmail.com, marco.antonio.sousa.reis@gmail.com,
{aleteia,mholanda}@unb.br

Abstract. Cloud computing is a suitable platform for running applications to process large volumes of data. Currently, with the growth of geographic and spatial data volume, conceptualized as Big Geospatial Data, some tools have been developed to allow the processing of this data efficiently. This work presents a cost-efficient method for processing geospatial data, optimizing the number of data nodes in a SpatialHadoop cluster according to dataset size. With this, it is possible to analyse and compare the costs for this type of application on public cloud providers.

Keywords: Big geospatial data · Spatial Cloud Computing
Spatialhadoop

1 Introduction

Big geospatial data is the emerging paradigm for the infinite amount of information available with the development and massive use of Geographical Information System (GIS) software, delivering hundreds of TiB up to several PiB per hour and there is some characteristics that distinguish it from other datasets [18]. These characteristics, known as the 5 Vs, are [20]: (i) *Variety* – referring to the different types of data, with more than 80% of them in an unstructured form; (ii) *Volume* – the tremendous amount of data generated each second; (iii) *Velocity* – the speed at which new data is being produced; (iv) *Veracity* – how trustworthy the data is; and, (v) *Value* – the importance of the data to the business.

The rise of cloud computing and cloud data stores have been a precursor and a facilitator to the emergence of big data. In this model, computational resources can be acquired quickly, and released with very little managing effort, or interaction with the service provider. Yang and Huang [19] proposed Spatial Cloud Computing, an infrastructure that could help conduct relevant computing and data processing with the characteristics of enough computing capability, a minimized energy cost, a fast response to spike computing needs, and a wide accessibility to the public when needed.

© Springer International Publishing AG, part of Springer Nature 2018
D. Ferguson et al. (Eds.): CLOSER 2017, CCIS 864, pp. 223–236, 2018.
https://doi.org/10.1007/978-3-319-94959-8_12

To be able to process these vast volume of geospatial data, particular methods were developed [18]. Among them, Apache Hadoop stands out for its effectiveness. It is a programming framework for distributed computing using the divide and conquer (or Map and Reduce) method to break down complex big data problems into small units of work, and process them in parallel.

Therefore, Big Geospatial data has demanded a lot of resources to store and process information. The amount of computational resources required by this vast volume of information grows in an asymptotic way and each wasted resource can represent a high monetary value that can be saved, once public cloud providers, such as Amazon AWS[1], Microsoft Azure[2], Google Cloud[3] and others, charge users on a pay-per-use basis.

With this, the primary challenge of working in a cloud environment is gauging the cost of processing big data in public cloud providers. According to Zhang et al. [3], cloud computing has impact where large companies, such as Google, Amazon and Microsoft strive to provide cost-efficient cloud platforms. Thus, the cost to execute the applications using these public providers is fundamental information for executing applications in a cloud [17]. In this context, this article presents a cost-efficient method and a comparative analysis for processing big geospatial data using SpatialHadoop on public cloud providers, with the goal of optimizing the use of computational resources to reduce costs.

The remainder of the article is divided into 7 sections. Section 2 covers concepts of Spatial Cloud Computing and Public Cloud Providers. SpatialHadoop is presented in Sect. 3; and some related works in Sect. 4. Section 5 presents the method to determine the number of data nodes in a cluster, based on dataset size. Information about system architecture is presented in Sect. 6. Tests and results are presented in Sect. 7. Finally, Sect. 8 contains the conclusion and some suggestions for future work.

2   Spatial Cloud Computing

Yang et al. [19] defines Spatial Cloud Computing as the cloud computing paradigm that is driven by geospatial sciences, and optimized by spatiotemporal principles for enabling geospatial science discoveries and cloud computing within a distributed computing environment. This is expected to supply the computational needs for geospatial data intensity, computing intensity, concurrent access intensity and spatiotemporal intensity.

With Spatial Cloud Computing, is possible to bypass the challenges for a computing infrastructure that needs: (i) support data discovery, access, use and process well, relieving scientists and engineers of IT tasks so that they can focus on scientific discoveries; (ii) provide real-time IT resources to enable real-time applications, such as emergency response; (iii) deal with access spikes; and (iv) provide

---

[1] https://aws.amazon.com.

[2] http://azure.microsoft.com/.

[3] https://cloud.google.com.

extremely reliable and scalable service for massive numbers of concurrent users to advance public knowledge [8].

The five essential characteristics for an cloud environment defined by NIST [14], namely, on demand self-service, broad network access, resource pooling, rapid elasticity, and measured service, demonstrates that cloud computing offers facilities that help overcome the challenges of a big geospatial data environment.

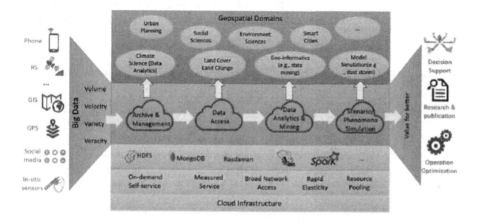

Fig. 1. Utilizing cloud computing to address big geospatial data applications [20].

Figure 1 presents the facilities offered by cloud computing which are essential to support big geospatial data applications that need to transform the input of 4 *Vs* (Volume, Velocity, Variety and Veracity) to an output with the last *V*, that is the Value that can be used by geospatial domains.

2.1   Public Cloud Providers

According to NIST [14], there are four deployment models for clouds, namely private, public, hybrid and community. Regarding public clouds, the authors define how the cloud infrastructure is provisioned for open use by the general public. These public providers offer two types of plans for the allocation of resources: on demand and reserved. With the on–demand plan, users are charged on a *pay-per-use* basis. The customer is charged for specific use (per hour, for example), which can include an increase or reduction of resources allocated according to the applications needs. With the reserved plan, users are charged fees and resources are allocated over an extended time period (one-time fee for available resources per year, for example). However, although is cheaper than the on–demand plan, the reserved plan is not suitable for applications that have ample variations in processing, since located resources may not be used, thereby wasting finances.

According to the Gartner Magic Quadrant for Cloud Infrastructure as a Service[4], Amazon AWS is the leading public cloud provider, followed by Microsoft Azure and Google Cloud.

For the processing of large volumes of data (Big Data), several providers offer specific services, given the complexity that an environment for this type of application requires. The main concept of this service is related to the provisioning and scaling of the cluster. A cluster is a resource pool consisting of a master server and one or more slaves servers. A comparison between Big Data services offered by the three public providers of cloud computing are presented in Table 1.

Table 1. Services for process *Big Data* applications on public cloud providers.

	Microsoft Azure	Google Cloud	Amazon AWS
Service	HDInsight	Dataproc	Elastic MapReduce (EMR)
Applications	Hadoop, Spark, Hive, HBase, Storm, Kafka e R	Hadoop, Spark, Pig e Hive	Hadoop, Spark, HBase, Presto e Flink
Charging unit	per minute	per minute	per hour

The life cycle of a cluster begins with its provisioning and ends when it is turned-off. Therefore, as seen in Table 1, charging fees by the hours (instead by the minute) can be a financial waste. Among the three services compared, only AWS EMR does not allow per-minute charging.

3   SpatialHadoop

Although Hadoop, an open-source project from the Apache community, is the most popular technique for working with big data, there are some limitations when working with big geospatial data related to the indexing of HDFS (Hadoop Distributed File System) files [8]. SpatialHadoop was developed as a fully-fledged MapReduce framework with native support for spatial data. It was built on Hadoop base code, adding spatial constructs and the awareness of spatial data inside the core functionality of traditional Hadoop.

SpatialHadoop comprises four main layers (shown Fig. 2), namely language, operations, MapReduce and storage. All of them execute in a cluster environment with one master node that breaks a MapReduce job into smaller tasks, carried out by slave nodes.

The Language layer uses the Pigeon programming language [7], a simple high-level SQL-like language, extended from Pig Latin [16]. The advantage is that it is compliant with the Open Geospatial Consortium's (OGC) simple feature

---

[4] www.gartner.com/doc/reprints?id=1\discretionary-2G2O5FC&ct=150519.

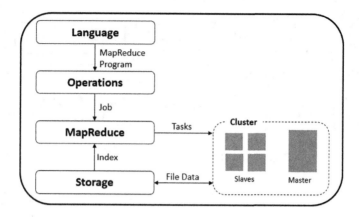

Fig. 2. SpatialHadoop high-level architecture.

access standard, supported both open source and commercial spatial Data Base Management System (DBMS). Pigeon also supports OGC standard data types including point, linestring and polygon, as well as OGC standard functions for spatial data.

The Operations layer encapsulates the implementation of various spatial operations with spatial indexes and the new components in the MapReduce layer. The Operations layer comprises: basic operations, range query, k-nearest neighbor (knn) and spatial join [8]; CG_Hadoop, a suite of scalable and efficient MapReduce algorithms for various fundamental computational geometry problems, namely, polygon union, skyline, convex hull, farthest pair, and closest pair [5]; and spatial data mining, operations developed using spatial data mining techniques.

The core layer of SpatialHadoop is the MapReduce layer (Figs. 3 and 4) because it is the query processing layer that runs MapReduce programs [8]. To be able to process spatial data, SpatialHadoop improves Hadoop systems with two main components: SpatialFileSplitter and SpatialRecordReader. The first one, exploits the global index in input files to perform early pruning of file

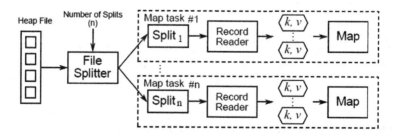

Fig. 3. MapReduce in traditional Hadoop [8].

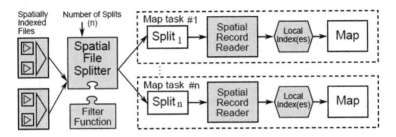

Fig. 4. MapReduce in SpatialHadoop [8].

blocks not contributing to answer. The second one reads a split originating from spatially indexed input files and exploits the local indexes to efficiently process it.

The Storage layer creates two index layers, global (on master node) and local (on slaves nodes). The SpatialHadoop supports the main spatial index structures [8]: grid file (Fig. 5a), a simple flat index that partitions the data according to a grid, such that, records overlapping each grid cell are stored in one file block as a single partition; R-tree (Fig. 5b), records are not replicated which causes partitions to overlap; and R+-tree (Fig. 5c), a variation of the R-tree where nodes at each level are kept disjointed, while records overlapping multiple nodes are replicated to each node to ensure efficient query answering.

(a)   (b)   (c)

Fig. 5. (a) Grid File Indexing. (b) R-tree Indexing. (c) R+-tree Indexing. [8].

4 Related Work

The comparison between cloud providers is a recurring theme, since new services are offered on this platform every day. In the work presented in [13], four public cloud providers were compared (Amazon AWS, Microsoft Azure, Google AppEngine, and Rackspace CloudServers) based on four functionalities considered essential by the authors (elasticity, storage persistence, cloud and wide access). In this scenario, a tool called *CloudCmp* was presented to compare both the performance and the cost of cloud providers, which, in the different case studies presented, showed a great disparity in between the costs of each provider. At the time of this work, there were still very few providers offering services for *Big Data* processing, so this type of service was not compared.

The use of a computational cloud environment for *Big Data* applications was also addressed by [10,11], focusing mainly on applications implemented by Hadoop. There are several challenges presented by [10] for improving the performance of large-volume data processing in a cloud environment through Hadoop applications. The first challenge is keeping down costs and the time required for data transfer. The second is optimizating iterations of jobs to avoid wasted processing. Finally, both there is the need for real–time processing for some applications, and the need for optimizations for join queries. The authors also pointed out that even with the straights computational power of cloud computing, applications need to be able to simplify information processing - indexing the databases to be processed, for example - to avoid wasting resources.

The work presented by [11] also proposes an optimization in the provisioning of resources to execute Hadoop jobs in the cloud environment. For this, the authors use adjustments in Hadoop parameters, such as the number of replicas of the data, the number of tasks executed in parallel etc., to estimate the appropriate resources for the execution of the application, maintaining performance and avoiding wasted resources. Although studies indicate that this optimization is independent of the cloud provider being used, there have not been any studies carried out to prove the effectiveness of the proposal in different providers.

The same objective was presented by [21], which proposes an algorithm called *Profit Optimization Resource Scheduling* for the optimization of resources allocated in cloud providers for the processing of *Analytics-as-a-Service* (AaaS). The tests to demonstrate the applicability of this algorithm were executed in the provider CloudSim[5], proving effective in the optimization of the utilization of the resources. There was, however, no results presented on the performance in other cloud providers nor any indication of an actual reduction in cost.

SpatialHadoop was presented in 2013 by Eldawy and Mokbel [6] as the first fully-fledged MapReduce framework with native support for spatial data. In this article, the authors used a demonstration scenario created on an Amazon AWS, with a 20 node cluster to compare SpatialHadoop and traditional Hadoop in three operations, namely, range query, knn and spatial join. In this paper, as in others, such as, Mokbel et al. [15], Alarabi et al. [1], Eldawy et al. [8] and Eldawy et al. [9], a static computational environment was used to validate tests. The increase of data nodes was done in a controlled way, without automation.

A modular software architecture for processing big geospatial data using SpatialHadoop on a cloud infrastructure was presented by Kramer and Senner [12]. Since the proposed framework does not distinguish whether the cloud environment is private or public, a third-party tool Ansible was used to execute provisioning scripts. Also related to Big Geospatial Data processing, in 2016, Das et al. [4] proposed a geospatial query resolution framework using an orchestration engine for clouds. However, the cloud environment used was private, and no dynamic allocation of computational resources was performed.

Finally, Yang et al. [20] presented work on the use of cloud computing to assist in the processing of large volumes of geographic data. The benefits of

---

[5] www.cloudbus.org/cloudsim.

the cloud platform, such as elasticity, service measurement, on-demand service and pay-per-use, were evidenced through four use cases, which were climate studies, mining knowledge, analysis of changes in the terrestrial surface and the simulation of storms. Cloud computing has proven to be very compliant and suitable for all the tests generated by the proposed use cases. However, the authors were not concerned with the costs of executing the tests, and focused solely on the computational power offered by the platform.

None of these works presents a method to optimize the use of computational resources, and reduce financial costs when using SpatialHadoop to process big geospatial data. Also, none of these works shows a cost analysis for big geospatial data applications on public cloud providers.

This paper presents a cost-efficient method for processing geospatial data, optimizing the number of data nodes in a SpatialHadoop cluster according to dataset size. Thus, it is possible to analyse and compare the costs for this type of application on public cloud providers.

5   Cluster Sizing

A very important task for Hadoop environment administrators is to define the cluster size infrastructure. The application must have a good performance and all computational resources must be not wasted. To solve this problem, the Formulas 1 and 2 presented by [2] must be used to calculate the quantity of data nodes based on dataset size for a SpatialHadoop environment on public cloud providers:

$$DN = \left\lceil \frac{T}{d} \right\rceil \tag{1}$$

DN represents the total number of data nodes needed; T is the total amount of data and d is the disk size in each node.

It is necessary to calculate T because the total amount of data used in a SpatialHadoop application is not only the volume of the dataset. To calculate T, the Formula 2 can be used:

$$T = \frac{C \times R \times S}{(1 - i) \times (1 + w)} \tag{2}$$

C represents the compression rate of the dataset, required, because Spatial-Hadoop can work with compressed files. When no compression is used, the value must be 1. R is the number of replicas of data in HDFS and S represents the size of the dataset. The notation i refers to the intermediate working space dedicated to temporarily storing results of Map Tasks. Finally, w represents the percentage of space left (wasted) to HDFS file system.

To demonstrate the use of these formulas, let us consider a real Open Street Map dataset of 96Gb of total size (2.7 billion records) available to download at http://spatialhadoop.cs.umn.edu/datasets. Without compression ($C = 1$), without replication ($R = 1$), considering $i = 25\%$ and $w = 20\%$, the value obtained for T is 106.67. Considering that each data node has a disk with

32 Gb ($d = 32$) it is possible to conclude that the ideal number of data nodes (DN) is 4.

6   System Architecture

An architecture composed of four layers, namely User Interface, Storage, Spatial-Hadoop and Management (Fig. 6), was created to support the test environment, and the proposed method were presented in [2].

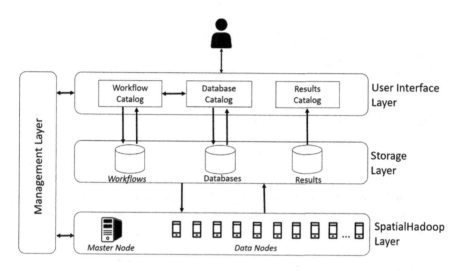

Fig. 6. System architecture overview [2].

The User Interface layer is a user-friendly interface to receive inputs and to show results. In this layer, the user selects an available dataset (or uploads one if it is new) using the Database Catalogue. The workflow to be executed is loaded or created through the Workflow Catalogue. A workflow contains information about queries and operations to be executed and file index type (Grid, R–Tree or R+–Tree). Results are available in Results Catalogue.

The Storage layer stores all datasets available, the workflows used, and the results saved after application execution.

The Management layer is responsible for provisioning the SpatialHadoop cluster with one master node and n data nodes. The quantity of data nodes is defined based on dataset size, as shown in Sect. 5. After all jobs were done, this layer will turn-off the cluster.

The SpatialHadoop layer is the core layer. This layer indexes the dataset (based on user choice in the Web Interface layer), processes queries and operations, and saves the results file back in the Storage layer.

7 Tests and Results

A SpatialHadoop environment was configured in each of the providers mentioned in Table 1, using clusters with virtual servers with 4 vCPUs, 14 Gb of memory and 2 SSDs with 40 GiB each one, to test the proposed method and analyse the total costs to process Big Geospatial Data on providers presented in Table 1.

The datasets used for tests were extracted from OpenStreetMap (OSM), which is a project for geographic information comprised of a world map built by volunteers, presented in Table 2. All datasets are available to download in http://spatialhadoop.cs.umn.edu/datasets.html.

Table 2. Datasets and their features.

Dataset	Description	Records	Size
Lakes	Boundaries of lakes in the world	20 millions	9.0 GB
Buildings	Boundaries of all buildings around the world	115 millions	26.0 GB
Objects	All extracted map objects	263 millions	96.0 GB

The clusters created for tests comprise one master node and the quantity of data nodes based on the formulas shown in Sect. 5, with $C = 1$, $R = 3$, $i = 25\%$ and $w = 20\%$. To compare the costs in each cloud provider, the on-demand (or pay-per-use) price was used. To all datasets presented on Table 2, the following steps were executed:

- Provisioning Cluster: a defined request is sent by the Management layer to the cloud provider with the number and type of master node and data nodes;
- Transfer Dataset: copies an existing dataset from the Storage layer to Data nodes;
- Index Dataset: applies the user-defined index type to dataset;
- Queries and Operations: executes the user-defined queries and operations;
- Save Results: saves the result file usually a text file on Storage layer to be accessed by the user;
- Turn-off Cluster: to avoid wasting of computational resources and to reduce financial costs, all the cluster (master node and data nodes) are turned off by the Management layer, unless some stickiness parameter was defined by the user.

Table 3 presents the runtime of each task executed on Amazon AWS. The values represent an average of 3 executions for each dataset. The queries KNN (with $k = 100$) and Range Query, and the indexing type *Grid* were chosen randomly.

Considering Amazon AWS alone, and the instances configurations presented on Table 4, given the cost of the cluster to support the Small Dataset (1 master node and 1 data node) as US\$ 0.63/h, the total cost to execute all the tasks presented on Table 3 was US\$ 0.19 (18 min). For the cluster to support the

Table 3. Time (seconds) measured in each task.

Task	Lakes (*Small*)	Buildings (*Medium*)	Objects (*Large*)
Provisioning cluster	262	262	262
Indexing (Grid)	602	3,543	15,361
KNN query	8	10	9
Range query	8	6	7
Turning-off cluster	164	164	164
Total time	1,044	3,985	15,803

Medium Dataset (comprising 1 master node and 2 data nodes), the cost per hour was US\$ 0.84, and the cost to process these tasks was US\$ 0,94 (1 h and 7 min). Finally, for the cluster to support the Large Dataset (1 master node and 4 data nodes) the cost per hour was US\$ 1.26, and the cost to process these tasks was US\$ 5.53 (4 h and 24 min). However, since on AWS users are charged by the hour, and not the minute, the cost for a small dataset is US\$ 0.63 (1 h), for a medium dataset was US\$ 1.68 (2 h). For a large dataset, the cost was US\$ 6.30 (5 h). This problem did not occur in others cloud providers tested - Microsoft Azure and Google Cloud - because these providers charge per minute of use.

Table 4. Cluster price on each provider.

Function	AWS	Azure	Google
Master node	0.42/h	1.24/h	0.23/h
Data node	0.21/h	0.62/h	0.23/h

If this cluster was created without considering the datasets size, and other parameters defined in the Formula 1, it would be necessary to consider the largest dataset available to ensure that any query or operation could be executed in this cluster. Considering all datasets available to download on the SpatialHadoop webpage, the largest dataset an OSM file with 137 Gb of size and 717 M records about road networks represented as individual road segments would require a cluster comprising 1 master node and 6 data nodes. Analysing all datasets available in SpatialHadoop webpage, and considering the scenario and parameters defined in our test environment ($C = 1$, $R = 3$, $i = 25\%$ and $w = 20\%$), only 7 out of a total of 33 datasets needed more than 1 data node to be executed. On the other extreme, only 1 dataset needed a 6-node cluster. Processing any other datasets would waste computational resources if the proposed Formula 1 is not applied.

A comparison of performance and costs for the Large Dataset was executed on the 3 providers and is presented in Fig. 7. In this case, although Microsoft Azure has the best performance time (154 min against 214 min from Google, and 262 min from AWS), the cost from Azure is more expensive (US\$ 9.58).

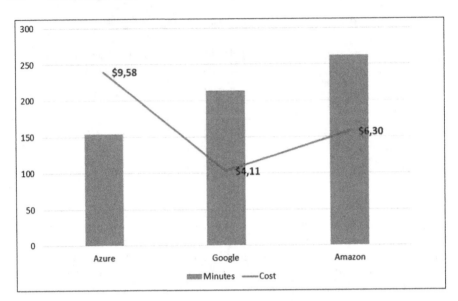

Fig. 7. Time and costs to execute big geospatial data queries on cloud providers.

The cost-efficient cloud provider for processing Big Geospatial Data, in this case, is Google Cloud, with a cost of (US\$ 4.11).

Other important information includes the amount of time spent by the indexing task. It is very important to ensure the SpatialHadoop is high performance,

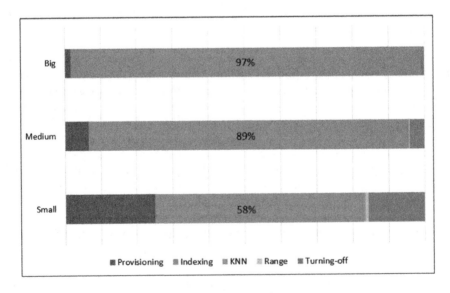

Fig. 8. Time for indexing task.

however it takes up most of the time, although later the queries are done very quickly. Figure 8 presents the percentage of time used to index the 3 sizes of datasets (Table 2) executed on Azure. The time necessary to index a dataset is related to the dataset's size, that is, for the biggest dataset, the time necessary to index representing 97% of the total time.

8   Conclusion and Future Works

The execution of applications for processing Big Geospatial Data is very adherent to cloud computing, since it requires vast computational resources and can be executed in distributed form through applications like SpatialHadoop. The services offered by the providers, which were compared in this article, demonstrate that it is possible to obtain a viable cost-benefit ratio.

A major advantage that leads organizations to seek the services offered by cloud providers is related to cost reduction, especially for applications that are executed sporadically, making investments in equipment with high computational power underutilized. Among these tasks is the indexing of datasets for the processing of Big Geospatial Data which, as shown, is very expensive, but is necessary to guarantee the performance of queries and geographic operations.

The method proposed in this paper achieves the goal of supporting a SpatialHadoop environment on public cloud providers, while avoiding the waste of computational resources. The formula to define the number of data nodes was validated in a test scenario.

Thus, among the three services evaluated, the Dataproc, offered by the provider Google Cloud, is the most cost-efficient one, while the HDInsight offered by the Microsoft Azure, was the most performative, but had the highest cost.

Testing with other databases, other virtual server specifications, other cluster configurations, or even other existing tools for processing Big Geospatial Data is suggested as future work.

References

1. Alarabi, L., Eldawy, A., Alghamdi, R., Mokbel, M.F.: TAREEG: a MapReduce-based web service for extracting spatial data from OpenStreetMap. In: Proceedings of the 2014 ACM SIGMOD International Conference on Management of Data, pp. 897–900. ACM (2014)
2. Bachiega, J., Reis, M., Araujo, A., Holanda, M.: Cost optimization on public cloud provider for big geospatial data: a case study using Open Street Map. In: Proceedings of the 7th International Conference on Cloud Computing and Services Science, pp. 54–62 (2017)
3. Chaisiri, S., Lee, B.S., Niyato, D.: Optimization of resource provisioning cost in cloud computing. IEEE Trans. Serv. Comput. 5(2), 164–177 (2012)
4. Das, J., Dasgupta, A., Ghosh, S.K., Buyya, R.: A geospatial orchestration framework on cloud for processing user queries. In: 2016 IEEE International Conference on Cloud Computing in Emerging Markets (CCEM), pp. 1–8. IEEE (2016)

5. Eldawy, A., Li, Y., Mokbel, M.F., Janardan, R.: CG_Hadoop: computational geometry in MapReduce. In: Proceedings of the 21st ACM SIGSPATIAL International Conference on Advances in Geographic Information Systems, pp. 294–303. ACM (2013)
6. Eldawy, A., Mokbel, M.F.: A demonstration of SpatialHadoop: an efficient mapreduce framework for spatial data. Proc. VLDB Endowment 6(12), 1230–1233 (2013)
7. Eldawy, A., Mokbel, M.F.: Pigeon: a spatial MapReduce language. In: 2014 IEEE 30th International Conference on Data Engineering (ICDE), pp. 1242–1245. IEEE (2014)
8. Eldawy, A., Mokbel, M.F.: SpatialHadoop: a MapReduce framework for spatial data. In: 2015 IEEE 31st International Conference on Data Engineering (ICDE), pp. 1352–1363. IEEE (2015)
9. Eldawy, A., Mokbel, M.F., Jonathan, C.: HadoopViz: a MapReduce framework for extensible visualization of big spatial data. In: 2016 IEEE 32nd International Conference on Data Engineering (ICDE), pp. 601–612. IEEE (2016)
10. Ji, C., Li, Y., Qiu, W., Awada, U., Li, K.: Big data processing in cloud computing environments. In: Pervasive Systems, Algorithms and Networks (ISPAN), 2012 12th International Symposium on. pp. 17–23. IEEE (2012)
11. Kambatla, K., Pathak, A., Pucha, H.: Towards optimizing hadoop provisioning in the cloud. HotCloud 9, 12 (2009)
12. Krämer, M., Senner, I.: A modular software architecture for processing of big geospatial data in the cloud. Comput. Graph. 49, 69–81 (2015)
13. Li, A., Yang, X., Kandula, S., Zhang, M.: CloudCmp: comparing public cloud providers. In: Proceedings of the 10th ACM SIGCOMM Conference on Internet Measurement, pp. 1–14. ACM (2010)
14. Mell, P., Grance, T., et al.: The NIST definition of cloud computing (2011)
15. Mokbel, M.F., Alarabi, L., Bao, J., Eldawy, A., Magdy, A., Sarwat, M., Waytas, E., Yackel, S.: A demonstration of MNTG-a web-based road network traffic generator. In: 2014 IEEE 30th International Conference on Data Engineering (ICDE), pp. 1246–1249. IEEE (2014)
16. Olston, C., Reed, B., Srivastava, U., Kumar, R., Tomkins, A.: Pig Latin: a not-so-foreign language for data processing. In: Proceedings of the 2008 ACM SIGMOD International Conference on Management of data, pp. 1099–1110. ACM (2008)
17. Rosa, M., Moura, B., Vergara, G., Santos, L., Ribeiro, E., Holanda, M., Walter, M.E., Araújo, A.: BioNimbuZ: a federated cloud platform for bioinformatics applications. In: 2016 IEEE International Conference on Bioinformatics and Biomedicine (BIBM), pp. 548–555. IEEE (2016)
18. Sagiroglu, S., Sinanc, D.: Big data: a review. In: 2013 International Conference on Collaboration Technologies and Systems (CTS), pp. 42–47. IEEE (2013)
19. Yang, C., Goodchild, M., Huang, Q., Nebert, D., Raskin, R., Xu, Y., Bambacus, M., Fay, D.: Spatial cloud computing: how can the geospatial sciences use and help shape cloud computing? Int. J. Digital Earth 4(4), 305–329 (2011)
20. Yang, C., Yu, M., Hu, F., Jiang, Y., Li, Y.: Utilizing cloud computing to address big geospatial data challenges. Comput. Environ. Urban Syst. 61, 120–128 (2017)
21. Zhao, Y., Calheiros, R.N., Bailey, J., Sinnott, R.: SLA-based profit optimization for resource management of big data analytics-as-a-service platforms in cloud computing environments. In: 2016 IEEE International Conference on Big Data (Big Data), pp. 432–441. IEEE (2016)

A Flexible Semantic KPI Measurement System

Kyriakos Kritikos[1](✉), Dimitris Plexousakis[1], and Robert Woitch[2]

[1] ICS-FORTH, 70013 Heraklion, Greece
{kritikos,dp}@ics.forth.gr
[2] BOC, Vienna, Austria
Robert.Woitsch@boc-eu.com

Abstract. Linked Data (LD) technology enables integrating information across disparate sources and can be exploited to perform inferencing for deriving added-value knowledge. As such, it can really support performing different kinds of analysis tasks over business process (BP) execution related information. When moving BPs in the cloud, giving rise to Business Process as a Service (BPaaS) concept, the first main challenge is to collect and link, based on a certain structure, information originating from different systems. To this end, two main ontologies are proposed in this paper to enable this structuring: a KPI and a Dependency one. Then, via exploiting these well-connected ontologies, an innovative Key Performance Indicator (KPI) analysis system is built that offers two main analysis capabilities: KPI assessment and drill-down, where the second can enable finding root causes of KPI violations. This system advances the state-of-the-art by exhibiting the capability, through the LD usage, of the flexible construction and assessment of any KPI kind, allowing experts to better explore the possible KPI space.

1 Introduction

Organisations formulate and realise both internal and external procedures in the form of business processes (BPs) in order to provide support or enable their core business. In this respect, corresponding process-aware information systems (PAIS) are embraced that enable the execution and management of these BPs to facilitate the delivery of core services and products. The traditional BP management lifecycle [1] comprises the four main activities of BP design, allocation, execution and evaluation. The first three activities focus on bridging the well-known business-to-IT gap and supporting BP execution. The evaluation activity supports deriving business intelligence (BI) information via conducting various analysis tasks to facilitate BP improvement, thus closing the BP lifecycle loop.

Key Performance Indicator (KPI) measurement and assessment is a well-studied BP evaluation task in the literature. A KPI specifies a condition over a BP quality metric, thus defining the minimum respective quality level to be sustained. The involved metric supplies all measurement details needed to measure a certain BP quality attribute, which can be categorised into 4 groups: (a) time,

© Springer International Publishing AG, part of Springer Nature 2018
D. Ferguson et al. (Eds.): CLOSER 2017, CCIS 864, pp. 237–261, 2018.
https://doi.org/10.1007/978-3-319-94959-8_13

(b) quality, (c) customer satisfaction, and (d) financial [2]. As such, an evaluation expert has the main goal to specify suitable KPIs, possibly spanning all four groups, which can be measured by the BP evaluation system and enable assessing the quality levels of BPs.

In this respect, various KPI measurement systems have been proposed which use different technologies, such as OLAP [3] or SQL query evaluation [4]. While such systems can rapidly perform the KPI assessment, we believe that their main goal should not be the KPI assessment speed but the assistance to evaluation experts in defining the most suitable KPIs for a BP. However, there is a lack of flexible and user-intuitive mechanisms for KPI definition in these systems. Such systems are also usually special-purposed as they are designed to serve only a fix set of KPI metric types, such that introducing a new metric can require re-engineering the underlying system database. Finally, they do not exploit sophisticated integration mechanisms to integrate any information source kind. Such an integration is essential to integrate information not only from internal information sources within a BP management system (e.g., from BP monitoring and execution components) but also external ones that can enable deriving suitable, added-value facts. For instance, a location ontology could certainly assist in deriving non-obvious location relations between KPI assessment facts such that, e.g., the deployment of a BP component in a certain cloud region leads constantly to KPI violations, thus enabling to derive of useful deployment facts.

The latter issue is critical in the context of not only traditional but also BPs that have been moved to the Cloud, i.e., BP as a Service (BPaaS). Such a migration has become a trend nowadays due to the great advantages that cloud computing offers, such as reduced cost and elasticity. As such, this migration must be suitably supported. This support can be realised via a BPaaS management system, able to control the whole BPaaS lifecycle, which comprises different environments, each responsible for a different lifecycle activity [5]. This inevitably well justifies the need to integrate information from many of these environments and their components to support the BPaaS monitoring and evaluation.

To realise the vision of a BPaaS by providing essential, flexible and user-intuitive support to BPaaS evaluation, this paper advocates the use of Linked Data (LD) technology for the following reasons: (a) it allows performing inferencing tasks to deduce added-value analysis information; (b) enables integrating information, even in unforeseen ways, across disparate information sources; (c) LD are represented via ontologies which are closer to human perception.

The information integration task is facilitated via introducing two ontologies: (a) a dependency ontology that captures the dependencies between BPaaS components, across different abstraction levels (BP, software and infrastructure), and their state. This ontology constitutes the major integration point for information coming from different systems, enabling its suitable correlation for supporting KPI analysis; (b) a KPI-based extension of the OWL-Q [6] ontology which enables formally and fully specifying how KPIs can be measured over which BPaaS hierarchy components. As such, via introducing KPI metric hierarchies that span the whole BPaaS hierarchy, the measurability of KPIs is guaranteed.

An innovative KPI measurement system has been built [7] over these two ontologies offering its facilities in the form of a REST service. This system can integrate information from many parts of a BPaaS management system and offers two KPI analysis capabilities: KPI measurement and drill-down. The KPI drill-down capability relies on relating via parent-child relations different KPIs at both business and technical levels which enables performing root cause analysis over a high-level KPI violation. This capability comes into two flavours depending on which KPI elements are related: the KPI itself or its metric. The proposed measurement system supports the on-the-fly KPI metric formula specification and assessment, provided that the relation of the formula to a certain context is given. This highlights the great flexibility in KPI measurement offered that greatly assists in the best possible exploration of the KPI metric space.

The rest of this paper is structured as follows. Section 2 reviews the related work. Section 3 offers background information enabling to better understand the main paper contribution. The two proposed ontologies are analysed in Sect. 4. Section 5 analyses the proposed system architecture and explains the way KPI analysis is performed. Finally, Sect. 6 concludes the paper and draws directions for further research.

2   Related Work

Work related to this paper spans KPI & dependency modelling and KPI analysis which is analysed in 3 respective sub-sections.

2.1   KPI Meta-Models

As KPI modelling is a pre-requisite for KPI assessment, a great amount of research was devoted in developing KPI meta-models, languages and ontologies, especially as currently there is no standardised BP language covering the BP context perspective (including goal-based and measurement information aspects) [8].

The related work evaluation in KPI modelling relies on a systematic approach which: (a) considers a comparison criteria set, (b) summarises the comparison based on these criteria in the form of an evaluation table, where rows map to the related work approaches, columns to the criteria and cells to the performance of an approach over a certain criterion, and (c) supplies a discussion over the evaluation results presented.

The following comparison criteria were considered: (a) *KPI coverage*: how well the notion of a KPI is covered; (b) *metric formulas*: computation formulas are provided to support the KPI metric measurement; (c) *measurability*: other aspects complementing metric specification are expressed to cover all measurement details (e.g., units, measured objects); (d) *goal coverage*: KPIs are connected to goals to enable assessing operational or even tactical goals satisfaction via performing goal analysis; (e) *semantics*: the meta-model/language should be semantic or allow semantic annotations to enable formal reasoning and reaching better evaluation accuracy levels; (f) *information sources*: both internal and

Table 1. Comparison table [7] over KPI modelling work.

Work	KPI Cov.	Metric formulas	Measur.	Goal Cov.	Semantics	Inf. Sources	Meas. Origin	Level
[9]	Moderate	Yes	Moderate	No	No	Internal	Probes	BP, SE
[10]	Low	No	Low	yes	No	Internal	-	BP, SE
[11]	Good	Yes	Low	yes	No	Internal	-	BP
[12]	Good	Yes	Moderate	No	No	Internal	Probes	BP
[13]	Moderate	No	Low	yes	No	Internal	Probes	BP, Inf
[14]	Low	Yes	low	No	No	Internal	Probes	BP
[15]	Moderate	Yes	Good	Yes	Yes	Internal	Probes	BP
[16]	Low	No	Low	No	Yes	Internal	probes	BP
[17]	Low	Yes	Low	No	no	Both	Probes	BP, Inf
OWL-Q KPI Extension	Good	Yes	Excellent	Yes	Yes	Both	All	BP, SE, Inf

external information sources should be exploited; (g) *measurement origin*: the coverage of measurements and their origin (probes, sensors, or humans); (h) *level*: the levels covered (BP, SE - service, Inf - Infrastructure) (Table 1).

The table evaluation results [7] show that not only our ontology scores well over all criteria but also exhibits the best performance for almost all of them. Thus, it can be considered as the most prominent. [15] maps to the sole modelling work close to ours. However, that work does not cover all levels and correlate measurements to human sources, it exploits only internal information sources and supplies a moderate KPI coverage. It also does not directly model the notion of a metric but intermixes it with that of an indicator. This is wrong as when the latter notion is re-used in the context of KPI computation formulas, it maps to a metric condition and not to the metric itself which represents all suitable measurement details to enable KPI computation. The metric formula definition in that work, though, is interesting as it involves a restricted natural language form. This might be more user-intuitive but loses on clarity and comprehension when recursive composite metric formulas must be specified. A pure mathematical form might be more suitable, an issue that we currently explore.

2.2   Dependency Meta-Models

Dependency modelling is a pre-requisite for system monitoring and adaptation. Without dependency knowledge, both monitoring can be limited, covering low abstraction levels as propagation to higher levels is prohibited, as well as respective adaptation capabilities.

By following the same analysis approach as in the previous sub-section, the following evaluation criteria have been devised: (a) *abstraction level*: the levels (denoted as BE, SE, Inf) in the BPaaS hierarchy covered; (b) *formalism*: the dependency model formalism used; (c) *runtime*: the capability to cover a dynamic or just a static system view. Dynamic views enable to record system

Table 2. Evaluation table [7] over dependency modelling work.

Work	Abst. Level	Formal.	Runtime	Detail level
SEE	BP, SE	Ontology	No	Good
GRU	SE, INF	Graph	Yes	Low
CUI	SE, INF	Graph	Yes	Mod.
HASS	SE, INF	Graph	Yes	Good
TOSCA	SE, INF	DSL	No	Good
CAMEL	SE, INF	DSL	Yes	Good
Ours	All	Ontology	Yes	Good

evolution and enable realising monitoring and adaptation mechanisms; (d) *detail level*: how well component dependencies are expressed.

The dependency modelling work, apart from ours, encoded in the table [7] is the following: (a) SEE [18], (b) GRU [19], (c) CUI [20], (d) HASS [21], (e) TOSCA[1] and (f) CAMEL[2].

The evaluation results show that our ontology covers all possible levels, covers runtime information and includes a good detail level for the dependencies captured. Thus, it is better than all other work. Sole competitors are approaches in [18,22] that do not cover all BPaaS hierarchy levels. Moreover, the approach in [18] does not capture runtime information, while [22] does not rely on semantics. Please also consider that: (a) an ontology-based approach is essential for better integrating dependency information from various information sources as well as enabling interesting inferencing over this information; (b) some modelling approaches must go beyond the good dependency detail level that they exhibit (Table 2).

Table 3. Evaluation table [7] over KPI analysis work.

Work	Analysis types	DB type	Evaluation technique	Drill-Down technique	Evaluation flexibility	Level
[4]	All	Relational	SQL queries	Decision trees	Low	BP
[23]	All	Relational	Formula comp	Decision trees	Low	BP, SE
[16]	Evaluation	Semantic	Formula comp	-	Low	BP
[24]	Evaluation	Semantic	WSML rules	-	Moderate	BP, SE
[3]	Evaluation	Warehouse	OLAP	-	Moderate	BP
[25]	All	Semantic	SPARQL queries	KPI-based	Moderate	BP
Our Framework	All	Semantic	SPARQL queries	Metric/KPI-based	Good	All

---

[1] http://docs.oasis-open.org/tosca/TOSCA/v1.0/TOSCA-v1.0.html.
[2] www.camel-dsl.org.

2.3   KPI Analysis Systems

The KPI analysis frameworks proposed employ techniques that mainly support KPI evaluation but also KPI drill-down in some cases. Most techniques employ relational or semantic dbs or data warehouses in order to appropriately structure the underlying database to support KPI analysis.

By following the same evaluation approach as in previous subsections, the following evaluation criteria have been devised: (a) *analysis types*: the KPI analysis kinds supported; (b) *db type*: type of db used to store the information relevant for KPI analysis; (c) *evaluation technique*: the KPI measurement technique used; (d) *drill-down technique*: the KPI drill-down technique used; (e) *evaluation flexibility*: the level of flexibility offered in the exploration of the possible metric space; (f) *level*: the BPaaS hierarchy levels covered.

The evaluation results in Table 3 [7] show that semantic dbs are do considered in more than half of the systems, indicating that their added-value is recognised: they better link information and enable various forms of reasoning. Almost half of the systems focus only on KPI evaluation, while the rest support KPI drill-down via two main techniques: decision trees and combination of metric & KPI hierarchies. The first technique is suitable for covering measurability gaps (disconnected metric trees). The second is suitable when measurability gaps do not exist and KPI hierarchies are formed, such that we can go down to more technical KPIs and then continue from there by exploring the respective metric hierarchies involved for finding the root causes of the high-level KPI violations considered.

Evaluation techniques greatly vary, from SQL queries, OLAP and event-based metric formula calculation to WSML rules and SPARQL queries. SPARQL queries, however, can be more expressive, even with respect to semantic rules, as they: (a) allow different ways to link the underlying semantic information; (b) have similar grouping and aggregation capabilities with SQL queries; (c) operate on the conceptual level which is closer to actual human perception.

Our system seems to be one step ahead in evaluation flexibility from the work in [3,24,25] as it does not only allow to map human-based formulations of metric formulas into SPARQL queries but also to experiment with the metric and condition context. Via combining this with the respective KPI ontology capabilities, it can also support exploiting various information sources, like metrics and service properties to enable better exploring the metric space. As such, our approach is more complete and user-intuitive than the other two systems.

Finally, the evaluation results show that only our system is able to cover all levels. In fact only three out of seven systems recognise the need to cover more than one BPaaS hierarchy level.

3   Background

As OWL-Q is the basis for the KPI ontology proposed, it is shortly analysed in this section. OWL-Q is a prominent [26] non-functional service specification ontology-based language that captures all necessary measurability aspects via the introduction of corresponding OWL-Q facets. Semantic rule also accompany OWL-Q to enable two semantic reasoning types: (a) semantic OWL-Q model validation based on the domain semantics; (b) added-value knowledge generation in the form of term equivalence facts. The 6 main facets of OWL-Q are now analysed by focusing more on those more relevant to this paper's work.

The core facet captures generic concepts and properties, such as *Schedule* and *name*. *Category* is one important generic concept, enabling to construct hierarchies of categories, i.e., partitions of this and other element types, like quality metrics and attributes. As such, this concept facilitates specifying structured quality models (see KPI categories in Sect. 1) that can be re-used in the context of non-functional capability and KPI description.

The attribute, unit and value type facets capture respective attribute, unit and value type elements. Attributes (e.g., *utilisation*) represent properties measurable by metrics. Units can be derived (e.g., *bytes/sec*), single (e.g., *sec*) or dimensionless (e.g., *percentage*). Different value types can be specified spanning both non-numeric (e.g., lists) and numeric (e.g., ranges) constructs. Such value types express the domain of values for metrics. As such, they can be used for measurement or metric condition threshold validation by checking whether such values are included in them.

The metric facet specifies how attributes can be measured via the conceptualisation of the *Metric* concept. A metric can be raw (e.g., uptime), computed from sensors or measurement directives posed over service instrumentation systems, or composite (e.g., availability), computed from formulas, i.e., function applications over a list of arguments, where an argument can be a metric, attribute, service property or another formula. Any kind of metric can be related to a respective context which details its measurement frequency and window.

The specification facet enables expressing non-functional specifications as sets of respective capabilities/requirements. Each capability/requirement is expressed as a constraint which can be either a logical combination of other constraints (i.e., a *CompositeConstraint*) or a simple condition imposing a certain threshold over a metric (i.e., a *SimpleConstraint*. A metric condition is related with two different contexts: the metric and condition ones. The condition context explicates which object (e.g., service or service input) is measured and the way the condition should be evaluated over this object's instances. In the latter case, it is expressed whether the measurements over all or a certain amount or percentage of object instances should be considered in the condition evaluation.

4   KPI and Dependency Ontologies

To enable conducting any KPI analysis kind, meta-models must be supplied that structure and link respective information on which the analysis relies. As such, to support BPaaS KPI analysis, 2 main ontologies have been developed: (a) the dependency ontology covering BPaaS dependency models; (b) the KPI ontology covering KPI modelling. These ontologies are interconnected in one major point, the actual BPaaS element measured within the BPaaS hierarchy. In this way, based on the BPaaS dependency model and interconnections between different BPaaS elements, measurement propagation hierarchies to cover measurability gaps can be deduced while root causes for KPI violation can be discovered. In the following, these two ontologies are analysed in separate sub-sections.

4.1   KPI Ontology

It has been decided to extend OWL-Q to cover the modelling of KPIs as it completely covers the specification of QoS profiles and SLAs. The OWL-Q extension developed builds upon OWL-Q constructs only a minimum but sufficient number of relevant new parts. It does not only involve extending the core OWL-Q ontology but also the rule set that has been originally specified for OWL-Q. The latter extension kind involved the development of validation and knowledge production rules which apply for the KPI domain and enable both the semantic validation of OWL-Q KPI models (to detect, e.g., that a parent KPI is measured by a metric which is not a parent of the metric used for the evaluation of a child

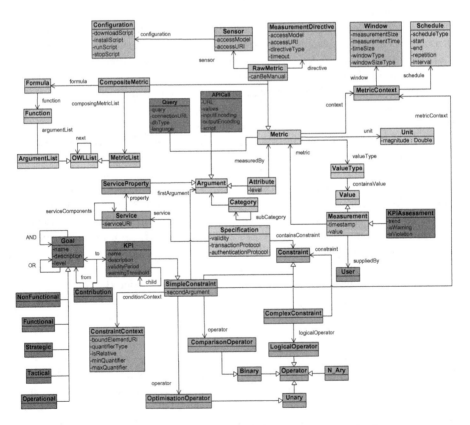

Fig. 1. OWL-Q KPI extension [7]. (Color figure online)

KPI) but also the production of new knowledge based on them (e.g., the kind of KPI violation for a certain KPI measurement based on the measurement value).

The current application of the overall OWL-Q extension over the Cloud-Socket project[3] use cases has led to the full modelling of all KPIs needed. This is a major evaluation step which validates the design of this OWL-Q extension.

Figure 1 [7] depicts the KPI OWL-Q extension, where the grey colour denotes core OWL-Q concepts, blue metric-related concepts, green specification-related concepts, and yellow a concept from the Dependency ontology, while red denotes the KPI extension concepts mapping to a sub-facet of the specification one.

A *KPI* represents an indicator signifying whether BP performance is satisfactory, problematic or erroneous. Thus, it maps to 3 possible states, captured by a warning and violation threshold. The BP performance for positively monotonic metrics is satisfactory when is above the warning threshold, problematic when is between the warning and violation ones, and erroneous when is below the violation threshold. In case of negatively monotonic metrics, the order between warning and violation thresholds is reversed and the state mapping is symmetric.

A KPI was modelled as a sub-concept of simple constraint which apart from the existing reference to a metric and (violation) threshold, it carries extra information spanning a human-oriented description (for human consumption), a validity period and the warning threshold.

OWL-Q enables the modelling of preference models which can represent the actual way measurements can be propagated from the lowest to the highest level by also providing weights to each node in the hierarchy signifying its relative importance and contribution to the higher-level quality of the parent node. Such weighting as well as the content of such preference models can be BPaaS or customer-specific and thus might be subjective. This also signifies that weights can be modified as suited at evaluation time to represent the change of (broker/customer) opinion or any kind of initial misjudgement.

In other KPI meta-models in the literature, weights are given to KPIs and not metrics. This is an alternative modelling for representing this nested metric structures. However, such a modelling caters for an ad hoc propagation (e.g., possibly with the on-the-fly grouping of KPIs in order to produce a certain higher-level quality value) of quality and not for a generic one.

While OWL-Q fully covers the specification of metrics, it was extended to address the issue of external information access via incorporating such information in metric formulas. By realistically assuming that all modern information sources are available in the form of REST APIs or database endpoints, this extension was implemented by introducing the *Query* and *APICall* as sub-concepts of *Argument*, enabling instances of these classes to be directly used as input arguments in metric formulas. A *Query* expresses in an implementation-independent way the information required to connect and query a db spanning: (a) the db connection URL; (b) the query language; (c) the actual query; (d) the db type.

On the other hand, an *APICall* expresses all information needed to call a REST API and retrieve back the result, spanning: (a) the API URL; (b) values to

---

[3] http://www.cloudsocket.eu.

all API input parameters for the call; (c) input information encoding; (d) output format (e.g., XML or JSON); (e) a JSON or XML-like script (e.g., in XPath) to operate over the output returned so as to return a single value focusing on a certain part within the retrieved output (e.g., the post-code for an email address).

In certain cases (e.g., *customer satisfaction* metrics) it is imperative to enable humans to manually provide measurements in the system. In this case, the measurement-to-user linkage should be modelled. When connected to certain aspects like human trust and reliability, such linkage can enable reasoning over measurements and their propagation to establish a so-called trust level over them and a more reliable and accurate way to aggregate them. This was realised in OWL-Q by not only associating a measurement to a specific sensor or directive but also to a human resource that might produce this measurement. Such a human resource could also be part of the BPaaS dependency hierarchy (e.g., the knowledge worker responsible for the execution of a certain BPaaS user task) which then makes this extension another connection point with the Dependency ontology proposed.

The drill-down from higher- to lower-level KPIs to support root-cause analysis is enabled by associating KPIs to each other via a parent-child relation. This relation must conform to the parent-child relation between the metrics of the involved KPIs (i.e., the parent KPI's metric should be a parent metric of the child KPI metric). For instance, a KPI for service response time could be related to KPIs mapping to the service execution time and network latency.

While such relations enable us to go down until low-level KPIs which could be blamed for a high-level KPI violation, the actual root cause of such a violation may not be clearly identified. Even in this case, the specification of metric hierarchies can suffice to enable going even further down to the actual problem by also observing the objects being involved. The inspection of the lowest level metric values could be subject to automatic analysis tools to produce the respective derivations needed or based on the experience of the analyst which can know what can be the improper measurement values for quite low-level metrics.

In KPI assessment, we are also interested in deriving other information, such as the value trend with respect to the previous assessments, by performing different analysis kinds. For instance, we could evaluate whether the BPaaS performance gets gradually reduced from the very beginning. To this end, to also make a connection to the original OWL-Q concept called *Measurement*, specifying a measurement's value and its timestamp, a new sub-concept named as *KPIAssessment* was developed, specifying additional information spanning the value trend and the KPI violation kind (warning or fatal) occurred.

By connecting a KPI to a business goal to be satisfied, we have the capability to assess the respective goal's achievement. In this way, such a linkage can enable performing goal-based analysis in order to reach interesting conclusions related, e.g., to the satisfaction of strategic goals from operational ones.

To this end, OWL-Q was further extended to both specify goals and their linkage to KPIs. First, the concept of *Goal*, representing any goal kind, along with respective sub-concepts mapping to strategic, tactical, operational, functional and non-functional goals were introduced. Any goal was associated with a name, description and application level, while operational goals were mapped to the BPs used to satisfy them (another connection point with Dependency ontology). Goals were also linked with each other via AND/OR self-relations or contribution relations to enable forming goal hierarchies from strategic to operational goals. The *Contribution* concept was modelled to express contribution relations by linking a goal with another goal or KPI and being mapped to a certain contribution level.

4.2   Dependency Ontology

Various analysis types over a certain system can be performed only if the evolution of the system dependency model is captured. This model reveals what are the system components, how they are interconnected and what is the interconnection direction. Such a direction indicates the way faults and measurements can be propagated from lower to higher abstraction levels. Following the opposite direction enables conducting root cause analysis, i.e., from a current, issue at a high-level component down to the actual component to blame in a lower-level.

The Dependency ontology proposed captures both deployment and state information about all components in a BPaaS hierarchy. It extensively covers many information aspects, thus becoming suitable for many different BPaaS analysis kinds, including: (a) KPI analysis; (b) (semantic) process mining [27], due to the coverage of (semantic) I/O information for tasks and workflows; (c) best BPaaS deployment analysis [28] as all possible deployment information across all levels is covered; (d) the detection of event patterns [29] leading to a KPI violation.

Figure 2 [7] depicts the Dependency Ontology which follows the well-known type-instance pattern, enabling to capture both the allocation decisions made as well as the whole BPaaS allocation history and evolution. The proposed ontology also captures organisational information. In particular, the *Tenant* concept was incorporated to model an organisation, also associated with a *User* set. Different kinds of tenants exist: (a) *Brokers* that offer a BPaaS, (b) *Customers* that can purchase a BPaaS, and (c) *Providers* which offer a cloud service supporting the BPaaS execution. A string type enumeration was also modelled to cover different kinds of customer organisations, like SMEs, start-ups or big companies.

Similar to the new design of OWL-Q [30], the Dependency ontology includes generic data properties which can be mapped to all or a subset of the concepts modelled, such as *id* properties to be attributed to any concept and *endpoint/URL* properties to be attributed only to services. As such, from now on, the analysis focuses on specific data properties that individually characterise aspect-specific concepts and not generic ones.

We follow a a top-down analysis for the ontology from the type to the instance level. The top concept at the type level represents a *BPaaS* which is associated with an *owner* and an executable *Workflow* to be run in the Cloud. The executable workflow is related in turn to its main *Tasks*.

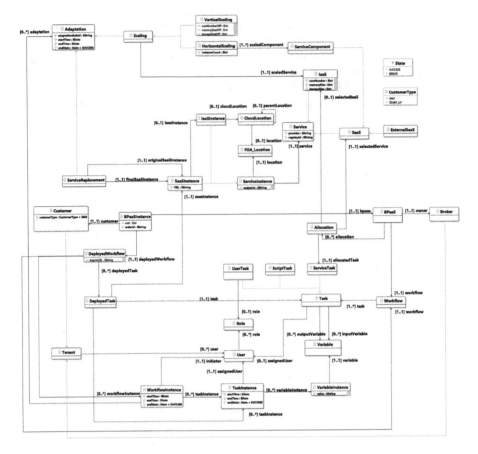

Fig. 2. Dependency ontology UML class diagram [7].

A task can have input and output *Variables* and is associated with a certain user or role that can be assigned to it. It can be further classified into a *Manu-alTask* (performed by human workers), a *ScriptTask* (performed automatically via a script) and a *ServiceTask* (performed automatically by calling a Software as a Service (SaaS)).

As stated, a BPaaS corresponds to an allocated executable workflow. This signifies that: (a) many BPaaSes can share the same workflow; (b) from these BPaaSes each BPaaS can be uniquely distinguished based on the specific set of allocations performed on that workflow. Such a distinction is enabled via the modelling of the *Allocation* concept which represents an allocation decision that is linked to a certain BPaaS and workflow. Such an allocation maps a service task in the workflow to a *SaaS*, either an *ExternalSaaS* or a (internal) *Service-Component*. In case of a *ServiceComponent*, the allocation is also associated to an Infrastructure as a Service (IaaS) which supports its deployment. A *IaaS* is characterised by the following properties: its number of cores and the main memory & storage size.

The top concept at the instance level is *BPaaSInstance* which represents an instance of a BPaaS associated with the *Customer* that has purchased it, its actual cost and the *DeployedWorkflow*. The latter concept represents the BPaaS workflow deployed on behalf of a customer upon successful purchasing of this BPaaS. The instances of this workflow are then associated with: (a) the instances of tasks (*TaskInstance*) created; (b) its start and end time; (c) its resulting state ("SUCCESS" or "ERROR"); (d) the user that has initiated it; (e) the adaptations performed on it to maintain the service level promised in the corresponding SLA signed with the customer. Instances of tasks of this workflow are associated with similar information that incorporates the user (if exists) executing them and the input/output *VariableInstances* that they generate. The latter map to the actual *Variable* concerned and include the respective values produced.

The Dependency ontoloy models two types of concrete allocations: (a) from a deployed workflow task to a *SaaSInstance* realising its functionality; (b) from an internal *SaaSInstance* to the *IaaSInstance* hosting it (in case of instances of internal service components). Both SaaS and IaaS instances are sub-concepts of *ServiceInstance* which encompasses their common features including the service's endpoint and its physical & cloud location. *IaaSInstances* further encapsulate certain hardware-specific information, such as the id and name of the image involved as well as the respective *OS* deployed, while they also map to respective *IP* on which they are available.

The FAO (United Nations Food and Agriculture Organisation) geopolitical ontology[4] has been used to capture physical locations and their hierarchies. In particular, the physical service location is mapped to the concepts of *geographical_region* and *self_governing* that represent geographical regions (e.g., continents), and all locations mapping to self governing countries, respectively. The *CloudLocation* concept was also used to structure arbitrary hierarchies of cloud locations to cover the hierarchy diversity across different cloud providers. The *Cloud* concept was also modelled in order to specify the cloud that is being offered by a certain *Provider* for which the corresponding location hierarchy applies.

Concerning BPaaS adaptation, the most usual types as reported in respective literature have been modelled, i.e., service replacement and scaling ones. Any kind of *Adaptation* is mapped to its start and end time, its final state and the adaptation rule triggered. A *ServiceReplacement* is additionally associated with the service instance being substituted and the service instance substituting it.

On the other hand, any kind of scaling maps to the IaaS to be scaled. Two main scaling types have been covered: (a) *HorizontalScalings* for which we specify one or more service components hosted by the IaaS to be scaled plus the amount of instances to be generated or removed; (b) *VerticalScalings* for which

---

[4] http://aims.fao.org/aos/geopolitical.owl.

we indicate the respective increase or decrease amount of the corresponding IaaS characteristic(s) scaled.

5   KPI Analysis System

In the following, we analyse the architecture of the KPI analysis system, then we provide some implementation details and finally we describe in detail the algorithms used for the KPI measurement and drill-down mapping to respective components of the system architecture analysed.

5.1   Architecture

The proposed system offers the following main features: (a) it supports multi-tenancy in the context of BPaaS brokers. This means that the system can support multiple BPaaS brokers in the conduction of KPI analysis tasks and also enforces the right access control such that no broker can conduct analysis tasks and see corresponding analysis results pertaining to other brokers; (b) it enables not only to evaluate the current value of KPI metrics but also the browsing and search over their measurement history; (c) it supports the dynamic evaluation of KPI metrics via the more flexible exploration of the possible metric space; (d) it supports the storage of the KPI measurements produced allowing the more efficient querying of the KPI evaluation history rather than its more time-consuming reconstruction; (e) it adopts a high-level language in the specification of the KPI metrics to be evaluated which is closer to the human perception.

Figure 3 depicts the service-oriented architecture of the KPI analysis system which comprises eleven main components and follows the known three-level implementation pattern of UI-business logic-database. In the following, we analyse the functionality of each system component in different paragraphs.

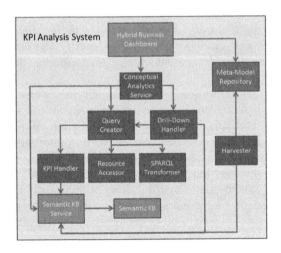

Fig. 3. Architecture of the KPI analysis system.

Hybrid Dashboard. This component constitutes the main entry point to the system from which respective analysis tasks can be performed and then their results are represented according to suitable visualisation metaphors.

Harvester. This composite component is responsible for the harvesting of information from different components of the BPaaS management platform. The information harvested at a particular frequency is further structured and linked according to the two ontologies proposed as well as stored in the *Semantic KB*. The population is performed periodically to not overwhelm the system but more frequently with respect to the way KPI measurements are assessed. The analysis of the internal architecture of this composite component is out of context of this paper but can be found here [31].

Conceptual Analytics Service. This component is a REST service offering the two main KPI analysis capabilities at the following URL: http://134.60.64.222/evaluation. As such, it can be exploited by external components to programmatically deliver these capabilities. The KPI measurement comes into two main forms: (a) measurement over certain KPIs which have been already defined for the BPaaS; (b) measurement over dynamically specified KPI metrics - here is where the flexibility in the evaluation is supported as the user can specify dynamically KPI metric formulas as well as play with the metric measurement schedule and window. For the first type of KPI measurement, there are two possibilities as mentioned in the main features of the KPI analysis system: either we directly measure the KPI or we just perform a query over its measurement/evaluation history. The first possibility is more appropriate in the case of the production of new KPI measurements while the second is more efficient in terms of evaluation response time in the context of browsing the evaluation history of a certain KPI.

Similarly, KPI drill-down comes into two forms: (a) KPI drill-down based on KPI parent-child relationships - here the whole KPI hierarchy is exploited in order to go from the violation of a high-level KPI to a low-level KPI which is to be blamed for this violation; (b) KPI drill-down based on the KPI metric parent-child relationships - here we follow the dependencies between KPI metrics in order to find the root causes of KPI violations. Another main differentiation with respect to the other drill-down type is the fact that the analysis can further go down into metrics over which KPIs have not been specified enabling to perform a deeper root cause analysis.

Apart from these two analysis capabilities, the *Conceptual Analytics Service* offers additional functionality which covers

1. the enumeration of all KPIs that can be evaluated for a certain BPaaS - this can enable a UI to visualise represent all these KPIs and assist the user in selecting the right KPI to evaluate for that BPaaS
2. the enumeration of all metrics that can be used for the construction of dynamic metric formulas for on-the-fly evaluation of new, more composite KPI metrics

3. the enumeration of all BPaaS customers for which a certain BPaaS applies - this enables the system to focus the analysis on a certain customer once this customer has been selected in the *Hybrid Business Dashboard*.
4. the supply of a SPARQL query which can be evaluated in the underlying semantic LD database. This latter functionality is more suitable for an expert which is aware of the two ontologies proposed for a more ad-hoc and specialised exploration of the possible metric space.

Underlying the *Conceptual Analytics Engine* lie two main components which are responsible in turn for the delivery of the two main KPI analysis functionalities: (a) the *Query Creator* and the *Drill-Down Handler*. These two components are now analysed in detail.

Query Creator. This component is responsible for the production of a SPARQL query for the evaluation of a certain KPI metric. This query is then issued by the *Conceptual Analytics Service* on the *Semantic KB* in order to produce the corresponding KPI measurement as a result that is finally compared against the KPI threshold in order to evaluate whether the KPI is violated or not. Internally, the *Query Creator* orchestrates the functionality of the following three components.

KPI Handler. This component is responsible for the management of the KPIs. In particular, this component extracts the KPI model of a certain BPaaS which is specified in OWL-Q into a list of KPI objects that can then be retrieved by the *Query Creator* component for their further respective processing and transformation into an SPARQL query. This extraction is supported by the OWL-Q processing library which is analysed in the implementation details subsection.

Resource Accessor. This component is responsible for accessing information resources from external information sources. In particular, each time a metric formula needs to be transformed into a SPARQL query, it is checked whether it accesses external information. If this holds, then this component takes care of accessing the DB or invoking the corresponding API exposed by the external information source in order to retrieve the respective information resource required. Subsequently, the retrieved information can be exploited as a constant in the SPARQL query used to evaluate the metric computation formula.

SPARQL Transformer. This component is responsible for the actual transformation of the KPI object into a SPARQL query. More details about how this transformation takes place is supplied in Sect. 5.3.

Drill-Down Handler. This component is responsible for the execution of the two main drill-down forms. Internally, it exploits the *Query Creator* in order to produce respective SPARQL queries when corresponding KPI metrics need to be evaluated. This is needed, for example, when we need to evaluate the KPIs within the hierarchy of a certain high-level KPI. More details about these two forms of KPI drill-down are supplied in Sect. 5.3.

Semantic KB. This component is a semantic Triple Store which enables the management and storage of semantic information, which is structured in our case based on the two ontologies proposed. To address the heterogeneity of different triple store implementations and their exchange, a *Semantic KB Service* was developed on top of this KB to offer a RESTful interface enabling LD management via methods that facilitate issuing SPARQL queries, inserting as well as updating RDF graphs.

Meta-Model Repository. This component includes basic information about BPs like their models and annotations to be exploited for visualisation and information harvesting reasons. In the current implementation prototype, this component is shared between the BPaaS Design and Evaluation environments in the corresponding BPaaS management platform (see CloudSocket project). This witnesses the closeness between the two BP lifecycle activities and the respective level of cooperation established between them.

5.2   Implementation Details

All the components were developed in the Java programming language. The development of the *Conceptual Analytics Service* relied on the Jersey library[5].

The transformation of a OWL-Q KPI model to KPI in-memory objects relied on the OWL-Q library. This library enables the domain code-based representation of OWL-Q models as well as their loading from and storage to the file system. Such a library can also be exploited for the production of a customised OWL-Q editor in order to provide a more user-intuitive way of editing and managing OWL-Q models with respect to generic OWL editors like Protege[6]. Such an editor would also enable the expert user not to possess any knowledge over OWL and ontology modelling for the production of KPI models. This would increase the mass of possible experts that can be involved in the production of KPI models based on OWL-Q.

The *Resource Accessor* is a Java-based component which encompasses drivers for the accessing of widely-known DBs like MySQL or Postgresql. It also relies on the Jersey library for the invocation of REST APIs for the accessing of external information needed in metric formulas.

The *Semantic KB* was realised based on the Virtuoso Triple Store[7]. This triple store is quite efficient in SPARQL query evaluation, especially as it relies on a column-based object database, The service on top of the *Semantic KB* was realised again via the Jersey as well as the sesame RDF management library[8]. This enabled us to exploit the sesame driver in Virtuoso for a more advanced and high-level handling of the SPARQL query evaluation.

---

[5] https://jersey.github.io/.

[6] protege.stanford.edu.

[7] https://virtuoso.openlinksw.com.

[8] rdf4j.org.

5.3 KPI Analysis and Drill-Down Algorithms

KPI Analysis. Independently of what is the KPI analysis form, a core KPI metric evaluation functionality has to be realised. To this end, a semantic approach for this realisation was selected for two main reasons: (a) evaluation accuracy is higher; (b) semantic linking enables better exploring the actual space of possible KPI metric computation formulas. The latter actually reflects the current KPI evaluation practice where, apart from some KPI metrics that can be fixed in advance (e.g., cross-domain metrics like *process duration*), the rest of the KPI metrics must be computed based on the knowledge and expertise of the (BP performance) evaluator.

Semantic linking enables a richer connection between different information aspects to facilitate the metric formula construction with respect to other forms of measurement storage and aggregation. On the other hand, other measurement system alternatives, like Time Series Data Bases, require an a-priori design of the measurement space and do not enable advanced forms of information linking and aggregation. This means that such systems suffer from a certain form of inflexibility while they do not offer a satisfactory level of dynamicity.

The most intuitive way to express metric formulas for a semantic approach that adopts LD technology is via SPARQL queries. However, SPARQL queries require deep knowledge about LD technology and great expertise in SPARQL query modelling which might not be possessed by a BP performance evaluation expert. Such an expert would rather prefer to specify the metric formula in mathematical terms via a simplified language. This observation has led us to adopting the OWL-Q KPI extension. By relying on an user-intuitive OWL-Q editor and the fact that ontologies represent human conceptualisations of a domain, the expert can more naturally specify the metric formula. This obstacle could be further overpassed by introducing a domain-specific language for pure mathematical metric formula expressions which is left as a possible future work direction.

Based on this (language) adoption, the challenge that still remains for a suitable KPI evaluation lies in the capability to transform OWL-Q models, and especially KPI metric formulas, into a SPARQL query specification. This metric formula to SPARQL query transformation comprises some specific hurdles that had to be overcome. First, it is differentiated based on the metric kind. Two metric kinds exist: (a) *customer-specific*, pertaining to a certain BPaaS instance purchased by a customer of the BPaaS broker at hand; (b) *broker-specific*, pertaining to the overall performance of the BPaaS offered across all customers. Customer-specific metrics have as their measurement space all the measurements produced for the customer's BPaaS instance, while broker-specific metrics have a broader measurement space spanning all measurements over all instances of a BPaaS purchased.

Second, two main factors harden the transformation: (a) it should not only consider the metric itself (i.e., the actual computation) but also the metric and condition context, which indicates that all such information should be linked together to obtain the right set of measurements to be aggregated; (b) the dynamic KPI evaluation kind envisioned, where the expert can experiment with formulas, metric kinds, evaluation (schedule & windows) and history periods, does not allow storing the measurements in the physical storage once they are derived. To this end, the way lower-level KPI metrics can be derived needs to be accounted for when attempting to compute a high-level KPI metric. This means that we might need to go down even to the level of low-level or resource metrics for which measurements are already produced to derive the measurements for a high-level KPI.

By taking into consideration the above two issues, a particular transformation algorithm has been produced which, depending on the input provided, attempts to generate dynamically the SPARQL query to be issued for deriving the respective metric measurement. Listing 1.1 depicts the pseudo-code of this algorithm.

Listing 1.1. Transformation & Drill-Down Algorithms pseudo-code.

```
ResultSet evalKPI{Metric m, Object object, BPaaS bpaas,
    DateTime start, DateTime end, String custID}{
  MetricFormula mf = expandFormula(m.formula);
  List<String> vars = getVars(mf);
  String clause = getClause(mf);
  String query = createQuery(vars,clause,object,bpaas,
    start,end,m.metricContext.schedule,custId);
  return runQuery(query);
}

String createQuery(List<String> vars, String clause,
    Object obj, BPaaS bpaas, DateTime start, DateTime end,
    Schedule schedule, String customerId){
  String query = insertPrefixes();
  query += applyClause(clause, getBrokerGraph());
  query += createMeasurementTriples(vars,obj.URI);
  query += createInterLink(bpaas,object,customerId);
  query += applyFilters(start,end,vars);
  query += applyGrouping(schedule,vars);
  return query;
}

Tree<ResultSet> kpiDrillDown(KPI kpi,
BPaaS bpaas, DateTime start, DateTime end,
String custId){
  Tree<ResultSet> result = evalKPI(kpi.metric,
    kpi.object,bpaas,start,end,customerId);
  Set<Tree<ResultSet>> results =
    measureKPIsInParallel(kpi.children,
      start,end,customerId);
  result.addChildren(results);
  return result;
}

Hashtable<Metric,ResultSet> metricDrillDown(Metric m,
    Object object, BPaaS bpaas, DateTime start,
    DateTime end, String custId){
  MetricTree mt = expandFormulaInTree(m.formula);
  Set<MetricNode> metrics = getLeaves(mt);
  Hashtable<Metric,ResultSet> results =
  new Hashtable<Metric,ResultSet>();
  while (!metrics.isEmpty()){
    for (MetricNode mn: metrics{
    if (mn.isLeaf()) results.union(evalKPI(mn.metric,
      object,bpaas,start,end,custId));
    else results.union(measureKPI(mn,object,start,
      end,custId,results));
    }
    metrics = getParents(metrics);
  }
  return results;
}
```

This algorithm (see **evaluateKPI** method) comprises four main steps: (a) metric formula expansion which includes the recursive substitution of component metrics, for which measurements are not stored in the *Semantic KB*, with their derivation formulas; (b) SPARQL query variable derivation from those metrics in the expanded formula, i.e., the leaf ones, for which measurements have been stored; (c) production of the (SPARQL) select clause from the expanded formula; (d) production of the whole SPARQL query.

The SPARQL query production (see `createQuery` method) involves executing the following steps: (i) creation of query prefixes; (ii) application of SELECT & FROM clauses by also taking into account the respective LD graph URI mapping to the individual RDF graph of the broker from which the relevant information for the query evaluation can be obtained; (iii) generation of the triple patterns mapping to the measurements of the leaf metrics/variables in the expanded metric formula; (iv) enforcement of the correlation between measurements according to the object being measured, the customer (if given as input) and the respective BPaaS instances mapping to these measurements; (v) application of the filtering (FILTER clause) over the history period to select measurements produced only on that period; (vi) application of SPARQL GROUP BY clauses based on the KPI metric evaluation period, i.e., its measurement schedule.

To exemplify this OWL-Q-to-SPARQL transformation algorithm and raise its understanding level, we now highlight its application on a specific example of a KPI metric by especially taking a closer look at the corresponding SPARQL query being generated.

Suppose that the *average availability* metric AVG_A has to be measured for the whole BPaaS workflow. This metric can be computed via the formula $\text{MEAN}(RAW_A)$, where RAW_A represents the instance-based availability metric for this workflow. Further suppose that: (i) the average availability metric should be calculated every 1 h, while the raw availability metric every minute; (ii) the history period is 1 day.

The first transformation algorithm step will expand the above computation formula based on the measurability of the component metrics of *average availability*. In particular, RAW_A is not stored in the *Semantic KB*, thus it is expanded into its derivation formula

$$\frac{UPTIME}{TOTAL\_OBSERVATION\_TIME}$$

where $UPTIME$ is a raw metric and $TOTAL\_OBSERVATION\_TIME$ is a constant. As such, the final expanded formula will take the following form:

$$\text{MEAN}\left(\frac{UPTIME}{TOTAL\_OBSERVATION\_TIME}\right)$$

Based on this formula, the next two algorithm steps will generate a set of one variable ("?uptime") and the select clause ("SELECT (AVG(?uptime/60) as ?value) (MAX(?uptime_ms_ts) as ?date)"). As uptime is calculated every second, please observe that 60 is the total observation time constant.

The fourth step will finally generate the actual SPARQL query depicted in Fig. 4 [7]. This SPARQL query is now explained by focusing over all the steps involved in the `createQuery` method and the content generated by them.

Lines 1–2 supply the prefixes of the two ontologies being exploited mapping to the first query generation step. Lines 3–4 depict the query SELECT & FROM clauses produced from the second step of the query generation sub-algorithm.

Lines 5–9 express a set of triple patterns, generated by the third query generation step, linking the uptime measurement to: (a) the *Uptime* metric; (b) its actual value used in the formula of Line 3; (c) the actual *dateTime* where this measurement was produced; (d) the URI of the object measured (i.e., a workflow instance in our case). These lines guarantee that we operate over *Uptime* measurements but do not provide suitable connections to other major information aspects, such as which BPaaS is actually concerned.

To this end, Lines 10–13, which map to the fourth query generation step, realise the needed connections from the object measured to both the BPaaS instance involving it and the current BPaaS at hand. Line 10 links the current BPaaS to one of its instances, while Line 11 connects this BPaaS instance with a deployed workflow. Line 12, currently commented, could link this instance to a certain client that has purchased it, in case we are dealing with a customer-specific metric. Finally, Line 13 links the deployed workflow to the actual workflow instance measured. Depending on the kind of object being measured, Lines 11–13 can be differentiated. For instance, if a task instance is to be measured, we need to add another triple pattern linking the workflow instance involved with this task instance.

Line 15, currently commented, mapping to the fifth query generation step, supplies a SPARQL FILTER constraint that can restrict the history period under investigation. In particular, the conjunction of two simple constraints is expressed over the *dateTime* of the measurement indicating that this date-Time should be greater or equal to the low bound *dateTime* of the considered period and less than or equal to the upper bound *dateTime* of this period. This line is commented as the whole evaluation history of the KPI metric is explored.

Finally, Line 17, generated by the last query creation step, supplies a grouping statement where the last sub-group directly relates to the evaluation period of the KPI metric (i.e., per hour). This statement groups first the results based on the month, then on the day and finally on the respective hour.

```
1: prefix eval: <http://www.cloudsocket.eu/evaluation#>
2: prefix owlq: <http://www.ics.forth.gr/ontologies/owlq#>
3: SELECT (AVG(?uptime / (60)) AS ?value) (MAX(?uptime_meas_ts) AS ?date)
4:     from <http://www.cloudsocket.eu/evaluation/bwcon> WHERE {
5:   ?uptime_meas a owlq:Measurement;
6:       owlq:metric owlq:Uptime;
7:       owlq:value ?uptime;
8:       owlq:timestamp ?uptime_meas_ts;
9:       owlq:boundElement ?obj.
10: eval:ChristmasCard ?bpaasInstance ?bpaasInt.
11: ?bpaasInst eval:deployedWorkflow ?depWf.
12:     #eval:customer eval:Customer1;
13:  ?depWf eval:workflowInstance ?obj.
14:
15:     #filter (?uptime_meas_ts <= "dateTime2"^^xsd:dateTime
        #&& ?uptime_meas_ts >= "dateTime1"^^xsd:dateTime)
16: }
17: GROUP BY (MONTH(?uptime_meas_ts) as ?month,
        DAY(?uptime_meas_ts) = ?day,
        HOUR(?uptime_meas_ts) as ?hour)
```

Fig. 4. Constructed SPARQL query for the example [7].

Drill-Down Algorithms. Two main forms of drill-down are supported by the KPI Analysis System proposed: (a) based on KPI parent-child relationships; (b) based on KPI metric parent-child relationships. It can be indicated that the first form is equivalent to the second one. This is not the actual case due to the fact that while KPI relationships might involve corresponding metric relationships, the latter relationships might not be complete in the sense that the metrics of the child KPIs cannot be solely used for the production of the measurement of the metric of the parent KPI. This indicates that possibly there is a component metric of a parent KPI metric for which a KPI has not been supplied. For instance, suppose that we have a parent KPI metric over BPaaS availability. This metric might be computed from other metrics that span the availability of the SaaS services exploited plus the availability of the workflow engine used to execute this BPaaS. Logically speaking, a BPaaS broker might express KPIs for all SaaS-based availability metrics but not for the workflow engine availability one. As such, the first form of KPI drill-down will be able to show the relationships between the KPIs and their respective evaluations. On the other hand, the second KPI drill-down form will show the relationships between the KPI metrics and their measurements. As such the first form is suitable until the point where KPI relationships clearly show the root causes of problems. However, the second form is a more elaborate one which is also able to bring the analysis until the lowest possible level. These two KPI drill-down forms are now analysed in the following paragraphs.

KPI Parent-Child Relationship based Drill-Down. This form of KPI drill-down is handled by the algorithm mapping to the `kpiDrillDown` method in Listing 1.1. In this form, the parent-child relations between KPIs are exploited. The main logic of this algorithm is quite simple: each KPI involved in the hierarchy of a top-level KPI needs to be evaluated. In this respect, the algorithm comprises two main steps: (a) processing of current KPI by producing its SPARQL query via the OWL-Q-to-SPARQL transformation and evaluation of the query in order to produce the respective measurement; (b) processing of the child KPIs of current KPI in parallel and storage of the respective measurements produced into a hierarchical tree-form where parent KPI measurement is described first and then followed by the measurement trees of all its children. Due to the recursive form of this algorithm we will be able in the end to produce the whole hierarchical measurement tree for the top-level KPI which could then enable the respective assessment of all the KPIs involved in the top-level KPI's hierarchy.

KPI Metric Parent-Child Relationship based Drill-Down. This KPI drill-down form is handled by the algorithm mapping to the `metricDrillDown` method in Listing 1.1. This algorithm exploits the OWL-Q-to-SPARQL transformation one by also considering the whole derivation tree of the current KPI metric at hand. It sequentially executes the following steps: (a) expand recursively the top metric's derivation list until leaf metric nodes are reached. This leads to producing a metric (derivation) tree which has as leaf nodes metrics for which measurements exist in the *Semantic KB*; (b) compute the needed intermediate metric (node) values based on the SPARQL-based transformation approach in a bottom-up way. This means that we proceed in a level-by-level basis in the computation of not yet processed metrics for which the child nodes map to metrics whose values have been already computed or map to measurements already stored in the *Semantic KB*. This procedure the propagates up the produced measurements in the tree until the top level metric is reached. Each time a KPI metric node is visited, its values are produced based on the metric formula involved and the already produced measurements. The produced measurements are stored in the hashtable, from metrics to measurement result sets, to support the higher-level metric computations plus the production of the drill-down results to be returned.

6   Conclusions

This paper has presented a service-oriented, multi-tenant KPI evaluation system which enables the intelligent and dynamic exploration of the whole KPI metric space. The system's evaluation and exploration capabilities rely on the semantic and human-oriented capturing of the KPI information and its linkage with respective BPaaS dependency information. The linked information is then stored into a semantic KB over which not only KPI evaluation but also other kinds of BPaaS analysis can be performed, such as process mining and best BPaaS deployment discovery. BPaaS evaluation relies on the transformation of KPI information into SPARQL queries which are then issued over the semantic KB. On the other hand, to support root-cause analysis, also two KPI drill-down forms are supplied by the system which rely on the appropriate capturing of KPI dependencies. The coverage of KPI & BPaaS dependency information is achieved via the introduction of two main ontologies: (a) a KPI extension of OWL-Q [6] and (b) a BPaaS dependency ontology.

Future work will pursue the following research directions. First, thoroughly evaluating the KPI analysis system according to both performance and accuracy aspects. Second, further validating the proposed ontologies to obtain suitable feedback to optimise them. Third, realising and injecting additional BPaaS analysis algorithms into the respective KPI analysis system so as to transform it into a full-fledged BPaaS evaluation environment.

Acknowledgements. This research has received funding from the European Community's Framework Programme for Research and Innovation HORIZON 2020 (ICT-07-2014) under grant agreement number 644690 (CloudSocket).

References

1. Karagiannis, D.: BPMS: Business Process Management Systems. SIGOIS Bull. **16**, 10–13 (1995)
2. Caplan, R.S., Norton, D.P.: The balanced scorecard measures that drive performance. Harvard Bus. Rev. **70**, 281–308 (1992)

3. Chowdhary, P., Bhaskaran, K., Caswell, N.S., Chang, H., Chao, T., Chen, S.K., Dikun, M., Lei, H., Jeng, J.J., Kapoor, S., Lang, C.A., Mihaila, G., Stanoi, I., Zeng, L.: Model driven development for business performance management. IBM Syst. J. **45**, 587–605 (2006)
4. Castellanos, M., Casati, F., Shan, M.C., Dayal, U.: IBOM: a platform for intelligent business operation management. In: ICDE, pp. 1084–1095. IEEE Computer Society, Washington, DC (2005)
5. Woitsch, R., Albayrak, M., Köhn, H., Utz, W., Ferrer, A.J., Iranzo, J., Leonforte, A., Gallo, A., Mihnea, V., Pacurar, R., Avasilcai, C., Arama, G., Boca, R., Griesinger, F., Seybold, D., Domaschka, J., Kritikos, K., Plexousakis, D.: D4.1 - First CloudSocket Architecture. CloudSocket European Project (2015)
6. Kritikos, K., Plexousakis, D.: Semantic QoS metric matching. In: ECOWS, pp. 265–274. IEEE Computer Society (2006)
7. Kritikos, K., Plexousakis, D., Woitsch, R.: Towards semantic KPI measurement. In: CLOSER, pp. 63–74. SciTePress, Porto (2017)
8. List, B., Korherr, B.: An evaluation of conceptual business process modelling languages. In: SAC, pp. 1532–1539. ACM, Dijon (2006)
9. Wetzstein, B., Karastoyanova, D., Leymann, F.: Towards management of SLA-aware business processes based on key performance indicators. In: BPMDS, Montpellier, France (2008)
10. Motta, G., Pignatelli, G., Florio, M.: Performing business process knowledge base. In: First International Workshop and Summer School on Service Science, Heraklion, Greece (2007)
11. Pierantonio, A., Rosa, G., Silingas, D., Thönssen, B., Woitsch, R.: Metamodeling architectures for business processes in organizations. In: Proceedings of the Projects Showcase at STAF, L'Aquila, Italy. CEUR (2015)
12. Friedenstab, J.P., Janiesch, C., Matzner, M., Muller, O.: Extending BPMN for business activity monitoring. In: HICSS, pp. 4158–4167. IEEE Computer Society (2012)
13. Frank, U., Heise, D., Kattenstroth, H., Schauer, H.: Designing and utilising business indicator systems within enterprise models: outline of a method. In: MobIS: Modellierung zwischen SOA und Compliance Management, Saarbröcken, Germany (2008)
14. González, O., Casallas, R., Deridder, D.: MMC-BPM: a domain-specific language for business processes analysis. In: Abramowicz, W. (ed.) BIS 2009. LNBIP, vol. 21, pp. 157–168. Springer, Heidelberg (2009). https://doi.org/10.1007/978-3-642-01190-0_14
15. del Río-Ortega, A., Resinas, M., Durán, A., Ruiz-Cortés, A.: Using templates and linguistic patterns to define process performance indicators. Enterp. Inf. Syst. **10**, 159–192 (2016)
16. Costello, C., Malloy, O.: Building a process performance model for business activity monitoring. In: Wojtkowski, W., Wojtkowski, G., Lang, M., Conboy, K., Barry, C. (eds.) Information Systems Development - Challenges in Practice, Theory, and Education, pp. 237–248. Springer, Boston (2008). https://doi.org/10.1007/978-0-387-68772-8_19
17. Liu, R., Nigam, A., Jeng, J., Shieh, C., Wu, F.Y.: Integrated modeling of performance monitoring with business artifacts. In: ICEBE, pp. 64–71. IEEE Computer Society, Shanghai (2010)
18. Seedorf, S., Schader, M.: Towards an enterprise software component ontology. In: AMCIS. Association for Information Systems (2011)

19. Gruschke, B.: Integrated event management: event correlation using dependency graphs. In: DSOM (1998)
20. Cui, Y., Nahrstedt, K.: QoS-aware dependency management for component-based systems. In: HPDC, p. 127. IEEE Computer Society (2001)
21. Hasselmeyer, P.: Managing dynamic service dependencies. In: DSOM, pp. 141–150. Inria, Nancy (2001)
22. Rossini, A., Kritikos, K., Nikolov, N., Domaschka, J., Griesinger, F., Seybold, D., Romero, D.: D2.1.3 - CloudML Implementation Documentation (Final version). Paasage project deliverable (2015)
23. Wetzstein, B., Leitner, P., Rosenberg, F., Brandic, I., Dustdar, S., Leymann, F.: Monitoring and analyzing influential factors of business process performance. In: EDOC, pp. 118–127. IEEE Press (2009)
24. Wetzstein, B., Ma, Z., Leymann, F.: Towards measuring key performance indicators of semantic business processes. In: Abramowicz, W., Fensel, D. (eds.) BIS 2008. LNBIP, vol. 7, pp. 227–238. Springer, Heidelberg (2008). https://doi.org/10.1007/978-3-540-79396-0_20
25. Diamantini, C., Potena, D., Storti, E., Zhang, H.: An ontology-based data exploration tool for key performance indicators. In: Meersman, R., et al. (eds.) OTM 2014. LNCS, vol. 8841, pp. 727–744. Springer, Heidelberg (2014). https://doi.org/10.1007/978-3-662-45563-0_45
26. Kritikos, K., Pernici, B., Plebani, P., Cappiello, C., Comuzzi, M., Benbernou, S., Brandic, I., Kertész, A., Parkin, M., Carro, M.: A survey on service quality description. ACM Comput. Surv. 46, 1 (2013)
27. de Medeiros, A.K.A., et al.: An outlook on semantic business process mining and monitoring. In: Meersman, R., Tari, Z., Herrero, P. (eds.) OTM 2007. LNCS, vol. 4806, pp. 1244–1255. Springer, Heidelberg (2007). https://doi.org/10.1007/978-3-540-76890-6_52
28. Kritikos, K., Magoutis, K., Plexousakis, D.: Towards knowledge-based assisted IaaS selection. In: CloudCom. IEEE Computer Society, Luxembourg (2016)
29. Zeginis, C., Kritikos, K., Plexousakis, D.: Event pattern discovery in multi-cloud service-based applications. Int. J. Syst. Serv. Oriented Eng. 5, 78–103 (2015)
30. Kritikos, K., Plexousakis, D.: Semantic SLAs for services with Q-SLA. In: ICWS, pp. 686–689. IEEE Computer Society, San Francisco (2016)
31. Kritikos, K., Zegkinis, C., Seybold, D., Griesinger, F.: D3.6 - BPaaS Monitoring and Evaluation Prototypes. CloudSocket European Project (2017)

A Framework for the Orchestration and Provision of Cloud Services Based on TOSCA and BPMN

Domenico Calcaterra, Vincenzo Cartelli, Giuseppe Di Modica,
and Orazio Tomarchio[✉]

Department of Electrical, Electronic and Computer Engineering,
University of Catania, V.le A. Doria 6, 95125 Catania, Italy
{Domenico.Calcaterra,Vincenzo.Cartelli,Giuseppe.DiModica,
Orazio.Tomarchio}@dieei.unict.it

Abstract. Cloud computing is a consolidated and high-maturity level paradigm which is capable of handling powerful computing environments and providing complex services in a flexible and scalable way. In order to compete in the cloud service market, one of the challenges Cloud providers are faced with is to efficiently automate the service "provisioning" activities through the use of Cloud orchestration techniques. The focus of this paper is the orchestration process. Starting with TOSCA, a well-known standard specification used to represent the complete structure of a Cloud service, we developed an orchestrator capable of automating the workflow of all the tasks required to build up such a service. What makes our approach novel is the definition of a converter component which takes as input a TOSCA service template and transforms it into a BPMN process model that is ready to be fed to a workflow engine. The BPMN notation is used to represent both the workflow and the data associated with each workflow step. To prove the viability of the YAML-to-BPMN conversion process, a software prototype of the system was developed and tested with a sample use case which is discussed in the paper.

1 Introduction

In the last few years, cloud computing platforms have been widely adopted to provide increasingly complex services in very different fields. From the cloud providers' point of view, a significant and increasing cost factor is related to the management and operational tasks needed for the provision of each cloud service. All the big cloud players are making a lot of investments to develop software tools and frameworks that support the automation of cloud services' delivery and maintenance. Also the scientific community has shown a growing interest around the topic of cloud provisioning and orchestration [4, 30, 36]. The lack of a common and established industry standard for defining composite applications, including

D. Ferguson et al. (Eds.): CLOSER 2017, CCIS 864, pp. 262–285, 2018.
https://doi.org/10.1007/978-3-319-94959-8_14

their orchestration and management, appears today as one of the critical issues preventing from a wider cloud's adoption, also affecting the actual portability of a cloud application.

In the panorama of standard initiatives, OASIS TOSCA (Topology and Orchestration Specification for Cloud Applications) [22] has become very popular. It is supported by many big cloud players and promises to cater for their need of streamlining cloud service orchestration and provisioning operations. Also, the standardization body has released a version of the specification which makes use of a very simple and human understandable language (YAML) that has contributed to speed up the standard adoption process.

The work described in this paper grounds on the TOSCA specification, extending the one presented in [7]. It leverages the TOSCA features to build up a cloud service orchestrator capable of automating the execution of tasks and operations required for the provisioning of a cloud application. The strategy adopted by the cloud orchestrator is to convert a TOSCA cloud application model into its equivalent BPMN workflow and dataflow model [25]. The orchestrator will then use a BPMN engine to enforce the operations specified in the BPMN model. The approach we propose clearly separates the orchestration of the provisioning tasks from the real provisioning services (i.e., the e-services that enforce the provisioning). In this work, we present the design of a cloud service provisioning framework, and discuss the design and implementation of a cloud orchestrator prototype. With respect to [7], in this paper we also describe the service provisioning architecture. Further, we discuss a real use case of a cloud application provisioning.

The remainder of the paper is organized in the following way. In Sect. 2 we report the related work. Section 3 provides a bird's eye view of the TOSCA specification. The core ideas of the proposed framework are presented in Sect. 4. The design and implementation details of the cloud orchestrator and provisioning services are discussed in Sects. 5 and 6, respectively. A real use case showing the potential of the proposed idea is discussed in Sect. 5.4. Section 7 draws some final considerations and suggests some future directions.

2 Related Work

This section presents a survey of all the recent and authoritative initiatives, both commercial and scientific, that address the cloud provisioning and orchestration topic.

Many **cloud industry** players have developed cloud management platforms [1,10,13–15,31,32] for automating the provisioning of cloud services. All platforms, to varying degrees, promise to provide automation in three fundamental steps: *cloud configuration, cloud provisioning* and *cloud deployment*. The more advanced platforms also offer services and tools for the management of cloud applications' lifecycle. None of these commercial products are open to the community, and the solutions they offer are not portable across third-party providers either.

The open source world has shown interest on this topic as well. Taking a look at the category of **configuration management** tools, DevOps Chef [9] is a software used to streamline the task of configuring and maintaining server applications and utilities. It is based on the concept of configuration "recipes", which are instructions on the desired state of resources (software packages to be installed, services to be run, or files to be written). Chef takes care of those recipes and makes sure that resources are actually in the desired state. Chef can integrate with cloud-based platforms such as Amazon EC2, Google Cloud Platform, OpenStack, Microsoft Azure and Rackspace to automatically provision and configure new virtual machines. Similar recipe-based approaches are proposed by other open-source solutions like Puppet [29] with its *Puppet manifests* and Juju [16] with its *Juju charms*. Speaking of **cloud orchestration** tools, OpenStack Heat [26] is a service to orchestrate composite cloud applications using a declarative template format - namely, the Heat Orchestration Template (HOT) - through both an OpenStack-native REST API and AWS CloudFormation-compatible API [1]. HOT describes the infrastructure for a cloud application in text files which are readable and writable by humans and software tools as well. Also, it integrates well with software configuration management tools such as Puppet and Chef. Very recently, orchestration concepts have been analyzed also in the context of *containers* [35]. Even if containers represent a portable unit of deployment, when an application is built out of multiple containers the setting up of a cluster of containers can actually become complex, because it is needed to make one container aware of another and expose several details required for them to communicate. As an example, Docker Compose, currently under active development, is one of the first tools for defining and running multi-container Docker applications [11].

With respect to **standardizing initiatives**, OASIS is the most active on the topic. TOSCA [22] is an OASIS open cloud standard supported by a large and growing number of international industry leaders. It defines an *interoperable description* of applications, including their components, relationships, dependencies, requirements, and capabilities, thus enabling *portability* and *automated management* across multiple cloud providers regardless of underlying platform or infrastructure. No commercial solution supports processing of the TOSCA specification at this moment. OpenTOSCA [3] is a famous open source TOSCA runtime environment. Although authors have been working on adding support to the TOSCA Simple Profile [28], only a few YAML elements are supported by the converter. At this moment, imports, inputs, outputs and groups are not supported, thereby limiting the description of application components. The reader may find some insight on the technical aspects of TOSCA in Sect. 3.

In the **scientific literature** a few works have addressed the TOSCA specification. In [18], *BPMN4TOSCA* was proposed as a domain-specific BPMN [25] extension to ease modelling of management plans by enabling convenient integration and direct access to TOSCA topology and provided management operations. Since the BPMN4TOSCA extension introduces new functionalities which are not natively supported by workflow engines, it leads to a non-standards-compliant BPMN and, therefore, needs special treatment, i.e., a transformation to plain BPMN. In [17], a *proof of concept* for the actual portability features of TOSCA on OpenStack and Opscode Chef has been presented. To that end, an execution runtime environment named *TOSCA2Chef* was developed to automate the deployment of TOSCA-based cloud application topologies to OpenStack by employing Chef and BPEL processes. An extension of the system to support different IaaS providers would require different data models reflecting new domain-specific attributes. Plus, the plan execution operation would need some adaptation to base its execution logic on the new model. In [37], a unified invocation bus and interface to be used by TOSCA management plans has been presented. Based on OpenTOSCA's architecture, a service bus (*Operation Invoker*) was implemented to provide a unified invocation interface for TOSCA plans to invoke operations without knowing what kind of technology is used in the background. When a particular operation is called through the Operation Invoker, it checks what kind of *Implementation Artifact* (IA) is available to execute the operation. Then, it checks whether there is a plugin registered that can execute IAs of the given type (e.g., SOAP or REST or script). In case there is a corresponding plugin, this plugin gets invoked, which itself invokes the corresponding IA. Plans need to communicate with the unified interface of the Operation Invoker, but they can only be modelled with the knowledge of it. On top of that, this solution is strongly linked to OpenTosca runtime environment, too. In [38], with the goal of achieving a seamless and interoperable orchestration of arbitrary artifacts, an integrated modelling and runtime framework has been introduced. After executable DevOps artifacts of different kinds get discovered and stored in DevOps knowledge repositories, they are transformed into TOSCA-based descriptions. OpenTOSCA was used as a deployment engine. However, this approach is still bound to the specific implementation of the runtime environment, which TOSCA specification does not cover. In [5], a process modelling concept to enable the integration of imperative and declarative provisioning models has been introduced with the goal of preserving the strengths of both flavours. The general modelling approach is based on extending imperative workflow languages such as BPMN and BPEL [21] by means of *Declarative Provisioning Activities*, which enable to specify declarative provisioning goals directly in the control flow of a workflow model. The data flow between provisioning activities is defined through *input parameters, output parameters* and *content injection*. A prototype based on the OpenTOSCA ecosystem and the BPEL workflow language was implemented. As the authors themselves underlined, a drawback is that process models often have to be created from scratch, while maintaining existing processes results in complex, time-consuming adaptations.

Several EU funded research projects, such as ARTIST [20], SeaClouds [6], PaaSage [33], MODAClouds [12] and PaaSport [2], also addressed cloud application portability in its essence. Most of these projects, instead of building a TOSCA engine, transform the TOSCA-based application specification into a single orchestration script, such as YAML, and execute it by a corresponding management tool, such as CAMP [23], Brooklyn [34], etc.

The work we propose grounds on the TOSCA standard as well. A distinctive feature of our approach is the clear separation between the *orchestration of the provisioning tasks*, intended as the scheduling of the logical steps to be taken, and the *provisioning services*, which are the services implementing the tasks' instructions. As for the orchestration aspect, we devised a mechanism that automatically builds a plain BPMN orchestration plan starting from a cloud application's TOSCA model.

3   The TOSCA Specification

TOSCA is the acronym for *Topology and Orchestration Specification for Cloud Applications*. It is a standard put together by OASIS that can be used to enable the portability of cloud applications and related IT services. This specification permits describing the structure of a cloud application as a *service template*, that is in turn composed of a *topology_template* and the types needed to build such a template. The topology_template is a typed directed graph, whose nodes (called *node_templates*) model the application components, and edges (called *relationship_templates*) model the relations occurring among such components. Each node of a topology can also be associated with the corresponding component's requirements, the operations to manage it, the capabilities it features, and the policies applied to it. Inter-node dependencies associate the requirements of a node with the capabilities featured by other nodes. TOSCA supports the deployment and management of applications in two different flavors: *imperative processing* and *declarative processing*. The imperative processing requires that all needed management logic is contained in the *Cloud Service Archive (CSAR)*, which stores all software artifacts required to provision, operate, and manage the application. *Management plans* imperatively orchestrate low-level management operations that are either provided by the application components themselves or by publicly accessible services (e.g., the Amazon Web Services API). These plans are typically implemented using workflow languages, such as BPMN or BPEL [21]. The declarative processing shifts management logic from plans to runtime, therefore no plans are actually required. TOSCA runtime engines automatically infer the corresponding logic by interpreting the application topology template. This requires a precise definition of the semantics of nodes and relations based on well-defined *Node Types* and *Relationship Types*. The set of provided management functionalities depends on the corresponding runtime and is not standardized by the TOSCA specification.

The TOSCA Simple Profile is a rendering of the TOSCA specification in the YAML language [24]. It aims to provide a more accessible syntax as well as a more concise and incremental expressiveness of the TOSCA language in order to speed up the adoption of TOSCA to describe cloud applications in a portable manner. The work described in this paper heavily grounds on the TOSCA standard and, specifically, on the TOSCA Simple Profile.

4   Design of a Cloud Service Provisioning Framework

This work addresses the design and implementation of a software framework that automates the processes pertaining to the operational management of cloud services. The stakeholders that may have a keen interest in the services provided through the framework are the Customers in need of cloud resources and applications (in a few words, "cloud services") and the Providers of cloud services. To the former, the framework offers tools to state functional requirements of the cloud service they are in need of; depending on those requirements, the framework takes the necessary actions for the service delivery to happen. The latter have the chance to offer their cloud services through the framework, while playing no active role in the service orchestration which the framework itself is in charge of.

The focus of this work is on the automation of the **cloud service provisioning process**, i.e., the process which is entrusted with setting up all the resources that build up the cloud service requested by the Customer. The framework has been designed to support more sophisticated operations such as, to cite a few, resource monitoring, resilience and scaling. Those specific operations are though out of the scope of the current work, and will be addressed in the future. As for the service provision, this work revolves around the design and implementation of an orchestrator which is capable of generating on the fly a *cloud provisioning process* made up of tasks that build up the ready-to-use service to be delivered. Specifically, the orchestrator coordinates the whole process and makes sure that every task's activity is performed with proper timing.

We inspected the literature for a well established and broadly accepted way of representing the cloud application requirements, i.e., a language or a meta-model the Customer may use to describe the stack of resources, and also, the way those resources need to get configured and coupled together in order to ensure that the final service will meet Customer expectations. As mentioned before, the approach we propose grounds on the *OASIS TOSCA* standard and, more specifically, on the *TOSCA Simple Profile* rendering. The TOSCA Simple Profile provides a meta-model written in YAML (a human friendly data serialization standard) which the Customer may use to define their **cloud application model**, i.e., to describe both the application topology and the artifacts needed by the application itself. We opted for a *workflow-based* solution which, starting from the cloud application model description, is capable of devising and orchestrating the flow of the provisioning operations to execute. Instead of developing a workflow engine from scratch, we decided to make use of a BPMN engine, i.e., an engine capable of executing workflows represented in the BPMN language. Since a YAML application model is not executable by a BPMN engine, we developed an ad-hoc YAML-to-BPMN converter. The reader may discover the details of the converter in Sect. 5. We chose the BPMN as workflow language since it is a robust standard and it also provides support for data modelling, a feature that we exploited to represent the application artifacts needed along the workflow.

A novelty introduced by this approach is the separation between the orchestration of the provisioning tasks and the provisioning services themselves. We propose a solution where the provisioning services may be supplied by third-party service providers, while the provisioning tasks orchestrated by the workflow engine will draw on those services in a SOA (Service Oriented Architecture) fashion. This enables a scenario of a market of services in which many providers are allowed to participate and where Customers can get the best combination of services that meet their requirements. The overall scenario described so far is best depicted in Fig. 1.

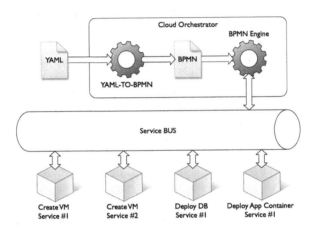

Fig. 1. Cloud orchestrator scenario [7].

We have designed and implemented a **TOSCA Orchestrator** which takes as input the application model and deploys the concrete application in the cloud. The Orchestrator takes the YAML model and transforms it into an equivalent BPMN model. The BPMN model is in turn fed to a BPMN engine that will instantiate and coordinate the relative process. The process will put in force all the provisioning activities needed to build up the application stack; as the reader may notice, the provisioning activities access a service bus in order to get the required services which are in turn supplied by third-party service providers. Finally, once the cloud application is up and running, the Customer is invited to take charge.

The framework we propose aims to offer tools and services that enable the scenario depicted in Fig. 1. Customers can use the YAML representation to express application requirements and push them into the framework. Providers can design their services according to specific templates and offer them to Customers through the framework. The framework is entrusted with orchestrating the provisioning activities and matching the services' offer and demand. In the current implementation, the framework cares just for functional requirements. Non-functional requirements, which call for enhanced service matchmaking mechanisms, are out of the scope of this work and will be addressed in future work.

5   Converting YAML to BPMN

This section discusses the features and the technical details of the software component we devised to convert a TOSCA Simple Profile into its equivalent BPMN process model. Starting from a TOSCA Simple Profile compliant service template, our software creates a *Provisioning Plan* which is fed into the workflow engine for the automated application deployment. This approach brings considerable benefits, among which (a) reusability of the process logic, since components of the same type use the same logic; (b) portability of the Plan, as the application can be deployed on a generic Cloud Provider; (c) efficiency in terms of streamlining Customer's work, because they only have to define their templates and fill them with the management functions of their choice, without caring about how Provisioning Plans will be created and executed on the Cloud Provider.

The proposed solution consists of three components: TOSCA-Parser, BPMN-Generator, and BPMN-Validator. The **TOSCA-Parser** deals with the service template by providing means to load, parse and validate the YAML file, and creates the *dependency graph*, a data structure containing the relationships between all of the nodes in the TOSCA template. Vertices in the graph represent nodes, while edges represent relationships occurring between them. The **BPMN-Generator** grounds the creation of the Provisioning Plan on the parsed service template and the dependency graph. The **BPMN-Validator** validates the automatically generated Plan against the BPMN specification. The following Sections will provide more details about these components.

5.1   TOSCA-Parser

The TOSCA Parser takes a TOSCA YAML template as input, with an optional dictionary of needed parameters with their values, validates it, and produces in-memory objects of different TOSCA elements with their relationship to each other. It also creates an in-memory graph of TOSCA node templates and their relationships. This software component is widely based on the OpenStack parser for TOSCA Simple Profile in YAML [27], a Python project licensed under Apache 2.0. In agreement with the overall structure of a *service template*, shown in Listing 1.1, the parser contains various Python modules to handle it including topology templates, node templates, relationship templates, data types, node types, relationship types, capability types, artifact types, etc. The *ToscaTemplate* class is an entry class of the parser and is of great importance, along with *TopologyTemplate*, *NodeTemplate* and *RelationshipTemplate*, in the construction of the *ToscaGraph*, which keeps track of all nodes and dependency relationships between them in the TOSCA template. This in-memory graph is, in turn, a milestone in the generation of the BPMN Provisioning Plan, and the entire process is covered in Sect. 5.2.

Listing 1.1. TOSCA Service Template grammar.

```
# Required TOSCA Definitions version string
tosca_definitions_version:
# Optional. default namespace (for type schema)
tosca_default_namespace:

# Optional metadata keyname: value pairs
metadata:
template_name:     # Optional name of the service template
template_author:   # Optional author of the service template
template_version:  # Optional version of the service template
# Optional list of domain specific metadata keynames

# Optional description of the definitions in the file.
description: <template_type_description>
# list of import statements for other definitions files
imports:
# list of YAML alias anchors (or macros)
dsl_definitions:
# list of repository definitions hosting TOSCA artifacts
repositories:
# list of TOSCA datatype definitions
data_types:
# list of node type definitions
node_types:
# list of capability type definitions
capability_types:
# list of relationship type definitions
relationship_types:
# list of artifact type definitions
artifact_types:
# list of interface type definitions
interface_types:

# topology template of the cloud application or service
topology_template:
  # a description of the topology template
  description:
  # input parameters for the topology template
  inputs:
  # node templates of the topology
  node_templates:
  # relationship templates of the topology
  relationship_templates:
  # output parameters for the topology template
  outputs:
  # logical groups of node templates within the topology
  groups:

  substitution_mappings:
    node_type: <node_type_name>
  capabilities:
    <map_of_capability_mappings_to_expose>
  requirements:
    <map_of_requirement_mapping_to_expose>
```

5.2 BPMN-Generator

The BPMN-Generator takes the aforementioned *ToscaGraph* and *ToscaTemplate* elements (e.g., Inputs, Outputs, NodeTemplates, RelationshipTemplates) as input and automatically generates the BPMN Provisioning Plan for the designated Cloud application. For clarity purposes, the service template shown in Listing 1.2 will be taken as a toy example to show what needs to be done to reach the goal. The BPMN generation is composed of the following two steps: (1) the creation of a *Workflow* modelling a detailed sequence of business activities to perform; (2) the creation of a *Dataflow* modelling the data to be read, written or updated during the Workflow execution.

Listing 1.2. SW Component - Service Template [7].

```
tosca_definitions_version: tosca_simple_yaml_1_0

description: >
  TOSCA simple profile with a software component.

topology_template:
  inputs:
    cpus:
      type: integer
      description: Number of CPUs for the server.
      constraints:
        - valid_values: [ 1, 2, 4, 8 ]
      default: 1

  node_templates:
    sw:
      type: tosca.nodes.SoftwareComponent
      properties:
        component_version: 1.0
      requirements:
        - host: server
      interfaces:
        Standard:
          create: software_install.sh
          start: software_start.sh

    server:
      type: tosca.nodes.Compute
      capabilities:
        host:
          properties:
            disk_size: 10 GB
            num_cpus: { get_input: cpus }
            mem_size: 1024 MB
        os:
          properties:
            architecture: x86_64
            type: Linux
            distribution: Ubuntu
            version: 14.04
```

The Workflow basically comprises a BPMN process made of Service Tasks, Sequence Flows and Gateways used to control how the process flows, with every single component being derived from all the node_templates and their requirements in the YAML Service Template. In particular, taking inspiration from normative node states and lifecycle operations of the Standard interface [22], each node_template in the YAML scenario leads to a new Service Task for every operation specified on that node. Such Service Tasks are related to each other by means of Sequence Flows and possible Gateways, whose creation depends on Service Tasks dependencies, which, in turn, depend on node_templates requirements. The *ToscaGraph*, which stores all nodes and dependency relationships between them in the TOSCA Template, is the reference point to determine such requirements. In this regard, the graph is traversed and for each node, represented by a vertex, the whole set of requirements is constructed in terms of relationships with other nodes, represented by related edges. Service Tasks dependencies are then obtained by taking into account the node requirements and the lifecycle operations they represent. Starting from such dependencies, it is possible to compute the execution order of all Service Tasks in the Provisioning Plan, i.e., the deployment order of all Cloud application components. This information is represented by numerical data: the lower the number is, the less priority that Service Task gets. Service Tasks with the lowest execution order, hereby collectively called *Service Tasks Endpoint*, don't feature in between any Service Task's required dependencies, whereas Service Tasks with the highest execution order, hereby collectively called *Service Tasks Startpoint*, don't feature any Service Task as a required dependency. With reference to our example scenario, the resulting data structures are shown in Listing 1.3.

Listing 1.3. SW Component - Tasks, Requirements, Order [7].

```
service_tasks = ['server', 'sw_create', 'sw_configure', 'sw_start']

service_tasks_requirements = {'sw_create': ['server'],
    'sw_configure': ['sw_create'], 'sw_start': ['sw_configure']}

service_tasks_order = {'server': 4, 'sw_create': 3,
    'sw_configure': 2, 'sw_start': 1}

service_tasks_startpoint = ['server']

service_tasks_endpoint = ['sw_start']
```

Service Tasks Endpoint and Startpoint are of paramount importance to define a proper execution flow, because they may lead to some degree of parallelism in the Workflow through *Parallel Gateways*, which are used to synchronize or create parallel flows. Specifically, they play a role in the creation of *Start Event*, *End Event* and *Service Tasks*. In the first case, an outgoing sequence flow must be created, having the Start Event as source and a Service Task as target when the Service Tasks Startpoint only contains one element, or a Parallel Diverging Gateway otherwise. In the second case, an incoming sequence flow must be created, having the End Event as target and a Service Task as source when the Service Tasks Endpoint only contains one element, or a Parallel Converging Gateway otherwise. In the third case, Service Tasks and related Sequence Flows are created by proceeding in ascending Service Tasks priority fashion (i.e., in their reverse execution order). From lowest to highest priority, each Service Task is created and then their incoming and outgoing paths are determined by distinguishing three further cases: (a) the Service Task belongs to Service Tasks Endpoint set, (b) the Service Task belongs to Service Tasks Startpoint set, (c) the Service Task belongs to neither of them. In case (a), the incoming path is calculated by analysing the Service Task dependencies: if there is just one of them, then a Sequence Flow must be created, having the required Service Task as source and the Service Task under consideration as target; if there is more than one of them, then a Parallel Convergent Gateway must be created, along with a Sequence Flow having the Gateway as source and the Service Task under consideration as target. The outgoing path is calculated by analysing the Service

Tasks Endpoint set: if it has just one element, a Sequence Flow must be created, having the Service Task under consideration as source and the End Event as target; if it has more than one element, a Parallel Converging Gateway must be created, along with a Sequence Flow having the Service Task under consideration as source and the Gateway as target. In case (b), the incoming path is calculated by examining the Service Tasks Startpoint set: if it has just one element, a Sequence Flow must be created, having the Start Event as source and the Service Task at hand as target; if it has more than one element, a Parallel Diverging Gateway must be created, along with a Sequence Flow having the Gateway as source and the Service Task at hand as target. The outgoing path is calculated by inspecting the set of all Tasks having the Service Task under consideration as a dependency: if it has just one element, a Sequence Flow must be created, having the Service Task at hand as source and that element as target; if it has more than one element, a Parallel Diverging Gateway must be created, along with a Sequence Flow having the Service Task at hand as source and the Gateway as target. In case (c), the incoming path is calculated in the same way as case (a), and the outgoing path is calculated just like case (b). As to our example scenario, the resulting BPMN Workflow is shown in Fig. 2.

Fig. 2. Output of the BPMN generator - Workflow [7].

The Dataflow simply consists of Data Inputs, Data Outputs and Data Objects, which are derived from node_templates and their data requirements in the YAML Service Template. Speaking of data requirements, the TOSCA standard allows template authors to customize Service Templates through the *inputs* section in the Topology Template, which represents an optional list of input parameters for the Topology Template. In a complementary way, the *outputs* section represents an optional list of output parameters for the Topology Template. Inputs and outputs can be used to parameterize node_templates properties or node_templates and relationship_templates lifecycle operations. Data Inputs, which capture input data that Activities and Processes often need in order to execute, are utilized to model such inputs; Data Outputs, which capture data that they can produce during or as a result of execution, are utilized to model such outputs. It should be noted that node_templates *attributes* can be used as parameters in the lifecycle operations as well. Data Objects are utilized to model this kind of data requirements, with Data Associations determining how information stored in Data Objects is handled and passed between Process flow elements. Data Inputs and Data Outputs integration involves the following steps: (1) define Data Inputs, InputSets, Data Outputs and OutputSets within the Workflow Process, (2) add Data Output Associations (one for each Data Input) to the Start Event and Data Input Associations (one for each Data Output) to the End Event, (3) define Data Inputs, InputSets, Data Input Associations, Data Outputs, OutputSets and Data Output Associations within Service Tasks of interest. Data Objects integration includes the following steps: (1) define Data Objects and Data Object References within the Workflow Process, (2) define Data Objects within Service Tasks of interest, i.e., define Data Outputs and Data Output Associations in Data Object source Service Tasks and Data Inputs and Data Input Associations in Data Object target Service Tasks. With reference to our sample template in Listing 1.2, there is only one input variable specified in the server *num_cpus* property. This leads to a Data Input and a Data Association between the Start Event and the server Service Task, as depicted in Fig. 3.

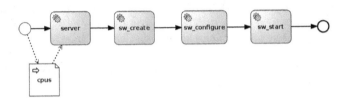

Fig. 3. Output of the BPMN generator - Workflow and Dataflow [7].

5.3   BPMN-Validator

The BPMN-Validator validates the BPMN Plan generated in the previous step against the BPMN XML Schema [25], with both of them being taken as input parameters. The validation is performed by means of *etree* module in Python *lxml* package [19]. More specifically, the BPMN XML Schema gets parsed and turned into an XML Schema validator, which checks if the previously parsed BPMN plan complies with the provided schema. If that is not the case, then a validation error is going to be raised.

5.4   Case Study

The Application model taken into consideration aims to deploy a WordPress web application on an Apache web server, with a MySQL DBMS hosting the database content of the application on a separate server. Figure 4 shows the overall architecture compliant with the TOSCA Simple Profile specification (although wordpress, php and apache node types are non-normative).

There are two separate servers: *app_server* for the web server hosting and *mysql_server* for the DBMS hosting. Both servers are configurable on *hardware side* (e.g., disk size, number of cpus, memory size and CPU frequency) and *software side* (e.g., OS architecture, OS type, OS distribution and OS version). The *apache* node features *port* and *document_root* properties, and is dependent upon the app_server via a *HostedOn* relationship as well. In the same way, the *php* node is dependent upon the app_server via a *HostedOn* relationship. The *mysql_dbms* node features *port* and *root_password* properties, and a *HostedOn* dependency relationship upon the mysql_server. The *mysql_database* node features *name*, *username, password* and *port* properties, and a *HostedOn* dependency relationship upon the mysql_dbms. Finally, the *wordpress* node features the *context_root* property, and depends on mysql_database and php by means of two *ConnectsTo* relationships and on apache by means of a *HostedOn* relationship, respectively.

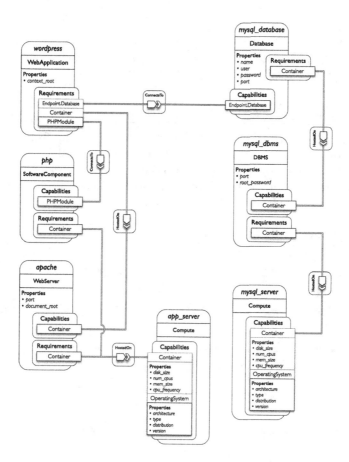

Fig. 4. Wordpress Deploy - TOSCA template [7].

For the sake of clarity, Listing 1.4 shows the apache node declaration in YAML. As mentioned above, the node takes the app_server as requirement and has *port* and *document_root* properties, whose values are retrieved from *apache_port* and *apache_doc_root* input parameters, respectively, by means of the *get_input* intrinsic function. Two lifecycle operations are also defined (i.e., *create* and *start*), with both of them taking *ip* as input parameter, whose value is retrieved from the *private_address* attribute of the app_server through the *get_attribute* intrinsic function.

Listing 1.4. Wordpress Deploy - Apache node [7].

```
apache:
  type: tosca.nodes.WebServer.Apache
  properties:
    port: { get_input: apache_port }
    document_root: { get_input: apache_doc_root }
  requirements:
  - host: app_server
  interfaces:
    Standard:
      create:
        inputs:
          ip: { get_attribute: [app_server, private_address] }
          port: { get_property: [SELF, port] }
          doc_root: { get_property: [SELF, document_root] }
        implementation: scripts/install_apache.sh
      start:
        inputs:
          ip: { get_attribute: [app_server, private_address] }
        implementation: scripts/start_apache.sh
```

In conformity with Sect. 5.2, the node transformation from YAML to BPMN leads to the creation of: (1) three Service Tasks (*apache_create*, *apache_configure* and *apache_start*); (2) two Data Inputs (*doc_root* and *port*) with their respective Data Input Associations in apache_create; (3) one Data Object (*app_server.private_address*) with its Data Input Associations in apache_create and apache_start.

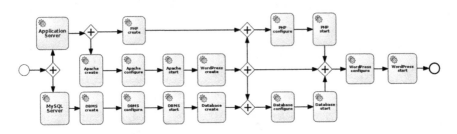

Fig. 5. Wordpress Deploy - Workflow [7].

Figures 5 and 6 show the overall Workflow and Dataflow-decorated Workflow, respectively. The workflow represented in Fig. 6 is then fed to a BPMN engine that will actually enforce the workflow's tasks.

6   Implementing the Provisioning Services

This Section explores the basic idea behind the design and implementation of the Provisioning Services. As anticipated in Sect. 4, our approach neatly separates the Provisioning Tasks from the Provisioning Services. On the one hand, the Provisioning Tasks orchestrated by the Workflow engine draw on the Provisioning Services supplied by third-party Providers to meet Customers' requirements. On the other hand, Providers can design their services according to specific

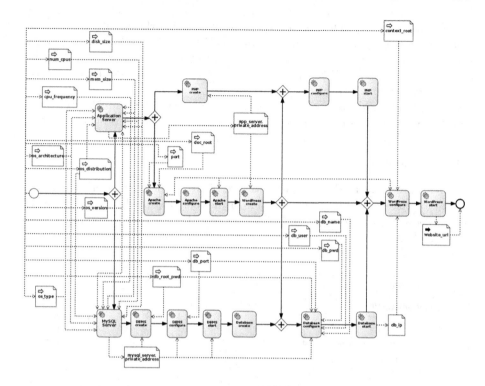

Fig. 6. Wordpress Deploy - Workflow and data flow [7].

templates and offer them to Customers through an *Enterprise Service Bus* (ESB) [8]. The ESB incorporates the features required to implement complex service-oriented architectures meeting challenges of integrating applications and providing a single, unified architecture.

There are mainly two categories of Provisioning Services that need to be integrated in the ESB: *Cloud Services*, provided by commercial Cloud providers by means of proprietary web interfaces, and *Packet-based Services*. The first category comprises the resources offered through any of the Cloud delivery models (IaaS, PaaS, SaaS), be them virtual machines, platforms or even software application instances hosted on a third-party provider's premises; by contrast, the second category includes all the downloadable software "packets" which require a pre-configured runtime environment to run (a database management system or a web server executable, to name a few). In order to integrate all the mentioned services in the ESB, we deploy a layer of *Service Connectors* which are responsible for connecting the requests coming from the Provisioning Tasks with the actual Provisioning Services. The connectors layer is meant to offer Providers a uniform way to publish their Provisioning Services, and to present Provisioning Tasks with a uniform way to invoke those services. To make it clearer, let us focus on the Cloud Services. Cloud Providers have different means to manage VMs or networks, different image formats that can be deployed on a physical host, or different interfaces. The Service Connectors layer interfaces with the specific IaaS management platforms (such as Amazon, Azure, OpenNebula, OpenStack) and provides the Provisioning Tasks with a uniform and standard way of managing the resources of a Cloud Provider, thus hiding away the peculiarity of each Cloud Service's invocation.

The following Sections will discuss the details of the ESB architecture and will describe the steps of the Provisioning Services' invocation process.

6.1   Architecture

Figure 7 shows the ESB-based architecture. The Connectors layer provides a unified interface model for the invocation of the services, which allows to achieve *service location transparency* and *loose coupling* between Provisioning BPMN plans (orchestrated by the *Process Engine*) and Provisioning Services.

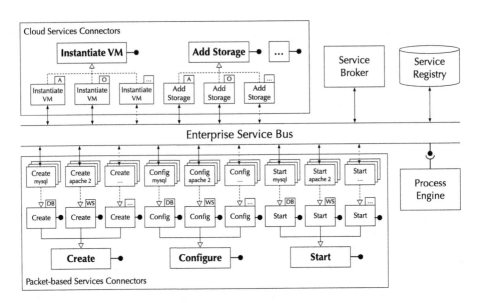

Fig. 7. Enterprise Service Bus and Service Connectors.

The *Service Registry* is responsible for the registration and discovery of the Connectors. At registration time, each Connector has to provide information regarding the service being provided such as service description, functional and non-functional properties of the service, service url. The *Service Broker* is in charge of taking care of the requests coming from the Provisioning Tasks. Its duty is to meet the expectation of the requestors by querying the Service Registry and selecting the Connectors which best fit requestors' need. The selection process of the "best" Connector is out of the scope of this work, and will be addressed in future work.

In Fig. 7 the Cloud and the Packet-based Service Connectors have been depicted. *Cloud Services Connectors* implement interactions with Cloud Providers for the allocation of Cloud resources (e.g., Virtual Machines, Virtual Storage). To serve this purpose, for each service type a specific Connector needs to be implemented. For instance, **Instantiate VM** represents the generic Connector interface to the instantiation of Cloud resources of "Virtual Machine" type. All concrete Connectors to real VM services (Amazon, OpenStack, Azure, etc.) must implement the **Instantiate VM** interface. Likewise, **Add Storage** is the interface of the generic Connector to storage services that concrete Connectors to real storage services in the Cloud must implement. By way of example, let us consider the *Instantiate VM* interface which exposes a **createvm** method in order to create and start a VM instance. Listing 1.5 shows the JSON Schema to validate the body of an HTTP-POST request to a RESTful-based /createvm web service. Three aggregated parameters are required: "host", "os" and "credentials". *Host* and *os* allow to specify the necessary hardware (i.e., number of CPUs, CPU frequency, disk size and memory size) and software (OS architecture, OS type, OS distribution and OS version) requirements, respectively; *credentials* enables to indicate the user's RSA public key to grant them private access to the VM, instead.

Listing 1.5. Instantiate VM - JSON Schema Request.

```
{
    "$schema": "http://json-schema.org/draft-06/schema#",
    "title": "VM",
    "description": "A VM instantiation",
    "type": "object",
    "properties": {
        "host": {
            "type": "object",
            "properties": {
                "num_cpus": {"type": "number"},
                "cpu_frequency": {"type": "string"},
                "disk_size": {"type": "string"},
                "mem_size": {"type": "string"}
            },
            "required": ["num_cpus", "cpu_frequency", "disk_size", "mem_size"]
        },
        "os": {
            "type": "object",
            "properties": {
                "architecture": {"type": "string"},
                "type": {"type": "string"},
                "distribution": {"type": "string"},
                "version": {"type": "string"}
            },
            "required": ["architecture", "type", "distribution", "version"]
        },
        "credentials": {
            "type": "object",
            "properties" : {
                "public_key": {"type": "string"}
            },
            "required": ["public_key"]
        }
    },
    "required": ["host", "os", "credentials"]
}
```

Packet-based Services Connectors are meant to implement interactions with all service providers that provide packet-based applications. As specified in Sect. 5.2, YAML to BPMN conversion implies that three types of BPMN service tasks are in place: "Create", "Configure" and "Start". To each of these tasks corresponds a generic connector interface (**Create**, **Configure** and **Start** in the bottom of Fig. 7). Those interfaces are then extended in order to manage many types of applications (DBMS, Web Servers, etc.). The latters are the ones that concrete Connectors must implement in order to interact with real packet-based application providers. To make an example, for the correct provisioning of a specific DBMS application, three connectors need to be implemented in order to create, configure and start the DBMS, respectively. Listing 1.6 displays a JSON Schema to validate the body of an HTTP-POST request to a RESTful-based /createdbms web service. Two parameters are required: "vm_url" and "workflow_id". *Vm_url* specifies the VM instance URL, whereas *workflow_id* uniquely identifies the provisioning workflow and allows Connectors to retrieve private application data (i.e., the DBMS root password to be set, in this particular case).

Listing 1.6. Create DBMS - JSON Schema Request.

```
{
    "$schema": "http://json-schema.org/draft-06/schema#",
    "title": "DBMS",
    "description": "A DBMS installation",
    "type": "object",
    "properties": {
        "vm_url": { "type": "string" },
        "correlation_key": { "type": "string" }
    },
    "required": ["vm_url", "correlation_key"]
}
```

For the DBMS provisioning to actually take place, the Connector needs to inject all the required instructions and parameters into the VM instance. Listing 1.7 shows a MySQL DBMS installation script for a VM with a Debian-based operating system.

Listing 1.7. Create MySQL - Example of installation script.

```
#!/bin/bash
#This script installs mysql server

apt-get update

debconf-set-selections <<< "mysql-server mysql-server/root_password password
    $db_root_password"
debconf-set-selections <<< "mysql-server mysql-server/root_password_again
    password $db_root_password"

apt-get -y install --fix-missing mysql-server
```

6.2   Invocation of Provisioning Services

In this Section a dynamic view of the system is provided by means of two UML Sequence Diagrams: the former models the instantiation of a VM (as an example of the allocation of Cloud resources), and the latter models the installation of a MySQL DBMS on a previously instantiated VM (as an example of the provisioning of packed-based applications).

Figure 8 shows the necessary steps that need to be taken for the instantiation of a VM. The BP engine, which is responsible for orchestrating the Provisioning Tasks, is the actor who initiates the interaction. To that end, the creation of a VM originates from the execution of a Service Task in the Provisioning Plan, through which the invocation of specific service is requested on the Service Broker. The Service Broker handles the request by querying the Service Registry in order to find the connector that meets as many requestor's requirements as possible. The Service Registry returns the URL of the selected connector (Amazon Instantiate_VM, in this case) to the Service Broker, which invokes the connector service. Then, the connector transparently interfaces with the Cloud Provider management APIs (Amazon AWS, in this case) which take care of the VM instantiation and return the VM access URL to the connector. Finally, the URL is forwarded from the connector to the Service Task passing through the Service Broker, thus determining the end of interaction with control being returned to the BP Engine.

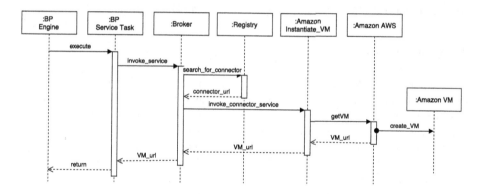

Fig. 8. Steps for the instantiation process of a VM.

Figure 9 exhibits the required steps for the installation of a DBMS on a previously instantiated VM. For the sake of clarity, the following assumptions are made: (a) MySQL is the DBMS of choice, (b) the VM is hosted on Amazon EC2, and (c) an Ubuntu Server distribution runs on the VM. As with the previous scenario, the BP engine is the actor who initiates the interaction. The installation of a DMBS starts from the execution of a Service Task in the Provisioning Plan, through which the invocation of specific service is requested on the Service Broker. The Service Broker manages the request by querying the Service Registry

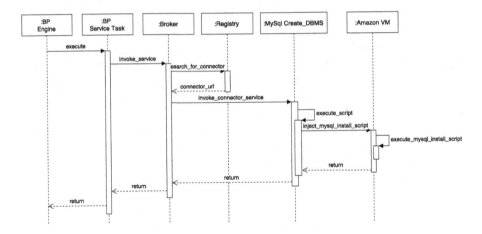

Fig. 9. Steps for the installation process of a DBMS.

in order to find the connector that suits the requestor's needs. The Service Registry returns the URL of the selected connector (MySQL Create_DBMS, in this case) to the Service Broker, which invokes the connector service passing as parameters the VM URL and information about the OS distribution running on it. Then, depending on this information, the connector injects the proper MySQL installation script into the VM where it gets executed. The interaction ends with control being ultimately returned to the BP engine.

7   Conclusion

In this paper we addressed the challenge that many cloud industry players are nowadays facing to reduce costs and improve flexibility in service provisioning: the automation of the operational management and orchestration of a cloud application. As shown, several different initiatives and tools have appeared to tackle the issue: very recently the TOSCA specification has emerged with the promise to facilitate the portable, automated, and reusable management of cloud services throughout their lifecycle. Our work leverages just on the TOSCA standard, by proposing a cloud orchestration and provisioning framework. Basically, the automation is carried out by a two-step process: (1) transforming a TOSCA cloud application model into a BPMN workflow; (2) getting the workflow executed on a workflow engine. The novelty of the approach consists in the definition of a data model that enriches the workflow and in the clear separation between the Provisioning Tasks and the Provisioning Services. In the future, the framework will be enhanced by providing support for non-functional requirements, also introducing advanced service matchmaking mechanisms.

References

1. Amazon: Amazon CloudFormation (2016). https://aws.amazon.com/cloudformation/. Accessed 15 Feb 2017
2. Bassiliades, N., Symeonidis, M., Meditskos, G., Kontopoulos, E., Gouvas, P., Vlahavas, I.: A semantic recommendation algorithm for the PaaSport platform-as-a-service marketplace. Expert Syst. Appl. **67**, 203–227 (2017). http://www.sciencedirect.com/science/article/pii/S0957417416305164
3. Binz, T., Breitenbücher, U., Haupt, F., Kopp, O., Leymann, F., Nowak, A., Wagner, S.: OpenTOSCA – a runtime for TOSCA-based cloud applications. In: Basu, S., Pautasso, C., Zhang, L., Fu, X. (eds.) ICSOC 2013. LNCS, vol. 8274, pp. 692–695. Springer, Heidelberg (2013). https://doi.org/10.1007/978-3-642-45005-1_62
4. Bousselmi, K., Brahmi, Z., Gammoudi, M.M.: Cloud services orchestration: a comparative study of existing approaches. In: IEEE 28th International Conference on Advanced Information Networking and Applications Workshops (WAINA 2014), pp. 410–416 (2014)
5. Breitenbücher, U., Binz, T., Kopp, O., Leymann, F., Wettinger, J.: A modelling concept to integrate declarative and imperative cloud application provisioning technologies. In: Proceedings of the 5th International Conference on Cloud Computing and Services Science, pp. 487–496 (2015)
6. Brogi, A., Carrasco, J., Cubo, J., Nitto, E.D., Durán, F., Fazzolari, M., Ibrahim, A., Pimentel, E., Soldani, J., Wang, P., D'Andria, F.: Adaptive management of applications across multiple clouds: the seaclouds approach. CLEI Electron. J. **18**(1) (2015). http://www.clei.org/cleiej/paper.php?id=326
7. Calcaterra, D., Cartelli, V., Di Modica, G., Tomarchio, O.: Combining TOSCA and BPMN to enable automated cloud service provisioning. In: Proceedings of the 7th International Conference on Cloud Computing and Services Science (CLOSER 2017), Porto, Portugal, pp. 187–196, April 2017. https://doi.org/10.5220/0006304701870196
8. Chappell, D.: Enterprise Service Bus. O'Reilly Media, Inc., Sebastopol (2004)
9. Chef: Devops Chef (2016). https://www.chef.io/solutions/devops/. Accessed 15 Feb 2017
10. Cisco: Cisco Intelligent Automation for Cloud (IAC) (2016). http://www.cisco.com/c/en/us/products/cloud-systems-management/intelligent-automation-cloud/index.html. Accessed 15 Feb 2017
11. Docker: Docker Compose (2017). https://docs.docker.com/compose/. Accessed 15 Feb 2017
12. Ferry, N., Almeida, M., Solberg, A.: The MODAClouds model-driven development. In: Di Nitto, E., Matthews, P., Petcu, D., Solberg, A. (eds.) Model-Driven Development and Operation of Multi-Cloud Applications. SAST, pp. 23–33. Springer, Cham (2017). https://doi.org/10.1007/978-3-319-46031-4_3
13. GigaSpaces: Cloudify (2016). http://getcloudify.org/. Accessed 15 Feb 2017
14. HP: HP Cloud Service Automation (2016). http://www8.hp.com/it/it/software-solutions/cloud-service-automation/. Accessed 15 Feb 2017
15. IBM: IBM Cloud Orchestrator (2016). http://www-03.ibm.com/software/products/it/ibm-cloud-orchestrator. Accessed 15 Feb 2017
16. Juju: Juju charms (2016). https://jujucharms.com/. Accessed 15 Feb 2017

17. Katsaros, G., Menzel, M., Lenk, A., Revelant, J.R., Skipp, R., Eberhardt, J.: Cloud application portability with TOSCA, Chef and Openstack. In: Proceedings of the 2014 IEEE International Conference on Cloud Engineering, IC2E 2014, pp. 295–302. IEEE Computer Society, Washington, DC (2014). https://doi.org/10.1109/IC2E.2014.27

18. Kopp, O., Binz, T., Breitenbücher, U., Leymann, F.: BPMN4TOSCA: a domain-specific language to model management plans for composite applications. In: Mendling, J., Weidlich, M. (eds.) BPMN 2012. LNBIP, vol. 125, pp. 38–52. Springer, Heidelberg (2012). https://doi.org/10.1007/978-3-642-33155-8_4

19. lxml: lxml project (2016). http://lxml.de/. Accessed 15 Feb 2017

20. Menychtas, A., Konstanteli, K., Alonso, J., Orue-Echevarria, L., Gorroñogoitia, J., Kousiouris, G., Santzaridou, C., Brunelière, H., Pellens, B., Stuer, P., Strauß, O., Senkova, T., Varvarigou, T.A.: Software modernization and cloudification using the artist migration methodology and framework. Scalable Comput. Pract. Exp. **15**(2) (2014). http://dblp.uni-trier.de/db/journals/scpe/scpe15.html#MenychtasKAOGKSBPSSSV14

21. OASIS: Web Services Business Process Execution Language Version 2.0, April 2007. https://www.oasis-open.org/committees/download.php/23964/wsbpel-v2.0-primer.htm. Accessed 15 Feb 2017

22. OASIS: Topology and Orchestration Specification for Cloud Applications Version 1.0, November 2013. http://docs.oasis-open.org/tosca/TOSCA/v1.0/os/TOSCA-v1.0-os.html. Accessed 15 Feb 2017

23. OASIS: Cloud Application Management for Platforms Version 1.1, November 2014. http://docs.oasis-open.org/camp/camp-spec/v1.1/camp-spec-v1.1.html. Accessed 15 Feb 2017

24. OASIS: TOSCA Simple Profile in YAML Version 1.0 (2015). http://docs.oasis-open.org/tosca/TOSCA-Simple-Profile-YAML/v1.0/csprd01/TOSCA-Simple-Profile-YAML-v1.0-csprd01.html. Accessed 15 Feb 2017

25. OMG: Business Process Model and Notation (BPMN 2.0), January 2011. http://www.omg.org/spec/BPMN/2.0/. Accessed 15 Feb 2017

26. OpenStack: OpenStack Heat (2016). https://wiki.openstack.org/wiki/Heat. Accessed 15 Feb 2017

27. OpenStack: OpenStack project (2016). https://github.com/openstack/tosca-parser. Accessed 15 Feb 2017

28. OpenTOSCA: OpenTOSCA project (2015). https://github.com/CloudCycle2/YAML_Transformer. Accessed 15 Feb 2017

29. Puppet: Puppet (2016). https://puppet.com/. Accessed 15 Feb 2017

30. Ranjan, R., Benatallah, B., Dustdar, S., Papazoglou, M.P.: Cloud resource orchestration programming: overview, issues, and directions. IEEE Internet Comput. **19**, 46–56 (2015)

31. RedHat: RedHat CloudForms (2016). https://www.redhat.com/it/technologies/management/cloudforms. Accessed 15 Feb 2017

32. Rightscale: Rightscale Cloud Management Platform (2016). http://www.rightscale.com/why-cloud-management-platform/benefits. Accessed 15 Feb 2017

33. Rossini, A.: Cloud Application Modelling and Execution Language (CAMEL) and the PaaSage workflow. In: Celesti, A., Leitner, P. (eds.) ESOCC 2015 Workshops. CCIS, vol. 567, pp. 437–439. Springer, Cham (2016). https://doi.org/10.1007/978-3-319-33313-7

34. The Apache Software Foundation: The Apache Brooklyn project (2016). https://brooklyn.apache.org/. Accessed 15 Feb 2017

35. Tosatto, A., Ruiu, P., Attanasio, A.: Container-based orchestration in cloud: state of the art and challenges. In: 9th International Conference on Complex, Intelligent, and Software Intensive Systems (CISIS 2015), pp. 70–75 (2015)

36. Weerasiri, D., Barukh, M.C., Benatallah, B., Sheng, Q.Z., Ranjan, R.: A taxonomy and survey of cloud resource orchestration techniques. ACM Comput. Surv. **50**(2), 26:1–26:41 (2017)

37. Wettinger, J., Binz, T., Breitenbücher, U., Kopp, O., Leymann, F., Zimmermann, M.: Unified invocation of scripts and services for provisioning, deployment, and management of cloud applications based on TOSCA. In: Proceedings of the 4th International Conference on Cloud Computing and Services Science, pp. 559–568 (2014)

38. Wettinger, J., Breitenbücher, U., Kopp, O., Leymann, F.: Streamlining DevOps automation for cloud applications using TOSCA as standardized metamodel. Futur. Gener. Comput. Syst. **56**, 317–332 (2016). http://www.sciencedirect.com/science/article/pii/ S0167739X15002496

Component Migration in a Trans-cloud Environment

Jose Carrasco, Francisco Durán[⊠], and Ernesto Pimentel

University of Málaga, Málaga, Spain
{josec,duran,ernesto}@lcc.uma.es

Abstract. The *trans-cloud* approach has recently been proposed to simplify the development and operation of cloud applications, and to minimize the *lock-in problem*. The three key ingredients of the *trans-cloud* approach are: agnostic topology descriptions, a unified API, and mechanisms for the independent specification of providers' services. We build on the trans-cloud mechanisms to propose a solution for the migration of stateless cloud components at runtime. In the context of our trans-cloud tool, we propose an algorithm for the migration of cloud applications' components between different providers, possibly changing their service levels between IaaS and PaaS. We present an implementation of our proposed solution, and illustrate it with a case study and experimental results.

1 Introduction

As an answer to the increasing demand of services in Cloud Computing [1,2], vendors are offering their own cloud solutions. Vendors have developed similar resources, which offer through their own APIs, defining their own service level agreements (SLA), non-functional requirements, add-ons, and quality of service (QoS) specifications. Such heterogeneity has derived into many interoperability and portability restrictions on cloud applications, often producing situations in which cloud developers are locked-in specific services from cloud providers.

We have recently witnessed how most of the interoperability issues have been solved thanks to the advances in the management of the connections between components deployed using different technologies and vendors (see, e.g., [3–5]). These advances have allowed the development of different deployment platforms, capable of distributing application modules using services from different providers. With these technologies, we can now deploy our applications using for each of the individual components the best alternative, with the best possible result for the operation of our applications. Trans-cloud environments [6] has been proposed as the last step in this direction, with the goal of providing the possibility of deploying applications combining IaaS and PaaS services, possibly provided by different vendors.

The selection of the service level and vendor to deploy each of the components of our applications, from the multitude of cloud offerings, is challenging

© Springer International Publishing AG, part of Springer Nature 2018
D. Ferguson et al. (Eds.): CLOSER 2017, CCIS 864, pp. 286–307, 2018.
https://doi.org/10.1007/978-3-319-94959-8_15

(see, e.g., [7–9]). Furthermore, since the context and required knowledge may change while applications are under operation, performing the required changes may result in additional costs to stop and re-started applications. This is part of life however. Even though developers may decide today, for example, to use a PaaS provider for a particular module because it is more cost effective, or because it requires less management effort, tomorrow they may require, e.g., to increase the security level of their services, or a better integration with their enterprise's infrastructure. These new operation requirements may force a change on the original decisions, since the new needs or business model requires more control over virtual machines. In this situation the best decision may be to move some component to IaaS services. Unfortunately, moving an application's component between different providers is problematic, and even worst between different abstraction levels.

With current technologies, provider or level changes may require a significant development effort [10,11], to adapt the components to the new service requirements and to their interaction with the rest of the components of the application, which may be running in other providers. Migration of individual components or entire applications may however be unavoidable over time, because of changes in the offered services, prices, security policies, or simply because a provider just stops providing its services. Once developers can take advantage of the features of different kinds of services, they will be interested as well in optimizing the cloud resources usage and improve their applications' performance.

To accomplish the correct movement of components, the migration of an application requires the orchestration of the entire environment where it is being executed. If we have to directly handle cloud interoperability and portability issues, the task becomes very complicated. Indeed, *live migration* of cloud applications pose a number of new key issues related to cloud resources and the control of the components of applications. Migration is currently being widely studied both at academia and at industry (see, e.g., [12,13]), and there have been several proposals for the live migration of cloud application's components (see, e.g., [14–16]). In some of these proposals, components of running applications are moved to different vendors or locations. However, they still present significant limitations, mainly due to the difficulties related to the cross-vendor portability of components, but also to their interoperability, which is typically solved by providing ad-hoc solutions. FurthermoreIn all these cases, solutions are limited to one specific service level, which may be IaaS or PaaS (cf. [15–17]).

To allow the migration of stateless components of cloud applications at runtime, we propose an orchestration algorithm. Our algorithm is *agnostic*, in the sense that it is not bound to a specific service level, nor any particular provider. In order to ensure this agnosticity, our algorithm is built over *trans-cloud* concepts [6]: agnostic topology descriptions, a unified API, and mechanisms for the independent specification of providers' services. The trans-cloud environment releases developers of most of the vendor lock-in issues, and facilitates the adaptation of running applications. Individual components may be moved independently of the target abstraction level. Specifically, [6] uses the TOSCA standard to model applications' topologies agnostically, without using any particularities of the target providers. The information related to the cloud service level, IaaS or PaaS, is added by means of *policies*, completely independent of the topology description. these specifications are then processed by the trans-cloud environment, which unifies IaaS and PaaS services of different vendors through an homogeneization API. Such unified API allows us to orchestrate the deployment and migration of applications over the required cloud services in a completely agnostic way. We focus on stateless components, the migration of components with state is left as future work.

The proposal for component-wise migration of applications at runtime was originally presented in [18]. Here we present an improved version of the approach and provide a detailed account on its implementation and use, with special attention to the extension of Apache Brooklyn, on which the trans-cloud environment was developed. Since our migration algorithm relies on the trans-cloud infrastructure for the management of each application module and the interaction with the used cloud services—to *stop*, *restart* or *move* the necessary components independently of the service level, IaaS or PaaS, the cloud technology or any other dependencies—in order to provide the necessary ground for the migration algorithm, an extensive presentation of the implementation of the trans-cloud infrastructure is provided before presenting the algorithm.

The rest of this paper is structured as follows. Preliminaries about trans-cloud deployment and its current implementation are presented in Sect. 2. The proposed migration algorithm is described in Sect. 3. Details on the implementation of the algorithm are presented in Sect. 4, together with some experimental results. Finally, Sect. 5 conclude the paper and presents some plans for future work.

2   A Brooklyn Basis for Trans-cloud

The trans-cloud tool presented in [6] is based on the TOSCA standard[1] for the description of agnostic topologies. Specifically, it builds on the Brooklyn-TOSCA open project for enabling an independent specification of the used services, and on the Apache Brooklyn project to provide a common API for the unified management of IaaS and PaaS services. Figure 2 shows an overview of the proposal in [6].

All concepts in the rest of the paper are illustrated on a running case study presented in Sect. 2. The example will be used in this section to illustrate Brooklyn and the main concepts in it (following the CAMP standard). Specifically, Sect. 2.3 presents Brooklyn's abstract architecture, and Sects. 2.4–2.7 its main elements, namely, entities, drivers, locations, and lifecycles. The same case study is later used to show the use of the our proposal in Sect. 3 and to evaluate it in Sect. 4.

---

[1] TOSCA (Topology and Orchestration Specification for Cloud Applications) is an OASIS standard for the description of cloud applications, the corresponding services and their relationships.

2.1   Trans-cloud Concepts

The main goal of the trans-cloud management proposal is to allow the development and deployment of applications without restrictions on the providers or service levels used for each individual component. A trans-cloud environment provides facilities for the use of available services and resources, at IaaS or PaaS levels, in accordance to the requirements and preferences of the applications.

The trans-cloud approach liberates developers from the usual infrastructure limitations while defining their applications, and significantly reduces all issues related to the portability and interoperability of applications and components. The key ingredients of the approach are:

Agnostic topology descriptions. Applications' components, configurations, interrelations, etc. are specified without details about cloud providers.
Target service specifications. Topology descriptions are kept agnostic and reusable by using topology-independent specifications of target providers. This independence allows the flexible specification of target services, IaaS or PaaS, for the deployment of individual components.
A unified API. IaaS and PaaS services management is unified under a common homogeneization API. Cloud heterogeneity is thus mitigated, providing a vendor-independent solution, which releases ourselves of proprietary tools, frameworks and technologies to manage IaaS and PaaS services of specific vendors.

Thanks to these key ingredients, given the definition of an application's topology and specifications of the target providers of each of its components, the deployment of the application can be carried out by using the unified API to operate with the selected services, IaaS or PaaS. And as for the provision of a unified cloud management, these concepts are also useful as an essential basis for the migration of components: the unified API may be used for the management of the necessary resources (using drivers for the cloud technologies and connectors) to adjust to a change of the target locations of a component in an application's description.

2.2   The Softcare Case Study

Softcare is a cloud-based clinical, educational, and social application, based on state-of-the-art technology developed by Atos Spain [19]. It is an innovative application for the social inclusion of elderly people and for the management of their medical problems. The main features of the application.

Figure 1 depicts Softcare's topology. It is composed of seven modules: SoftwareWS, Forum, Multimedia, and SoftwareDashboard are web modules over respective Tomcat servers (note the Tomcat icons), and SoftcareDB, ForumDB, and MultimediaDB are MySQL databases (note the database icons). The main graphical user interface is provided by the Softcare Dashboard component, which depends on the SoftwareWS, Forum, and Multimedia modules. The Forum module provides a

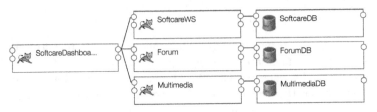

Fig. 1. Brooklyn-TOSCA Softcare's topology [19].

forum service to the web platform, the Multimedia module is responsible for the management of the multimedia content, and the SoftcareWS module provides the business logic. The ForumDB and MultimediaDB databases store the forum's messages and the multimedia content, respectively. The rest of the application's data is stored in the SoftcareDB database.

2.3   Brooklyn's Abstract Architecture

Brooklyn is a framework for modeling, monitoring, and managing cloud applications. It quite closely follows the OASIS CAMP standard,[2] an API for managing public and private cloud applications. Indeed, current Brooklyn blueprints conform to the OASIS CAMP v1.1 Public Review Draft 01 [20]. Most concepts and terminology in its definition, such as entities, locations, drivers or policies, come from the standard.

In this section, we present some details on Brooklyn's architecture and operation. The complexity of Brooklyn makes it really challenging to present all the details of its architecture. Instead, for our explanation of Brooklyn, as for the presentation of our extension in Sect. 2.8, we will focus on a small set of classes and interfaces, as well as the relationships between them, that gives an insight into its design, enough to understand the extension we have developed. Figure 3 depicts a few classes and interfaces as in the actual Java implementation of Brooklyn. Further details on Brooklyn and its implementation may be found in its official documentation [21].

To be precise, the open-source Apache Brooklyn project is a multi-cloud application management platform for the management of the provisioning and deployment of cloud applications. Although Brooklyn provides a unified API that enables cross-computing features, its current official release only handles IaaS services. As can be seen in Fig. 2, in [6] Brooklyn's API was extended with new mechanisms for the management of PaaS services. PaaS providers and mechanisms have been added to allow the deployment and management of application components on PaaS services as well as on IaaS services. Our extension builds on the flexibility and genericity of Brooklyns API, which has the independency between application descriptions and cloud services used in their operation as one of its goals. As a prototype for the PaaS support, and to allow

---

[2] Information on the use of standards in Brooklyn can be found at https://brooklyn. apache.org/learnmore/theory.html.

components to be deployed using both IaaS and PaaS, we initially integrated CloudFoundry-based platforms, like IBM Bluemix, Pivotal Web Services, etc.

The other key ingredient of our proposal for trans-cloud is the open project Brooklyn-TOSCA, whose main goal is to extend the Brooklyn tool with capabilities for the deployment and management of cloud applications and resources using TOSCA concepts. In Brooklyn-TOSCA, agnostic TOSCA topologies are built by expressing the target services using TOSCA policies.

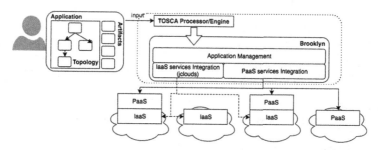

Fig. 2. Trans-cloud approach [6].

To illustrate the agnostic description of applications' topologies, the TOSCA YAML topology schema of the Softcare case study is shown in Listing 1.1. For brevity, only some elements are described. This definition follows the Brooklyn-TOSCA initiative that allows target cloud services to be specified by means of policies (brooklyn.location), as can be seen in lines 29–37. In this example specification, one group of components is to be deployed on AWS (Ireland's cluster) and another one on SoftLayer (London's cluster). Although in this case both target location are IaaS, we can observe the separation between the topology description and the provider specifications. If we decided to use different providers to redeploy the application, changing the corresponding locations would be enough, with no need for modifying the original topology. Listing 1.2 shows an excerpt of the corresponding TOSCA YAML description using Pivotal (PaaS) as target location for the deployment of some of the components.

Our agnostic algorithm for the migration of application's component build on the trans-cloud approach, which provides a set of useful basic mechanisms.

2.4 Brooklyn Entities

In Brooklyn, *entities* represent agnostic pieces of software, such as cloud resources, applications, and application modules (servers, databases, etc.), with the purpose of managing their deployment and operation. A cloud application is an entity that has a collection of other entities forming a hierarchy of application modules: its children. The parent-child relationship of entities does not represent any dependency between the software artifacts modeled by the entities, but a *control* dependency, meaning that a parent entity is responsible for

```
1   tosca_definitions_version: tosca_simple_yaml_1_0_0_wd03
2   ...
3   topology_template:
4     node_templates:
5       SoftcareDashboard:
6         type: org.apache.brooklyn.entity.webapp.tomcat.TomcatServer
7           ...
8         requirements:
9         − endpoint_configuration:
10            node: SoftcareWS
11            ...
12        − endpoint_configuration:
13            node: Forum
14            ...
15        − endpoint_configuration:
16            node: Multimedia
17            ...
18      SoftcareWS:
19        type: org.apache.brooklyn.entity.webapp.tomcat.TomcatServer
20          ...
21        requirements:
22        − endpoint_configuration:
23            node: SoftcareDB
24            ...
25      SoftcareDB:
26        type: org.apache.brooklyn.entity.database.mysql.MySqlNode
27          ...
28          ...
29    groups:
30      add_compute_locations:
31        members: [SoftcareDB, ForumDB, MultimediaDB, Forum]
32        policies:
33        − brooklyn.location: aws−ec2:eu−west−1
34      add_web_locations:
35        members: [SoftcareDashboard, SoftcareWS, Multimedia]
36        policies:
37        − brooklyn.location: softlayer:lon02
```

Code 1.1. Softcare's TOSCA description [6].

controlling its children entities. For example, if an entity, such as a cluster, is to be started, it will also have to start its children. In Brooklyn, each entity of an application may be deployed on a different location, supporting what is known as multi-cloud deployment.

An entity represents the core of any deployable artefact, so it can be extended to model new concrete software pieces, such as web servers, DBMSs, etc. For illustration purposes, Fig. 3 shows interfaces TomcatServer and MySqlNode, which model, respectively, the software modules Tomcat server and MySql server. Of course, Brooklyn also provides concrete software representations for JBoss servers, clusters, and many others. As shown in the diagram, the Entity interface is extended by the SoftwareProcess interface, which is described as the basis of any

```
1    ...
2    groups:
3     add_compute_locations:
4      members: [SoftcareDB, ForumDB, MultimediaDB, Forum]
5      policies:
6       − brooklyn.location: aws−ec2:eu−west−1
7     add_web_locations:
8      members: [SoftcareDashboard, SoftcareWS, Multimedia]
9      policies:
10      − brooklyn.location: pivotal−ws
```

Code 1.2. New locations for some of the web modules [6].

software process, that is, a piece of software to run somewhere. This interface is extended for each specific piece of software.

Following the interface-based architectural pattern, Brooklyn provides classes implementing each of these interfaces. For example, TomcatServerImpl implements TomcatServer. These specializations form themselves a new hierarchy inheriting from AbstractEntity, an abstract class that provides the behavior of Brooklyn entities. Inheriting from it, we find SoftwareProcessImpl, which implements the SoftwareProcess interface and provides the management logic of any software process.

The management of entities is performed through their provided endpoints, to know their status (*sensors*) and operate on them (*effectors*). Sensors allow entities to expose data. For example, a server can offer the number of requests per second or its running time; a cluster can offer the current number of server

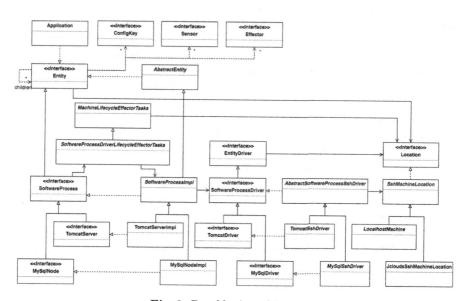

Fig. 3. Brooklyn's architecture.

instances it handles. Effectors are used to model the actions that can be applied on an entity. For example, effectors are used for starting an entity using offered cloud resources, or for stopping an entity in a VM. Although sensors and effectors are independent, entities are responsible for the connection and updating of their sensors and effectors (as for any other entities depending on them). Effectors and sensors can be injected into an entity at runtime, following the classical Abstract Factory and the Strategy patterns [22], and allowing a useful elasticity. These mechanisms are very helpful for improving the extensibility and flexibility of entities. In a similar vein, configuration keys are used to model their configuration, for the establishment of dependencies between components in provider-independent application specifications.

2.5   Locations

Each entity has an associated *location*, which defines where the entity is or is to be deployed. A location represents a cloud service or a deployment resource, and contains the necessary information to access and to use the referenced elements. Thus, a local VM or an AWS datacenter will be modeled by different locations. Furthermore, these classes have to provide the necessary mechanisms to manage the target services and resources. For example, an AWS EC2 location should contain the necessary methods to connect to the specific AWS datacenter and to use the necessary services, such as creating and launching a VM, and configuring network resources.

On the right-hand side of Fig. 3, we show the Location hierarchy. Locations represent the cloud services and providers where entities are to be deployed. Some examples are a remote or local virtual machine, remote hosts (BYONS), public and private datacenters to provision virtual machines on-demand, and so forth. The diagram shows some location classes in the Brooklyn implementation. For instance, the SshMachineLocation class implements the Location interface, and represents machines that can be managed using the ssh protocol. This technology is very useful in IaaS environments, where a very wide range of virtual and physical machines are accessed using this protocol. Locations have to include the necessary mechanisms to manage the represented element. Thus, SshMachineLocation offers methods to establish a connection with any machine reachable by ssh, to copy files, to execute commands, etc.

Two different SshMachineLocation specializations are depicted in Fig. 3. The first one is LocalhostMachine, which represents the machine where the Brooklyn instance is running. Deploying an entity using LocalhostMachine is straightforward, since the location exists and can be easily reached. The second specialization is JcloudsSshMachineLocation, for jclouds locations. Brooklyn relies on jclouds to, with a single location, manage all providers supported by jclouds[3] in an unified way.

---

[3] The list of providers supported by jclouds is available at https://jclouds.apache.org/reference/providers/.

Brooklyn has been developed in an extensible and flexible way. To allow the addition of new elements, the different entities, locations, and drivers are discovered and injected at runtime in accordance with the requirements of the applications. In the case of locations, Brooklyn offers the LocationResolver interface, which must be implemented by each location in order to enable its discovery and usage at runtime. Then, Brooklyn uses resolvers to create instances of the expected locations. For instance, given the Brooklyn locations above, we find resolvers LocalhostLocationResolver and JcloudsLocationResolver.

The current location hierarchy of Brooklyn includes other location classes. For example, the ProvisioningLocation class models locations where new VMs can be provisioned and launched, such as cloud datacenters. If we wanted Brooklyn to support further cloud offerings, either services, providers, or resources, then we would have to develop corresponding new implementations of Location and LocationResolver.

2.6   Drivers

The location of a SoftwareProcess defines where the modeled piece of software will be deployed and run. For example, if a JBossServer has a LocalhostMachine as location, then it will be deployed on the machine where the Brooklyn instance is running. Moreover, with this approach, entities may operate on their corresponding locations if they need to carry out some of their tasks. Of course, they will be the implementations AbstractEntity, SoftwareProcessImpl, TomcatServerImpl, etc., and not the entity interfaces, the ones with the references to locations and the ones that provide the endpoints to manage them. However, to avoid requiring an intimate knowledge or management of any concrete location, these implementations have been developed generically by delegating the location management to another hierarchy of elements: the *drivers*. A driver contains the code to allow a specific entity to operate over a specific location. This scheme allows the location-independent definition of entities. Moreover, it is very useful if a new kind of location has to be supported, since in that case just a new driver will be required, which will be able to manage the entity in the new location, satisfying the open/closed principle. In other words, entities use a Strategy pattern [23] to delegate the necessary behavior to carry out the location's management.

Class SoftwareProcessImpl implements the DriverDependentEntity interface, which determines that an entity must have a driver implementing SoftwareProcessDriver. To enable the management of different kinds of drivers, each entity declares a driver interface that the given driver will implement. For instance, TomcatServerImpl demands a specific driver, which will focus on a specific location, that implements TomcatDriver. This leads to a new hierarchy of driver interfaces, as shown in Fig. 3. With this approach, implementations of SoftwareProcess just see a driver interface, which hides the fine-grained details of each specific driver. Of course, although SoftwareProcessImpl follows a driver-based approach, by appropriately implementing DriverDependentEntity, other implementations of the SoftwareProcess interface could be provided.

Corresponding specializations of SoftwareProcessDriver are provided for the deployment and management of entities on each location. For illustrative purposes, Fig. 3 shows the sub-hierarchy of locations based on SshMachineLocation. In it, we find a driver TomcatSshDriver that handles the deployment of TomcatServer entities on SshMachineLocation. More precisely, this class contains operations to download, install, configure and run Tomcat servers on machines accessed through ssh. That is to say, the driver contains the capability to place and manage a piece of software on a specific location. The driver specializations in Fig. 3 extend AbstractSoftwareProcessSshDriver, which implements the SoftwareProcessDriver interface. Indeed, the AbstractSoftwareProcessSshDriver class is extended by class AbstractSoftwareProcessDriver, which is in charge of implementing the SoftwareProcessDriver interface.

2.7   Entities' Life Cycles

Although a driver contains the necessary knowledge to deploy and run an entity on a location, drivers operate in the context of an entity, which means that drivers expect configured locations to operate on. For instance, according to the entity restrictions, some ports are required for SshMachineLocation. For example, a MySqlNode will require port 3306, which is the one normally used by MySQL servers. Machine-based location management is extracted to an abstract class MachineLifecycleEffectorTasks, which defines the life cycle to carry out. This life cycle is responsible for different tasks, such as configuring the machines, adding the necessary information to the entities, and even machine provisioning. This class focuses on machine management, but SoftwareProcess will require it to form part of this life cycle in order to be deployed and run. Then, class MachineLifecycleEffectorTasks is extended by class SoftwareProcessDriverLifecycleEffector, which specializes the machine life cycle by adding driver management and improving the integration of the life cycle with the entity. Thus, we can say that life cycles handle the different entities' processes, because they manage the location, the drivers and even the entity itself.

Life cycles define the operations to handle the deployment of entities, to manage machines and any other required infrastructure in a systematic and generic way, using specific effectors. For IaaS-based life cycles, the only ones supported in Brooklyn, life cycles assume the Startable interface, which forces entities to offer effectors such as start, stop and restart. During the initialization of an entity, the operations of its effectors are modified by injecting appropriate body effectors, which are defined by the lifecycle, to manage a certain kind of location. After that, the entity is ready to support locations based on machines and use the drivers to carry out the deployment and management of the entity in the desired machine-based location. Specifically, the SoftwareProcess interface extends the Startable interface, and when a subclass of SoftwareProcessImpl is created, its effectors' default behavior is overridden with the appropriate effector bodies during the initialization phase of their life cycle.

Thus, the start, stop and re-start effectors executed by the life cycle will be those injected into the corresponding SoftwareProcessImpl entity. The (start routine of the) start effector is in charge of managing the entity's location and driver, which is described by SoftwareProcessDriverEffectorTasks. It begins by getting the necessary flags to configure the machine, open ports, etc. Once the machine is running, the start effector will create the expected driver, and will add it to the entity. The configuration of the entity is completed with some final details, e.g., the creation of sensors offering the address and the host's name for the entity. Then, the start effector manages the entity's children. By default, they are started using the location of their parent. Once its children have started, the entity's driver is executed, which takes care of installing, configuring and launching the entity's software in its location. Finally, the entity's sensors are connected. The stop effector is in charge of disconnecting the entity's sensors, and stopping their children. Then, the entity driver is used to stop the software which is running on the location. Once the software has been stopped, the machine is released if necessary. The re-start effector uses the previous effectors. First, it stops the entity using the stop effector, without releasing the machine, and then it uses the start effector to start the entity software again in the target location.

Although effectors are injected during the initialization phase of an entity's life cycle, as defined in the Startable interface, the start effector takes a location as parameter. This location will be used to start the entity on it. As a result of this, an entity does not fix the specific location where it will run until the start effector is invoked, which allows it to start an application in a location different to the one it was designed for, or, more interestingly, postponing the assignment of a given location until its start. When SoftwareProcessImpl-based entities are initialized, their effectors are replaced by SoftwareProcessDriverEffectorTasks effector bodies, which are intended to manage machine locations. This means that, although SoftwareProcessImpl entities assume a MachineLocation-based management, the specific target location (JcloudsSshMachineLocation, LocalHostLocation, etc.) to use will not be specified until the start effector is called. This mechanism will be key for the agnostic definition of entities in our extension, since we will use this possibility, not only to change the specific location, but also to change the entire life cycle.

In summary, in order to enable the deployment on PaaS locations, the PaaS life cycle we have developed and added to Brooklyn's API for PaaS entities, is responsible for: (1) injecting effector logic to allow interaction with PaaS platforms, (2) creating drivers and adding them to entities, and (3) defining the key steps for managing application processing (deployment, stopping, removing, etc.) on the target PaaS platform. As explained, life cycles are agnostic pieces and do not know about final providers' management, so they require the specification of drivers to manage entities on target locations. For instance, an entity requires PaaS-based drivers for signing in to the target platform and using the required services.

2.8 Extended Architecture

As explained in the previous sections, Brooklyn provides an API for the management of IaaS cloud services for a significant number of providers, and establishes a life cycle for the management of IaaS services and applications. We have extended Brooklyn by adding some new elements to this API in order to facilitate the management of PaaS services, provided by platforms such as Cloud Foundry, thus providing an homogeneous access to IaaS and PaaS services.

The Apache Brooklyn tool presented in the previous sections was extended in several ways, but keeping its architecture. To be able to handle PaaS locations, it is not enough providing the corresponding locations and drivers to manage them. More importantly, PaaS services follow a completely different life cycle to orchestrate application deployment. The new locations allow PaaS platforms to be modeled inside Brooklyn, allowing the creation of a new family of PaaS-based drivers. These new drivers contain the logic to enable the deployment and management of entities on PaaS platforms. However, as for the management of IaaS locations, SoftwareProcess instances require a new PaaS-based life cycle. Indeed, to manage IaaS and PaaS behaviors at runtime many other classes and patterns were developed.

Our migration algorithm (see Sect. 3) was developed and integrated into Brooklyn as an independent piece of the customized Brooklyn described in Sect. 2. The algorithm is accessed as part of a set of available trans-cloud mechanisms, its public API, which provides support for the management of cloud providers and resources. These operations perform activities such as stopping, starting, restarting, etc.

Brooklyn, as the customized Brooklyn presented in Sect. 2, have a limited support for the management of relations between components. Although relationships are specified in the TOSCA descriptions of applications' topologies and on the configuration of components, the explicit knowledge about the relations was not shared with the trans-cloud API. This basically means that it does not offer the operations to identify, and manage the relations and functional dependencies between components, which are necessary for the development of the proposed migration algorithm: we cannot get these dependencies, for example to re-establishment the connections, to find the components that depend on another (parents), or retrieve all the dependencies of one of them (children).

Our trans-cloud infrastructure was therefore extended to enable the explicit management of functional relationships of application's components. In our extended implementation of Brooklyn, when Brooklyn-TOSCA processes the TOSCA relationships to configure the component's relations, this information is added to the trans-cloud API. This functionality was provided by adding mechanisms that enable the management of relationships, and by providing operations to find the children and parents of a given component.

A particularly interesting type of functional dependencies are composition relations. In the case of composition relations, a component is in charge of the management of its sub-components. For example, the relation between a cluster and the servers it controls is modeled by a composition relation. Then, if a stopping or starting operation is applied to a cluster, the same operation must also be applied to all its children, in order to maintain the consistency of the topology. For this reason, a composed element, like a cluster or other elastic components, can be considered and managed as a bundle, which represent a set of sub-components.

Regarding our migration algorithm, if an operation must be carried out on a bundle, the algorithm takes care of ensuring that the same operation is applied to all its sub-components. For instance, if the migration algorithm requires to stop a cluster, this cluster itself ensures that all its component servers will also be stopped. This simple mechanism maintains the integrity of the topology during the migration process and ensures that the algorithm orchestration is delivered to all the components of the application.

Our Brooklyn-based trans-cloud tool, including its source code, is publicly available at https://github.com/scenic-uma/brooklyn-dist/tree/trans-cloud. Some additional documentation, examples and evaluation are available at https://trans-cloud.firebaseapp.com.

3   Migration Algorithm

In this section, we present our algorithm for the reconfiguration of cloud applications' components. The algorithm allows connecting the components in a convenient way, provisioning the necessary cloud resources, making the required operations (stop, start, and release), and respecting functional dependencies.

3.1   Description of the Algorithm

In this section we provide some insights on how the algorithm works by illustrating it on our case study. Specifically, we describe how the Forum component of the Softcare case study can be migrated step by step.

Let us assume that we have deployed the Softcare application following the trans-cloud approach. That is, we have an agnostic description of the application and all its components, for instance using TOSCA, such as it was made in Sect. 2. In that description, we used policies to specify the concrete locations on which the components were deployed, what also includes information about the service level, IaaS or PaaS. The trans-cloud infrastructure is in charge of managing the module to be deployed or migrated, as well as the required resources. The application developer does not have to worry about the management of the components, vendors, or abstraction levels. The infrastructure is therefore responsible of guaranteeing the integrity of the topology. It will identify and handle the interdependencies between components, both during deployment and migration.

As in the deployment plan in Sect. 2, we assume that the Forum component of the Softcare application is running in AWS EC2 (IaaS). The diagram in Fig. 4 shows the sequence of steps followed when migrating the Forum component to Pivotal Web Services (PaaS). In the sequence diagram se can observe how the

Migration Orchestrator controls the migration process fired by the request to migrate the Forum component.

To avoid having active components depending on non-active ones, all elements that have functional dependencies with the Forum component are stopped by the migration orchestrator upon the reception of the migration request. Notice that collecting all parents of a module might be a complex task, because of the variety of mechanisms for configuring and establishing connections between components: environment variables, configuration files, etc. In the trans-cloud approach, however, all the relations and dependencies are specified in the description of the application's topology, which allows to quickly identify and process all the relations between components.

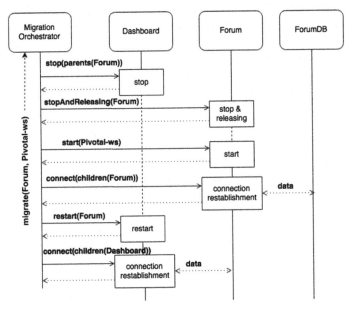

Fig. 4. Forum migration process [18].

The execution of an operation over a component depends on the specific vendor and level, PaaS or IaaS, of the service the component is running on. For instance, if a server is running on a PaaS environment, to stop it, a concrete REST web service of the platforms API should be called; however, if the server was running on a VM in IaaS, a specific command should probably be executed on the VM using ssh. Nevertheless, the trans-cloud approach greatly simplifies the management of different cloud services, because it hides the cloud heterogeneity through its unified API.

Once all parents have been stopped, the component to be migrated must be stopped. We can see how in the Step 2 in the diagram in Fig. 4, the Forum component is stopped. Since the resources used by the Forum component in AWS will not be used after the component is moved to its new location, the trans-cloud infrastructure takes care of releasing all these resources. This allows us to stop a component without having to worry about the resources use by the component, or the vendor and abstraction level of the services used.

Step 3 shows how, once the component has been stopped and the resources used released, a new instance of the component is started in its new location. Again, the trans-cloud infrastructure greatly simplifies this task. The information about the structure of the application included in the specification of the topology of the application is used to deploy the component in its new location by using the information on the target providers. In this case, the description of the Forum component and its associated resources, and the new target location (Pivotal Web Service), are provided as arguments to the operations in the unified API in charge of the task.

Once the component is in its new location, in Step 4, the connections of its functional dependencies are re-established, in order to maintain the structural integrity of the application. In our example, once the Forum component in running in Pivotal, its connection with the ForumDB component is re-established. The trans-cloud environment analyzes the application topology, finds the necessary relations for the newly migrated component, and re-establishes the connections with the other components in the topology, independently of the cloud environments components are running in. Continuing with our ample, since Pivotal offers PaaS services, environment variables are used to handle the connections between components.

The process concludes with the re-start of all the components of the application that were stopped in Step 1. Once more, the trans-cloud infrastructure greatly simplifies the re-starting of the necessary components and the re-establishment of their connections (see Steps 5 and 6). Thanks to the information on the topology of the application, the Dashboard component, only parent of the Forum component, is re-started. Finally, the new Forum component's endpoint, now provided by Pivotal, is used to re-establish the connection.

3.2   Specification of the Algorithm

Since the trans-cloud infrastructure takes care of the diversity of the cloud and the complex management of applications' components, we can provide a migration algorithm that completely abstracts from details from vendors and service levels. The Algorithm 1 can therefore be reduced to a process orchestrator. Given an application, the component to be migrated, and the target location for such a component, the algorithm generates a plan for the migration process, delegating all the management details to the trans-cloud infrastructure.

The operation MIGRATE(a, c, l) takes three parameters: the application to operate on (a), the component to be migrated (c), and the target location (l). The process to migrate a component starts by stopping all its input dependencies (lines 2–3). STOPPARENTS (lines 10–13) is a recursive procedure that stops all the ancestors of a given component following a top-down strategy, that is, it stops a component once all its parents have been previously stopped. The *stop*(*a, c*) operation (line 15), provided by the trans-cloud infrastructure, stops an application's component.

Once all parent components have been stopped, the trans-cloud operation *stopAndReleaseResources*(*a, c*) is used to stop the component to be migrated and to release all its bound resources (line 4). Then, the target component is started in its new location and all its connections are re-established (lines 6–8). The trans-cloud operations *start*(*a, c, l*) and *reestablishRelations*(*a, c, child*) are used to deploy and start the component in its new location, thus hiding the complexity of managing the different services.

In a last step, all components stopped in previous steps are re-started (lines 9–10). The recursive function RESTARTPARENTS(*a, parent*) (lines 17–22), which follows a bottom-up strategy, is in charge of re-starting all the stopped ancestors. This procedure ensures that all dependencies of a component are available before re-starting it, and thus concluding the migration process.

Algorithm 1. Migration Algorithm.

Input: *a : application*
Input: *c : component to migrate*
Input: *l : new location for the component*

1: **procedure** MIGRATE(a, c, l)   ▷ Main function
2:     **for** *parent: parents*(*a, c*) **do**
3:         STOPPARENTS(*a, parent*)

4:     *stopAndReleaseResources*(*a, c*)
5:     *start*(*a, c, l*)
6:     **for** *child: children*(*a, c*) **do**
7:         *restablishRelations*(*a, c, child*)

8:     **for** *parent: parents*(*a, c*) **do**
9:         RESTARTPARENTS(*a, parent*)

10: **procedure** STOPPARENTS(a, c)   ▷ STOPPARENTS auxiliary function
11:     **for** *parent: parents*(*a, c*) **do**
12:         STOPPARENTS(*a, parent*)

13:     *stop*(*a, c*)

14: **procedure** RESTARTPARENTS(a, c)   ▷ RESTARTPARENTS auxiliary function
15:     *re − start*(*a, c*)
16:     **for** *child: children*(*a, c*) **do**
17:         *reestablishRelations*(*a, c, child*)

18:     **for** *parent: parents*(*a, c*) **do**
19:         RESTARTPARENTS(*a, parent*)

---

4   The Tool in Practice

Our migration algorithm has been integrated into our proposal for trans-cloud deployment and management as an effector of cloud entities. In this section, we evaluate our proposal by focusing on two aspects: the effort required for migrating one component from one location to another, and the times taken for the execution of two different migration scenarios.

4.1   The Effort Required for Migration

Whereas the migration from on-premise applications to the cloud has been studied by many researchers [12], not much work has been published on changes in target providers for migration. Moreover, there seems not be a consensus on how to compare alternative deployments. We use the approach in [24] to compare and analyze, in terms of portability and effort, the feasibility of the migration of an application using several different vendors.

In the analysis in [24], for an application with modules similar to those used in our case study, the deployment steps needed for several PaaS providers are very different. Although for the different vendors these steps are semantically similar, they must be executed using proprietary tools, each of which requires its own set of steps and information. The experiments in [24] show that, on average, a migration operation may require an effort of 17 actions, with a maximum spread of 14 and a standard deviation of 5. In their analysis, a low number of steps is offset by a complex configuration of the initial code repository, which increases the complexity of the initial deployment.

In their analysis, this effort is reduced to 1 when they use a bidimensional cross-cloud approach to orchestrate the migration of components and interact with the different providers. This is also true in our case, although with our algorithm in a trans-cloud environment this is the case, not only for migrations between locations in the same level, but also for any combination of IaaS and PaaS vendors used for each of our application's modules.

The encapsulation inside the customized Brooklyn of the knowledge to interact with a specific provider and to handle application topologies, like relations, allows the reduction of the effort required for the migration of an application component to 1. Because of this, given an initial effort to provide the TOSCA specification of the topology of our application, our trans-cloud-based algorithm allows any application's component to be migrated between different providers with no effort.

4.2   The Time Required for Migration

We illustrate the performance and reliability of our algorithm by showing the results of a trans-cloud migration. We have carried out experiments with two different scenarios. We assume the Softcare application has previously been deployed using different services, and then we migrate the Forum component to a different provider: (1) in the Aws-to-Pivotal case the Forum component is moved from AWS EC2 to Pivotal Web Services, and (2) in the Pivotal-to-Aws case the Forum component is moved from Pivotal Web Services to AWS EC2.

To follow their evolution along time, the tool was instrumentalized to gather information at each sub-task of the process for each module. Then, each migration scenario was executed 10 times using our algorithm. Following the process explained in Sect. 3.2, we identified in both cases tasks Dashboard.stop, Forum.stop, Forum.start, Dashboard.restart, and gather the times at which they were performed (all times are in seconds).

Figures 5(a) and (b) show, respectively, box plots for the migration times in the Aws-to-Pivotal and Pivotal-to-Aws scenarios. We can observe that both show similar times for the stopping of the Dashboard component. However, since the

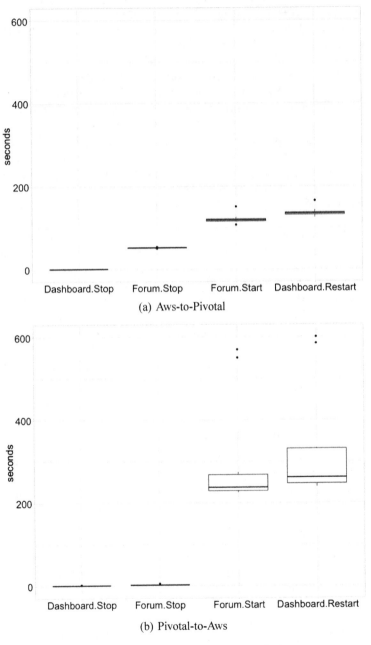

(a) Aws-to-Pivotal

(b) Pivotal-to-Aws

Fig. 5. Forum migration process [18].

releasing of cloud resources on IaaS takes more time than releasing of PaaS, we observe different delays in the stopping and releasing of the Forum component (Forum.stop).

When the Forum component is deployed on IaaS (AWS EC2), it requires provisioning and configuring a new virtual machine, and then executing the necessary commands to deploying the component, etc. However, the process is much simpler on PaaS. The Forum.start event represents the re-deployment of the Forum component in its new location and the reconnection of its dependencies. Figure 5(a) present smaller time values for Forum.start, and smaller dispersion, than Fig. 5(b).

Although the Dashboard component is running on AWS EC2 in both cases, the Dashboard.restart event shows a greater delay in Fig. 5(b) due to the accumulated dispersion in previous steps.

5   Conclusions

This paper presents an algorithm to orchestrate the migration process of stateless components of applications. The algorithm is based on a trans-cloud infrastructure (also proposed by the authors), allowing it to abstract from vendor, technology and service-level.

The proposed algorithm takes significant advantage of the capabilities provided by the trans-cloud infrastructure. This allows greatly simplifying the management of the different cloud solutions and abstraction levels. In turn, this abstraction reduces portability and interoperability issues related to the vendor lock-in problem. In fact, the algorithm is fully *agnostic*, and it can be applied to any stateless application component, independently of the service level (IaaS or PaaS) it uses, as far as the component and the target provider are in Brooklyn's catalog.

The algorithm completely automates the migration process. The process is initiated by a migration request with the component to migrate and its target location as parameters. The operation is handled as an autonomous task. It does not need to be integrated in the application modeling or its management lifecycle.

The algorithm presented in this paper is intended for the migration of a single stateless component of an application. We are currently working on extending the algorithm to support the concurrent migration of a number of components of an application. A discussion on related work may be found in [18].

Acknowledgements. We are grateful to our partners in the SeaClouds project, and in particular to our colleagues Alex Heneveld, Andrea Turli, and the rest of Cloudsoft, and Francesco D'Andria and Roi Sucasas from Atos Spain. This work has been partially supported by MINECO/FEDER projects TIN2014-52034-R and TIN2015-67083-R, and Universidad de Málaga, Campus de Excelencia Internacional Andalucía Tech.

References

1. Armbrust, M., Fox, A., Griffith, R., Joseph, A.D., Katz, R., Konwinski, A., Lee, G., Patterson, D., Rabkin, A., Stoica, I., et al.: A view of cloud computing. Commun. ACM **53**, 50–58 (2010)
2. Youseff, L., Butrico, M., Silva, D.D.: Toward a unified ontology of cloud computing. In: IEEE Grid Computing Environments Workshop (GCE), pp. 1–10 (2008)
3. Kritikos, K., Plexousakis, D.: Multi-cloud application design through cloud service composition. In: International Conference on Cloud Computing (CLOUD), pp. 686–693 (2015)
4. Paraiso, F., Haderer, N., Merle, P., Rouvoy, R., Seinturier, L.: A federated multi-cloud PaaS infrastructure. In: International Conference on Cloud Computing (CLOUD), pp. 392–399 (2012)
5. Grozev, N., Buyya, R.: Inter-cloud architectures and application brokering: taxonomy and survey. Software Pract. Exper. **44**, 369–390 (2014)
6. Carrasco, J., Cubo, J., Durán, F., Pimentel, E.: Bidimensional cross-cloud management with TOSCA and Brooklyn. In: 9th IEEE International Conference on Cloud Computing (CLOUD), pp. 951–955 (2016)
7. Androcec, D., Vrcek, N., Kungas, P.: Service-level interoperability issues of platform as a service. In: World Congress on Services (SERVICES), pp. 349–356 (2015)
8. Moustafa, A., Zhang, M., Bai, Q.: Trustworthy stigmergic service composition and adaptation in decentralized environments. IEEE Trans. Serv. Comput. **9**, 317–329 (2016)
9. Brogi, A., Ibrahim, A., Soldani, J., Carrasco, J., Cubo, J., Pimentel, E., D'Andria, F.: SeaClouds: a European project on seamless management of multi-cloud applications. ACM SIGSOFT Software Eng. Notes **39**, 1–4 (2014)
10. Petcu, D.: Portability and interoperability between clouds: challenges and case study. In: Towards a Service-Based Internet, pp. 62–74 (2011)
11. Di Martino, B.: Applications portability and services interoperability among multiple clouds. IEEE Trans. Cloud Comput. **1**, 74–77 (2014)
12. Jamshidi, P., Ahmad, A., Pahl, C.: Cloud migration research: a systematic review. IEEE Trans. Cloud Comput. **1**, 142–157 (2013)
13. Zhao, J.F., Zhou, J.T.: Strategies and methods for cloud migration. Int. J. Autom. Comput. **11**, 143–152 (2014)
14. Binz, T., Leymann, F., Schumm, D.: CMotion: a framework for migration of applications into and between clouds. In: International Conference on Service-Oriented Computing and Applications (SOCA), pp. 1–4. IEEE (2011)
15. Boyer, F., Gruber, O., Pous, D.: Robust reconfigurations of component assemblies. In: International Conference on Software Engineering (ICSE), pp. 13–22 (2013)
16. Durán, F., Salaün, G.: Robust and reliable reconfiguration of cloud applications. J. Syst. Software **122**, 524–537 (2016)
17. Zeginis, D., D'Andria, F., Bocconi, S., Cruz, J.G., Martin, O.C., Gouvas, P., Ledakis, G., Tarabanis, K.A.: A user-centric multi-paas application management solution for hybrid multi-cloud scenarios. Scalable Comput. Pract. Exp. **14**, 17–32 (2013)
18. Carrasco, J., Durán, F., Pimentel, E.: Component-wise application migration in bidimensional cross-cloud environments. In: Ferguson, D., Muñoz, V.M., Cardoso, J.S., Helfert, M., Pahl, C. (eds.) CLOSER 2017 - Proceedings of the 7th International Conference on Cloud Computing and Services Science, Porto, Portugal, 24–26 April 2017, pp. 259–269. SciTePress (2017)

19. Brogi, A., Carrasco, J., Cubo, J., Nitto, E.D., Durán, F., Fazzolari, M., Ibrahim, A., Pimentel, E., Soldani, J., Wang, P., D'Andria, F.: Adaptive management of applications across multiple clouds: the SeaClouds approach. CLEI Electron. J. **18**(1), 1–14 (2015)
20. OASIS: CAMP: Cloud application management for platforms (v. 1.1) (2012). http://docs.oasis-open.org/camp/camp-spec/v1.1/camp-spec-v1.1.html/
21. Brooklyn: Brooklyn 0.9.0 Documentation (2016). https://brooklyn.apache.org/v/0.9.0/
22. Gamma, E.: Design patterns: elements of reusable object-oriented software. Pearson Education India (1995)
23. Gamma, E., Helm, R., Johnson, R., Vlissides, J.: Design Patterns: Elements of Reusable Object-oriented Software. Addison-Wesley, Reading (1995)
24. Kolb, S., Lenhard, J., Wirtz, G.: Application migration effort in the cloud. In: International Conference on Cloud Computing (CLOUD), pp. 41–48 (2015)

A Lexical and Semantical Analysis on REST Cloud Computing APIs

Fabio Petrillo[1(✉)], Philippe Merle[2], Francis Palma[3], Naouel Moha[4],
and Yann-Gaël Guéhéneuc[1]

[1] Concordia University, Montréal, Canada
fabio@petrillo.com
[2] Inria Lille - Nord Europe, Villeneuve d'Ascq, France
[3] Linnaeus University, Växjö, Sweden
[4] Université du Québec à Montréal, Montréal, Canada

Abstract. Cloud computing is a popular Internet-based computing paradigm that provides on-demand computational services and resources, generally offered by Cloud providers' REpresentational State Transfer (REST) APIs. Developers use REST APIs by invoking these APIs by their names and, thus, the lexicons used in the APIs are important to ease the developers' comprehension. In this paper, we study the lexicons and the linguistic (anti)patterns from 16 providers of REST Cloud Computing APIs. We observe that, although the 16 REST APIs describe the same domain (Cloud computing), contrary to what one might expect, their lexicons do not share a large number of common terms and 90% of the terms (3,561/3,947) are just used by one provider. Thus, the APIs are lexically heterogeneous and there is not a consensus on which terms to use in Cloud computing. Further, we observe that the majority of the URIs, 54%, follow the *Contextualised Resource Names* pattern, which is considered a good practice in REST API design. However, a majority of the URIs, 62.82%, suffer from the *Non-pertinent Documentation* antipattern. Thus, we present three main contributions: (1) a tooled approach, called CLOUDLEX, for extracting and analysing REST Cloud computing lexicons; (2) our analysis of the terms used in 16 REST APIs in 59,677 term occurrences; (3) our analysis of the linguistic (anti)patterns in more than 23,000 URIs of the 142 services of the 16 Cloud providers. We also show that CLOUDLEX has an average precision of 84.82%, recall of 63.57%, and F1-measure of 71.03% on one complete API, `Docker Engine`, which confirms the accuracy of our semantic analyses for the detection of linguistic (anti)patterns.

1 Introduction

Cloud computing has transformed the information-technology industry [2] by hosting applications and providing resources (*e.g.,* CPU and storage) as services on-demand over the Internet [23]. Cloud providers, such as Google Cloud Platform (a commercial public Cloud) and OpenStack (an open-source stack for

© Springer International Publishing AG, part of Springer Nature 2018
D. Ferguson et al. (Eds.): CLOSER 2017, CCIS 864, pp. 308–332, 2018.
https://doi.org/10.1007/978-3-319-94959-8_16

building public/private Clouds), usually offer these services in the form of REST (REpresentational State Transfer) [7] APIs, the *de facto* standard adopted by many software organisations for publishing their services.

Most of Cloud providers, such as Google Cloud Platform or OpenStack, propose their own proprietary APIs. Conversely, open and standard Cloud APIs have also been proposed, such as the Open Cloud Computing Interface (OCCI) [14], which is a vendor-neutral cloud standard.

This observed variety of cloud APIs may decrease developers' comprehension, especially within such a complex and technical context as Cloud computing. Moreover, well-designed and well-named REST APIs may attract client developers to use them more than poorly designed and named ones, particularly in the current open market, where Web services are competing against one another [13]. Indeed, client developers must understand the providers' APIs while designing and developing applications that use these APIs.

Therefore, the understandability of REST APIs are two major quality characteristics, which are reachable when best practices for REST APIs design [13] and naming are followed. Because developers' comprehension is essential for Cloud computing adoption [21], we claim that this comprehension requires quality lexicons in the APIs and the URIs used to access these APIs.

Consequently, we study 16 different and well-known REST APIs to investigate and organise their lexicons. We also study the linguistic (anti)patterns on REST APIs of 16 cloud providers, extending and complementing our previous work [17]. Linguistic antipatterns represent poor solutions to recurring naming problems, which may hinder (1) the consumption of APIs by client developers and (2) the maintenance/evolution of APIs by the API developers. In contrast, linguistic patterns are good solutions to recurring naming problems—they facilitate the consumption and maintenance of APIs [15].

For the semantic analysis of Cloud REST APIs, we apply the SARA approach [15]. We rely on WordNet[1] and Stanford CoreNLP[2] as English dictionaries with a combination of Latent Dirichlet Allocation (LDA) topic modeling technique [3] and second-order semantic-similarity metric [11,12]. LDA is a popular technique in the natural-language processing domain. The second-order semantic-similarity metric is based on the distributional similarity between terms to decide their semantic similarities.

The remainder of the paper is organised as follows. Section 2 presents the main concepts about natural-language processing and the second-order semantic-similarity metric. Section 3 presents the key concepts of CLOUDLEX, our approach to analyse lexically and semantically Cloud computing REST APIs. Sections 4 and 5 present our results, answer the research questions, and discuss threats to validity. Section 6 presents some related work. Finally, Sect. 7 concludes the paper with future work.

This paper is an extension of our previous conference paper [17]. We extended our paper with (1) a dataset sixteen Cloud computing providers (thirteen more

---

[1] wordnet.princeton.edu.
[2] nlp.stanford.edu/software/corenlp.shtml.

that the previous paper; (2) a larger analysis of the terms used in 16 REST APIs in 59,677 term occurrences; (3) an analysis of the linguistic (anti)patterns in more than 23,000 URIs of the 142 services of the 16 Cloud providers. Moreover, we addressed new quality dimensions and three new research questions. Finally, our analysis confirm and corroborate the previous results presented in our conference paper.

2 Background

The second-order semantic-similarity metric [11,12] and the Latent Dirichlet Allocation (LDA) algorithm [3] are applied in natural-language processing, *e.g.*, [15] for various purposes. We now present them briefly because we use them to analyse the linguistic quality of Cloud APIs.

2.1 Second Order Semantic Similarity

The second-order semantic-similarity metric helps finding *distributionally* the most similar terms among a set of terms and computes similarity scores for the terms based on the second-order terms vectors [11,12]. Two terms are distributionally similar if they have multiple co-occurring terms in the same syntactic relations.

Table 1. Window set up for the calculation of window-position triples (WPT).

−3	−2	−1	-	+1	2	3
social	media	and	newsportal	are	more	popular
online	social	and	newsportal	are	beyond	those

Table 1 shows an example of the analysis of the term *newsportal*. If we consider *window_size* as ±3, it gives us two occurrences of *newsportal*. When we consider the position, the term *newsportal* has eight unique features (without stop words, *e.g.*, "are", "beyond", "and") as shown in Table 2 in the WPT column. If we do not consider the window position, then the term *newsportal* has seven different features without stop words, as shown in the Co-occurrences column.

By moving the window over the corpus, we can get the terms vectors for each term. Using the terms vectors and normalising the counts [12], we can compute the distributionally similar terms used in similar contexts. For example, if *newsportal* co-occurs with three terms {*social*, *online*, *media*, and both the terms *print*} and *media* co-occur with those three terms, then the terms *newsportal*, *print*, and *media* are said to be distributionally similar.

We can obtain the list of the *n* most similar terms for a given input by using this technique. We can use this list as the *second order* term vector for a given term, which contains the terms that occur together in similar contexts. We can apply a similar technique to compare the *second order* terms vectors and

Table 2. Examples of the window-position triples and co-occurrences for the example in Table 1.

WPT		Co-occurrence	
$<newsportal, -3, social>$	1	$<newsportal, social>$	2
$<newsportal, -3, online>$	1	$<newsportal, online>$	1
$<newsportal, -2, media>$	1	$<newsportal, media>$	1
$<newsportal, -2, social>$	1	$<newsportal, are>$	1
$<newsportal, +1, are>$	2	$<newsportal, more>$	2
$<newsportal, +2, more>$	1	$<newsportal, popular>$	1
$<newsportal, +3, popular>$	1	$<newsportal, those>$	1
$<newsportal, +3, those>$	1		

compute the *second-order semantic-similarity* metric [11,12]. Compared to WordNet [4,12], this metric allows going beyond the *is-a* relationships between nouns and verbs because WordNet only contains synonyms (warm–hot), meronyms (car–wheel), and antonyms (hot–cold).

2.2 Latent Dirichlet Allocation

In natural-language processing, topic models describe documents as aggregations of latent topics. Latent topics are clustered set of terms [3]. The LDA algorithm extracts topic models from a corpus of terms built from documents. These topic models are low-dimensional representations of the contents of the documents. The cardinality of each topic model, its dimensionality or size, k is set beforehand as an input to building topic models using LDA. LDA allows binding multiple topic models to a single document, which gives flexibility in deciding if a document or part thereof belongs to a topic.

However, LDA is impeded by the sizes of the vocabulary, the numbers of terms, inherent to the majority of documents corpora [3]. Consequently, a new document may contain new and unobserved terms to be classified that were not initially present in the training corpus. This problem along with the *bag-of-words* assumptions motivate us to define an approach combining LDA and second-order semantic-similarity metric. The former allows obtaining a low-dimensional representation of a corpus and the later measures the semantic similarity between the terms in the corpus.

2.3 Linguistic Patterns and Antipatterns

We now describe four linguistic (anti)patterns: *Contextualised vs. Contextless Resource Names* [8] and *Pertinent vs. Non-pertinent Documentation* [15], which we will study in the rest of this paper.

Contextualised vs. Contextless Resource Names. URIs of Cloud resources defined by Cloud providers should be *contextual, i.e.,* it is a good practice for URIs to be in semantically-related or similar contexts. The *Contextless Resource Names* linguistic antipattern is introduced when API developers do not design URI nodes within the same semantic context. An example of *Contextless Resource Names* linguistic antipattern is `www.provider.com/server/research/stock?id=01` where the terms "server", "research", and "stock" are not from semantically-related contexts. In contrast, `www.provider.com/server/memory?size=1024` is an example of *Contextual Resource Names* pattern because "server" and "memory" belong to semantically-related contexts (assuming that the statement "server has memory" is true). The consequences of the *Contextless Resource Names* antipattern include not providing a clear context for a Cloud resource and misleading the cloud API clients, which reduce API understandability [8].

Pertinent vs. Non-pertinent Documentation. The *Non-pertinent Documentation* linguistic antipattern occurs when the documentation of a Cloud resource URI is not consistent with its set of nodes. Therefore, this antipattern involves both the URI and its documentation. Contrary to this antipattern, a well-documented URI describes its goals and functions using relevant semantic terms. An example of a *Non-pertinent Documentation* is `/v2/tenant_id/flavors/flavor_id/os-extra_specs/key_id` – Gets the value of the specified key from OpenStack, in which the URI and its documentation have no semantic similarity. In contrast, from the same Cloud provider, `/v2/software_deployments/` – Lists all available software deployments. is an example of *Pertinent Documentation* pattern as this URI–documentation pair shows a high semantic similarity. As a consequence of the *Non-pertinent Documentation* linguistic antipattern, Cloud API consumers may make incorrect assumptions on the URIs, which can hinder their comprehension. In addition, for Cloud API providers, this may hinder understandability during the maintenance and evolution [15].

3   Approach

We now present CLOUDLEX, our approach to building the lexicon of Cloud computing REST APIs. First, we introduce a conceptual model of Cloud computing REST APIs. Second, we describe our approach to extract and analyse lexicons from Cloud APIs. Finally, we describe our semantic analysis of Cloud APIs.

3.1   Conceptual Model for Cloud Computing REST APIs

Cloud computing is the root concept of this model composed of the key concepts of **Provider, Service, Resource,** and **Action,** their main attributes and aggregation relationships. Figure 1 sketches our conceptual model. In our conceptual model, we abstract Cloud computing actors (companies, implementations,

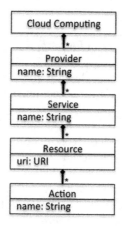

Fig. 1. Conceptual model of cloud computing REST APIs [17].

and standards) under the single concept of **Provider**. Each provider supplies a set of REST APIs. For example, in Google Cloud Platform, each API is in fact a commercial Google *product*, such as `compute` and `sql`.

Independently of the name used by Cloud providers (product, API, extension), each provider's REST API exposes conceptually useful services, *e.g.,* managing virtual machines, networks, databases, or applications, orchestrating their deployment, controlling their access, etc. The number and contents of these services are extremely heterogeneous for each provider: hundreds of services in Google Cloud Platform, more than one hundred in OpenStack, and five in OCCI. In our conceptual model, we abstract this diversity of functional services under the single concept of **Service**.

Each provider's service manages a set of computing resources implemented as REST resources. A service is characterised by a unique resource identifier, *e.g.,* URI, URL, etc., and usually a documentation to describe the service. For example, virtual machines are accessible through the URI /project/zones/zone_id/instances/instance_id in the `compute` service of Google Cloud Platform and the URI /tenant_id/servers/server_id in the `os-compute-2` service of OpenStack. Our conceptual model abstracts this diversity of computing resources under the single concept of **Resource**.

Each resource supports common CRUD operations (Create, Retrieve, Update, and Delete) and some specific business behaviours, like starting and stopping a virtual machine, attaching a disk to a virtual machine, etc. Our conceptual model abstracts this diversity of operations and behaviours under the single concept of **Action**.

To instantiate this conceptual model, we designed a tooled approach for identifying automatically **Service**, **Resource**, and **Action** from Cloud computing REST APIs of any **Provider** and then extracting and analysing the lexicons of these APIs.

3.2 CLOUDLEX

The CLOUDLEX approach divides in four steps:

Step 1. Collecting Documentation. The first step consists in collecting manually the documentation of a provider's Cloud computing REST API.

Step 2. Parsing Documentation. The second step parses all the provider's documentation to identify the **Service**, **Resource**, and **Action** of the conceptual model automatically to create the `Cloud Dataset` of our conceptual model.

Step 3. Extracting Lexicon. The third step extracts the lexicon of each provider from its associated `Cloud Dataset`. The lexicon of each provider contains the names of all the services, the terms extracted from the path of the URIs of all provided resources, and the names of all the actions defined on the resources

For example, the URI /project/zones/zone_id/instances/instance_id contains five segments: {`project`}, `zones`, {`zone_id`}, `instances`, and {`instance_id`}. We keep in the lexicon all segments not enclosed by braces, *e.g.,* `zones` and `instances`. Other segments enclosed by braces identify specific resources, usually as identifiers, such as {`project`} and all {`instance_id`}.

Step 4. Analysing Lexicon. The fourth step analyses automatically the lexicons. We use various analyses to count occurrences of each term in the lexicons, identify nouns and verbs, singular and plural terms, and lower/upper/camel cased terms.

The lexicons are encoded as CSV files (Comma-Separated Values). This implementation choice fosters the *reusability* of the lexicons by researchers and practitioners. Most of the CLOUDLEX parsers, extractors, and analyses are implemented in Python, a dynamic scripting language providing simple libraries to get and parse HTML pages/Swagger files, and read/write CSV files. The implementation of the CLOUDLEX approach is freely available at https://github.com/Spirals-Team/CloudLexicon.

3.3 Semantic Analysis of Cloud APIs

The semantic analysis of Cloud APIs requires four automatic steps shown in Fig. 2. The first step involves the collection of API documentation and performing a pre-processing phase, for example to remove stop words. The second step processes URI nodes to their base form (*a.k.a.*, lemmatisation) using the Stanford Core NLP. The third step involves the extraction of topic models using LDA. In the final step, we compute the second-order semantic-similarity metric between the obtained topic models and the nodes in a URI. We illustrate with a running example the semantic analysis, showing the detection of the *Contextless Resource Names* antipattern and *Contextual Resource Names* pattern.

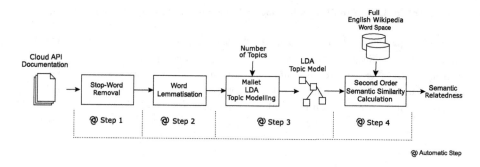

Fig. 2. The Semantic analysis method applied to cloud APIs from [15].

Semantic Analysis. To infer the contextual relationships between nodes in URIs, we rely on Mallet LDA topic modeling[3]. LDA forms a model for a given document, which represents a URI and its documentation. Our proposed approach applies Mallet topic modeling to build topic models by accepting resource identifiers and descriptions of Cloud resources as input.

Table 4 shows an excerpt of the LDA topic model created during our analysis of the Cloud API provider `Docker Engine`. The complete topic model consists of ten topic clusters and we consider the ten most relevant terms in each topic, *i.e.,* the top ten terms. We can use this set of topics to measure similarity between resource identifiers, if two URI nodes are semantically related. URI nodes are semantically related if they are from the same topic [19] (Table 3).

Table 3. List of extracted topics in `Docker Engine`.

List of topics
auth
build
commit
containers
events
exec
images
info
ping
version

To compute the semantic similarity between terms, we use the second-order semantic-similarity metric. We rely on the distributional second-order similarity

---
[3] http://mallet.cs.umass.edu.

Table 4. Top ten terms for `Docker Engine` topic model with $k=10$.

Topic0	Topic1	Topic2	Topic3	Topic4	Topic5	Topic6	Topic7	Topic8	Topic9
copy	resize	image	amp	container	create	search	ping	container	json
unpause	start	version	restart	info	attach	height	history	top	exec
commit	tag	event	wait	push	log	log	change	change	load
build	build	width	width	width	stop	stop	auth	auth	kill
		pause	pause	pause	pause	pause	pause	pause	export

because the nodes in the URI can be slightly different from the terms used for their description (structure and form). A pair of terms are distributionally similar if they have common co-occurring terms, *i.e.*, terms that appear frequently with the same set of terms as neighbors. As described in Sect. 2.1, the computation of this similarity is based on the corpus of terms extracted from the URI dataset, which we analyse to find the terms that occur together within a context of $\pm window\_size$ terms. We then process the resulting terms matrix to build terms vectors that represent the distribution of a term in the corpus and show the terms sharing a maximum number of co-occurrences. We use these to compare two terms by analysing the extent to which these two terms have similar second-order terms vectors [12]. We use DISCO [11] to compute such distributional similarity between terms.

Identifying Antipatterns. To compare the context of every pair of nodes in a URI, we measure the second-order semantic similarity between each node with the ten top terms of each topic. Based on the similarity value, we determine to which topics a node belongs. We consider that a node belongs to a topic if the average second-order semantic similarity value is greater than a predefined *threshold*, *i.e.*, 0.3, for any terms in each topic. We simulate over several threshold values and choose the minimum with reasonable results based on our simulation results and comprehension. And, finally, we choose the same threshold based on the work in [15] where the authors reasoned their detection accuracy over this threshold value.

If, for a given nodes pair of a URI, the intersection of topic sets to which each node belongs is empty (*i.e.*, there is no common topic for that pair of nodes in the URI), then we report the URI as a *Contextless Resource Names* antipattern. Otherwise, if each pair of nodes in the URI share at least one common topic, then we report the URI as a *Contextual Resource Names* pattern.

Table 5 shows the results for a resource URI from the `Docker Engine` API `https://docker.engine.com/images/search`. The base forms of each node (*i.e.*, `image` and `search`) appear in Topic2 and Topic6 shown in Table 4. Hence, we report the URI as a *Contextual Resource Names* pattern. As shown in Table 5, we have two nodes in base forms: `image` and `search`. We compare the second-order similarity for each node with each terms of the obtained topic model shown in Table 5. The first column shows the second-order similarity values between the first node `image` and the topic model, and the second column shows the values

Table 5. Example of analysis of a URI from the `Docker Engine` API.

Node: image	Node: search	Topic average
https://docker.engine.com/images/search		
URI Nodes: /images/search		
image *vs.* **Topic0**	**search** *vs.* **Topic0**	
copy: 0.45550877	copy: 0.31544656	
unpause: −2.0	unpause: −2.0	
commit: 0.0	commit: 0.098813675	
build: 0.32840174	build: 0.01179231	
Max Result Topic 0: 0.45550877	Max Result Topic 0: 0.31544656	0.385477665
image *vs.* **Topic1**	**search** *vs.* **Topic1**	
resize: 0.2891726	resize: 0.57163477	
start: 0.012896833	start: 0.018111441	
tag: 0.101503715	tag: 0.1996914	
Max Result Topic 1: 0.2891726	Max Result Topic 1: 0.57163477	0.430403685
image *vs.* **Topic2**	**search** *vs.* **Topic2**	
image: 2.0	image: 0.2916552	
version: 0.2870915	version: 0.24986088	
event: 0.0743737	event: 0.042658847	
width: 0.12692761	width: 0.011248095	
pause: 0.07810811	pause: 0.09917007	
Max Result Topic 2: 2.0	Max Result Topic 2: 0.2916552	1.1458276
image *vs.* **Topic3**	**search** *vs.* **Topic3**	
amp: 0.032073073	amp: 0.011314062	
restart: 0.011473239	restart: 0.031095618	
wait: 0.036101706	wait: 0.09236097	
Max Result Topic 3: 0.0	Max Result Topic 3: 0.0	0
image *vs.* **Topic4**	**search** *vs.* **Topic4**	
container: 0.1470323	container: 0.070620485	
info: 0.23985307	info: 0.5876746	
push: 0.04289078	push: 0.078571856	
Max Result Topic 4: 0.23985307	Max Result Topic 4: 0.5876746	0.413763835
image *vs.* **Topic5**	**search** *vs.* **Topic5**	
create: 0.16315852	create: 0.19966161	
attach: 0.21755742	attach: 0.015138787	
log: 0.16914968	log: 0.31177378	
stop: 0.017904773	stop: 0.100144744	
Max Result Topic 5: 0.21755742	Max Result Topic 5: 0.31177378	0.2646656

(*continued*)

Table 5. (*continued*)

https://docker.engine.com/images/search		
URI Nodes: /images/search		
Node: image	Node: search	Topic average
image *vs.* **Topic6**	**search** *vs.* **Topic6**	
search: 0.2916552	search: 2.0	
height: 0.15941465	height: 0.0106301615	
Max Result Topic 6: 0.2916552	Max Result Topic 6: 2.0	1.1458276
image *vs.* **Topic7**	**search** *vs.* **Topic7**	
ping: 0.0	ping: 0.0	
history: 0.06135501	history: 0.05444772	
change: 0.11254101	change: 0.13595133	
auth: 0.04527525	auth: 0.28564966	
Max Result Topic 7: 0.11254101	Max Result Topic 7: 0.28564966	0.199095335
image *vs.* **Topic8**	**search** *vs.* **Topic8**	
container: 0.1470323	container: 0.070620485	
top: 0.18044263	top: 0.0	
Max Result Topic 8: 0.18044263	Max Result Topic 8: 0.0	0.090221315
image *vs.* **Topic9**	**search** *vs.* **Topic9**	
json: 0.11969886	json: 0.4653473	
exec: 0.073554516	exec: 0.2546377	
load: 0.14074977	load: 0.13070202	
kill: 0.0	kill: 0.13537067	
export: 0.022680383	export: 0.051750746	
Max Result Topic 9: 0.14074977	Max Result Topic 9: 0.4653473	0.303048535
Maximum Average		**1.1458276**

between the second node `search` and the topic model. The third column shows the average second-order similarity for each topic for both nodes. We obtain the maximum average of 1.1458 as the second-order semantic-similarity metric. Topic6 has the maximum average vale for the nodes, which is higher than the predefined threshold. Thus, we report these two nodes as contextual. We repeat this process for all the URIs and Cloud APIs to decide if the nodes in URIs are from the same context.

4   Cloud Lexical Analysis

Using CloudLex presented in Sect. 3.2, we extract a total of **3,947 different terms** in the REST APIs of **16 Cloud computing providers**. We analyse the terms to answer two main research questions as follows.

4.1 RQ1: Do RESTful Cloud APIs Follow Good Practices?

We analyse automatically the quality of the terms along five dimensions. We group the terms based on these dimensions, counting how many terms belong to each dimension. Table 6 shows the result of the grouping from which we observe several findings.

1. **Parts of Speech:** we classified the parts of speech of each term as *Noun* or *Verb*.
2. **Number:** we classified the terms as *Plural* or *Singular*.
3. **Casing:** we classified the terms as *Camel*, *Lower*, or *Upper* cased.
4. **Hyphenation:** we classified the terms based on the presence or not of hyphens.
5. **Underscoring:** we classified the terms based on the presence or not of underscores.

First, we find that 69% of the terms are nouns (3,323/4,843) and 31% verbs (1,520/4,843) and that the majority of the APIs avoid using extensively verbs. Second, we observe that 56% of the terms are plural (2,127/4,843) and 44% are singular (2,716/4,843). Third, the analysis of the APIs shows that 52% of the terms use camel casing (2,517/4,843), close to 48% are lowercase (2,313/4,843), and only 0.27% are upper case (13/4,843). Finally, 98% of the terms do not include hyphens (4,735/4,843) or underscores (4,753/4,843).

Petrillo et al. [18] compiled a catalog of 73 best practices in the design of REST APIs. In the catalog, there are five best practices directly related to URI

Table 6. Number of terms by provider and quality dimensions.

Provider	Terms Ocurrences by Provider	Parts of Speech		Quantity		Case			Hyphens		Underscores	
		Noun	Verb	Plural	Singular	Camel	Lower	Upper	No	Yes	No	Yes
1and1	42	93%	7%	64%	36%	0%	95%	5%	60%	40%	100%	0%
Cloud Foundry	75	93%	7%	64%	36%	0%	100%	0%	52%	48%	100%	0%
CloudStack	565	2%	98%	28%	72%	99%	1%	0%	100%	0%	100%	0%
Digital Ocean	46	52%	48%	54%	46%	0%	100%	0%	72%	28%	100%	0%
Docker	32	34%	66%	16%	84%	0%	100%	0%	97%	3%	100%	0%
Google Cloud	349	47%	53%	48%	52%	51%	49%	0%	100%	0%	100%	0%
Heroku	14	79%	21%	64%	36%	0%	100%	0%	93%	7%	100%	0%
IBM Bluemix	52	67%	33%	52%	48%	0%	100%	0%	100%	0%	96%	4%
Kubernetes	16	94%	6%	75%	25%	0%	100%	0%	100%	0%	100%	0%
Microsoft Azure	622	67%	33%	63%	37%	58%	42%	0%	100%	0%	100%	0%
OCCI	46	70%	30%	0%	100%	0%	100%	0%	74%	26%	100%	0%
OpenStack	160	76%	24%	54%	46%	8%	89%	3%	92%	8%	68%	32%
Oracle Cloud	1,518	88%	12%	52%	48%	60%	40%	0%	100%	0%	99%	1%
OVH	1,014	79%	21%	23%	77%	48%	52%	0%	100%	0%	100%	0%
Rackspace	146	81%	19%	51%	49%	5%	94%	1%	95%	5%	92%	8%
VMWare	146	81%	19%	51%	49%	5%	94%	1%	95%	5%	92%	8%
Total	4,843	69%	31%	44%	56%	52%	48%	0%	98%	2%	98%	2%

lexicons: (1) *lowercase letters should be preferred in URI paths*; (2) *a singular noun should be used for document names*; (3) *a plural noun should be employed for collection names*; (4) *a verb or verb phrase should be used for controller names*; (5) *underscores should not be used.* Our results show that the APIs, in general, follow these five good practices.

We thus conclude that **the lexicon of the analysed Cloud computing REST APIs contains a majority of nouns, which are equally singular or plural, and are mainly in lower case, following REST API best practices.**

4.2   RQ2: Which Lexicon Is Adopted by Cloud Computing Providers?

We count the number of providers that adopt a same term, observing that although the 16 studied REST Cloud APIs describe the same domain, contrary to our expectation, they do not share a large number of common terms. In fact, 90% of the terms (3,561/3,947) are used by one provider only, 5% of the terms (198/3,947) are adopted by two providers, and 5% of the terms (198/3,947) are adopted by three providers or more. If we define **consensus** when all providers adopt a term, there is no term that is consensual in the 16 studied APIs.

Although a majority of the terms are adopted just by one provider, we can highlight 23 terms that are used by seven[4] or more providers: images (used by 11 providers), events (10), users (9), services (9), stop (9), resources (8), logs (8), roles (8), snapshots (8), restore (8), actions (8), restart (8), instances (7), domains (7), volumes (7), credentials (7), config (7), export (7), start (7), tags (7), validate (7), and resume (7).

Thus, **we conclude that the 16 Cloud APIs are lexically heterogeneous, with few common terms. There is not a consensus on which terms to use in Cloud computing REST APIs.**

5   Semantic Analysis of Cloud APIs for the Detection of Linguistic (Anti)patterns

In this section, we assess the effectiveness of our semantic analysis approach on Cloud APIs by (1) verifying if linguistic (anti)patterns do occur in Cloud APIs and (2) analysing the detection accuracy for the detected linguistic (anti)patterns. In this paper, we perform the validation study on more than 23,000 URIs from 16 Cloud API providers.

5.1   Subjects and Objects

The subjects of our semantic analysis are the four linguistic patterns and antipatterns described in Sect. 2.3 and the objects of our analysis are the 23,062 URIs

---

[4] We chose at least seven providers to show a short list of terms (around of 20 terms). The full list is available at https://github.com/Spirals-Team/CloudLexicon.

Table 7. Number of URIs tested from each Cloud API provider.

Cloud API providers	Test URIs
1and1 Cloud Server	161
Apache CloudStack	563
Cloud Foundry	233
Digital Ocean	131
Docker Engine	40
Google Cloud Platform	505
Heroku	30
IBM Bluemix	113
Kubernetes	114
Microsoft Azure	1,820
OCCI	204
OpenStack	588
Oracle Cloud	11,264
OVH	4,229
Rackspace	479
VMware	2,588
Total	**23,062**

from the 16 Cloud API providers. Table 7 summarises the numbers of URIs per provider.

5.2 Research Questions

We propose two research questions to assess the effectiveness of our semantic analysis for the detection of linguistic (anti)patterns:

RQ_1 *To what extent do the analysed Cloud APIs contain the linguistic patterns and antipatterns (defined in Sect. 2.3)?*
By answering RQ_1, we show the quality of the URIs.
RQ_2 *How accurate are the detected linguistic patterns and antipatterns?*
By answering RQ_2, we show whether our identification process is accurate.

5.3 Validation Process

For the validation, we collected URIs and their corresponding documentations for each Cloud APIs and subsequently applied the detection rules of linguistic patterns and antipatterns [15] in the form of detection algorithms using CLOUDLEX. We validated detection results in two parts: (1) for *Contextless vs. Contextual Resource Names*, 50 randomly-selected URIs from the 16 Cloud APIs and for *Pertinent vs. Non-pertinent Documentation*, 25 randomly-selected

URI–documentation pairs to measure the overall precision and (2) to measure precision and recall for one Cloud API provider, we chose `Docker Engine` with its reasonable number of URIs, *i.e.*, other providers have high numbers of URIs up to 11,264.

We involved three professionals, who are expert in Android, iOS, and Cloud development, to identify the true positives and false negatives to define a gold standard for `Docker Engine`. They also assisted in our validation process where we calculate overall precision by randomly choosing 50 URIs and 25 URI–documentation pairs. For the validation purposes, we provided them with the online descriptions[5] of the linguistics patterns and antipatterns, the sets of 50 randomly selected URIs, the set of 25 randomly selected URI–documentation pairs, and all the URIs and URI–documentation pairs from `Docker Engine`. We involved odd number of professionals to resolve their conflicts with majority decision.

5.4   Detection Results

Table 8 shows detection results for the first 15 URIs from `Docker Engine`. As shown in Table 8, all the URIs from `Docker Engine` are detected as *Contextualised Resource Names* pattern.

Table 8. Detection results of *Contextless vs. Contextualised Resource Names* for the first 15 URIs from `Docker Engine`.

URI	Detected as
`https://docker.engine.com/auth`	Pattern
`https://docker.engine.com/build`	Pattern
`https://docker.engine.com/commit`	Pattern
`https://docker.engine.com/containers/create`	Pattern
`https://docker.engine.com/containers/{id}/start`	Pattern
`https://docker.engine.com/containers/{id}/stop`	Pattern
`https://docker.engine.com/containers/{id}/top`	Pattern
`https://docker.engine.com/containers/{id}/logs`	Pattern
`https://docker.engine.com/containers/{id}/attach`	Pattern
`https://docker.engine.com/containers/{id}/exec`	Pattern
`https://docker.engine.com/containers/{id}/json`	Pattern
`https://docker.engine.com/containers/{id}`	Pattern
`https://docker.engine.com/containers/{id}/unpause`	Pattern
`https://docker.engine.com/containers/{id}/export`	Pattern
`https://docker.engine.com/containers/{id}/wait`	Pattern

---

[5] http://sofa.uqam.ca/resources/antipatterns.php.

Table 9 shows the detection results for the first 20 URI–documentation pairs of the `Docker Engine` API. All these pairs are identified as *Pertinent Documentation* except two. Those two pairs: (1) `https://docker.engine.com/containers/id/json` – [inspect a container] and (2) `https://docker.engine.com/containers/json` – [List containers] are `Non-pertinent Documentation`. The rationale behind this outcome could be the absence of the specific term "json" in both their documentations and, in the first documentation, the term "inspect" seems important but the URI does refer to it. All our analyses results are available on our project Web site at https://github.com/Spirals-Team/CloudLexicon.

In the following sections, we answer our two research questions on the presence of patterns and antipatterns in Cloud APIs (RQ_1) and on the accuracy of our identification approach (RQ_2).

Table 9. Detection results of *Pertinent vs. Non-pertinent Documentation* for the first 20 URI–documentation pairs of `Docker Engine`.

URI	Description	Detected as
`https://docker.engine.com/auth`	Check auth configuration	Pattern
`https://docker.engine.com/build`	Build an image from Docker file via stdin	Pattern
`https://docker.engine.com/commit`	Create a new image from a containers changes	Pattern
`https://docker.engine.com/containers/create`	Create a container	Pattern
`https://docker.engine.com/containers/{id}/start`	Start a container	Pattern
`https://docker.engine.com/containers/{id}/stop`	Stop a container	Pattern
`https://docker.engine.com/containers/{id}/top`	List processes running inside a container	Pattern
`https://docker.engine.com/containers/{id}/logs`	Get container logs	Pattern
`https://docker.engine.com/containers/{id}/attach`	Attach to a container	Pattern
`https://docker.engine.com/containers/{id}/exec`	Image tarball format	Pattern
`https://docker.engine.com/containers/{id}/json`	Inspect a container	Antipattern
`https://docker.engine.com/containers/{id}`	Remove a container	Pattern
`https://docker.engine.com/containers/{id}/unpause`	Unpause a container	Pattern
`https://docker.engine.com/containers/{id}/export`	Export a container	Pattern
`https://docker.engine.com/containers/{id}/wait`	Wait a container	Pattern
`https://docker.engine.com/containers/{id}/pause`	Pause a container	Pattern
`https://docker.engine.com/containers/json`	List containers	Antipattern
`https://docker.engine.com/containers/{id}/changes`	Inspect changes on a containers file system	Pattern
`https://docker.engine.com/containers/{id}/restart`	Restart a container	Pattern
`https://docker.engine.com/containers/{id}/copy`	Copy files or folders from a container	Pattern

Table 10. Summary of the semantic analyses of the 16 Cloud APIs.

API providers	URIs tested	Contextless	Contextual	Pertinent	Non-pertinent
1and1 Cloud Server	161	2 (1.24%)	159 (98.76%)	72 (44.72%)	89 (55.28%)
Apache CloudStack	563	0 (0%)	563 (100%)	0 (0%)	563 (100%)
Cloud Foundry	233	5 (2.15%)	228 (97.85%)	-	-
Digital Ocean	131	35 (26.72%)	96 (73.28%)	46 (35.11%)	85 (64.89%)
Docker Engine	40	0 (0%)	40 (100%)	35 (87.50%)	5 (12.50%)
Google Cloud Platform	505	248 (49.11%)	257 (50.89%)	58 (11.49%)	447 (88.51%)
Heroku	30	5 (16.67%)	25 (83.33%)	14 (46.67%)	16 (53.33%)
IBM Bluemix	113	8 (7.08%)	105 (92.92%)	91 (80.53%)	22 (19.47%)
Kubernetes	114	3 (2.63%)	111 (97.37%)	-	-
Microsoft Azure	1,820	1,744 (95.82%)	76 (4.18%)	-	-
OCCI	204	4 (1.96%)	200 (98.04%)	-	-
OpenStack	588	57 (9.69%)	531 (90.31%)	476 (80.95%)	112 (19.05%)
Oracle Cloud	11,264	4,717 (41.88%)	6,547 (58.12%)	-	-
OVH	4,229	2,702 (63.89%)	1,527 (36.11%)	-	-
Rackspace	479	62 (12.94%)	417 (87.06%)	-	-
VMware	2,588	1,003 (38.76%)	1,585 (61.24%)	-	-
Total	23,062	10,595	12,467	792	1,339
Average for APIs		23.16%	76.84%	48.37%	51.63%

5.5   RQ$_1$: To What Extent Do the Analysed Cloud APIs Contain the Linguistic Patterns and Antipatterns?

Table 10 shows the summary of our detection results in the 16 Cloud APIs. Figures 3 and 4 show the total numbers of linguistic patterns and antipatterns for each Cloud API. All the Cloud APIs follow the *Contextualised Resource Names*

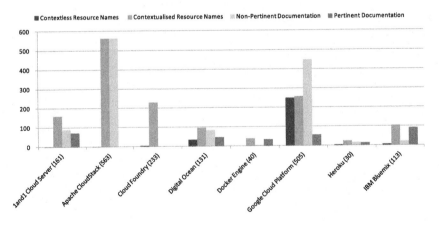

Fig. 3. Detection results of the four patterns and antipatterns in the 16 Cloud APIs (part-I).

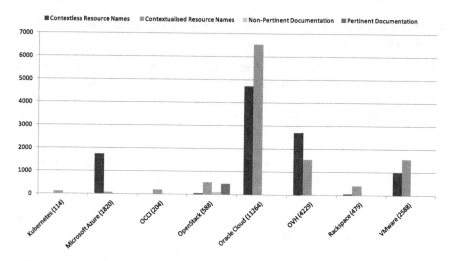

■ Contextless Resource Names   ■ Contextualised Resource Names   ■ Non-Pertinent Documentation   ■ Pertinent Documentation

Fig. 4. Detection results of the four patterns and antipatterns in the 16 Cloud APIs (part-II).

pattern. We identified two APIs following the *Contextualised Resource Names* pattern for all of their URIs, *e.g.*, Apache CloudStack and Docker Engine. Around 50%–98% of the URIs from remaining 14 Cloud APIs follow this pattern. In addition, we identified the *Contextless Resource Names* antipattern in some large Cloud APIs, including Google Cloud Platform (248 occurrences, 49%), IBM Bluemix (8 occurrences, 7%), Microsoft Azure (1,744 occurrences, 95%), Oracle Cloud (4,717 occurrences, 41%), and VMware (1,003 occurrences, 38%). In summary, out of 23,062 URIs, 10,595 (45.94%) are *Contextless Resource Names* and 12,467 (54.06%) are *Contextualised Resource Names*.

Moreover, of the eight Cloud APIs in which we identified the *Pertinent vs. Non-pertinent Documentation* (anti)patterns, we report that they all have *Non-pertinent Documentation*. In particular, 89 occurrences (55.28%) of 1and1 Cloud Server, 563 occurrences (99.98%) of Apache CloudStack, 85 occurrences (64.89%) of Digital Ocean, 5 occurrences (12.50%) of Docker Engine, 447 occurrences (88.51%) of Google Cloud Platform, 16 occurrences (53.33%) of Heroku, 22 occurrences (19.47%) of IBM Bluemix, and 112 (19.05%) occurrences of OpenStack have *Non-pertinent Documentation*. Thus, out of 2,131 pairs of URIs–documentations, 1,339 (62.82%) have *Non-pertinent Documentation*.

These findings suggest that majority, *i.e.*, 54%, of the analysed URIs follow *Contextualised Resource Names* pattern that is a good practice in API design. In contrast, a majority, *i.e.*, 62.82%, of the analysed URI–documentation pairs suffer of the *Non-pertinent Documentation*.

We can positively answer RQ_1: analysed Cloud APIs contain the linguistic patterns and antipatterns. The majority of the analysed URIs have *Contextualised Resource Names*—a good design practice. Our findings also show that the majority of the analysed URI–documentation pairs have *Non-pertinent Documentation*.

5.6   RQ₂: *How Accurate Are the Detected Linguistic Patterns and Antipatterns?*

Table 11 shows that our approach identified 22 URIs as antipatterns, 14 of them were true positive as validated manually. Therefore, we obtained an accuracy of 63.64%. Together with *Contextualised Resource Names* pattern (with 78.57% accuracy), we obtain an overall precision of 71.10% for *Contextualised vs. Contextless Resource Names*. Similarly, for *Pertinent vs. Non-pertinent Documentation*, we obtain an average precision of 77.27% with the manual validation for randomly selected 25 URI–documentation pairs from the 2,131 pairs. Thus, for the first validation, we obtain an average precision of 74.19%.

Table 11. Validation summary on 50 randomly-selected URIs and 25 randomly-selected URI–documentation pairs of the 16 Cloud APIs.

Antipatterns/patterns	P	TP	Validated	Precision	Average precision for anti(pattern)
Contextless Resource Names	22	14	20	63.64%	71.10%
Contextualised Resource Names	28	22	30	78.57%	
No detection	0	0	0	-	
Non-pertinent Documentation	11	6	6	54.55%	77.27%
Pertinent Documentation	14	14	19	100%	
No detection	0	0	0	-	
Average Precision					**74.19%**

While the goal of our first validation is to measure the overall accuracy of our approach for linguistic analysis, in this second validation, we want to show not only the precision but also the recall of our approach. Professional developers manually validated all 40 URIs from `Docker Engine` Cloud API for *Contextualised vs. Contextless Resource Names* and all 40 URI–documentation pairs from `Docker Engine` for *Pertinent vs. Non-pertinent Documentation*. Table 12 shows that we did not identify any occurrence of *Contextless Resource Names* but the manual validation revealed instances of contextless nodes in three URIs. Therefore, our detection process missed all three true positives (*i.e.*, recall of 0%) for this antipattern. However, we obtained 100% of precision. On average, for the *Contextualised vs. Contextless Resource Name*, we obtain an average precision of 92.5% and an average recall of 50% with F1-measure of 64.91%. Similarly, for the *Pertinent vs. Non-pertinent Documentation*, we obtain an average precision and recall of 77.14% with F1-measure of 77.14%.

We conclude that, as shown in Table 12, our approach has a global average precision of 84.82% and a global average recall of 63.57% with an average F1-measure of 71.03%. Thus, we can positively answer RQ₂ on the detection accuracy of linguistic patterns and antipatterns.

Table 12. Validation summary on the URIs and URI–documentation pairs of `Docker Engine`.

Antipatterns/patterns	P	TP	Validated	Precision	Avg. precision	Recall	Avg. recall	F1-measure
Contextless Resource Names	0	0	3	-	92.5%	0%	50%	64.91%
Contextualised Resource Names	40	37	37	92.50%		100%		
No detection	0	0	0	-		-		
Non-pertinent Documentation	5	3	5	60%	77.14%	60%	77.14%	77.14%
Pertinent Documentation	35	33	35	94.29%		94.29%		
No detection	0	0	0	-		-		
Average Precision					**84.82%**			
Average Recall							**63.57%**	
Average F1-measure								**71.03%**

5.7 Threats to Validity

As with any empirical study, threats exist that reduce the validity of our results, which we attempted to mitigate or had to accept. We now discuss these threats and the measures that we took on them.

Threats to the Construct Validity. These threats concern the relationship between theory and observations. We assumed that good naming practices [18] improve the quality of the REST APIs of the Cloud providers [23]. Although these assumptions are legitimate and have been withheld by many researchers and works, for example that of Zhang and Budgen [22], future work should study whether these good naming practices apply universally to all Cloud services. Also, we argued that the lexicons should be homogeneous to help developers' comprehension but this argument should be validated experimentally.

Threats to Internal Validity. These threats concern confounding factors that can affect our dependent variables. Although we did not carry any statistical analysis on the characteristics of the studied REST APIs, we assumed that the lexicons were a feature of the REST APIs. However, there may be other terms that describe more accurately these REST APIs and that impact their comprehension, in particular their documentations. Future work includes analysing and contrasting more APIs with more terms and documentations.

Threats to External Validity. These threats concern the generalization of our results. Although we presented, to the best of our knowledge, the largest study on the lexicons of Cloud computing REST APIs, we cannot generalise our results to all Cloud computing REST APIs. Future work is necessary to analyze more REST APIs, from other Cloud providers, open-source implementations, and standards to confirm and–or infirm our observations.

6   Related Work

Recently, there is a growing interest in the design quality evaluation of REST APIs. However, to the best of our knowledge, few studies made specifically a lexical evaluation of REST APIs in general, and none in the domain of cloud computing.

In related work for the general design quality evaluation of REST APIs, we can cite the research work of Hausenblas [10], who studies some widely used REST Web APIs in terms of URI space design, resource representations, and hyperlinking support. Rodríguez et al. [5] evaluated also the conformance of good and bad design practices in REST APIs from the perspective of mobile applications. They analysed large data logs of HTTP calls collected from the Internet traffic of mobile applications, identified usage patterns from logs, and compared these patterns with best design practices. Zhou et al. [24] showed how to fix design problems related to the use of REST services in existing Northbound networking APIs in a Software Defined Network and how to design a REST Northbound API in the context of OpenStack. These previous work made contributions to the design evaluation of REST APIs for general or specific domains, mobile and networking, while we consider the domain of cloud services.

Palma et al. [16] evaluated the linguistic aspects of several REST APIs based on REST patterns and anti-patterns, which correspond to good and bad practices in the design of REST services. However, the APIs evaluated were selected from different and general domains. They included Facebook, Twitter, Dropbox, and Bestbuy. So, it was not possible to compare and discuss the results among the APIs. Moreover, the list of patterns and anti-patterns was really compared to this focused study.

Petrillo et al. [18] evaluated three cloud computing REST APIs using a catalog of 73 general best practices. However, this catalog was mainly dedicated to the design of REST APIs from a conceptual and syntactic point of view, but not necessarily lexical. The present paper specifically focuses on a lexical evaluation of cloud computing REST APIs.

Researchers have analysed Cloud APIs to verify if the developers properly use them [9,20]. However, no study were conducted in the literature to assess the linguistic quality of Cloud APIs. In the following, we discuss some relevant research done on assessing the structural correctness of APIs [9,20] or the use of Cloud ontology [1,21] for comprehension.

Developers repeatedly need to manually ensure that they are building HTTP requests using correct URIs while developing framework-based JavaScript Web applications, which is error-prone. Wittern *et al.* [20] proposed an approach for statically checking request URIs in JavaScript-based applications by extracting their URLs, HTTP methods, and the corresponding request data. The authors evaluated if request URIs in JavaScript files conform to their publicly available specifications. With analysing more than 6,000 request URIs, the approach achieved the detection accuracy of more than 95%. This study ensures developers use URI correctly, however, does not analyse the linguistic quality which we perform in our work.

Haupt *et al.* [9] proposed a framework for structural analysis of REST APIs based on their online specifications. The authors considered this proposed framework as a first catalog of REST APIs describing structural characteristics that comprises a set of metrics and graphical representation for each API. Moreover, this framework comes useful in identifying the non-conformity of REST APIs to the REST design principles and architectural style. Similar to our work in this paper, the proposed framework in [9] considers the API descriptions and the structure of REST APIs. The authors also proposed a meta-model for REST APIs describing the structure of REST APIs. However, this study only verifies structural correctness of APIs but does not verify their linguistic quality.

Androcec *et al.* [1] provided a global view of Cloud computing ontology after a systematic review. The authors classified the relevant studies into four main categories: cloud resources and services description, cloud security, cloud interoperability, and cloud services discovery and selection. The authors found that the studies from 'cloud resources and services descriptions' category applied Cloud ontologies to describe Cloud resources and services, classify the current services, and pricing models. The Cloud interoperability category consisted of the studies that use ontologies to achieve interoperability among different Cloud providers and their offered services. The authors concluded that Cloud Computing ontologies are primarily applied in the discovery and selection of the best candidate service in accordance with users' computing requirements and the specifications of Cloud resources and services.

In another study, Youseff *et al.* [21] proposed a detailed Cloud ontology to facilitate the comprehension of the Cloud technology as, the authors suggested, it would enable the community to design more efficient cloud applications. Based on the fact that the current state-of-the-art in Cloud computing research lacks the thorough understanding of the classification of the cloud systems, the authors presented a classification of Cloud components, their relationships, and their dependency on concepts from other service computing domains. According to the proposed ontology, the Cloud computing systems fall within *applications, software environments, software infrastructure, software kernel*, and *hardware* categories. However, both the studies [1,21] focused on ontology aspect of REST APIs. The linguistic aspect of the Cloud APIs is not considered in these studies.

Last but not least, Chalitta *et al.* [6] defined formal-based framework for semantic interoperability in multi-clouds, organizing a catalogue of formal models that mathematically describe cloud APIs, describing their concepts and semantic interoperability.

7   Conclusion and Future Work

Cloud computing is a popular Internet-based computing paradigm that provides on-demand computational services and resources, generally offered by Cloud providers' REpresentational State Transfer (REST) APIs. Developers use REST APIs by invoking these APIs by their names and, thus, the lexicons used in the APIs are important to ease the developers' comprehension. We claimed that

Cloud computing lexicons reflect the nature of their APIs and the automatic detection of "linguistic" antipatterns could further boost the adoption of Cloud computing.

We presented three contributions. First, we introduced CLOUDLEX, an approach to build the lexicons of Cloud computing REST APIs, based on a conceptual model and providing a toolkit to extract and analyse these lexicons. Second, we extracted and studied the lexicons of 16 REST Cloud Computing APIs. Finally, we analysed semantically the (anti)patterns in 1,297 URIs of the 142 services of the 16 Cloud providers.

We showed that the 16 APIs form **a lexicon of 3,947 different terms** to express all provided services. We found that this lexicon contains a majority of nouns, which are equally singular or plural, and are mainly in lower case, following REST API best practices.

We observed that, although the 16 studied REST Cloud APIs describe the some domain (Cloud computing), contrary to what one might expect, they do not share a large number of common terms. In fact, 90% of the terms (3,561/3,947) are used by only one provider, 5% of the terms (198/3,947) are adopted by two providers, and the other 5% of the terms (198/3,947) are adopted by three providers or more. Thus, we conclude that the 16 APIs are lexically heterogeneous, which point that there is not a consensus on which terms to use in Cloud computing.

We also showed that, through our semantic analysis of the Cloud APIs, 54% of the URIs follow the *Contextualised Resource Names* pattern, which is considered a good practice in API design. However, 62.82% of the URIs suffer from the *Non-pertinent Documentation* antipattern. We also reported the detection accuracy on one complete API, Docker Engine, with a global average precision of 84.82% and a global average recall of 63.57% for an average F1-measure of 71.03%, which confirms the accuracy of our semantic analyses for the detection of linguistic patterns and antipatterns.

In future work, we plan to build an ontology of Cloud computing APIs, establishing semantic joins between services and resources from different providers to deal with semantic interoperability between Clouds. Further, future work is necessary to analyze more REST APIs, from other Cloud providers, open-source implementations, and standards to confirm and–or infirm our observations.

Acknowledgment. This work is partially supported by the OCCIware research and development project (http://www.occiware.org) funded by French Programme d'Investis sements d'Avenir (PIA). It is also co-funded by the Natural Sciences and Engineering Research Council of Canada (NSERC).

References

1. Androcec, D., Vrcek, N., Ševa, J.: Cloud Computing Ontologies: A Systematic Review, September 2017
2. Armbrust, M., Stoica, I., Zaharia, M., Fox, A., Griffith, R., Joseph, A.D., Katz, R., Konwinski, A., Lee, G., Patterson, D., Rabkin, A.: A view of cloud computing. Commun. ACM **53**(4), 50 (2010)

3. Blei, D.M., Ng, A.Y., Jordan, M.I.: Latent Dirichlet allocation. J. Mach. Learn. Res. **3**(4–5), 993–1022 (2003)
4. Budanitsky, A., Hirst, G.: Evaluating WordNet-based measures of lexical semantic relatedness. Comput. Linguist. **32**(1), 13–47 (2006)
5. Rodríguez, C., Baez, M., Daniel, F., Casati, F., Trabucco, J.C., Canali, L., Percannella, G.: REST APIs: a large-scale analysis of compliance with principles and best practices. In: Bozzon, A., Cudre-Maroux, P., Pautasso, C. (eds.) ICWE 2016. LNCS, vol. 9671, pp. 21–39. Springer, Cham (2016). https://doi.org/10.1007/978-3-319-38791-8_2
6. Challita, S., Paraiso, F., Merle, P.: Towards formal-based semantic interoperability in multi-clouds. In: 10th IEEE International Conference on Cloud Computing (CLOUD), Honolulu, Hawaii, USA, June 2017. https://hal.inria.fr/hal-01519831
7. Fielding, R.T.: Architectural styles and the design of network-based software architectures. Ph.D. thesis, University of California, Irvine (2000)
8. Fredrich, T.: RESTful Service Best Practices: Recommendations for Creating Web Services, May 2012. http://www.restapitutorial.com/resources.html
9. Haupt, F., Leymann, F., Scherer, A., Vukojevic-Haupt, K.: A framework for the structural analysis of REST APIs. In: Proceedings of the 1st IEEE International Conference on Software Architecture, ICSA 2017, 3–7 April 2017, Gothenburg, Sweden, pp. 55–58. IEEE Computer Society (2017)
10. Hausenblas, M.: On entities in the web of data. In: Wilde, E., Pautasso, C. (eds.) REST: From Research to Practice, pp. 425–440. Springer, New York (2011). https://doi.org/10.1007/978-1-4419-8303-9_19
11. Kolb, P.: DISCO: a multilingual database of distributionally similar words. In: Proceedings of 9th Conference on Natural Language Processing KONVENS 2008, Berlin, Germany, no. 2003, pp. 37–44 (2008)
12. Kolb, P.: Experiments on the Difference between Semantic Similarity and Relatedness. In: 17th Nordic Conference of Computational Linguistics, Odense, Denmark, NODALIDA 2009 (2009)
13. Masse, M.: REST API Design Rulebook, vol. 53. O'Reilly Media, Sebastopol (2011)
14. Nyren, R., Edmonds, A., Papaspyrou, A., Metsch, T., Parak, B.: Open Cloud Computing Interface - Core. OCCI-WG Specification Document 1.2, Open Grid Forum (2016). https://redmine.ogf.org/attachments/217/core.pdf
15. Palma, F., Gonzalez-Huerta, J., Founi, M., Moha, N., Tremblay, G., Guéhéneuc, Y.G.: Semantic analysis of RESTful APIs for the detection of linguistic patterns and antipatterns. Int. J. Coop. Inf. Syst. **26**(02), 1742001 (2017). http://www.worldscientific.com/doi/abs/10.1142/S0218843017420011
16. Palma, F., Gonzalez-Huerta, J., Moha, N., Guéhéneuc, Y.-G., Tremblay, G.: Are RESTful APIs well-designed? Detection of their linguistic (anti)patterns. In: Barros, A., Grigori, D., Narendra, N.C., Dam, H.K. (eds.) ICSOC 2015. LNCS, vol. 9435, pp. 171–187. Springer, Heidelberg (2015). https://doi.org/10.1007/978-3-662-48616-0_11
17. Petrillo, F., Merle, P., Moha, N., Guéhéneuc, Y.G.: Towards a REST cloud computing Lexicon. In: ScitePress (ed.) 7th International Conference on Cloud Computing and Services Science, CLOSER 2017, pp. 376–383. INSTICC, Porto, April 2017. https://hal.archives-ouvertes.fr/hal-01480593
18. Petrillo, F., Merle, P., Moha, N., Guéhéneuc, Y.G.: In: Proceedings of 14th International Conference on Service-Oriented Computing, ICSOC 2016, Banff, Canada, 10–13 October 2016 (2016)

19. Steyvers, M., Griffith, T.: Probabilistic topic models. In: Landauer, T., McNamara, D., Dennis, S., Kintsch, W. (eds.) Latent Semantic Analysis: A Road to Meaning. Laurence Erlbaum, Mahwah (2007)
20. Wittern, E., Ying, A.T.T., Zheng, Y., Dolby, J., Laredo, J.A.: Statically checking Web API requests in JavaScript. In: Proceedings of the 39th International Conference on Software Engineering, ICSE 2017, pp. 244–254. IEEE Press, Piscataway (2017). https://doi.org/10.1109/ICSE.2017.30
21. Youseff, L., Butrico, M., Silva, D.D.: Toward a unified ontology of cloud computing. In: 2008 Grid Computing Environments Workshop, pp. 1–10, November 2008
22. Zhang, C., Budgen, D.: What do we know about the effectiveness of software design patterns? IEEE Trans. Softw. Eng. **38**(5), 1213–1231 (2012)
23. Zhang, Q., Cheng, L., Boutaba, R.: Cloud computing: state-of-the-art and research challenges. J. Internet Serv. Appl. **1**(1), 7–18 (2010)
24. Zhou, W., Li, L., Luo, M., Chou, W.: REST API design patterns for SDN northbound API. In: 2014 28th International Conference on Advanced Information Networking and Applications Workshops. pp. 358–365. IEEE, May 2014. http://ieeexplore.ieee.org/lpdocs/epic03/wrapper.htm?arnumber=6844664

Author Index

Printed in the United States
By Bookmasters